Volume I

A Terrible Truth
Anthology of Holocaust Drama

Albert Speer
David Edgar

Ghetto
Joshua Sobol

Rose
Martin Sherman

Z
Anne Szumigalski

Sammy's Follies
Eugene Lion

A Terrible Truth

Anthology of Holocaust Drama
Volume I

compiled by

Irene N. Watts

introduction by Adrienne Kertzer

Playwrights Canada Press
Toronto • Canada

A Terrible Truth: Anthology of Holocaust Drama, Volume I © copyright 2003 Irene N. Watts
Introduction © Adrienne Kertzer 2003 • *Albert Speer* © David Edgar 2000
Ghetto © Joshua Sobol 1989 • *Rose* © Martin Sherman 1999
Z: a meditation on oppression, desire & freedom © Anne Szumigalski 1994
Sammy's Follies: a criminal comedy © Eugene Lion 2003
The authors assert moral rights.

Playwrights Canada Press
215 Spadina Avenue, Suite 230, Toronto, Ontario CANADA M5T 2C7
416-703-0013
orders@playwrightscanada.com • www.playwrightscanada.com

CAUTION: These plays are fully protected under the copyright laws of Canada and all other countries of The Copyright Union, and are subject to royalty. Changes to the script are expressly forbidden without the prior written permission of the author. Rights to produce, film, or record, in whole or in part, in any medium or any language, by any group, amateur or professional, are retained by the author. For amateur or professional production rights, please contact Playwrights Canada Press.

No part of this book, covered by the copyright hereon, may be reproduced or used in any form or by any means—graphic, electronic or mechanical—without the prior written permission of the publisher except for excerpts in a review. Any request for photocopying, recording, taping or information storage and retrieval systems of any part of this book shall be directed in writing to Access Copyright, 1 Yonge St., Suite 1900, Toronto, Ontario CANADA M5E 1E5 416-868-1620.

Playwrights Canada Press acknowledges the support of the taxpayers
of Canada and the province of Ontario through
The Canada Council for the Arts and the Ontario Arts Council.

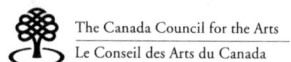

Cover illustration "Terezín's Street" by Bedřich Fritta. Pencil, Chinese ink. Eine Gasse in Theresienstadt, Tuschzeichnung.
Production Editor/Cover Design: Jodi Armstrong

National Library of Canada Cataloguing in Publication

A terrible truth : anthology of Holocaust drama / compiled by Irene N. Watts.

ISBN 0-88754-694-3 (v. 1).—ISBN 0-88754-714-1 (v. 2)

1. Holocaust, Jewish (1939-1945)—Drama. 2. English drama—20th century.
I. Watts, Irene N., 1931-

PN6120.H73T47 2003   822'.914080358   C2003-905701-1

First edition: January 2004.
Printed and bound by AGMV Marquis at Quebec, Canada.

Albert Speer
Albert Speer © copyright David Edgar 2000
Published by Nick Hern Books – www.nickhernbooks.demon.co.uk – London, England.
Reprinted with permission.
Afterword © David Edgar, 2000
Albert Speer: His Battle with Truth by Gitta Sereny first published in Great Britain in 1995 by Macmillan, published in paperback by Picador in 1996
Applications for performance should be made to:
Alan Brodie Representation, 211 Piccadilly, London W1J9HF.

Ghetto
Ghetto © copyright Joshua Sobol 1989
English by Ron Jenkins.
Based on a literal translation from the Hebrew by the author.
Lyrics by Vilna Ghetto translated by Jeremy Sams © 1989.
Applications for performance should be made to:
Mitch Douglas, ICM, 40 West 57th Street, New York, NY 10019, USA
1.212.556.5720 fax 1.212.556.5665

Rose
Rose © copyright Martin Sherman 1999
Published by Methuen.

Z
a meditation on oppression, desire & freedom
Z: a meditation on oppression, desire & freedom © copyright Anne Szumigalski 1994
Published by Signature Editions, Winnipeg, Manitoba.

Sammy's Follies
a criminal comedy
Sammy's Follies: a criminal comedy © copyright Eugene Lion 2003
For performance and all other rights please contact:
isisarts@magma.ca (Canada)

Dedicated to John Neville

TABLE OF CONTENTS

Introduction:

On the Other Hand: The Paradox of Holocaust Theatre
    by Adrienne Kertzer   iii

Plays:

Albert Speer
    by David Edgar   1

Ghetto
    by Joshua Sobol   165

Rose
    by Martin Sherman   257

Z: a meditation on oppression, desire & freedom
    by Anne Szumigalski   291

Sammy's Follies: a criminal comedy
    by Eugene Lion   355

On the Other Hand: The Paradox of Holocaust Theatre
by Adrienne Kertzer

— — • — —

> *"The Holocaust performative acknowledges that there is nothing to say to goneness and yet we continue to try and mark it, say it, identify it, memorialize the loss over and over."* (Patraka 7)

Despite the box-office success of numerous Holocaust films and plays, we are often told that something about the Holocaust—opinions vary as to what that something is—defies our traditional expectations of theatre. Critics regularly observe that the success of Steven Spielberg's "Schindler's List," Roberto Benigni's "Life is Beautiful," and Frances Goodrich and Albert Hackett's *The Diary of Anne Frank* is inextricably linked to the way each work masks and distracts us from the horrific facts of state-organized annihilation. It is not that "terror, real terror, can never be represented on stage" (Isser 15), or that we are disturbed by the ethics of deriving pleasure from others' pain. *Oedipus Rex* dramatizes terror, and watching that tragedy, we do indeed derive pleasure from someone else's pain. Nevertheless, statements regarding the risks of Holocaust theatre are commonplace. They are often advanced as though the failure of civilization, that for many the Holocaust has come to represent, is necessarily followed by a failure of art—that symbol of civilization's highest achievements—to speak adequately to the disaster. "Never again" has become the slogan of Holocaust memory; for Holocaust drama and other artistic responses, a more appropriate catch phrase might be "nevertheless."

In his "Author's Note," playwright David Edgar characterizes Albert Speer, Hitler's Minister of Armaments and War Production, as "a man whose long life was dominated by the defining event of the twentieth century." Edgar's statement implies that dramatists, if they are adequately to address that century, cannot avoid confronting the Holocaust. Basing his play, *Albert Speer*, on Gitta Sereny's magisterial biography, *Albert Speer: His Battle with Truth*, in his "Afterword" he both praises Sereny and defends the dramatist's task: "If Gitta Sereny hadn't written her book about Albert Speer, his slave-workers would still have died, but we would be less able to understand why. For that reason alone, it [is] worth taking the risk of putting his story on stage." Edgar recognizes that in dramatizing Speer's life he risks evoking sympathy for a high-ranking Nazi official sentenced at Nuremberg to twenty years in Spandau prison. The risk is that understanding how men like Speer remained loyal to Hitler for so long can lead us to slide from sympathy to tolerance or even to indifference that opens the way for writers who challenge the historical reality of the Holocaust. During the rehearsals of the original London production of *Albert Speer*, the David Irving trial was taking place. Ironically, the play reveals that Irving's discovery more than thirty years earlier of an unedited record of Speer's activities during the war helped to challenge Speer's lifelong insistence that he knew nothing during the war regarding Nazi treatment of Jews.

Dramatizing Albert Speer as a tragic villain, Edgar caters to neither those who deny the Holocaust, nor to those who assert that the Holocaust cannot be understood. The understanding he takes from Sereny's account is precise – insight into the psychology of Albert Speer, swept up by the Faustian temptation offered by a Mephistopheles/Hitler who offers him the world. It is also general – recognition that the man judged at Nuremberg was not so different from the rest of us: "To give in to personal ambition, to realize a moral and ideological error too late, and to spend the rest of your life making inadequate sense of that failure is all too recognizable." If Speer escaped hanging at Nuremberg because he claimed not to know about the Final Solution, the play displays little interest in his assertions during the trial; the dramatic focus lies elsewhere, in the story he relentlessly tells himself both before and after the trial.

The psychological drama of how we come to believe in the stories we tell ourselves not only remains relevant to our understanding of history; it makes Speer a figure worth dramatizing, someone whose evil does not separate him from the rest of us. Believing that understanding the tragic villain demands both "recognition and even empathy," Edgar treats Speer as a Faust diabolically tempted not with beautiful women and luxury, but with the opportunity to create magnificent and beautiful buildings. Speer conceptualized his attraction to Hitler as æsthetic; the magic spell died in March 1944 when suddenly the Hitler whose gaze could hypnotize him was just an ordinary and rather ugly man. Speer insists that this was the moment he realized that Hitler had betrayed his ideals. In contrast, in June 1940 when Hitler conquered France and asked him to plan the reconstruction of Berlin, Speer tells Georges Casalis that the invitation completed their Mephistophelean bargain: "How could I not be his, then, body and soul?"

Casalis is the Calvinist pastor who meets Speer in Spandau and offers him a different bargain, the possibility of a new future if he tells the truth about his past. The focus of the play becomes the distance between what Speer remembers—how he imagines himself to be the man he never was—and the counter-evidence of historical witness, as provided by oral testimony and Nazi documents. Edgar always respects the gap between Speer's statements and Casalis's reactions. Casalis serves as a model for the audience's response. Both are sympathetic to Speer's interpretation ("the only way he could admit what he admitted was by denying what he had denied") and both are skeptical of the story Speer tells him ("I believe that's what you remember"). Casalis continually challenges Speer, never doubting that Speer believes in the story he tells, but always questioning his premises. Speer becomes obsessed with denying that he was present in 1943 when Heinrich Himmler delivered his notorious Posen speech about the need to exterminate the Jews. Although the play demonstrates that Speer's alibi is not convincing, Speer remains unwilling to acknowledge that, even if he were absent during the Posen speech, he is still lying to himself. He insists, "I could have known. I should have known. I didn't know." The drama of the play thus lies in the tension between Speer's "Not-yet"—his refusal to tell himself the truth—and Casalis's "And yet"— the hope that Speer still can change. Thus Speer remains, as he tells his fellow Spandau inmate, Rudolf Hess, someone who "marched obstinately in a circle for decades." Only in a deathbed visionary confrontation with Hitler does Speer admit that he knew. His admission is imaginary and secret, a fantasy created by the dramatist; if the real Albert Speer ever reached this moment, he never told anyone. The words of Himmler haunt the play's ending: "you will keep the knowledge to yourselves." Himmler rightly predicted that those present at Posen would "take the secret with us to our graves."

Edgar is not the only playwright who recognizes the risks of Holocaust drama, but chooses to take up the challenge. As is evident by the production dates of most of the plays in Volume I of *A Terrible Truth*, dramatists' interest in the Holocaust shows no signs of abating. All but one of the plays in this volume were first produced less than ten years ago and employ a broad spectrum of approaches, ranging from the epic theatre of *Albert Speer* to the one woman show of Martin Sherman's *Rose*. Edward R. Isser warns that "[p]lays that use the Holocaust to make a symbolic point, frame a conventional drama, or push a political agenda risk falling into the abyss of Holocaust representation" (173). But how can plays avoid doing so? To argue that Holocaust plays must not be like other theatre is characteristic of a dominant response to the burden of Holocaust knowledge, and to the way it can produce a catalogue of prohibitions premised upon the failure of all representations. Predictably, Isser argues that the plays that best succeed "acknowledge... the impossibility of the task" (173). Anyone familiar with Theodor Adorno's pronouncement—No poetry after Auschwitz—or with Elie Wiesel's observation—"A novel about Auschwitz is not a novel, or else it is not about Auschwitz" (qtd. in Horowitz 15)—will not be surprised by Isser's conclusion.

Like Robert Skloot who judges Holocaust plays "as both moral texts and theatrical events" (*The Darkness* xiii), Isser describes the ideal Holocaust dramatist as possessing a triple expertise: as moralist/ethicist, historian, and dramatist. Such expectations far exceed those we expect in playwrights who write on other topics. While Claude Schumacher acknowledges that there is no single "model of representation" (8) for Holocaust theatre, he also asserts that a successful Holocaust play "disturbs, offers no comfort, advances no solution" (8). The play "leaves the reader or spectator perplexed, wanting to know more" (8). Instead of applause, the play "generates stunned silence" (8).

If this is the case, we might ask not only why dramatists are willing to write about the Holocaust, but also why audiences are willing to attend their plays. Granted that many theatre patrons are content to limit their interest in Holocaust drama to endless revivals of Goodrich and Hackett's *The Diary of Anne Frank*; their behaviour is less puzzling than the motivation of those who attend a wider range of plays. Is it because these theatregoers desire a theatre of ideas and want, in Schumacher's terms, to know more? But if the Holocaust produces a situation in which no knowledge is ever enough, if it produces a theatre that provides no answers, surely Schumacher's objective of "stunned silence" does not accurately describe what theatregoers experience today. In an age in which metaphors of the Holocaust are easily invoked, we might debate whether this usage proves Holocaust knowledge or ignorance, but it definitely seems to preempt stunned silence.[1] Those who attend Holocaust drama already know the Holocaust happened. Surely when they attend, they will not be stunned by what they already know.

But if the time for stunned silence is long gone, "[i]t is possible to live in a twilight between knowing and not knowing" (Sereny vii).[2] This only aggravates the question of what it means to know the Holocaust. As an answer, dramatists increasingly foreground the multiple and linked problems of Holocaust representation, including the problem of what will constitute knowledge in the future. In 1994, Anne Szumigalski in *Z: A Meditation on Oppression, Desire and Freedom* drew attention to the dilemma of dramatizing the Holocaust fifty years after the war. *Z*'s opening line acknowledges that the dramatist's objective must be something other than the production of new knowledge: "And I'll tell you again and again the same story." Szumigalski describes one of her central characters, Itzak, as an "ex-comedian and storyteller," the "ex" encouraging us to think that humour is impossible in the concentration camp even as Itzak continues to tell stories (and jokes) within the camp. A story, Itzak explains, "is not responsible for answers. A story merely poses questions." Itzak initially justifies his self-serving role as Kapo because the storyteller must survive: "I must live to tell the tale." This statement, which recurs in so many survivor memoirs, is immediately questioned as Itzak asks: "What does a story matter? What does anything matter if it's not a story?" In the incantatory poetic form of *Z*, Szumigalski repeats Itzak's words, and then has Horst, the German guard and former schoolteacher, triply challenge them.

Even if Itzak survives to tell the tale, other questions follow, and with time, perhaps, become more important: "Who will listen?" "Who will believe?" and "Who will care?" Itzak's answer to these questions—"Nevertheless"—recalls Galileo's words, "*E pur si muove*" (And yet it moves), after he was forced by the Inquisition to recant his theory of planetary movement. Just as the earth still moves around the sun, dramatists still write Holocaust plays. Certainly Itzak's response reflects Szumigalski's own practice. Act Two of *Z* is set in the 1960s; Forest Grove Concentration Camp site has become Forest Grove Memorial Park, which tourists interested in experiencing "One day of hell" can visit. Act Two proves very ambiguous in its answers to Horst's questions. For the tourists' inability to imagine the Holocaust—"We all know there's no worse pain than pinched feet"—challenges the audience to imagine a far worse pain. The tourists are determined to "enjoy the gardens," to see the camp the "Heidegger way." Titillated by visiting a site of past horrors, they are unable to escape the present. In contrast, the audience sees on stage what the tourists cannot see, a different setting where Itzak and Horst continue to argue and Itzak insists, "there is no such thing as the last story." Schumacher's description of the ideal Holocaust play is echoed during an interview with Szumigalski and the play's original director, Tom Bentley-Fisher. The director observes, "Those people who come to theatre with a very comfortable idea of what the theatre is and should be didn't like this production." Bentley-Fisher also includes a personal justification in his foreword to the posthumously published *Z*: "*Z* is Anne's first play, inspired by her experiences working with victims in a newly liberated concentration camp at the end of World War II. But the play is not only, nor perhaps even primarily, about the Holocaust."

Eugene Lion is another dramatist who questions whether Holocaust drama that produces "stunned silence" is adequate to the task and whether such plays are ever primarily about the Holocaust. Why people attend Holocaust drama is a central issue in Lion's play, *Sammy's Follies: A Criminal Comedy*, in which the trial of Franz Ferdinand Höss, Commandant at Auschwitz, is presented as theatrical games played in a bar.[3] Höss is accused of indifference, a crime that extends to both the contemporary characters that perform the trial and the audience that views it: "EVERYBODY'S ON TRIAL HERE." Because most of his "witnesses are dead... [t]o lend their testimony credibility," the prosecuting attorney argues that he requires "graphic reenactments." *Sammy's Follies* is highly self-conscious and reflexive regarding its performance of history; it reveals that such performances are always trials in which theatrical conventions limit the kind of testimony the spectators—witnesses to the performance of witnessing—are willing to accept. The play repeatedly draws attention not just to its performance of history, but also to the problematic limits in that performance. In Act One, the characters perform a hanging, leading Sammy to announce the act's conclusion with the words, "Our first atrocity is complete." When the defense attorney protests that such enactments are in questionable taste, the prosecuting attorney replies "hangings are, by definition, morbid and always in questionable taste." In Act Two, a stripper performs the testimony of a woman who must remove her clothes before she is gassed, and the other characters become aroused by her performance. Through such performances, *Sammy's Follies* compels us to interrogate our own watching. What does it take to offend us? What do we do if we are offended? What does it mean, if we are not?

In addition, by deliberately setting the play when the bar is closed because of an election—"Break time! Who's for stuffing ballot boxes?"—Lion destabilizes the play's focus. Whatever the outcome of the trial (Lion provides three different endings depending on the way the jurors [a group selected from the audience] vote), corruption and indifference continue. The play thus concludes not with the conventional sentencing of the accused (Höss "was hanged in Auschwitz I by the Poles on April 16, 1947" [Epstein and Rosen 129]) but with an accusation directed at the audience. One of the actors steps out of his role and challenges the audience to stop being spectators of the world: "Sit on your collective ass in your collective silence—or stand up, collectively stricken, and, collectively, do nothing!" Why people attend theatre about historical atrocity, and what they do after the performance, are what matters. At the play's end, Sammy, the bartender, appeals for applause, proof that "indifference belongs to history and not to the theatre!" The audience has "survived" the performance, and the actors, Sammy tells us, are preparing a different show: "Next month we do Rwanda!"

Jokes about Rwanda? The angry satire of *Sammy's Follies* may well offend some viewers. Robert Skloot has written that Holocaust drama will fail "if it demeans the suffering or memory of the mass of Holocaust victims... [or] if it distorts or denies history for the purpose of advancing otherwise unrelated causes" (*The Darkness* 116). In the 1980s, Skloot generalized that there were "five objectives of serious playwrights... honouring the victims, teaching history to audiences, evoking emotional responses, discussing ethical issues, and suggesting solutions to universal, contemporary problems" (10). But a list of objectives does not explain what these objectives entail, or how Holocaust theatre in 2003 might have different answers than those provided earlier. The outrageousness of *Sammy's Follies* also exemplifies how Holocaust theatre during the last twenty years tests many of the theatrical conventions Skloot initially analyzed. In 1998, writing the introduction to his second volume of *The Theatre of the Holocaust*, he drew attention to remarkable developments in Holocaust drama in the eighties and nineties. The contributions made by and about "new and different voices" (3) i.e., plays by and about survivors and their children, as well as a greater cultural willingness to recognize how "postmodern theatre forms may use history differently yet still ethically" (30) made Skloot modify his earlier list of objectives. Putting quotation marks around universality, Skloot concluded that, "we not only know more about the Holocaust, but we know it differently as well" (4).

The plays collected in the two volumes of *A Terrible Truth* provide insight into what it means to know the Holocaust differently. In Alvin Goldfarb's "Select Bibliography of Holocaust Plays, 1933-1997," an annotated list of 256 plays, which is itself a revision made necessary by the number of plays that appeared after his first bibliography published eleven years earlier, only five plays are by Canadians. None of the Canadian plays Irene Watts has selected is mentioned, in most cases simply because they were neither published nor produced by 1997. Like the Canadian plays (Jason Sherman's *None Is Too Many*, Anne Szumigalski's *Z*, Theresa Tova's *Still the Night*, Jonathan Garfinkel's *The Trials of John Demjanjuk: A Holocaust Cabaret*, and Eugene Lion's *Sammy's Follies*), Martin Sherman's *Rose* and David Edgar's *Albert Speer* are less than ten years old. The three older plays chosen by Watts, C.P. Taylor's *Good*, Joshua Sobol's *Ghetto*, and Arthur Miller's *Playing for Time*, were produced and published in the 1980s.[4] Although *Good*, *Ghetto*, and *Playing for Time* all have their own special focus, they share a concern that the Nazis used performance, music, and theatre as instruments of control and humiliation. The case of Vilna, known before the war as the Jerusalem of Lithuania, and dramatized by Sobol's *Ghetto*, offers a good example. News of the first concert in Vilna was greeted by the protest sign, "*oyf a beysoylom shpilt men nit kayn teater*" (in a cemetery no theatre is to be performed). The relationship between drama and the Holocaust has always been controversial.

Sobol examines both the ambivalence and opposition to the Vilna Ghetto Theatre, and utilizes the metaphor of performance as emblematic of everyone's life in the ghetto. He turns to the testimony found in Herman Kruk's *Diary of the Vilna Ghetto* for evidence that the inhabitants of this ghetto were highly sensitive to their roles as performers, compelled at the whim of the Nazi commandant to don costumes that were the detritus of the dead. He makes Kruk a character who contests the ghetto leadership's approval of the theatre, and frames the play's action with an 1983 interview during which a Holocaust survivor with only one hand is asked about his past.[5] The survivor, Srulik, identifies himself as the former artistic director of the theatre. Asked to recount the last performance, he insists that he can "remember nothing" yet immediately contradicts himself by setting the last performance at a precise time: "the night before Kittel murdered Gens," ten days before the ghetto was liquidated. Remembering only fragments, joking that like the Greek philosopher, Diogenes, the ghetto inhabitants were searching for justice, Srulik enters the past of his memories as the walls of his apartment vanish to reveal a setting in which a truck dumps a pile of clothing. Kittel, the Nazi officer as God, enters and announces, "Let there be light!" He soon orders a desperate woman to dress up. Discovering that under her slip she is hiding some beans, Kittel proposes that she repay the debt of the missing beans by performing for him. Fond of theatre as well as delighting in jazz (he later paints blackface on the Jewish actors and compels them to play the banned Gershwin), full of contempt for Lithuanian Vilna but claiming to admire Jewish art, Kittel is the sadistic puppet master who can do with the inhabitants what he will.

In contrast to Kittel, Srulik is a timid ventriloquist who relies upon a Dummy to express what he is afraid to say. He knows that he is powerless to stop Kittel's abuse; he is merely a performer. When Kittel threatens to shoot the woman, the Dummy shouts, "Wait! Halt! *Arretez! Stoi!*" but Srulik complains "Don't do that! You're a hero, it's me who gets shot in the head." If the Dummy's indirect speech is representative of the silencing of the other ghetto inhabitants, Gens, the head of the ghetto, is obviously perceived as Kittel's puppet. Srulik tells Gens "This is no time to start a theatre"; three weeks earlier "fifty thousand Jews were massacred here." Tormented by what he must do, and yet convinced that the "intellectuals" who condemn the theatre are misguided, Gens defends the creation of the theatre as both pragmatically and morally the right choice, a practical way to save the lives of actors who will die without work permits, and a spiritual way to defy the Nazi contempt for their humanity. He knows that their time is limited, that the performance will soon be over, but he insists that until then, he will collaborate in order to save as many Jews as he can. Gens cherishes no illusions about how others in the ghetto view him; he imagines himself in the future submitting to "Jewish justice" and despairs whether future generations will understand his behaviour. Forced to make choices, like the ghetto doctors who debate how to ration their limited supply of insulin, fully knowing that eventually the supply will run out and everyone will die no matter how they arrange their "selection," Gens acts his part with as much skill as he can.

The trial that Gens longs for never takes place, or if it does, it occurs only through Sobol's dramatization. For Gens's words are clearly directed at the audience: "You with your morality. There's dirt, there's filth, you look away. If you survive, you'll show your hands – clean." In the final scene, seemingly empty Nazi uniforms satirize both the Jewish ghetto puppets and the Nazi puppets that have power over them. Beginning with a parody of Shylock's speech, "Hath not a Jew eyes?" the Nazi uniforms proceed to mutilate the Dummy and then spray him with DDT. After applauding the performance—"As satire, that was outstanding. And I'm an expert. I used to perform in satirical cabaret in the thirties"—Kittel demands final payment for the missing beans. Since the woman who stole the beans has escaped the ghetto, presumably to join the resistance, he insists that new orders now apply. In a reminder of who is the real puppet master, Kittel states, "One hand washes the other" and demonstrates that he is the ultimate dramatist. Feeding the starving performers first, and then shooting them all, Kittel even shoots the Dummy when it sings in his face. Only Srulik survives the massacre, bereft of the hand that held the Dummy. The memory of the shooting shocks Srulik back to the present and the play ends where it began as though only through an endless rehearsal of his traumatic memories can Srulik hope to get the story right and find the justice he is seeking. But if one hand washes the other, how can a one-handed man ever hope to wash away the past?

Sobol's acknowledgement that no performance will conclusively answer our questions about the ethics of theatre in the Vilna Ghetto is characteristic of the complexity of recent Holocaust theatre. What has changed since *The Diary of Anne Frank* was first performed nearly fifty years ago is manifold. It includes increasing interest in second and third generation stories (*Rose*), and the willingness to examine the psychology and history of perpetrators (*Albert Speer*) and the responsibility of bystanders (*Sammy's Follies*). We might generalize that Holocaust theatre increasingly concentrates on gray zone matters, such as the degrees of collaboration enacted in *Ghetto* and *Sammy's Follies*. In *The Diary of Anne Frank* no Nazis appeared on stage. Although Nazis do not appear in all the plays included in Volume I, dramatists today appear more willing to risk representing Nazis, to set their dramas within the camps, and to represent the specific violence of the Holocaust while relating it to other questions of twentieth-century history.

Another striking characteristic of the plays in this collection, if not of all contemporary Holocaust drama, is that no dramatist opts for the upbeat tone that characterizes the final scene of *The Diary of Anne Frank*. In that scene, Otto Frank completes his reading of his dead daughter's diary by recollecting, "It seems strange to say this, that anyone could be happy in a concentration camp. But Anne was happy in the camp in Holland where they first took us. After two years of being shut up in these rooms, she could be out... out in the sunshine and the fresh air that she loved" (86-87). Contemporary Holocaust drama avoids the sentimental, particularly the sentimentality that is unintentionally comic. What it does not avoid is the deliberately comic. Dramatists are increasingly challenging the long held taboo on Holocaust laughter. The comedy can be grotesque and jarring, as in *Sammy's Follies*. The jokes in *Ghetto* are equally dark:

KITTEL
> Tell me, what is the difference between partial liquidation and total liquidation?

WEISKOPF
> Kill fifty thousand Jews and not me, that's partial liquidation. Kill me, that's total.

The comedy of Martin Sherman's *Rose* is more extended and sophisticated. It is also deceptive: the opening words, "She laughed," take on a radically different meaning at the end. Sherman's language is also deliberately misleading, for the protagonist's words that follow the opening, "The bullet struck her forehead. It caught her in the middle of a thought. She was nine," do not refer, as we expect, to Rose's baby daughter casually murdered by a soldier in the Warsaw Ghetto decades earlier. Despite the statement that appears early in Rose's monologue— "Nothing happened yesterday. Trust me"—something did happen that explains why the eighty-year-old Rose is sitting on a bench mourning the death of a child.

Rose sits shivah for the Palestinian child killed the night before by her Israeli grandson, Doron. The anonymity of the television coverage of violence—"Someone attacked someone. Someone threw a stone. Someone was knifed"—is dispelled the moment Rose recognizes Doron. She knows that sitting shivah for the Palestinian child, speaking Yiddish to her, is absurd and "meaningless." She recollects that her Israeli son, Abbie, tells her, "You only think you're sitting shivah for this girl. That's not what you're sitting shivah for." But when so many have died, sometimes Rose forgets for whom she is sitting shivah.

In a one-woman play that examines issues of Jewish identity, memory, and history, in a dramatic structure that tricks us with its deceptively rambling nature, Rose recollects the horrifying tale of her life and of the twentieth century. The practice of shivah, which Rose describes as a week in which "you laugh, cry, argue as you remember the dead... and it reminds you that you belong to a people, a race, a culture of sore behinds and complainers and heated discussions" perfectly describes Sherman's approach. Rose debates everything, concludes nothing, and is always willing to admit another point of view. She and Abbie argue over who has the right to condemn Doron. Telling her that Israel is their future—"We have nothing else.... Everything else is gone"—Abbie begs her to recognize that the burden of Holocaust memory is too much: "You have to let us go, Mama. Your shadows will choke us to death." The Holocaust is clearly central to Rose's narrative and yet to say that the play is "about the Holocaust" excludes too much. What is the play not about? When her life has taken her from Ukraine, Poland, Germany, across Europe to Palestine, back to France, then Germany, Atlantic City, Miami Beach, Israel, and back to the USA, Rose rightly concludes that she has "lived through some of the most tumultuous events of this century."

But when one has lived so long and experienced so much, how can Rose be sure "if [her] memory is of the actual event or a scene from the movie"? The trip to Palestine in 1947 was on the ship *Exodus*; Rose clearly recalls seeing a sign with the ship's name and date, but then questions the basis for this memory: "Am I remembering the newsreels or the movie with Paul Newman?" She rejects the commonplace that "the elderly are supposed to remember the past with dreadful clarity, but the present – hardly at all." Even the memory of her first pogrom is confused; she regards it as the end of her childhood, but whether the Cossacks she remembers are her own memories or images left over from her later watching of *Fiddler of the Roof* is uncertain. Rose knows that historians question the accuracy of survivors' memories, but on this point she refuses to back down: "Years later, a history professor told me they couldn't have been Cossacks; Stalin had pacified the Cossacks, he said. Well, there were a few left over." As for the America to which she immigrates after the war, it too has its pogroms during the McCarthy hearings: "As Americans were no longer very good on horses, they conducted their pogroms around committee tables and under television lights."

Believing that "Judaism's greatest contribution to mankind was asking questions that can't be answered," Rose defines the essence of that gift as "the invention of the phrase 'on the other hand.'" Examples of "on the other hand" keep appearing in a life account that is both horrific and comic. The tone is flat: "Well, then. The war was over. One day Nazis were marching into Warsaw.

Another day, Russians." Running away from the Russians, unable to comprehend what has happened, Rose flees to Germany and witnesses in Dresden "[a] child with no arms.... The goodies had conquered the baddies, and had saved what remained of our lives, but the child had no arms."

Sitting shivah for her life and that of the century, for all the children whose lives were destroyed, Rose recalls accompanying her grandchildren to a play about "teenagers in the Warsaw Ghetto." Disappointed at the prettiness of the play—"There was no stench. It was utterly foreign to the audience, it could have been a fairy tale. Where was the smell, I wondered"—she is equally disappointed when her Israeli grandchildren laugh at the play's representation of Yiddish culture (the sentimental as unintentionally comic). The dilemma of how to dramatize the Holocaust, the question of what kind of laughter is the right laughter, the focus on the audience's response – these concerns persist. Rose tells us repeatedly that she wishes to die in the middle of a sentence, and for once, she is granted her wish. She dies in the middle of a memory and a thought: "On the other hand..." As in all Holocaust literature, the ellipses symbolize both what cannot be said and how much more remains to be said. Dramatists continue to write plays about the Holocaust, looking for ways beyond the stunned silence that is no longer sufficient. On the other hand, whether we are spectators in the theatre or in the world, was it ever the right answer?

— — • — —

Adrienne Kertzer is a professor of English at the University of Calgary. Her many articles on Holocaust representation include "*Fugitive Pieces*: Listening as a Holocaust Survivor's Child," *English Studies in Canada* 26 (2000): 193-217 for which she received the F.E.L. Priestley Prize. Her book, *My Mother's Voice: Children, Literature, and the Holocaust*, Broadview Press, 2002, won the Canadian Jewish Book Award for Scholarship on a Jewish Subject.

Notes

[1] As an example of the questionable use to which we put Holocaust metaphors, an official at a Canadian university recently referred to the consequences of a public school strike, in which high school students might not be able to write their final examinations, as a holocaust.

[2] Gitta Sereny uses these words by W.A. Visser 't Hooft as part of her epigraph for *Albert Speer: His Battle with Truth.* See also Sereny 335.

[3] Eric Joseph Epstein and Philip Rosen identify Rudolf Hoess as the "kommandant of Auschwitz I... responsible for enlarging the camp's capacity and introducing Zyklon-B" (129).

[4] Volume II of *A Terrible Truth* will include *None Is Too Many, Still the Night, The Trials of John Demjanjuk: A Holocaust Cabaret, Good,* and *Playing for Time.*

[5] *Ghetto* is the third of Sobol's plays set in the Vilna Ghetto. It was first staged in Israel in 1984, five years before the David Lan English production. The other two plays are *Adam* and *Underground.*

Works Cited

Epstein, Eric Joseph and Philip Rosen. *Dictionary of the Holocaust: Biography, Geography, and Terminology.* Westport, CT: Greenwood P, 1997.

Goldfarb, Alvin. "Select Bibliography of Holocaust Plays, 1933-1997." Schumacher 298-334.

Goodrich, Frances and Albert Hackett. *The Diary of Anne Frank.* 1956. Toronto: Irwin, 1964.

Horowitz, Sara R. *Voicing the Void: Muteness and Memory in Holocaust Fiction.* SUNY Series in Modern Jewish Literature and Culture. Albany: State U of New York P, 1997.

Isser, Edward R. *Stages of Annihilation: Theatrical Representations of the Holocaust.* London: Associated University Presses, 1997.

Patraka, Vivian M. *Spectacular Suffering: Theatre, Fascism, and the Holocaust.* Unnatural Acts: Theorizing the Performative. Bloomington: Indiana UP, 1999.

Schumacher, Claude. ed. *Staging the Holocaust: The Shoah in Drama and Performance.* Cambridge: Cambridge UP, 1998.

Sereny, Gitta. *Albert Speer: His Battle with Truth.* New York: Knopf, 1995.

Skloot, Robert. *The Darkness We Carry: The Drama of the Holocaust.* Madison, WI: U of Wisconsin P, 1988.

—. Ed. *The Theatre of the Holocaust.* Vol. 2. Madison, WI: U of Wisconsin P, 1999.

Albert Speer

based on the book
Albert Speer: His Battle with Truth
by Gitta Sereny

David Edgar

ABOUT THE AUTHOR

David Edgar was born in Britain in 1948 into a theatre family. After a period in journalism, he took up writing full time in 1972. He founded and directed Britain's first post-graduate course in playwriting studies, at the University of Birmingham, from 1989 to 1999.

Other plays include: *Entertaining Strangers* and *The Shape of the Table* (National Theatre). *Destiny, Maydays, Pentecost*; adaptations of *The Jail Diary of Albie Sachs, Dr. Jekyll and Mr. Hyde* and *Nicholas Nickleby* (Royal Shakespeare Company).

David Edgar has also written several plays for the BBC, including the three-part serial *Vote for Them*; *A Movie Starring Me*; *Buying a Landslide*; *Talking to Mars* and a dramatization of Eve Brook's *The Secret Parts*. He wrote the biographical *Citizen Locke* for television and the film *Lady Jane*, for Paramount (1986). His libretto *The Bridge* was performed at the Northern College of Music and as part of the Covent Garden Festival in 1998.

David Edgar writes and reviews for a wide variety of journals. A collection of his non-dramatic writings, *The Second Time as Farce*, was published by Lawrence and Wishart in 1988. He edited and introduced a book of contributions to the Birmingham Theatre Conference, *State of Play*, in 1999.

Albert Speer by David Edgar, based on Gitta Sereny's book *Albert Speer: His Battle with Truth*, was first performed in the Lyttelton at the National Theatre in May 2000, with the following company:

Albert Speer	Alex Jennings
Nuremberg Prosecutor	William Gaunt
Nuremberg Judge	John Nolan

Spandau Prison, 1947

French Officer	Patrick Baladi
Russian Director	Charles Millham
Guard	Stephen Ballantyne
Soviet Guard	Patrick Marlowe
Konstantin von Neurath, foreign minister	Pip Donaghy
Admiral Karl Dönitz	Martin Chamberlain
Baldur von Schirach, Hitler Youth leader	David Weston
Rudolf Hess, Hitler's Deputy	Sylvester Morand
Walther Funk, economics minister	Iain Mitchell
Admiral Erich Raeder	Benny Young
Georges Casalis, Calvinist pastor	Jonathan Cullen

Germany and the Occupied Territories, 1931–45

Rudolf Wolters, architect	Simon Day
Hans Tessenow, architect	Pip Donaghy
Architecture students	Patrick Baladi, Stephen Ballantyne, Giles Smith, Chris Vance
Adolf Hitler	Roger Allam
Colonel Nicolas von Below, adjutant	Adrian Penketh
Karl Hanke, party official, later Gauleiter	Iain Mitchell
Margret Speer, Speer's wife	Jessica Turner
Anne-Marie Wittenberg (later Kempf), Speer's secretary	Christine Kavanagh
Julius Schaub, adjutant	John Nolan
Dr. Fritz Todt, Minister of Armaments	Pip Donaghy
Speer's Father	William Gaunt
Frau Maria von Below	Imogen Slaughter
Eva Braun	Cathryn Bradshaw
Frau Anni Brandt	Tilly Blackwood
First Adjutant	Stephen Ballantyne
Fräulein Johanna Wolf, secretary	Sally Ann Burnett
Second Adjutant	Charles Millham
Fräulein Christa Schröder, secretary	Elizabeth Conboy
Theodor Ganzenmüller, railway official	Patrick Baladi
Major in Ukraine	Benny Young
Ukrainian Tufties	Chloe Angharad, Sally-Ann Burnett, Elizabeth Conboy, Imogen Slaughter
Speer Construction Workers	Martin Chamberlain, Patrick Marlowe, Giles Smith, Chris Vance
State Secretary, Ministry of Armaments	John Nolan
His Assistant	David Weston
Ernst, Speer's brother	Stephen Ballantyne
Dr. Professor Friedrich Koch	David Weston
Heinrich Himmler, Reichsführer-SS	Benny Young

Germany and England, 1966–81

Role	Actor
Hans Flachsner, Speer's lawyer	David Weston
Pressmen	Martin Chamberlain, Charles Millham, John Nolan, David Weston, Chris Vance, Benny Young
Heckler	Iain Mitchell
Albert, Speer's son	Stephen Ballantyne
Hilde Schramm, Speer's daughter	Cathryn Bradshaw
Ulf Schramm, her husband	Iain Mitchell
Ruth, Albert's wife	Sally Ann Burnett
Arnold, Speer's son	Chris Vance
Fritz, Speer's son	Giles Smith
Margret Nissen, Speer's daughter	Elizabeth Conboy
Hans Nissen, her husband	Adrian Penketh
Ernst, Speer's son	Patrick Marlowe
Waitresses	Chloe Angharad, Imogen Slaughter
Wolf-Jobst Siedler, Speer's publisher	William Gaunt
Mrs Winteringham	Tilly Blackwood
Publishers	Elizabeth Conboy, Charles Millham
Chair of University Meeting	Sally-Ann Burnett
Hecklers	Stephen Ballantyne, Chris Vance, David Weston
Questioners	Patrick Marlowe, Elizabeth Conboy, John Nolan, Martin Chamberlain, Benny Young
Robert Raphael Geis, Rabbi	Pip Donaghy
David, his assistant	Patrick Baladi
Hotel Waiter	Patrick Marlowe

Directed by Trevor Nunn
Set Designer: Ian MacNeil
Costume Designer: Joan Wadge
Lighting Designer: Rick Fisher
Video Design: Chris Laing
Music: Steven Edis
Movement Director: Kate Flatt
Sound Designer: Chris Shutt
Company Voice Work: Patsy Rodenburg
Associate Set Designer: Paul Atkinson

AUTHOR'S NOTE

Gitta Sereny's *Albert Speer: His Battle with Truth* is a 720-page book, written with the utmost historical rigour, about a man whose long life was dominated by the defining event of the twentieth century. In order to write a stage play based on this work I have had to conflate characters, combine scenes and concentrate the incidents on which they are based.

As ever, the aim of this is better to reveal the truth. This is a vulnerable procedure in a play based on a biography in which the truth is pursued but also questioned. I am hugely grateful for the chance to retell the story Gitta Sereny has told so authoritatively in her book. For the consequences of doing so in a very different medium, I am responsible.

In addition to Gitta Sereny herself, I am indebted to Michael Eaton and Hilary Norrish for their contribution to the shape and content of the play as it developed through treatment into draft. As with our earlier stage collaboration, *Nicholas Nickleby*, Trevor Nunn had an immense influence on the structure, substance and meaning of the text, both before and during rehearsals.

Finally, two practical notes. In order to counter the notion that Nazism could only have happened in a foreign language, I've anglicized most of the ranks and titles in the play. The ones left in German are those for which an English translation is misleading: "Führer" doesn't mean the same as "Leader," "Gauleiter" implies something different from "Governor," and while "Herr" does mean "Mr." it is often used in conjunction with other titles in a way which sounds odd to an English ear. Second, where lines are broken in the text, I have indicated the point at which the next character interrupts by a slash. The rest of the first character's line does not have to be completed: it is there to provide some overlap but also to indicate to the actor where the interrupted sentence was going.

CHARACTERS

Albert SPEER
Nuremberg PROSECUTOR
Nuremberg JUDGE

Spandau Prison, 1947
FRENCH OFFICER
RUSSIAN DIRECTOR
GUARD
SOVIET GUARD
Konstantin von NEURATH, foreign minister
Admiral Karl DÖNITZ
Baldur von SCHIRACH, Hitler Youth leader
Rudolf HESS, Hitler's Deputy
Walther FUNK, economics minister
Admiral Erich RAEDER
Georges CASALIS, Calvinist pastor

Germany and the Occupied Territories, 1931–45
Rudolf WOLTERS, architect
Hans TESSENOW, architect
Adolf HITLER
Karl HANKE, party official, later Gauleiter
MARGRET Speer, Speer's wife
ANNEMARIE Wittenberg (later Kempf), Speer's secretary
Colonel Nicolas VON BELOW, adjutant
Julius SCHAUB, adjutant
Dr Fritz TODT, Minister of Armaments
Speer's FATHER
FRAU Maria VON BELOW
EVA BRAUN
FRAU Anni BRANDT
Two young ADJUTANTS (at the Berghof)
FRÄULEIN Johanna WOLF, secretary
FRÄULEIN Christa SCHRÖDER, secretary
Theodor GANZENMÜLLER, railway official
MAJOR in Ukraine
Six members SPEER construction SQUAD
STATE SECRETARY, Ministry of Armaments
His ASSISTANT
ERNST, Speer's brother
DR Professor Friedrich KOCH
Heinrich HIMMLER, Reichsführer-SS

Germany and England, 1966–81
Hans FLACHSNER, Speer's lawyer
ALBERT, Speer's son
HILDE Schramm, Speer's daughter
ULF Schramm, her husband
RUTH, Albert's wife
ARNOLD, Speer's son
FRITZ, Speer's son
MARGRET (JNR) Nissen, Speer's daughter
HANS Nissen, her husband
ERNST (JNR), Speer's son
Wolf-Jobst SIEDLER, Speer's publisher
MRS WINTERINGHAM
Young PUBLISHERS
CHAIR of University Meeting
Two HECKLERS
Five QUESTIONERS
Robert Raphael GEIS, Rabbi
DAVID, his assistant

Architecture Students
Ukrainian Tufties
Staff Officers
Adjutants
Pressmen and Hecklers
Publishers and Partygoers
Audience at University Meeting

Albert Speer
based on the book *Albert Speer: His Battle With Truth* by Gitta Sereny
by David Edgar

Act One

"For five years I lived in this world of plans,
and in spite of all their defects and absurdities
I still cannot entirely tear myself away from it all."
—Albert Speer, *Inside the Third Reich*

1.1.1   Heidelberg, 1970s

Around 70 years old, ALBERT SPEER sits in a chair, sleeping and dreaming. He remembers the charges and sentences passed at the Nuremberg trial of the Nazi leaders.

PROSECUTOR
The Defendant Speer – between 1932 and 1945 was: A member of the Nazi Party, Reichsleiter, member of the Reichstag, Reich Minister for Armaments and Munitions, \ Chief of the Organization Todt, General Plenipotentiary for Armaments in the Office of the Four Year Plan, and Chairman of the Armaments Council.

JUDGE
In accordance with Article 27 of the Charter, the International Military Tribunal will now pronounce the sentences on the defendants convicted in this indictment. Defendant Joachim von Ribbentrop, on the counts of the indictment on which you have been convicted, the Tribunal sentences you to death by hanging. Defendant Ernst Kaltenbrunner, the Tribunal sentences you to death by hanging.

PROSECUTOR
The defendant Speer used the foregoing positions and his personal influence in such a manner that: \ He participated in the military and economic planning and preparation of the Nazi conspirators for Wars of aggression and Wars in Violation of International Treaties, Agreements, and Assurances set forth in Count One and Count Two of the Indictment…

JUDGE
Defendant Julius Streicher, the Tribunal sentences you to death by hanging.

PROSECUTOR
…and he authorized, directed, and participated in the War Crimes set forth in Count Three of the Indictment…

JUDGE
Defendant Fritz Sauckel, the Tribunal sentences you to death by hanging.

PROSECUTOR
...and the Crimes against Humanity set forth in Count Four of the Indictment, including more particularly the abuse and exploitation of human beings for forced labour in the conduct of aggressive war.

JUDGE
Defendant Albert Speer! On the counts of the indictment on which you have been convicted, the Tribunal sentences you to death by hanging!

SPEER wakes in terrible agitation.

SPEER
Not – yet.

1.2.1 Spandau, 18 July 1947

The RUSSIAN DIRECTOR and a FRENCH OFFICER and GUARDS await prisoners in a reception hall in Spandau prison. Seven concentration camp uniforms set out. A door opens and a GUARD admits Konstantin von NEURATH, wearing shabby civilian clothes.

RUSSIAN DIRECTOR
(from a list, to NEURATH, emphatically, but with terrible pronunciation)
Konstantin von Neurath. Foreign Minister. Fifteen year.

FRENCH OFFICER
On admission, the prisoners will undress completely. Prisoners will be addressed by their convict number, in no circumstances by name.

RUSSIAN DIRECTOR
Now you are Number one.

NEURATH undresses. KARL DÖNITZ is admitted.

Grand Admiral Karl Dönitz: ten year. Number Two.

DÖNITZ undresses. Baldur von SCHIRACH is admitted.

Baldur von Schirach. Hitler youth leader, twenty year. Number Three.

SCHIRACH undresses. HESS is admitted.

Ah. Hess. Hitler Deputy, till 1941. Sentence to life. Is number four.

HESS doesn't undress. SPEER admitted. He is 42.

Albert Speer, Arm Minister, 20 year.

SPEER sizes up the situation.

I say a lucky man.

GUARD
(*shouts to HESS*) Undress!

RUSSIAN DIRECTOR
His number five.

> *HESS and SPEER begin to undress. We sense hostility from the other PRISONERS to SPEER. Walter FUNK is admitted.*

(*to FUNK and RAEDER*) Walter Funk, Reichsminister for Economics. Number six, for life.

Erich RAEDER is admitted.

And Admiral Erich Raeder is number seven. Also life.

> *As the later PRISONERS finish undressing, the FRENCH OFFICER continues to read out the rules. GUARDS gesture to them to go and dress in the concentration camp uniforms. HESS is swaying.*

FRENCH OFFICER
The discipline of the institution requires that prisoners should adopt a standing position whenever approached or in the presence of prison officers. They will salute by standing at attention at the same time removing their headgear.

> *HESS gestures to the GUARD who goes to speak to him. A GUARD goes and whispers to him.*

The prisoners may approach an officer or warder only if ordered to do so or if they want to make a request.

RUSSIAN DIRECTOR
(*in Russian*) Ftchyom tam dela? [What's the problem?]

GUARD
(*nodding to HESS*) This man says he will faint.

RUSSIAN DIRECTOR
(*Russian*) Poost syadit. [Let him sit down.]

GUARD
(*to HESS*) You must sit down.

HESS sits on the floor. The other PRISONERS continue to dress.

FRENCH OFFICER
(*continues*) Prisoners shall at all times wear the clothing provided for them. Imprisonment shall be in the form of solitary confinement. Approaching any window—including those in the cells—is strictly prohibited. The Prisoners may not talk or associate with one another except with special dispensation from the Directorate. However religious services and walks in open air will be carried out together.

RUSSIAN DIRECTOR
Form line!

The PRISONERS form up in their concentration camp uniforms.

(*Russian*) Zaklyutchyonnym vazzmozhina boodit intiressna oozznat shto etoo adezhdoo nasseeli oozniki konstlagirey. [The Prisoners may be interested to learn that these clothes were worn by prisoners in concentration camps.]

GUARD
(*translates*) The Prisoners must like to know that these cloths are worn by prisoners in concentration camp.

No response from the PRISONERS.

RUSSIAN DIRECTOR
(*Russian*) Im shto, ni panyatna? [Do they understand that?]

GUARD
(*translates*) Do you understand?

The PRISONERS give slight nods. HESS nods and is helped to his feet.

RUSSIAN OFFICER
So, gentlemen. Welcome to Spandau.

As the DIRECTOR, OFFICER, GUARDS and PRISONERS leave, and the next scene is set up, SPEER speaks out front.

SPEER
You ask me how I felt? That I was getting what I deserved.
What, did I really feel that? Well, my feelings then were complex. I am putting them in simple terms for you.
But I can assure you, at that moment, nothing could have been better designed to make me feel very humble indeed.

1.2.2 Spandau, October 1947

GEORGES CASALIS has come in to a double cell which has been appointed for use as a chapel. He carries a suitcase. There is one table and the cell lavatory. CASALIS, a young Calvinist pastor, opens the case, takes out a wooden cross and places it on the table. He takes out a Bible and finds himself a black cassock. He takes off his jacket and is putting the cassock on when he hears the rumble of an approaching congregation.

He hurries to finish dressing as a SOVIET GUARD leads in RAEDER, FUNK, DÖNITZ, SCHIRACH, NEURATH and SPEER, dragging chairs. There is a moment when the SOVIET GUARD and the SIX PRISONERS stand watching a YOUNG MAN having a fight with his cassock. CASALIS wins, looks round for someone he recognizes and holds out his hand to DÖNITZ.

CASALIS
Herr Dönitz.

After a moment, DÖNITZ puts his chair upright and shakes CASALIS's hand.

(to the next man) Herr Schirach?

SCHIRACH
Yes.

Shake hands.

CASALIS
(to FUNK) And – Raeder?

FUNK
Funk.

CASALIS
Herr Funk.

FUNK
(shaking hands, nodding to the next man) Raeder.

RAEDER
Admiral Raeder.

CASALIS
(shaking hands) How do you do. And... Herr von Neurath.

NEURATH shakes, pleased that CASALIS used the "von."

And of course, Herr...

SPEER
Speer.

CASALIS
Herr Speer.

Shakes hands. To the GUARD.

Herr Hess?

The GUARD is baffled.

NEURATH
(Russian) Nommerr chetyrree. [Number Four.]

SOVIET GUARD
He is in cell. No religion. "Mumbo jumbo."

He indicates by the universal gesture that HESS is mad.

CASALIS
Please gentlemen be seated.

The PRISONERS sit on their chairs. The SOVIET GUARD sits on the lavatory.

My name is Georges Casalis. I am minister to the Protestant French community here in Berlin. I was asked if I would be prepared to serve as pastor to the prisoners of Spandau, on the grounds I fear of my linguistic rather than my spiritual skills.

No laugh.

So, as required of me: your regular Saturday dose of mumbo jumbo.

No laugh.

The text on which I wish to speak today is taken from Luke's gospel: "While he was in a certain city, there came a man full of leprosy–"

The PRISONERS glance at each other.

"–and when he saw Jesus he fell on his face and begged him: Lord, if you will, make me clean."

SCHIRACH a bark of a laugh. DÖNITZ leans over and whispers to FUNK.

Now, you may ask, why I have chosen this passage to discuss with you today.

The PRISONERS are chuntering. CASALIS looks up from his notes, deciding to confront the atmosphere directly.

But before I say anything more to you, I sense that you have something you want to say to me.

RAEDER stands. The SOVIET GUARD stands too.

RAEDER
Herr Pastor, we must protest.

CASALIS
Uh – why?

RAEDER
It is entirely inappropriate to address us in this way.

CASALIS
In what \ way?

FUNK
As lepers.

CASALIS
Ah.

Slight pause. SCHIRACH stands.

SCHIRACH
We are here not as criminals, but because we have been unjustly condemned.

DÖNITZ
(stands) As men who only did their military duty.

FUNK
(stands) Therefore we protest, in the strongest possible terms.

RAEDER
And if our protest should prove ineffective–

NEURATH
–we shall take official action.

A moment of standoff. NEURATH stands. SPEER stands.

CASALIS
Gentlemen–

DÖNITZ
And so good morning, Herr Pastor.

> *DÖNITZ leads the group, picking up their chairs and dragging them to the exit.*

SOVIET GUARD
You want be take to cell?

DÖNITZ
"We want be take to cell."

> *SPEER is following the group.*

CASALIS
But gentlemen–

> *The GUARD calls up the corridor to other GUARDS.*

SOVIET GUARD
(in Russian) Kapitan Razzinskiy! Mne noozhna vasha pomashch! Dvaa tchelaveka! [Captain Rozinsky! I need your help! Two men!]

CASALIS
But, gentlemen, I don't know what to do.

> *The PRISONERS look back at him, a little contemptuously.*

If the words of the Bible are an offence to you, how can I be of help?

> *The other GUARDS arrive.*

I had hoped we were to set out on a journey, to find common ground between us and our inner selves. Tomorrow, I shall deliver the sermon I have not delivered here, to my own congregation. Next week I planned to speak to you and then to them from Mark: "Those who are well have no need of a physician."

> *He puts the Bible and the cross in the suitcase, and slams it shut.*

That is, to anyone who wants to hear me.

RAEDER
We shall see.

DÖNITZ leads the PRISONERS out. SPEER lingers. When the others have gone, the SOVIET GUARD gestures for him to follow. SPEER demurs. CASALIS is picking up his suitcase.

SPEER
Well, that put the cat among the pigeons.

CASALIS realizes that SPEER wants to speak to him. He puts down his suitcase.

CASALIS
That was not of course \ my intention–

SPEER
You should however pay no attention to that little spectacle.

CASALIS
I fear \ that's not as easy–

SPEER
Your sermons *should* upset us. You should not spare anybody's feelings.

CASALIS
No. Well, thank you.

Pause.

Herr Speer, would you like to join your comrades?

SPEER
Oh, come now, Herr Pastor. You have done your homework. You know that even if I saw those gentlemen as comrades, they would hardly think that way of me.

Pause.

CASALIS
(to GUARD) Please, leave us for a moment.

After a beat, the GUARD understands, and leaves, shutting and locking the door behind him.

Your defence at Nuremberg: Your position in the government was merely technical. You made no ideological statements. You were aware that people were evacuated but you had no idea that they were being systematically put to death.

SPEER
But nevertheless…

CASALIS
Nevertheless it was your duty to assume your share of the responsibility for the catastrophe of the world war. Insofar as Hitler gave you orders and you obeyed them, you must share the blame.

SPEER
Well done.

CASALIS
(aware of being patronized) Well, thank you.

SPEER
So it will be no surprise that number five is hardly number one in the affections of his fellow-prisoners.

CASALIS
No.

SPEER
In the same way as I would imagine you are hardly popular with your associates.

CASALIS
I beg your pardon?

SPEER
I wondered what your comrades in the French Resistance think about your present ministry?

CASALIS
You've done your homework too.

SPEER acknowledges with a gesture.

I think they are suspicious of its premise.

SPEER looks questioningly.

Which is, that the greatest sinner can repent. And now Herr Speer, I think you should tell me what you want to say or go back to your cell.

Pause.

SPEER
I want to know if they are right. You spoke about a journey to becoming someone else. I wondered if you felt that anyone can leave their past behind, and become a different man. Or if there are crimes—and criminals—so terrible there is no price too high for them to pay.

CASALIS
What is the past self that you want to leave behind?

SPEER
The man who thinks it's possible to be merely technical.

CASALIS
And what price do you think your crimes deserve?

SPEER
That is the question.

Slight pause.

CASALIS
Herr Speer. I don't think I am looking at a man who wished he'd died at Nuremberg.

SPEER looks questioning.

But perhaps... a man who thinks he ought to have wanted to die.

Slight pause.

And yes. The crimes for which you took responsibility were terrible. In the scale of justice, maybe, for a judge, a jury, yes, there is no price too high. But I am not a lawyer, I am not here to judge, to probe or to interrogate. I am a priest, and as such I am not concerned with balancing your suffering against the suffering for which you were undoubtedly responsible. All I see before me is an individual soul. Alone, alive, and thus, yes, capable of change.

SPEER
And is this a journey I must make alone?

Pause.

CASALIS
Not if you'd prefer to walk in company.

Slight pause.

But only if you tell the truth, to me and to yourself. For although it's possible that a man be born again, to do so he must confront the truth of what he was before.

1.3.1 Germany, 1920s

SPEER out front:

SPEER
And so I tried to do so. Starting with my childhood, how at school I shone at mathematics, how my father nevertheless persuaded me to follow him into an architectural career. And how despite, yes, some initial disappointment, this course of study took me from provincial Heidelberg to Munich, to new interests and new friends.

Enter RUDOLF WOLTERS, a couple of years older than SPEER, now in his 20s. He tosses SPEER his informal 1930s clothes, into which SPEER changes, as:

WOLTERS
Say, you know your problem, Albert? You don't do any work, you dress like a tramp, you're always late and you can't draw. Correct those faults, and you might make something of yourself in architecture.

SPEER
(to CASALIS) Which of course was absolutely \ true.

WOLTERS
Oh, and that's not to mention spending all your time with girls far too pretty for you doing pointlessly exhausting things in boats, down rivers and up mountains.

SPEER
Which was also true. The woman, naturally, was to become my wife. But this was after I had followed Rudi Wolters to the capital, falling under the influence of the great Heinrich Tessenow...

WOLTERS
...whose deep knowledge of the classical tradition...

SPEER
...love of peasant culture and hostility to internationalism...

WOLTERS
...inspires us all.

TESSENOW appears, bringing young ARCHITECTURE STUDENTS in his wake.

TESSENOW
So what is simple?

STUDENTS
Simple is not always good.

TESSENOW
But what is good?

STUDENTS
It's always simple.

TESSENOW
And where will we find good and simple?

STUDENTS
Not in the cities! With the peasants! In the countryside!

SPEER
He told us in his classes in Berlin.

TESSENOW
And so what three things unite the principles of Germanic peasant architecture with those of Agrigento, Paestum and the Parthenon?

The STUDENTS are all keen to answer but TESSENOW silences them with a raised finger.

Herr Speer?

SPEER
Simplicity.

SPEER momentarily stumped. WOLTERS gestures at his own body.

The proportions of the human form. And um...

WOLTERS holds up three fingers.

The rule of three.

TESSENOW
Exactly and precisely and entirely so.

TESSENOW sweeps off, followed by the STUDENTS, echoing:

STUDENTS
Exactly and precisely and entirely so...

SPEER
But what changed my life and fortunes was a chance meeting with the head of my party district.

CASALIS
You are in the party now?

SPEER
Yes, I joined in 1931.

CASALIS
Two years before Hitler came to power.

SPEER
Yes.

CASALIS
You will understand that for me that needs some explanation.

SPEER
Oh, Herr Pastor, just the chaos and despair of the depression. The six million unemployed.

CASALIS
Of course. But, still...

SPEER
And a meeting I had been persuaded by my fellow students to attend.

> *Massive applause. YOUNG NAZIS run in to catch a glimpse of a MAN in a blue suit, surrounded by an entourage of MINDERS, striding purposefully across the stage. SPEER finds himself caught up in their enthusiasm. Finally, the group rushes forward to the front of the stage, saluting and chanting:*

YOUNG NAZIS
Sieg heil! Sieg heil! Sieg heil!

> *On the last of which SPEER finds himself joining in. The YOUNG NAZIS withdraw.*

CASALIS
And do you remember what he said?

SPEER
Well, as I recall, he concentrated on the way in which the war had eliminated the best, leaving the inferior in charge.

CASALIS
And what you felt?

SPEER
Well, I'd expected a vulgar rabble-rouser. In fact, he seemed quite quiet, almost shy...

CASALIS
But what you *felt*?

Slight pause.

SPEER
I felt he was a human being. That here was somebody who cared for us, the young. Who loved us. Individually. And afterwards I drove into the country, to the woods. And walked all night. And joined the Party.
And as the only member of my section with a car, and thus perforce a member of the Party's motorists' association, I was immediately appointed section head, and thus came to the notice of Karl Hanke, then a rising star.

1.3.2 Railway Station, Berlin, July 1932

KARL HANKE enters in party uniform. Also SPEER's wife MARGRET, with a PORTER, and the luggage of a boating holiday—collapsible boats and all—on his trolley.

HANKE
Speer.

SPEER
Who one day in 1932 pursued me to the Lehrter railway station.

HANKE
Thank God I've found you. They told me at your lodgings you had gone away.

SPEER
That's right, I have. On holiday.

MARGRET approaches.

MARGRET
Albert, the train is leaving.

HANKE
On holiday? For Christ's sake, where?

SPEER
East Prussia. We're going faltboating.

MARGRET
In fact, in less than five \ minutes–

HANKE
And all this – stuff–

SPEER
Is our equipment. My dear, this is Party Comrade Hanke.

MARGRET
I am very pleased \ to meet you.

HANKE
But Speer you cannot possibly.... You know that we have taken over premises in the Voss Strasse?

SPEER
Yes.

HANKE
Which the Doctor wishes to refurbish. Instantly.

SPEER
Uh – yes?

HANKE
Speer, you claimed you were an architect.

SPEER
I am.

A whistle blows.

MARGRET
Um, Albert–

SPEER
And yes of course I will.

HANKE
Good man, good man. Thank God.

HANKE goes out. SPEER looks at MARGRET and the luggage.

MARGRET
The Doctor?

SPEER
Goebbels.

MARGRET
Ah. So we don't go on holiday.

MARGRET goes out with the luggage.

CASALIS
So, effectively, your career began with Goebbels.

SPEER
And continued with him, yes.

1.3.3 Voss Strasse, Berlin, July 1932

ANNEMARIE WITTENBERG appears, carrying files and office equipment. She is 18.

ANNEMARIE
Herr Speer. My name is Annemarie Wittenberg.

SPEER
How do you do?

ANNEMARIE
You are the man who painted the outer office red?

SPEER
That's right.

ANNEMARIE
And Party Comrade Hanke's office yellow?

SPEER
Yes.

ANNEMARIE
I work in Dr. Goebbels' office. I am very happy there. But now, apparently, I have to work for you.

She goes out.

SPEER
And then in 1933, I saw some drawings on Karl Hanke's desk.

1.3.4 Voss Strasse, Berlin, April 1933

Enter HANKE with design drawings.

HANKE
What are you saying? This appears to be "The backdrop for 'a shooting match'"?

SPEER
Well, I said, the decoration for a rifle meeting. Not for a May Day rally to be addressed by the Chancellor of Germany.

HANKE
(looking at another design) And you think that this is better. Just these… three big flags.

SPEER
Well, they are are tall. But like the pillars of the Parthenon, they are proportionate.

HANKE hands him the drawings.

HANKE
Well, then. Why not.

HANKE goes out.

SPEER
(out front) And I have to say that the effect was considered something of a triumph.

We see the flags.

So much so, that Goebbels claimed it as his own idea. And when the time came to design the annual party rally at Nuremberg in 1933, I was called to Munich.

1.3.5 Munich, June 1933

Enter HESS, now 39, who takes the drawings from SPEER and looks at them.

HESS
It is an eagle.

SPEER
Yes.

HESS
Around 20 metres wide?

SPEER
That's right. Of course…

HESS
And mounted…

SPEER
On a truss. With nails.

HESS
Just like a butterfly.

SPEER
The idea is to overwhelm the viewer with its power and strength.

HESS
Hm. Only the Führer can decide if this will do.

A decision.

You will go and see him. He is here in Munich, in his apartment on the Prinzregentenstrasse. That will do.

HESS gives SPEER back the drawings and goes out. We see a MAN's back, sitting at a desk. SPEER approaches him.

SPEER
(*to CASALIS*) And so there he was. Sitting, looking at a pistol he'd dismantled on his desk. He didn't look up once. I put the drawing down, he looked at it, and said:

HITLER
Agreed.

And now we see the great eagle too.

CASALIS
And that was it? How did you feel?

SPEER
I felt – well, maybe, just a little disappointed. But he was the Chancellor of Germany. And then having finished Goebbels' flat in record time, I was asked to join the team rebuilding the Chancellor's apartments. Out of which arose an incident which was far from disappointing.

1.4.1 Chancellory apartments, Berlin, October 1933

SPEER goes out as HITLER enters, at speed, followed by his adjutant Julius SCHAUB and other AIDES. SCHAUB is 35, currently a Sergeant, though he will rise to General by 1945 without substantially changing his role. There could be painters and plasterers at work.

HITLER
When is this happening? I was assured that this was happening. Ah. It has happened.

He looks upwards.

Yesterday this room had not been plastered. Now it has. The ceiling moulding's very handsome.

ANNEMARIE and WOLTERS rush in.

And the windows? When will they be glazed?

WOLTERS
(*looking in panic at a sheaf of worknotes*) Um – I... I believe that they are due...

SPEER enters in a hurry. He now wears a waistcoat, collar and tie. He has a large plaster mark on his coat.

ANNEMARIE
(*prompting*) The windows.

SPEER
Yes. The glazing in this section will begin on Friday.

HITLER
Will *begin*?

SPEER
And will be completed.

HITLER
And is the work on schedule, as a whole?

SPEER
It is.

Pause.

HITLER
I am in a hurry. All I have now are the state secretary's apartments. How am I supposed to invite anybody there? It's ridiculous how penny-pinching the Republic was. The entrance! And the elevator!

Slight pause. Suddenly, looking straight at SPEER.

You say this will be done on time?

SPEER
   Yes, my Führer.

HITLER
   So many people tell me what I need's impossible.

SPEER
   This is absolutely possible.

   HITLER looks piercingly at SPEER.

HITLER
   You are the man who refurbished Dr Goebbels' flat. And designed the flags for the May Day rally at the Tempelhof?

SPEER
   Yes, my Führer. But here of course I am merely making sure that the work's completed in the timescale you have set.

HITLER
   Of course. Well, you must come to lunch.

SPEER
   Thank you my Führer. I look forward to it.

   SPEER gives a slight bow. HITLER works out SPEER's mistake.

HITLER
   I meant, today.

   SPEER's second thought is the plaster on his jacket. He can't stop looking down at it.

   Don't worry about that.

   He turns and goes. SPEER turns to his colleagues.

WOLTERS
   Who would have thought...

ANNEMARIE
   Herr *Speer*.

SPEER
   Well, I...

SCHAUB
   Herr Speer, I think the Führer means that you should follow him.

SPEER
Ah. Right.

SPEER hurries out, followed by SCHAUB, into:

1.4.2 Hitler's apartments

HITLER has a blue jacket with a party badge pinned on to it. SPEER hurries in.

SPEER
I'm sorry, I \ didn't realize you intended–

HITLER
Now, do you think that this will do?

He hands SPEER the jacket.

SPEER
But surely, this is \ your own special–

HITLER
Please.

SPEER hurries to change.

So tell me, how did you complete the Goebbels project by that deadline?

SPEER
Well, naturally, my team were all infused \ with commitment to the task–

HITLER
–with National Socialist ardour. Naturally. And?

SPEER
And I persuaded them to work around the clock.

HITLER
But even so...?

SPEER
I had to dry the plaster every night, with an industrial fan I borrowed from a laundry.

HITLER
Then I have made the right decision.

SPEER has changed his jacket. HITLER looks fixedly into SPEER's eyes. After a moment, SPEER turns away.

Or have I?

SPEER turns back, staring into HITLER's eyes. Enter SCHAUB, allowing both SPEER and HITLER to break the stare.

SCHAUB
Your guests await, my Führer.

HITLER
Good. Come, let me introduce you to the Merry Chancellor's Café.

HITLER hands SCHAUB SPEER's old jacket and leads him out towards:

1.4.3 Hitler's dining room in the Chancellory apartments

The LUNCH GUESTS are standing, waiting for HITLER's arrival. They are all men, mostly in Party or military brown: they include DÖNITZ, SCHIRACH, the elegant and patrician Colonel Nicolas VON BELOW (25) and the bull-necked and balding Dr Fritz TODT (44). They could also include NEURATH and FUNK. HITLER comes in, SPEER following. The conversation dries up as HITLER quickly works the room.

HITLER
Party Comrade Schirach.

SCHIRACH
Heil, my Führer.

HITLER
Dr Todt.

TODT
My Führer.

HITLER
(to DÖNITZ) Admiral.

Enter HESS, clearly late. He sees SPEER standing nervously on the edge of things, in HITLER's jacket.

HITLER
(to VON BELOW) Colonel.

VON BELOW
Führer.

HESS
Speer what are you wearing?

EVERYONE turns and looks.

Speer, this will not do. That is the Führer's party badge!

HITLER
Yes, and the Führer's jacket too. Herr Speer's was soiled in his morning's work.

HESS
My Führer, I apologize for lateness.

HITLER, going to his place at the table:

HITLER
No matter. No doubt you had last minute orders for your "special cook."

Laughter.

I have the best vegetarian chef in Germany.

He sits. Others sitting. SPEER doesn't know where to go.

And yet here I am… surrounded by eaters of burnt carrion! Herr Speer, please, sit by me.

After a moment, SPEER hurries over to sit by HITLER, who turns to HESS.

Now, Hess, you know Herr Speer.

HESS
I do.

HITLER
He refurbished Dr. Goebbels' rooms in record time. And he conceived the podium display at the May Day rally.

HESS
Not to mention the eagle design at Nuremberg.

HITLER
Ah.

SPEER
Indeed, my Führer, you did me the honour of approving my design in person.

HITLER looks to SPEER, a little surprised. Then he turns back to the company.

HITLER
I am asked why I am so concerned with beauty, and I answer with a question.

Slight pause. No one likes to volunteer the question.

It is this. How could the great betrayal have occurred, in 1918, quite so quickly, so dramatically?

Slight pause.

And the answer is, as I have said a thousand times, that the best of Germany had been destroyed, shot to blazes by French niggers in the trenches. So but the weakest elements remained. Leaderless, feminized, and naturally prey to any revolutionary bacillus Jewish agitators might care to spread among them. That is why our only duty is to purge the nation of this pestilence, to pass on a healthy Germany to future generations. That is why I surround myself with young men who are passionately committed to the pure and to the beautiful. Those for whom the word "impossible" does not exist!

He turns to SPEER, gazing into his eyes.

Of course. I remember you exactly.

1.4.4 Berlin, April 1934

The lunch party disappears. SPEER breaks forward, to CASALIS, handing HITLER's jacket to SCHAUB:

SPEER
So do you see? Do you understand? At the age of 28, to be plucked from nothing, to be chosen as the brightest and the best of my profession, by the man who, as we saw it, was the saviour of Germany.

CASALIS
"Saviour." "Chosen."

SPEER
Yes.

A social affair. Enter HANKE with MARGRET in formal dress. HANKE hands SPEER his jacket.

HANKE
Well, go on, Speer. Now is the moment.

SPEER
  (*to* CASALIS) The privilege of being in his closest circle.

HANKE
  Introduce her.

SPEER
  And yes, the thrill of being close to power.

  HITLER comes over.

HITLER
  Speer. You are able to grace us with your presence. Can this mean that we've run out of work for you?

SPEER
  No of course not. Führer, may I present my wife?

HITLER
  Your wife?

  Slight pause.

  Of course. I am enchanted by the privilege of your acquaintance. Frau Speer, how do you do.

  He kisses her hand.

MARGRET
  I am very well, my Führer.

HITLER
  A redoubled pleasure, being unaware for all these months of your existence.

  MARGRET flashes a look at SPEER.

SPEER
  Um I...

HITLER
  You will forgive me, madam, if I ask how long...?

MARGRET
  Six years, my Führer.

HITLER
  What? Six *years*?

SPEER
Um, I...

HITLER
And may I ask if there is any more concealment? Have you children?

MARGRET
No, my Führer, not as yet.

SPEER
In fact, my Führer, as it happens \ we are planning–

HITLER
What, six years married and no children? *Speer.*

Slight pause.

On this occasion I can hardly praise your prompt delivery.

EVERYONE laughs.

Frau Speer, your husband is going to make me buildings that will last a thousand years.

He looks at SPEER, bows, turns and goes. SPEER turns to CASALIS.

1.4.5 Spandau, 1947–1950

SPEER
And from then on, it was one task after another. Buildings. Pavilions. The Chancellory. And of course the party congresses.

CASALIS
The searchlights in the sky.

SPEER
The cathedral of light, as it was called.

Which emerges from the darkness behind SPEER.

Which served to dramatize the spectacle, while concealing the unattractive paunches of the party bureaucrats. It's funny, isn't it, that if anything, it will be these, dramatics, that I'll be remembered for?

CASALIS
Does that concern you?

SPEER
Do you think it should? Sometimes I feel quite stirred, that the most successful creation of my life is an immaterial phenomenon.

CASALIS
Well, I can understand that. Dealing also as I do with immaterial phenonema. What is not there, as well as what is there.

SPEER
What do you mean?

CASALIS
I mean that perhaps those searchlights concealed more than the bellies of the bureaucrats.

SPEER
In Nuremberg, they had psychologists. They showed us inkblots. We had to tell them the first thing that we thought of.

CASALIS
And?

SPEER
I said: "You've got it upside down."

Behind SPEER, Germania is beginning to materialize.

CASALIS
Yes of course. It is possible to read too much into these things. Please do go on.

SPEER
And then one day in 1936 I was told there was another job for me. "The greatest and the best of all." Well, even he had got to be impressed with *this*.

CASALIS
(*surprised*) Uh – Hitler?

SPEER
(*suddenly aware of his slippage*) My father.

1.5 General Inspectorate, Berlin, 1938

Suddenly through the darkness we see a vision of the new Berlin at night. In fact, it is the model of SPEER's design for the city HITLER would call Germania, 100 metres long, erected in the basement of the General Inspectorate of Buildings, SPEER's office in Berlin. We understand this when what initially appears to be a giant appears behind the huge, domed hall at the end of the main north-south axis. It is SPEER's 75-year-old FATHER. He has a scrap of paper he tries to look at in the gloom. He looks at the model. Then he calls:

FATHER
I am looking... I understand this is... I am looking for the headquarters of the General Inspectorate...

Lights come on, illuminating the model. Enter WOLTERS followed by ANNEMARIE.

WOLTERS
Herr Speer, how good to see you.

ANNEMARIE
We didn't know that you'd arrived.

ANNEMARIE nods to WOLTERS to go off and find SPEER. WOLTERS goes.

FATHER
I lost... I must have come round the wrong way. There was a garden and a little door...

ANNEMARIE
My name is Annemarie Wittenberg. I am your son's secretary.

FATHER
He has a secretary?

ANNEMARIE
Oh, he has a staff of 85!

She sees SPEER coming in and goes to him.

SPEER
Sir, you're here.

ANNEMARIE
(whispers) He came in through the Chancellory entrance.

SPEER is going to his FATHER. They shake hands.

FATHER
Albert.

SPEER
You are welcome, sir.

Pause. SPEER waits for his FATHER to acknowledge the model.

FATHER
You're not in party uniform.

SPEER
No, I wear civilian clothes.

Pause.

FATHER
(*to* ANNEMARIE) He was always slovenly in dress, as a young man.

SPEER
Sir, you will remember Rudi Wolters.

FATHER looks to the only person WOLTERS can be.

FATHER
Yes. I think I do.

WOLTERS
How are you sir?

FATHER
I am so-so.

SPEER is growing desperate.

SPEER
How is my mother?

FATHER
She is in good spirits. As are both your brothers.

Slight pause.

How is your family?

ANNEMARIE can't bear it any more.

ANNEMARIE
Herr Speer, this is the model for the new Berlin.

FATHER
Yes so I see.

A telephone rings offstage.

ANNEMARIE
Herr Wolters, I'm sure Herr Speer would welcome a short interpretation.

ANNEMARIE goes out to answer the telephone. The FATHER looks at the model as WOLTERS starts the usual pitch.

WOLTERS
Well, sir. The overall principle is the intersection of four thoroughfares of equal width, themselves linked \ at their extremities with the autobahn–

FATHER
So where's the south station?

Re-enter ANNEMARIE in some concern.

SPEER
Well, sir, in fact, the reordering of rail is Herr Wolters prime responsibility. / I'm sure–

FATHER
And the Tiergarten?

SPEER
But the major feature is the north-south axis flanked by state and representative buildings, 120 metres wide and five kilometres long running from–

FATHER
Ah. the figures. Always Albert and his figures. You know he wanted to do mathematics as a life career?

SPEER
Yes, sir. And it was you who persuaded me to change my mind.

ANNEMARIE
(whispers) The Chief is on his way.

SPEER
(whispers) He's what?

FATHER
Rather than end up at a dead-end university, cramming little mediocrities to scrape through their exams.

SPEER
Well, I think we can agree that between us we took the right decision. But now, sir, I am told that we have guests…

FATHER
What at this hour?

The door at the back opens and Colonel VON BELOW admits HITLER with FRAU VON BELOW, 20, FRAU ANNI BRANDT, 33, and EVA BRAUN, 26.

HITLER
Come, come, this is much better.

SPEER
Yes, at this hour.

EVA BRAUN
(*seeing the model*) Oh, look!

FRAU VON BELOW
(*to VON BELOW*) What's this?

HITLER
(*barring the model*) Stop. Now.

VON BELOW
The Führer \ will outline–

HITLER
–will explain. I have always said: a new nation needs new buildings, most especially in its capital. Ladies and gentlemen, Germania.

A "reveal" gesture.

EVA BRAUN
Well, look at that.

FRAU VON BELOW
Aha.

HITLER
And, see – here is its creator.

FRAU BRANDT
Good evening, Herr Speer.

SPEER
(*trying to introduce his FATHER*) My Führer, / may I introduce–

HITLER
We have all been looking at some movie. It is stupid. I ring Goebbels, "what is this stupid film? In the bin with it, in the bin!" Now shall you explain it or shall I?

SPEER
My Führer, \ I would like you–

HITLER
(*prompting*) The principle...

SPEER
(*giving up*) The principle is the meeting of four equal thoroughfares, linked \
at their extremities–

HITLER
Yes, yes, yes. But *this*.

SPEER
Well, starting with the east-west axis, running \ along what is now–

HITLER
No. No. Starting with the north-south axis, here, Frau von Below, five kilometres long, 120 metres wide, do you know what that is wider than?

FRAU VON BELOW
No, I don't my Führer.

HITLER
The Champs Elysées! Come, Frau Brandt, look here...

FRAU BRANDT
And those presumably are trees?

HITLER
But unlike Paris, not flanked with plutocratic utilitarian buildings, not by banks, but by monumental architecture, theatres, opera houses.... Come, Fräulein Braun, Frau von Below, come, look here.

EVA BRAUN
Um, where?

> *HITLER is making FRAU BRANDT, FRAU VON BELOW and EVA BRAUN look through the arch up the boulevard to the domed palace.*

HITLER
No, bend, through there...

FRAU BRANDT
Oh, yes, do you see, Fräulein Braun?

HITLER
The view through Speer's triumphal arch.

SPEER
Your triumphal arch, my Führer.

EVA BRAUN
Yes, I can see, my Führer.

FRAU VON BELOW
Quite magnificent.

HITLER
Itself 72 metres taller than the Arc de Triomphe, bearing the names of the 1.8 million German war dead, leading to…

He runs up the north-south axis.

…the largest building in the world. Speer, Speer, tell us the dimensions.

SPEER
Well, it is designed to be 290 metres high.

HITLER
And seating…

SPEER
My Führer, you always have these figures at your fingertips.

HITLER
One hundred and eighty thousand people!

FRAU VON BELOW
Goodness.

EVA BRAUN
(whispers to ANNEMARIE) What are those?

ANNEMARIE
They're fountains, Fräulein.

FRAU BRANDT
The trees are very beautiful.

HITLER
While here is my new Chancellory, which Speer has promised me will be ready on the 10th of January 1939.

SPEER
As it will be.

HITLER
And do you know *how* Herr Speer will make this ready for the 10th of January next year?

EVA BRAUN
No, my Führer.

HITLER
By placing orders first for those items which take longest to produce. Which are?

FRAU VON BELOW
I've really no idea.

HITLER
The carpets! Can you believe that? It's the carpets. With a logistic sense like that, this man should head the General Staff!

SPEER
My Führer, I am quite content with my present duties.

HITLER
But you must introduce me to your father.

ALL look at SPEER's FATHER.

FRAU BRANDT
Ah.

HITLER
Who taught you, I have no doubt, everything you know.

HITLER goes to the FATHER, gives a kind of bow. Nervously, the FATHER puts his hand out. HITLER shakes it, but holds on, cupping the FATHER's elbow and turning the gesture into a kind of embrace.

May I introduce Frau Brandt, who is married to my doctor. Fräulein Braun, who is visiting from Munich. My military adjutant, Colonel von Below and Frau von Below. Ladies and gentlemen, the father of my architect!

He turns back to focus on SPEER's FATHER, who remains struck dumb.

They say I am obsessed with height and width and depth. But it is all your son. I say – 200 metres. He says – why not three?

He looks into SPEER's FATHER's eyes.

Now. You have the Führer. And his architect. And his plan to build a capital that will outshine even Paris, the greatest capital existing in the world. Is there anything you want to ask?

Pause.

FATHER
I would... I... as you raise the matter of the future, I would be interested to know... where the people, in the houses you are going to demolish... where they will go.

HITLER suddenly snaps round to SPEER.

HITLER
Well? That's a question!

SPEER
(unusually thrown) Um...

During this SCHAUB enters and comes forward.

WOLTERS
(to the rescue). There is of course a comprehensive plan for the rehousing of those persons who are dispossessed. Garden suburbs will be built in which these people can be housed. Overall, the housing plan for the new Berlin \ will accommodate–

SPEER
(back on track) The plan overall is to house eight million people.

HITLER
(to the FATHER) There. You have the answer.

SCHAUB
My Führer. They have found another film.

HITLER
Well, let's hope it's better than the last.

The company, a little relieved, is moving to go. Again suddenly, HITLER returns to SPEER's FATHER.

My esteemed Herr Speer. Your son is a philosopher. He builds with distant posterity in mind. He makes drawings of how the ruins of his buildings might appear when overgrown, abandoned, in a thousand years from now. Like the Pyramids or Agrigento or the Parthenon. What is left of a great age but its monuments? Your son has understood that. He is creating them.

SPEER's FATHER is looking down, a kind of strange bow.

I too was a son who told his father that he yearned to be an artist. There the similarity ends. He told me that this was unthinkable. No! Never! What a thought!

SPEER's FATHER is shaking.

Well, I have always said, my mission is to realize the hitherto unthinkable.

HITLER puts out his hand to SPEER's FATHER, who does not respond. Quickly, turning to go.

What a father! What a son!

HITLER walks to SPEER, cups his arm, and walks quickly out.

FRAU BRANDT
Goodnight, Herr Speer. I hope… your father…

FRAU BRANDT, EVA BRAUN, VON BELOW, SCHAUB follow HITLER out. SPEER goes to his FATHER, tries to take his arm, but his FATHER pulls his arm away.

ANNEMARIE
Perhaps, Herr Speer… it's very late.

SPEER
(to ANNEMARIE) Go and call the car.

ANNEMARIE goes out.

(to his FATHER) He always likes to better me on figures.

FATHER
Hm.

SPEER
But once, I had to tell him that he was in error. We were discussing plans for the development of the Olympic Stadium. I pointed out that the athletic field did not conform to the dimensions laid down by the Federation. He replied that in 1940 the games will be in Tokyo. But after that, for all time to come, they will be here. And it will be us who will decide the necessary dimensions.

Re-enter ANNEMARIE.

ANNEMARIE
The car is here.

Slight pause.

SPEER
So, sir. What do you think?

FATHER looks at SPEER.

FATHER
I think – you've all gone insane.

He goes quickly out. ANNEMARIE looks back wide-eyed and then follows. SPEER to WOLTERS.

WOLTERS
He's wrong.

SPEER
I showed Tessenow the designs for Nuremberg. He said: "They're big, that's all."

WOLTERS
They are both wrong. How could they not be?

Slight pause.

You have not begun, Herr General Inspector.

SPEER smiles, and clasps his friend.

SPEER
"To have young men about me, for whom the word impossible…"

WOLTERS turns to go.

Will you do the lights?

WOLTERS
Of course.

WOLTERS turns down the lights to a night effect and goes. SPEER looks at the model in the "moonlight." Suddenly the door at the back opens. HITLER re-enters.

HITLER
Well, the second film was rubbish too. What did he think?

SPEER
It is hard for people of his age.

HITLER
Of course. And you are pulled two ways. You love your father, as your father. But your greater love is for your Fatherland. You must not feel guilty, it is rightly so.

Pause. HITLER looks at the model, bathed in the moonlight.

I can tell so few. My mission is to unify a single people in a single state. We are going to create a vast new Empire, combining all Germanic peoples, from Norway down to northern Italy. And your buildings, here, will crown that great achievement. Do you understand now why they must be huge? The capital of the Germanic Reich?

He goes and puts his hand on the top of the dome.

There are two possibilities. To win through, or to fail. If I win, I will be the greatest man since Charlemagne. If I lose – well, all this might just as well be dust. Goodnight.

SPEER
Heil, my Führer.

HITLER
Heil Speer.

HITLER goes out.

1.6.1 Spandau, 1947–50

Enter CASALIS to SPEER.

CASALIS
So what do you suppose he meant?

SPEER
Hitler?

CASALIS
Your father.

SPEER
He meant that he didn't understand, like so many of his generation.

CASALIS
I meant, what did your father mean by saying nothing?

SPEER smiles and shrugs, as if this is all a little metaphysical.

You said, when Hitler spoke to him, he bowed and trembled and said nothing. And when afterwards you tried to take his arm he pulled away.

SPEER
Yes?

CASALIS
I wondered if he sensed something that you didn't sense, yourself, till later.

SPEER
What, a "sense of evil?"

CASALIS acknowledges.

Herr Pastor, this was 1938.

CASALIS
So Hitler was not evil at that stage?

SPEER
Look. Of course, we knew that Hitler sought world domination. What my father didn't understand, and you don't understand, is that at the time we asked for nothing better. Eighty million Germans didn't follow Hitler because he was going to murder people in lime ditches and gas chambers. They didn't follow him because they knew that he was evil, but because they thought he was extremely good.

SPEER puts on his leather overcoat and cap.

And I'm afraid, most strongly in June 1940, at the fall of France. When in defiance of the whiners and the moaners, he had the world before him. And he laid it at my feet.

1.6.2 Paris, June 1940

The German anthem. HITLER and his entourage stride forward in a line, joined by SPEER. CASALIS watches.

HITLER
I tell you. It was always my dream, to be permitted to see Paris. Haussman's Boulevards. Les Invalides. I could have walked around Charles Garnier's opera in blindfolds.
In three months, London will be rubble. And when you have finished, even Paris will be but a shadow.

SPEER turns back to CASALIS.

SPEER
It was his dream. Though of course if you want to visit Paris it isn't strictly necessary to overthrow the government of France.
And then and there he ordered me to draw up a decree for the commencement of the reconstruction of Berlin. How could I not be his, then, body and soul?

HITLER looks at SPEER in triumph, turns and goes.

CASALIS
So you had your Mephistophilis.

SPEER
And he had his Faust.
And then one evening in his mountaintop retreat, when we had thought he'd long since gone to bed, he told me how he planned to crown his Paris triumph with an even greater victory.

1.6.3 Berghof, Obersaltzberg, July 1941

Two YOUNG ADJUTANTS, two SECRETARIES—FRÄULEIN JOHANNA WOLF and FRÄULEIN CHRISTA SCHRÖDER—run in, followed by FRAU BRANDT and MARGRET. The FIRST ADJUTANT holds a large peaked cap. There is a piano in the room.

FRAU BRANDT
No you *mustn't*.

FIRST ADJUTANT
I'm shaking! It's heavy in my hands!

MARGRET
What's going on?

FRAU BRANDT
Very schoolboyish behaviour.

FRÄULEIN SCHRÖDER
Oh for God's sake give it here.

She takes the cap.

There are, after all, but two possibilities.

SECOND ADJUTANT
One being that no one puts his hat on.

FRÄULEIN SCHRÖDER
And the other is that someone does.

FRAU BRANDT
Well, on your own heads be it.

FRÄULEIN SCHRÖDER puts the cap on. It's far too big. The others laugh and applaud.

FRÄULEIN SCHRÖDER
Tara tara. Who's next?

FIRST ADJUTANT
In such times one cannot use Salvation Army methods.

He puts the cap on. It's far too big.

FRÄULEIN SCHRÖDER
Extreme times call for extreme measures!

The FIRST ADJUTANT puts the cap on. It's far too big. He looks round for the next person to try it.

FIRST ADJUTANT
And now, Frau Brandt...

FRAU BRANDT
Oh no.

FRÄULEIN WOLF
Herr Speer?

SPEER diffident.

SPEER
Um... I...

MARGRET
Albert.

FRÄULEIN WOLF
(*winningly*) Herr Speer.

Pause. SPEER takes the cap.

SPEER
Well, I have always said, my mission is to bring the unthinkable about.

He puts the cap on. It fits. Surprised applause. EVA BRAUN has entered.

EVA BRAUN
Dear Herr Speer, what are you doing?

She gestures offstage just in time for SPEER to rip the cap from his head and put it behind his back, before HITLER and VON BELOW enter, the latter carrying sheet music.

HITLER
Ladies and gentlemen, my profound apologies.

FRAU BRANDT
Well, it's past bedtime...

Suddenly HITLER goes to MARGRET, kisses her hand.

HITLER
My own Frau Speer. Gracious ladies. Gentlemen.

Everyone takes this as a dismissal.

MARGRET
Goodnight, my Führer.

She goes out, the others follow, murmuring "Goodnight" and "Goodnight, my Führer." HITLER a slight gesture to SPEER to stay.

HITLER
Perhaps you too, my little applecake. Colonel, please.

EVA BRAUN shrugs. She goes to SPEER.

SPEER
Goodnight, Fräulein Braun.

With a slight gesture to SPEER.

EVA BRAUN
Goodnight, oh my dear Herr Speer. And goodnight my Führer.

She turns back and smiles at HITLER, taking the cap from SPEER with her back hand. She goes.

VON BELOW sits at the piano and plays a fanfare from Liszt's "Les Preludes."

SPEER
It's Liszt?

HITLER
Yes. It's from "The Preludes." So what d'you think of it?

SPEER
I suppose, my Führer, that depends on what it's for.

HITLER
This will be "for" the decisive confrontation of our epoch. Of course I am told I must "negotiate" with our enemies. That traitor Hess flies off to Scotland to sue for peace with that alcoholic gangster Churchill. But I say that we are now engaged in the final battle between Western civilization and the international Jew-Bolshevik conspiracy. Our aim must be nothing less than the complete destruction of that criminal conspiracy, with implacable and iron zeal. Naturally I am told this is unthinkable. But I say, one good strong German kick, and the whole rotten edifice falls in.

SPEER
Russia.

HITLER
Yes.

He looks at SPEER. It's the stare game. Without taking his eye off SPEER.

The victory fanfare. You will hear it frequently.

He holds the stare.

And for those who make the final sacrifice, your Germania will stand as their memorial for ever; the names of our heroic fallen carved on every stone.

Finally, HITLER breaks the stare, then goes to SPEER and cups his elbow.

And you will have all the granite and the marble that you need.

The fanfare continues orchestrally. Exit HITLER and VON BELOW. SPEER turns to CASALIS. Behind him, a dark void from which snow billows.

SPEER
But it was clear within months of the actual invasion of the Soviet Union that there were much more immediate construction needs.

1.7.1 Ukraine, February 1942

Outside, at night, in the winter snow. SPEER in a heavy overcoat. Enter WOLTERS, also heavily overcoated. Enter a young railway engineer, Theodor GANZENMÜLLER, with a mess-tin of caviar and spoons.

GANZENMÜLLER
Ah, Herr Wolters, please try this.

WOLTERS
What is it?

GANZENMÜLLER
It's the real stuff.

WOLTERS
Herr Ganzenmüller, this is General Inspector Speer.

GANZENMÜLLER
Welcome to the Ukraine, sir. Please try some caviar.

WOLTERS
Herr Ganzenmüller is performing miracles with what we must call for want of any better term the Ukraine railway system.

SPEER
Well, I'm all for miracles.

He takes caviar.

That's good.

Enter a group of SPEER CONSTRUCTION WORKERS and SOLDIERS, led by a MAJOR, MUSICIANS and two TUFTIES—young Ukrainian women—with trays of glasses and vodka.

MAJOR
Now after so many cheerful days with the Speer Construction Squad can this be Herr Speer himself? Tufty One, vodka for Herr Speer!

SPEER
Tufty?

WOLTERS
Ukrainian girls.

MAJOR
You will find this a change from building palaces and opera houses.

SPEER takes vodka from one TUFTY, as the other hands vodka out to the rest.

SPEER
It is a change which I enthusiastically proposed, Herr Major. Over half my workforce is assisting with reconstruction work in Russia.

MAJOR
A toast! In acknowledgement of Herr General Inspector's visit from Berlin! To our matchless constructional facilities! To our Repair Sheds!

FIRST SPEER SQUAD
Water tanks.

MAJOR
To our insulated water tanks!

SECOND SPEER SQUAD
Lumber!

THIRD SPEER SQUAD
Tracking!

FOURTH SPEER SQUAD
Nails!

All drink. Recovering from the hit:

SPEER
Well, in that case, all these things will be provided instantly. Herr Wolters, see to it at once.

Cheers, on the edge of mockery, but ambiguous enough for the MAJOR to move on.

MAJOR
Then – music!

Sad music is played. The men move upstage.

SPEER
(*to GANZENMÜLLER*) So the problem is supplies.

GANZENMÜLLER
Supplies of the right thing at the right time. Guns, no ammo. Tanks, no fuel. Troops, no trains.

SPEER
You mean it's not production, it's logistics.

GANZENMÜLLER
Of course I needn't tell you this. The man who worked out that the first thing that you have to order for a building is the carpeting.

SPEER
(*smiles*) Yes.

GANZENMÜLLER
Apparently, the war economy was two days from collapse through a shortage of ball-bearings.

He does a gesture – a machine turning.

Work it out.

SPEER
Oh, I don't need to.

GANZENMÜLLER is fearful he may have gone too far.

GANZENMÜLLER
But then again, we both know the order: "Everyone need only know what is going on in his domain."

The MAJOR approaches.

SPEER
And may I ask, is all this typical? This gloomy music?

Pause.

GANZENMÜLLER
It is typical of men so far from home.

SPEER
In circumstances such as these.

MAJOR
And up against what they are up against.

WOLTERS
The elements?

MAJOR
The enemy.

SPEER looks surprised.

Oh yes, Herr Speer. First thing you learn about the Ivan, don't underestimate his natural resourcefulness. Give him an axe, in a few hours time he'll have knocked up anything. A sledge, an igloo.... And the way they use that damned T-34.

WOLTERS
The tank.

MAJOR
The tank... the pillbox, the bivouac, the bulldozer.... And Army Group Centre enters Russia with 2,000 different types of vehicle.

GANZENMÜLLER
And a million spare parts.

MAJOR
And all they're issued with is fuel and ammo. So if they need spare parts, they rip 'em from the wrecks. Oh, yes, despite the propaganda, we have an enemy.

SPEER
The propaganda?

MAJOR
Surely you've heard the shit. "One good strong kick, and the whole rotten edifice falls in."

A moment of stand off, between SPEER and the MAJOR.

And you know they say you have to kill each Ivan twice. And no one who draws blood here leaves the place alive.

SPEER
And I'm sure you discourage such defeatist talk, Herr Major. Concentrating solely on ensuring that these brave young men are properly supplied. As will I.

MAJOR
But of course, Herr General Inspector.

The MAJOR goes out.

GANZENMÜLLER
And now you will forgive me. Tomorrow I have to open up a railway line as far as Sinelnikovo. With the assistance of the Speer Construction Squad, and a goodly slice of the surrounding peasantry.

SPEER
And they are collaborative?

GANZENMÜLLER
Collaborative and numerous. Goodnight, Herr Speer.

He goes out.

WOLTERS
Apparently, the chaps say that the Jewish details are the best. They work double shifts, even voluntarily. Of course, they know \ that if they don't–

SPEER
That Ganzenmüller is presumably the best man we have.

WOLTERS
A man for whom the word impossible does not exist?

SPEER
Exactly and precisely so.

They stand listening to the music for a moment.

I have a brother, out here, somewhere, Rudi.

The scene disperses.

And so on the evening of the 7th February I arrived at Hitler's eastern field HQ, hoping to report to the Minister of Armaments, Dr. Todt, who had built the autobahns and to whom I was, in a sense at least, now working. But when I arrived I was informed that Dr. Todt had been with Hitler for some time. And later that he was in the operations room.

1.8 Operations Room of Rastenberg barracks, 7 February 1942

Dominated by a huge table map of Europe, the room bears evidence of a long day – papers, half eaten pastries, trays of coffee long since gone cold. At the back are two young STAFF OFFICERS taking information from telephones; occasionally they move forward to move a flag on the map. At the moment, the room is empty apart from TODT who stands looking at the map, a brandy glass in his hand. Enter SPEER with a bottle of champagne and two glasses.

TODT
Champagne?

SPEER
Champagne.

SPEER pours TODT a glass of champagne and hands it over, as:

TODT
Maybe we should have stuck to France.

SPEER
Ah, but I hear the Georgian wines are marvellous.

TODT
Oh, well, then. Let's plough on.

SPEER laughs, as a STAFF OFFICER moves forward with an intelligence report.

SPEER
How is the Chief?

STAFF OFFICER
Heil Hitler, Herr Reichsminister.

TODT
'Hitler.

TODT doesn't want to answer SPEER's question with someone listening. The STAFF OFFICER moves a flag on the map, as:

So how long are you here for?

SPEER
I should leave tomorrow. On that ghastly train.

The STAFF OFFICER withdraws.

TODT
Speer, have you actually read *Mein Kampf*?

SPEER
Well, not exactly. In fact, I told the Chief. He said not to bother, it had been overtaken by events.

TODT
Well, yes, in some respects. However.

He takes out a notebook and reads from it.

"The task of diplomacy is to ensure that a nation does not heroically perish, but that measures are taken to preserve it."

Pause.

SPEER
So what's the relevance of that?

TODT
It is relevant to what I've spent the last two hours trying to explain to him.

SPEER
Which is?

TODT
That if we haven't beaten Russia by Christmas then we've lost the war.

SPEER has to ask the question:

SPEER
So, why?

TODT
American technology, and Russian space. I mean, just look at it.

SPEER
Well, yes \ but on the other–

TODT
Oh, and your housekeeper.

SPEER
My housekeeper?

TODT
You have one?

SPEER
Yes.

TODT
And your maid. And maybe a governess?

SPEER
I've got five children.

TODT
We are in the third year of what is now a world war. And we employ the same number of domestic servants as we did in 1939. And when you raise the possibility of mobilizing women workers, *like* the Russians, *like* the British, you are told about the moral threat to German womanhood. Oh, and look.

There's a tray of coffee things. He picks up a paper-wrapped sugar cube from the sugar bowl.

We're still wrapping sugar-cubes in pretty paper.

SPEER
I understand you were two days away from running out of ball-bearings.

TODT
No, worse. We were nearly out of screws.

SPEER
Who'd have your job?

TODT
Oh, Speer.

The other STAFF OFFICER comes forward, to move a flag. SPEER and TODT notice that he moves the flag that his colleague moved forward back. TODT is a little drunk.

Hey. You don't want that shitty train. I'm flying to Berlin at daybreak. Want a ride?

The STAFF OFFICER withdraws. SPEER, trying something out:

SPEER
Of course... in fact, there's millions. Men *and* women. In the east. Collaborative and numerous.

TODT
Aha. The "Slav subhumans."

SPEER
Yes. But what I meant \ was that they might—

TODT
I'm sorry. You're a young man. You think solutions. I just — brood.

SPEER smiles, as if to say "don't worry."

I'll see you on the plane.

TODT goes. SCHAUB enters. During the following, the young STAFF OFFICERS go too.

SCHAUB
Herr General Inspector. You're still up.

SPEER
Yes. Though I think I'm going to bed.

SCHAUB
He wants to see you.

SPEER
(looks at his watch) Oh, can't you tell him...

SCHAUB
He is on his way.

Enter HITLER. SCHAUB salutes.

'Hitler!

> *HITLER acknowledges. SCHAUB goes out. HITLER is still ruffled from his conversation with TODT, but suppressing it.*

HITLER
My dear Speer. How are you?

SPEER
My Führer. Very well. Perhaps a little tired.

HITLER
How are Frau Speer and your family?

SPEER
I fear I haven't seen them in a while.

HITLER
You have been in the Ukraine. Now don't remind me. Albert, Hilde… Fritz, Margaret… Ernst.

SPEER
Arnold. Who is nearly two. Ernst is my brother.

HITLER
(that explains it) Ah.

SPEER
Who is a little more than two.

HITLER
And presumably…

SPEER
Serves in the sixth at Krasnograd.

HITLER
Ah. There are bold and heroic deeds in prospect for the Sixth. So, Arnold nearly two.

SPEER
(smiling) In fact, I'm going home tomorrow.

HITLER
Not by train I trust. I will have von Below get you on a flight.

SPEER
Thank you, my Führer. But I have arranged a lift with the minister of armaments first thing.

HITLER
Oh, have you?

Slight pause.

SPEER
I saw him earlier.

HITLER
Yes, so did I.

Slight pause.

SPEER
He seemed...

HITLER
Speer, we live in times when only optimists can achieve anything. The trouble with Herr Todt is that he is fundamentally and unshakably a pessimist. Whose pessimism extends beyond his own domain, to matters which do not concern him.

SPEER
I think he is worried about the labour problem.

HITLER
I know. But I will *not* drive German women from their homes.

SPEER takes the sugar cube from his pocket.

SPEER
I think he feels that under total war \ there are some things–

HITLER picks up a sugar cube and eats it.

HITLER
And I will not deny them some at least of the things that make life civilized and elegant.

SPEER puts the sugar cube back in his pocket.

SPEER
When of course... we have twenty million potential men and women workers under our control.

HITLER
Well exactly. Twenty million Slav subhumans. Leaderless, supine, with no defence against the Jew-Communist embrace. I tell you, Speer, now is not the time to use Salvation Army methods! Set them all to work!

SPEER
Well, of course it is not precisely my area of responsibility–

HITLER
No. You are not Dr. Todt.

HITLER goes to SPEER and pats his shoulder.

Your charming wife. Your lovely family. From Albert down to Arnold nearly two. Yet your absolute priority? The greater German good.

Slight pause.

I am adamant about the women. But it may be… that we should ensure that production for the civilian market… is in proportion to the national need.

SPEER
Well, I'm sure \ that would be–

HITLER
What is the time?

SPEER
I fear \ it's very late–

HITLER
(looks at SPEER's watch) You're going to fly in three hours' time?

SPEER
Well, I…

HITLER
It's up to you.

Pause.

Sometimes, I regret what history requires of me. One cannot be the Führer all one's life. This war is robbing me of my best years. Sometimes I think, I should hang up my field grey jacket and go home to Linz, my birthplace on the Danube, where my remains will lie…. But I have burnt my bridges. So have you.

Slight pause.

You know, it may well be… that I will need to speak with you tomorrow.

He looks at SPEER.

Shall I have von Below call the pilot?

62 / David Edgar

SPEER
No, I'll do it.

HITLER
Well.

> *Slight pause.*

You're right. Twenty million foreign workers. Teach them to read roadsigns. Tell them the capital of Germany's Germania. And work them all like dogs to death. Goodnight.

SPEER
Heil my Führer!

HITLER
And Heil Speer.

> *HITLER goes. Darkness. We hear the sound of an airplane taking off and then immediately spiralling down to crash.*

1.9.1 Courtyard of the Ministry of Armaments, 9 February 1942. Morning

> *It's snowing. A microphone has been set up in the courtyard. ANNEMARIE and WOLTERS enter. OFFICIALS from the Ministry of Armaments have gathered, including the senior STATE SECRETARY and his young male administrative ASSISTANT. As SPEER enters to the microphone, he takes off his overcoat. He is in uniform, with a swastika armband. He hands his coat to ANNEMARIE.*

ANNEMARIE
But, Herr Speer...

SPEER
It's all right, Wittenberg.

> *ANNEMARIE glances questioningly at WOLTERS, who shrugs, as SPEER begins to speak.*

Party Comrades! Esteemed employees of the Ministry of Armaments! It is my sad duty to report that at the zenith of his labours, your leader Reichsminister Professor Todt was taken from you yesterday in a plane crash in East Prussia.

> *Shock.*

The Führer has placed me in charge of all Dr Todt's roles and functions.

People look at each other.

I have proposed—and the Führer has agreed—to free our war production industries from the shackles of duplication and bureaucracy. I have recommended—and the Führer has enthusiastically approved—the severest penalties for the use of materials, machinery or manpower for unauthorized or private purposes. With the Führer's keen endorsement, I have ordered the full mobilization of up to twenty million workers from the conquered territories.

A little applause; alarm from the STATE SECRETARY.

I have nothing else to say. We have a war to win and we shall win it. Sieg Heil!

SPEER leaves the microphone.

STATE SECRETARY
Well, congratulations, Herr Reichsminister.

The rest dispersing. We see an army private, on the edge of the crowd, waiting. It is SPEER's brother ERNST.

SPEER
Thank you, State Secretary. Rudi, have Wittenberg call up that railway engineer we met in the Ukraine.

STATE SECRETARY
However, I must respectfully enquire \ about the matter of–

WOLTERS
You mean, the one for whom the word "impossible…?"

SPEER
Precisely so.

STATE SECRETARY
…as to what specifically is meant by "freeing war production from duplication and bureaucracy." \ As of course–

SPEER
I think he is about to be promoted. Yes, State Secretary?

STATE SECRETARY
And… exactly what is meant by it.

SPEER
Well, certainly, I am eager to discuss all aspects of the new production policy. Do I have an office?

STATE SECRETARY
Yes of course.

ANNEMARIE
Herr Speer, there is something I must ask you.

SPEER
I will be with you in a moment.

WOLTERS and the STATE SECRETARY go.

SPEER
Of course, I didn't realize at first. I thought he meant for me \ to take over Todt's construction work –

ANNEMARIE
Herr Speer, do you intend for me to remain your secretary in your new post?

SPEER
Of course.

ANNEMARIE
Because if so I would like a day or two to think about it.

ERNST
Albert.

SPEER
What?

He turns to see ERNST.

ANNEMARIE
And as I have already booked a holiday...

SPEER
Why – Ernst.

ANNEMARIE
Perhaps you wouldn't mind...

SPEER
Please, Wittenberg... a moment.

ANNEMARIE thrown by the sight of SPEER's brother.

ANNEMARIE
Yes of course.

SPEER
Ernst, why are you here?

ANNEMARIE
But it is Frau Kempf, Herr Speer. As you may recall, you commissioned me to buy a present for my wedding.

She goes out, leaving SPEER and ERNST alone.

ERNST
Here in Berlin? On leave. Here at your ministry? Our mother telephoned me with your news. She said that I should come at once so you could get me out.

Enter the STATE SECRETARY's ASSISTANT.

ASSISTANT
Reichsminister, I have to tell you that the State Secretary is waiting.

SPEER
I will be with him in a moment. What d'you mean?

The ASSISTANT goes out.

ERNST
I mean that you get me transferred to the west.

SPEER
Oh Ernst you know I can't do that.

ERNST
Whyever not? You're the Minister of Armaments.

SPEER
But I have been appointed quite specifically to stamp out \ special favours—

ERNST
Our mother said you would. She said you'd do this for her sake.

Enter WOLTERS.

WOLTERS
Albert, the natives are \ getting restless—

SPEER
One *moment*. Ernst, I'll do my best. I shouldn't but I will.

ERNST
To do what?

SPEER
To get you transferred to the west. Now, Rudi...

ERNST
Oh, Albert. When?

SPEER
Well, obviously, at the end of this campaign.

ERNST
(*desperate*) I'm sorry...?

SPEER
Rudi, please tell them that I'm on \ my way...

ERNST
Well, then, that's that. We are preparing the advance towards the Volga.

The STATE SECRETARY is coming out into the courtyard.

STATE SECRETARY
Now, I am so sorry, Herr Reichsminister–

ERNST
So, till we meet again, Herr Professor Speer.

He salutes.

SPEER
Ernst, please, a moment–

STATE SECRETARY
But if you are to alter Ministry practices and protocols to the extent that you imply, then I will need to know on what authority \ these proposals have been made and who will be deemed responsible–

ERNST
I'm sorry. I will miss my train.

SPEER
Ernst, stay. State Secretary, it is not me implying anything. It is implementing what the Führer has commanded. That is "my authority."

ERNST
Heil Hitler!

He clicks his heels, salutes, turns, and goes quickly out, SPEER turns back to him.

SPEER
Ernst.... What?

Turning back.

Do you see?

Outflanked, the STATE SECRETARY senses that he must leave and be followed.

STATE SECRETARY
I await you in your office, Herr Reichsminister.

He goes out.

WOLTERS
Your brother?

SPEER
Yes. He's a private with the sixth.

WOLTERS
I know, you told me. So what really happened in East Prussia?

SPEER
(*still looking after ERNST*) I thought he meant I was to take on Todt's construction work. I didn't know he wanted me to be the Minister of Armaments.

WOLTERS
I meant, what happened to Herr Todt?

SPEER turns back to his old friend.

SPEER
Apparently, there was diminished visibility.... It's thought the pilot couldn't make out the horizon.

WOLTERS
Ah.

SPEER
But of course... this matter isn't our domain.

1.9.2 Berlin, November 1942

SPEER turns to CASALIS.

SPEER
So what was I to do? I didn't even shake his hand. And then as the weeks went by there was my father.

SPEER's FATHER appears.

FATHER
He's in an advanced observation unit. He is ill. He is your brother. Surely you, you of all people, can get him out.

SPEER
And as the months, my mother.

FATHER disappears, ANNEMARIE appears.

ANNEMARIE
She rang again today. Five times. She said you can't do this to him.

ANNEMARIE disappears.

SPEER
I had been given what was probably the second most important job in Germany, at a time of national peril. And I was supposed to put my family before my country?

CASALIS
Your country?

SPEER
Yes of course.

CASALIS
Or your career.

SPEER
And my career. Yes. And why not?

CASALIS says nothing.

But still... when as the battle raged, I was invited to the grand reopening of the Berlin State Opera, sumptuously restored...

Enter MARGRET, pregnant, in an evening gown. SPEER joins her in their row of seats at the opera. They speak quietly to each other.

MARGRET
Albert, what's Sixth Army disease?

SPEER
Jaundice. My mother telephoned.

MARGRET
More than once. Apparently your brother's in a field hospital. With whatever.

SPEER
I know. He wrote to me.

MARGRET
Why can't they fly him out?

SPEER
Because… it's not that simple.

MARGRET
Albert, is there something going wrong?

SPEER
No, of course not. Have we ever lost a battle? Have the Russians ever won?

MARGRET
Well, that's all right then. So, what opera are we seeing?

SPEER
The Magic Flute.

MARGRET
Oh good. A fairy tale.

As the overture begins, SPEER to CASALIS.

SPEER
And so we sat there in our box in those softly upholstered chairs among this festive audience, and all I could think about was the crowds at the Paris opera during Napoleon's retreat from Moscow.

CASALIS
Did he survive?

SPEER
Towards the end, I asked the people who were flying supplies in to the troops at Stalingrad to try and find him. Apparently, he'd left the so-called field hospital, and dragged himself back to his observation post. And in fact there was one last letter, full of bitterness and rage, against me, his brother.

Pause.

But no they never found him. And my mother told me the wrong brother died.

The opera breaks up and MARGRET goes.

1.10.1 Germany 1943

CASALIS
And after Stalingrad? Did you think that maybe Dr. Todt was right? And that far from being saviour of Germany, Hitler's actions would destroy your country and its people?

SPEER
Herr Pastor, I have to tell you, that there is an intoxication in the very fact of power. To have the final word, to deal with expenditure in billions.... But I knew the war would not be won if we continued to refurbish hunting lodges and manufacture ladies' summer outerwear. As I was forced, over the coming months and years, to repeat *ad nauseam*. Until I finally confronted the assembled Gauleiters of Greater Germany, at the lovingly and lavishly refurbished castle Posen in the Warthegau.

SPEER is moving to a lectern, lit by candelabra. A little afterthought.

Where my friend Karl Hanke, now Gauleiter of Lower Silesia, had been primed to put a question.

SPEER to the lectern. A group of GAULEITERS sit in ornate chairs, among them HANKE.

Yes?

HANKE
Herr Reichsminister. Are you seriously suggesting that those Gauleiters who are not prepared immediately to shut down all consumer goods production in our provinces might face arrest and and even – penal servitude? In concentration camps?

SPEER
Yes, that is exactly what I mean. As the Reichsführer-SS Himmler will underline this afternoon. Next question?

CASALIS
That doesn't answer me.

SPEER
It was the only way to see it, at the time. I was Hitler's Minister of Armaments.

SPEER leaves the lectern. Enter HITLER, furious, to SPEER, waving a document.

HITLER
So what is this?

SPEER takes the document.

SPEER
It is a memorandum, on the manganese situation.

HITLER
Which you copied to my chief of staff.

SPEER
My Führer, it's good news. It confirms we have eleven month's supply in Germany.

HITLER
This is intolerable. I have ordered all forces to be concentrated in defence of Nikopol, to the last man and at any cost, precisely to protect its vital manganese. Now I appear a liar and what's worse a fool. You will *not* communicate directly with my chief of staff. You will *not* proceed beyond your own domain.

SPEER
(*thrown*) My Führer, naturally, I had no intention \ of giving out a false–

HITLER
Your fault! Your responsibility! Why not admit it, just this once? There are those who say you are the second man in Germany. Do not delude yourself, Herr Speer!

HITLER storms out.

CASALIS
But surely the important thing was not your relationship with Hitler but the twenty million foreign workers you had commandeered. Who unlike the Gauleiters were really subject to arrest and servitude in concentration camps.

SPEER
Yes, some of them, of course. This was not the Salvation Army.

CASALIS
And did you know that Hitler ordered physical destruction of the commissars in Russia? That this order was extended to the Jews and gypsies? That his troops were told they would not be held responsible for killing innocent civilians in defiance of the rules of war?

SPEER
No. I did not know of this order.

CASALIS
But surely you had seen a concentration camp?

SPEER
I visited Mauthausen, I think, in March of 1943. But of course, you are a VIP. You see what you are shown. There was a quarry.

CASALIS
Whereas of course thousands of civilians were being sent to camps where the "special treatment" they received was very different.

SPEER
Of which of course I knew nothing at the time.

CASALIS
But you knew that women, children, old men, were transported...

SPEER
Yes of course I did. Every day, as I drove down to the Ministry, I would see crowds of people on the platform of the Nikolassee station. Wearing yellow stars. Presumably, awaiting... transportation as you say.

Behind SPEER we see, through the smoke of the railway station, a WOMAN and her elderly FATHER, not badly dressed but with meagre luggage and wearing the yellow star.

CASALIS
And did you not imagine what might lie in store for them?

SPEER
As I said, I had no idea what happened inside concentration camps.

CASALIS
What no idea? From anything you saw or any place you visited? What, no idea at all?

Pause. Now, the WOMAN and her FATHER have gone, and further back in the darkness, through clouds of dust, we can see a long tunnel, full of still, emaciated creatures, and hear the insistent sounds of a cement mixer and an electric saw.

SPEER
It was the worst place I had ever seen.

Pause.

It was code-named Dora. It was the plant that made the V-2 rocket, built in caves and tunnels in the Harz Mountains. It was worked by prisoners from a nearby concentration camp. Which had of course all kinds of security advantages.
I visited in December 1943. The condition of the prisoners was utterly... well, the word barbaric is.... Typhoid was rampant. The prisoners were quartered there, in the sodden caves, and of course mortality was extremely high. Not least because... their "rations" were rancid slop. And the sanitary arrangements.... There were these barrels, with planks, they had to sit on, literally on top... and of course, from time to time, apparently, they'd slip and fall into.... And of course, the *smell*...

As the vision fades, SPEER is tottering.

So, what? Did I "imagine?"

CASALIS
And that was in December 1943? And you fell ill in January?

SPEER collapses. WOLTERS and ANNEMARIE rush in to him. As, helped by ORDERLIES, they take him out, CASALIS turns to the entering MARGRET.

1.10.2 Hohenlychen Hospital, February 1944

MARGRET and Dr. Professor Friedrich KOCH, with NURSES, looking down on SPEER's hospital bed. An SS-MAN stands in the corridor.

MARGRET
Herr Doctor, how is my husband?

KOCH
Well, his temperature and pulse are very high.

MARGRET
He's spitting blood?

KOCH
He's hæmorrhaging, yes.

MARGRET
So this is not what Himmler's doctor diagnosed? This is not "rheumatism?"

KOCH
Frau Speer, your husband is extremely ill.

MARGRET
Will he survive?

KOCH
His temperature has stabilized.

Slight pause.

Yes, I think, now, that he will survive.

Pause. MARGRET breathes deeply. Then she recovers.

KOCH
Frau Speer. In the midst of... the crisis which we hope has passed.... Your husband looked up to me, quite suddenly and said: "I've never been so happy."

1.10.3 Spandau, 1947-1950

KOCH, MARGRET and the NURSES still looking down on SPEER's bed. SPEER, standing watching, turns to CASALIS when he speaks.

CASALIS
Do you remember saying that?

SPEER
No, but I remember feeling... no.

CASALIS
What do you remember feeling?

SPEER
Things which I fear you would respond to with a healthy scepticism. As did my wife.

CASALIS
Try me.

Pause. During this the group round the bed gradually turn to look at SPEER.

SPEER
Well, apparently, it's fairly common. It was on the worst night, in the hospital, when my temperature and pulse were God knows what, I was hæmorrhaging, my skin was blue. And I was suddenly above myself, and

looking down, and seeing everything so clearly... the doctors and the nurses, hovering, my wife, looking soft and slim, quite beautiful... and the ceiling, which was plain and white, was suddenly magnificently ornate, like a mediæval castle, like indeed the mediæval castles which my colleagues had so lovingly restored.... And feeling, yes, that I had never been so happy in my life. But then quite clearly... and for me, then, sternly and implacably, I heard two words. "Not yet."

Slight pause.

You don't believe me.

CASALIS
I believe that's what you remember.

SPEER a little laugh. The hospital scene breaks up behind him.

And I believe that your illness was the result of things outside you.

SPEER
Herr Pastor, my illness began with the recurrence of a knee injury, on a Christmas trip to Lapland.

CASALIS
Your wife thought you were wrongly diagnosed.

SPEER
I was. And then I was correctly diagnosed.

CASALIS
And other people feared you had been poisoned.

SPEER
Herr Hess believes he's being poisoned every day.

CASALIS
But nevertheless. You nearly died.

SPEER
And nevertheless, recovered.

CASALIS
And when you had recovered, changed?

Pause.

SPEER
You are trying to connect my illness with the things I'd seen. Of course, I understand. It is the fashion of the age.

Slight pause.

And yes, things changed. But the change did not originate with me.

1.10.4 Klessheim Castle, 19 March 1944

HITLER enters to SPEER, who sits in a wheelchair in a dressing gown with a blanket over his knees. MARGRET there.

HITLER
My dear Speer, how are you?

SPEER
(to CASALIS) He was in Austria for a conference with the Hungarians.

HITLER
I am delighted that you are recovered.

SPEER
As ever, he kissed my wife's hand.

HITLER kisses MARGRET's hand.

HITLER
Now you see, what I have always told your husband, dear Frau Speer. It is this love of sliding down the sides of mountains in the snow. These long boards on your feet – it's madness! In the fire with them! Please assure me, Speer, you will throw them all away!

HITLER holds out his hand. SPEER does not take it, but speaks again to CASALIS.

SPEER
And it was his face.

HITLER
And I believe... it is your birthday?

SPEER
And I looked at him – his sallow skin, his ugly nose, and thought – how could I not have seen?

HITLER smiles, pats SPEER's arm.

HITLER
Well, then. Well, there it is. Well done.

HITLER and MARGRET go out. SPEER stands, takes off his dressing gown, puts on his overcoat.

SPEER
And for the first time, the magic hadn't worked. And I thought: who is this man, who had meant so much to me?

CASALIS
So this was – essentially æsthetic?

SPEER
It was the moment that I realized – he'd changed. That he'd betrayed those great ideals with which he had inspired us all.

CASALIS
And you don't think that this was connected \ with the labourers–

SPEER
With the workmen in the mountains? No. I wish it was. Mine was not a moral opposition. It was because from that point on—as the Russians, British and Americans closed in on us—he extended his intentions to *my* area of responsibility.

We begin to sense the fireworks display of a distant air-raid, coming closer.

And I finally realized that he intended to pull the German people down into perdition with him. That far from saving it, he was preparing to destroy his Fatherland.
And worst of all that there were people—good people, friends—prepared to let him drag them down.

1.11 The Town Hall, Breslau, late January 1945

The air-raid continues. Enter HANKE to SPEER.

HANKE
Speer. Welcome.

SPEER
Hanke, my dear friend. This is so beautiful.

HANKE
We begin by refurbishing a Karl Friedrich Schinkel building on the Wilhemsplatz, all those years ago. And we end destroying one in Breslau.

Looking out.

Well, if the Americans don't do it first.

SPEER
"Destroy?"

HANKE
The order is quite clear. Monuments. And palaces, castles, telephone exchanges. Theatres, opera houses, industrial plants. I have it pinned up on every noticeboard.

SPEER
What, alongside "every man need only know what is going on in his domain?"

HANKE
So you think the war is lost?

SPEER
But if it isn't lost... then why destroy what we must recapture?

Pause.

HANKE
"The enemy will be defeated by weapons that are superior to his."

SPEER
I have told Goebbels he must stop promising ultimate salvation through miracle weapons which do not exist. We must face up to what is happening and not destroy our people's vital means of life.

HANKE
And leave a perfect Schinkel building to be trashed by the Red Army?

SPEER
I believe that beauty is a vital means of life. And we have to stick to not destroying it, whatever we have to face up to, in the future.

HANKE
Sometimes I wonder – if the Führer only knew...

SPEER
Oh, Karl. My friend.

A moment.

HANKE
(*gesturing around him*) All right. For you. I'll leave your precious Schinkel standing. Prove your point.

Pause. The bombing very loud, the explosions lighting up the sky.

SPEER
My friend. Your name will live in the German Pantheon forever. You are going to a fine and worthy end.

HANKE
You know, there is a kind of… dreadful beauty in all this.

SPEER
I know. As does the Führer.

> HANKE *looks at* SPEER, *then turns and goes quickly out.* SPEER *turns to* CASALIS.

But it got worse. On the 19th of March Hitler issued another decree, ordering the physical destruction of all German industry, and the forcible evacuation of the German population in the west ahead of the advancing American and British armies. And so whatever the risks to me and to my family, I knew I had to go back to the ruined Chancellory to make one final effort to persuade him to relent.

1.12.1 The Bunker, 29 March 1945

> SPEER *turns to see* FRÄULEIN WOLF, *hurrying along a corridor in the bunker. She is not pleased to see* SPEER.

SPEER
Ah, Wolf, I have a document for \ the Führer–

FRAULEIN WOLF
He has your document, Herr Speer.

SPEER
Reichsminister. This is another document, I want you to type up on the 12 point typewriter…

FRÄULEIN WOLF
I can't, Reichsminister.

SPEER
Whyever not?

FRÄULEIN WOLF
I have been ordered not to.

> *She hurries on.* SCHAUB *appears.*

SCHAUB
Follow me.

SPEER
And so I was led along the narrow corridors, surrounded as I knew by walls 3.6 metres thick, beneath the five metre, solid concrete roof, to the room where he awaited me.

1.12.2 The Bunker, 29 March 1945

The room where the pieces of the Germania model are now kept. SPEER enters to HITLER, who sits on the base of the great domed hall, holding a document.

HITLER
Well, Herr Speer, you see that despite the efforts of the enemy above us we may still converse surrounded by your architecture.

SPEER nods graciously. HITLER puts on his spectacles.

An irony, in view of your defection to the ranks of the whiners and fainthearts.

SPEER
Um \ may I ask–

HITLER
Yes, here it all is, your report, the usual stuff.... Final collapse of the German war economy... war cannot continue on the military plane... our obligation to maintain the people's means of life.... We have no right, it is not our duty, no one can take the viewpoint that the fate of the German people as a whole is tied to his fate personally.

He takes his spectacles off and glares at SPEER.

SPEER
My Führer. I am merely echoing what you yourself said so eloquently in Mein Kampf...

HITLER
You haven't read Mein Kampf.

SPEER
You will not wish me to deceive you.

HITLER
It is not a matter of what you say to me. I am told that you have told the Ruhr Gauleiters that the war is lost. Are you aware that that is treason? And what measures I would have to take? If you were not my architect?

SPEER
My Führer you must act as you think fit. Without consideration for my person.

Pause.

HITLER
I must act "without consideration for your person."

A sudden change of tack.

Speer, you have worked too hard. You should take some leave.

SPEER
No, my Führer. I am fit and well. If you want to get rid of me, you must dismiss me.

HITLER
You know I can't do that.

SPEER
Nor can I remain the Minister in name if I desert my post.

Pause. HITLER doesn't know what to do. He sits and looks away. SPEER sits.

HITLER
All right.

Pause.

You know, in some ways the enemy's advance is a great help to us. People fight fanatically when they have the war at their front door.

SPEER
My Führer, as I pointed out in my memorandum the enemy's military superiority \ means that–

HITLER
I sometimes think, the luck. I was always lucky. And then that dreadful early winter in 1941. And the allies get blue skies for Normandy. But, yet, despite all of that, we struggle on, with unshakable determination. You—what—you doubled tank production in two years. You trebled airplanes and munitions. Artillery, quadrupled. When naturally the moaners and whiners said it was impossible.

Pause.

Which is why I will give you one more chance.

SPEER
I'm sorry?

HITLER
If you can assure me that the war can still be won, then you can keep your post.

Pause.

SPEER
My Führer, the war is lost.

HITLER
Or indeed, if you still had faith the war might still be won.

Pause.

Or even… that you *hoped* that we aren't lost. At least you could say that. And then I would be satisfied.

SPEER
My Führer, how could I lie to you? It would be like lying to myself.

HITLER stands.

HITLER
You think about it. And then let me know.

SPEER
Um… "think about it?"

HITLER
Whether you're prepared to hope the war might still be won.

SPEER
But I…

HITLER
You know, when the whiners and the fainthearts say that it's impossible, then I say – look at Speer.

HITLER hits SPEER with the glare. It holds a long time.

You can say it in your own words. Any way you like.

SPEER turns away. HITLER pleased to have won, but furious that SPEER has not done what he asked.

Well, there it is.

He turns to go. Suddenly.

SPEER
My Führer, how could you doubt me. I stand unconditionally behind you.

HITLER turns back to SPEER. We don't know how he will react. After a long moment, it is HITLER who turns away, nodding, his eyes brimming with tears. He comes to SPEER putting out his hand. SPEER puts out his hand, HITLER takes it and converts it into the elbow cupping gesture.

HITLER
Well. Heil Speer.

SPEER
(pressing his advantage) My Führer. Will you do one thing for me?

HITLER looks quizzically at SPEER.

Will you give me and my ministry sole responsibility for implementing your decree of March 19?

HITLER
For implementing? Not for changing it?

SPEER
For implementing it, my Fuhrer. Absolutely and entirely.

SPEER takes a paper from his pocket.

It will require a sentence.

HITLER
Yes of course.

SPEER gives the piece of paper to HITLER.

Very well.

HITLER takes the document to a table to sign it.

A glass of wine?

SPEER
That would be very welcome.

HITLER calls.

HITLER
Schaub!

To SPEER, as he signs.

My hands are shaking. Lately it's been hard for me to write even a few words.

Enter SCHAUB.

SCHAUB
'Führer.

HITLER
Schaub, can you have them get a glass of wine for the Reichsminister.

SCHAUB goes out. HITLER stands, turns back to SPEER.

You know, if the war is lost then the people will be lost, and it is not necessary to worry about their needs. For the garbage left over after this will be only the inferior, as the best are dead. And the future belongs entirely to the hard men of the east.

SPEER
What?

HITLER hands him the document.

HITLER
We will leave this world in flame. I am confident in assigning this last duty to my Minister of Armaments.

HITLER disappears.

1.12.3 Berlin, 29–30 March 1945

WOLTERS and ANNEMARIE enter to SPEER. CASALIS is there.

ANNEMARIE
Thank God.

SPEER
(handing WOLTERS the document HITLER signed) Five thousand copies.

WOLTERS
New orders?

SPEER
Yes. And are \ the vehicles I ordered–

WOLTERS
(reading the document) Yes, as you ordered.

ANNEMARIE
Cars, trucks, lorries, motorbikes, and bicycles…

WOLTERS
…standing by.

SPEER
Excellent.

WOLTERS
(reading) So you got the old man to sign over everything to us.

SPEER
The Führer assigned me this last duty, yes.

WOLTERS
To countermand his general order as and when we think it fit.

SPEER
No.

WOLTERS
But that is what you plan to do.

SPEER
I plan to stop the destruction of the factories and farms and mines on which our people's future life depends.

SPEER turns to go.

WOLTERS
Where are you going first?

SPEER
East.

WOLTERS
A question.

SPEER
Yes?

WOLTERS
What happens if you turn the corner and run into an enemy patrol?

Slight pause.

SPEER
　　Oh, I've got that all worked out. It's simple. I'd surround them.

　　The tension between them is broken. WOLTERS laughs, turns and goes out.

CASALIS
　　And did it work?

SPEER
　　Yes. It saved German industry.

CASALIS
　　By betraying Hitler.

SPEER
　　As he and those who followed his last orders had given up the German people.

CASALIS
　　So despite your efforts there was destruction?

SPEER
　　Yes, sadly. For instance, I discovered that despite his pledge Karl Hanke had in fact blown up the Schinkel building. And everything besides. And then escaped from an inferno of his own creation.

CASALIS
　　Your old friend.

SPEER
　　Yes.

CASALIS
　　And so did you see Hitler, once again?

SPEER
　　Yes, on the 25th of April… I flew in and landed on the east-west axis and I was taken down into the bunker, where at approaching midnight I was told I was invited for refreshments.

　　SCHAUB enters.

SCHAUB
　　Please follow me.

SPEER
　　And so I did.

1.13.1 Eva Braun's room, bunker, 25 April 1945

SPEER enters EVA BRAUN's room. She looks rather guilty.

SPEER
Eva.

EVA BRAUN
Oh good it's you.

She retrieves a lit cigarette she's just hidden.

SPEER
I didn't know you smoked.

EVA BRAUN
Extreme circumstances call for extreme measures. Do you want one?

SPEER
No.

EVA BRAUN
If "someone" comes in and detects the smell, it's yours. But I bet you'd like some cake and some champagne.

SPEER
You're the first person to think I might be hungry.

EVA BRAUN
Everybody's got things on their minds.

SPEER
As have you.

Pause. She busies herself with cake and wine.

EVA BRAUN
Do you recognize your furniture?

SPEER
Of course.

EVA BRAUN
It too is a comfort to me in these times.

SPEER
I'm pleased.

EVA BRAUN
It's so sad, what's happened to all those lovely rooms upstairs.

SPEER
Yes, it is. But is not the saddest.

EVA BRAUN
Pop!

She pours champagne.

So how's Frau Speer, and all the children?

SPEER
She's very well. I've moved them to a place of safety, in the… in the area the British are attacking now.

EVA BRAUN
Good man. D'you want some cake?

SPEER
I saw Goebbels earlier. He appears to think that we can make a separate peace with the British and Americans.

EVA BRAUN
(cutting cake) Oh, is that right?

SPEER
Well, I'm not sure it's entirely realistic…

EVA BRAUN
(handing SPEER a piece of cake) Hey, have you heard the latest?

SPEER
No?

EVA BRAUN
(stubs out her cigarette) His ministry is putting out fake horoscopes. Do you want a peppermint?

SPEER
Fake *what*?

EVA BRAUN finds a newspaper.

EVA BRAUN
Look here, it's true.

She opens the newspaper, pops a peppermint into her mouth.

Now, what are you?

SPEER
Professionally?

EVA BRAUN
Your birth sign, Herr Reichsminister.

SPEER
Well, I was born on March 19.

EVA BRAUN
Ah. Pisces. "You are going through a term of trial but if you are steadfast and your will remains unshakable you will prevail against all odds." So what's Frau Speer?

SPEER
Well… she's September…

EVA BRAUN
Oh, *Albert*.

SPEER
(*guessing*) The 28th.

EVA BRAUN
Libra. And yes. Sometimes she must fear she's on the wrong path but nevertheless she will reach her final destination. So – you've done the right thing there.

SPEER
And you?

EVA BRAUN
Well, I'm Aquarius. And although things may look black I must be assured that they who love and care for me are acting always for the best. Isn't it priceless?

Pause. Delicately, she puts her hand on SPEER's arm.

You know he had decided to stay here, and I am staying with him. Like everyone, he wanted me to go to Munich. But I'm happy to be here. And you know the rest, of course.

Slight pause.

So my dear Albert, please, no pestering! I have reached my destination.

SPEER smiles. EVA BRAUN eats another peppermint.

EVA BRAUN
He was so pleased you came.

SPEER
Yes. Though I fear he would be less pleased if he knew \ what I've been–

EVA BRAUN
(*interrupting*) He thought that you had gone against him, like the others.

SPEER
You see, I have been countermanding \ orders to destroy–

EVA BRAUN
(*interrupting*) But I know that you will always stand behind him, unconditionally.

Pause.

SPEER
But surely. We must surely, all of us, feel there were things that shouldn't have occurred. Things said or done, or left undone.

EVA BRAUN
You mean, not having children?

Pause.

Well, perhaps. But after all, I am the Mother of the Nation.

SPEER smiles, a little wanly, giving up. EVA BRAUN yawns.

Well, I must go to bed. And you must go to... to your family.

They look at each other.

I told him – Speer will not betray you. Well, my case is proved, I think. Don't you?

SPEER says nothing. EVA BRAUN puts her hand out to SPEER.

EVA BRAUN
Well. So long.

SPEER
So long.

She shakes his hand. SPEER turns and goes out of the room.

1.13.2 Corridor, bunker, 25 April 1945

SPEER meets HITLER, looking at a map, and VON BELOW.

SPEER
Heil, my Führer.

HITLER
Ah, Speer, you're leaving?

SPEER
Yes, my Führer.

HITLER
Ah.

HITLER looks at SPEER. For a moment, the same, blinding look.

Well, then. Well, there it is. Goodbye.
(to VON BELOW) Will you get Keitel? If we're going to split the two commands, then we must do it now, while there's still a corridor...

HITLER goes out with VON BELOW following.

1.14.1 Hamburg, 1 May 1945

SPEER turns to CASALIS, as ANNEMARIE enters with a small bag. She opens the bag, takes out a red leather case, opens it, sets up a picture of HITLER in a silver frame. As SPEER takes off his coat:

SPEER
So that was it. No wishes to my family, no... statement, affirmation. No good luck. Nothing beyond... goodbye. And he was gone.
And so I went north, to join Dönitz, who was trying to negotiate surrender with the British. I was assigned a small room in a navy barracks. Frau Kempf had packed a small overnight bag for me, in which she'd put a portrait photograph of the Führer, in a silver frame, which he had given me six weeks before.

ANNEMARIE goes out with the jacket. SPEER goes and looks at the picture.

CASALIS
And presumably that's where you heard about his death?

SPEER can't answer. He nods.

And may I ask – what did you feel?

> SPEER *says nothing. Instead he starts to sob. He can't stop it, it goes on and on, until he is literally too exhausted to sob any more. He looks to CASALIS.*

SPEER
I felt that I was free of him at last.

1.14.2 Spandau, 1950

CASALIS
You felt that you were free of him? At last?

> SPEER *a little wearily, taking his prison jacket from the case and putting it on:*

SPEER
I've said. I realized too late.

CASALIS
Of course. You were an expert, not a politician.

SPEER
Yes.

CASALIS
You had sought where possible to improve the conditions of your workers.

SPEER
Yes.

CASALIS
You had visited one concentration camp.

SPEER
Yes.

CASALIS
You were ignorant of a systematic plan \ to murder–

SPEER
Yes.

CASALIS
But what do you think you would have done, if you *had* known?

> *Pause.*

SPEER
This is of course the question. And the answer doesn't help me sleep at night. I fear I would have said: "You're killing them? But that's insane. I need them for my factories."
That is why I came to you, and asked you to help me to become a different man. And you said you could and would if I told you the truth.

CASALIS
And do you think you have?

SPEER
Why, do you think I've been lying to you all this time?

CASALIS
No, Herr Speer. I don't think you've been lying. But I must tell you the questions that remain. You have told me you were let down by this man who had promised you so much. But was it really that? Was it not rather a playing out of what was there from the beginning? Is it not the case in truth that the hope was always false because the choice was always wrong? That there was a straight line from your building of the new Berlin to the blasting of that tunnel by those miserable slave-workers in the mountain. That the granite for Germania was quarried by the inmates of Mauthausen. That the searchlights which obscured the stomachs of the party bureaucrats at Nuremberg also blinded you to what was being thought and said and planned. Herr Speer, you have presented me the story of a man who was inspired by great ideals and saw those great ideals betrayed. And yet. I see a man with all the intellectual, yes, and all the moral strength to have seen through all of this. Surely, when you look back to the first time when you looked into those eyes, don't you ask yourself, how in God's name was I taken in by that?

SPEER is appalled.

SPEER
Look, Pastor. You had a simple war. Dangerous of course. Unenviable in many ways. But simple in that in hindsight there's no doubt at all that you were right. Now put yourself in my shoes. Ask yourself what hindsight asks of me. Had I done what was required of me by posterity in the war I would have been shot by Hitler. Had I admitted what I was asked to admit after the war, I would have hanged at Nuremberg. My crime consisted of not knowing and not asking what I didn't know, about an evil we will perish if we do not understand. For that – I have been condemned as a war criminal, robbed of my freedom, tortured with the knowledge that I based my life upon a catastrophic error. If you demand of me that I should have done more than I did, then you must be sure that if—God forbid—it came to that for you, you would make and meet the same demands on yourself. Till then…
I must repeat. I could have known, I should have known. I didn't know. I was blinded by what I felt about him at the start to what he reall–. To what he had become.

CASALIS
But still, you see, you cannot say: "to what he really always was."

CASALIS realizes he has gone too far.

I'm sorry. I should not have.... It is not my job to judge \ or to cross-examine you–

SPEER
So what *is* your job? If it is not "to judge to probe and to interrogate."

CASALIS
It is to repeat those two words. To a man who thought he should have died at Nuremberg.

SPEER
What words?

CASALIS
"Not yet." To a man who now may have begun to live.

SPEER
Begun?

CASALIS
Like his garden here in Spandau, he has cleared the undergrowth. Now the time has come to plant new seeds in fresh soil.

Enter HESS with a chair.

HESS
Ah. There you are.

SPEER
Herr Hess?

HESS
I've something for you.

SPEER
Yes?

HESS
I broke my chair. You lent me yours.

SPEER
I did.

HESS
　I understand you take your chair to religious service every Sunday. So you will have need of it. I mended mine. The whole thing's mumbo-jumbo, anyway.

　He goes out, leaving the chair.

SPEER
　In fact it is not my chair. It's Neurath's. It was found for him to help his back. But oddly enough, it is my chair in another sense. In that it was my own design.

　Pause.

CASALIS
　Well.

SPEER
　Herr Pastor, God preserve your strength.

CASALIS
　And yours. Please – stay. You have your chair.

　CASALIS goes. SPEER turns out front.

SPEER
　And he was gone. To complete his doctorate at Strasbourg.

　Pause.

　I said that when I heard of Hitler's death I felt that I was free of him at last. But as you know that isn't true at all.
　Yes. Yes. That's when the dreams began.
　Dreams of his knowing what I did, dreams of his knowing what I thought. And I realized he wasn't really dead at all.

1.15.1 Germany

　SPEER is dreaming. Suddenly, the sky is full of fire. Through it walks VON BELOW.

VON BELOW
　In October 1942, I was approached by a young lieutenant of the communications corps, who'd been working on a cable transfer somewhere in the Ukraine. He'd come upon a troop of SS, shooting men and women in a trench.
　I naturally investigated this. I was advised that this was not a matter of concern for me.

Now the fire feels like the torches of the Nuremberg rallies. Enter GANZENMÜLLER.

GANZENMÜLLER
On the 28th of July 1942, yes, I appear to have signed a letter to SS General Wolff. "With reference to our telephone conversation of 16th July, I am able to inform you that since 22 July one train a day, with 5,000 Jews, is going from Warsaw to Treblinka…"

Now the torches are topped by SPEER's Cathedral of Light, through which walks HANKE.

HANKE
All right. I'm going to say this once – and you're going to say nothing. There's a place, in Upper Silesia, on the Vistula near Crakow. It's vast, goes on for ever. I.G. Farben has a plant there. In the Polish it's Oswiecem and we call it Auschwitz. And if you're invited there – don't go. I can't describe it. I am not permitted to describe it. Just don't go.

1.15.2 Posen, 1943

Then the light becomes candelabra in the darkness and a small man enters, now alone, to a lectern. Finding it hard to see through the gothic gloom, he blinks, and cleans his glasses. Then he begins.

HIMMLER
I want to speak now, in this most restricted circle, about a matter which you, my party comrades, have long accepted as a matter of course, but which for me has become the heaviest burden of my life – the matter of the Jews. The brief sentence "The Jews must be exterminated" is easy to pronounce, but the demands on those who have to put it into practice are the hardest and the most difficult in the world.
We, you see, were faced with the question "What about the women and children?" And I decided, here too, to find an unequivocal solution. For I did not think that I was justified in exterminating—meaning kill or order to have killed—the men, but to leave their children to grow up to take revenge on our sons and grandchildren.
For the organization which had to carry out this order, it was the most difficult one we were ever given. I think I can say that it has been carried out without damaging the minds and spirits of our men, or of our leaders.

Blackout.

Act Two

— • —

"People cannot find a place in their imagination
(or allow themselves to remember) unimaginable horror.
It is possible to live in a twilight between knowing and not knowing."
—W.A.Visser 't Hooft, Dutch theologian
(quoted in Gitta Sereny, *Albert Speer: His Battle with Truth*)

2.1.1 Spandau Garden, August 1966 and September 1954

A bench on one side. On the other, SPEER kneels, looking down. We might think he is praying, or in a state of abject misery. In fact, he is planting a flower with a trowel. He looks up. He is 60 years old.

SPEER wears a corduroy prison suit stamped with the number five on the breast, back and knees. He stands and speaks.

SPEER
So who is this old man? Well, he was first an architect, whose works proclaimed his country's power to the world. And then a Minister, building armaments to dominate the world. But now he is a gardener... who built a place of beauty in the midst of all the dust and rubble, which he pretended was the world.
Who is he? Well, he's all these things. But most importantly, he is your father.

HESS enters. He is in his 60s, as he was in 1954. His corduroy uniform is stamped four.

It was Herr Hess who gave me the idea.

HESS sits on the garden bench.

So how are you today, Herr Hess?

HESS
Oh, pretty bad.

SPEER
(out front) He was Hitler's deputy. And frankly he'd been pretty screwy even then.

HESS
However. I've decided I was wrong to think my food was being doctored to give me stomach cramps. After all, I can take any one of the seven bowls that are standing on the table.

SPEER
So you've got over your obsession.

HESS
Oh, no. That would never do. If I got over it, it wouldn't be obsessive.

SPEER looks at HESS, fascinated by this logic.

SPEER
We all have our eccentricities. Do you know that I'm collecting kilometres? Don't you think that's crazy, writing down the distances I've walked each day?

HESS
Why not, if you enjoy it?

SPEER
But every week, I add them up, and calculate the weekly average, and enter the results.

HESS shrugs.

And even to start off I had to calculate my walking course, by measuring my foot, 31 centimetres, then walking heel to toe, 870 times, to work out my track.

HESS
Sounds logical to me.

SPEER
But it gets worse. Now I plan to walk to Heidelberg! 616 kilometres! That's Two Thousand Three Hundred and eighteen point fifty two circuits of my track! Isn't this completely mad?

HESS
Well only if \ you want to–

SPEER
And the worst thing is, my real obsession is that I'll miscount and get there late. Can you believe that? That I could have been sitting in my favourite pastry shop but I'm still trudging through the outskirts in the rain!

HESS stands and goes out.

Herr Hess? Have I offended you?

HESS returns with a tin.

HESS
Here. Take 30 beans. Put them in your left pocket. Then every round drop one into your right pocket. And at night you count them up. You understand?

SPEER
Yes. Thank you, Hess.

HESS
Don't mention it.

He makes to go.

A thought. Why stop at Heidelberg?

HESS goes out.

2.1.2 Spandau Garden, August 1966

SPEER turns out front.

SPEER
And so from Heidelberg I walked to Munich. Then across the mountains to Vienna. And all the time, I was thinking, when I got back to my cell, and found a scrap of paper, what I'd write to little or as time passed not so little Hilde.
When you were young, about how I first met your mother, and some jokey stories about life in prison in my "magazine" for you, the *Spanish Illustrated*. Then later, when I made our secret rule: that if something's wrong, but you don't want to say so, then put the word "nevertheless" before the sentence. Thus if you say, "Nevertheless, I'm fine," it means you are not fine at all. Meanwhile, I walk on. My record for one day so far is 24.7 kilometres, my best pace 5.8 kilometres an hour. To aid me, the person who I call "my friend" has obtained for me by our secret channel maps, travelogues, art history... he warns me of all natural barriers, raging rivers, glaciers, mountains, and sends me descriptions of the wonders I will pass.
You ask about the Nazis. You say how could an intelligent person go along with such a thing.
This morning I left Europe and crossed the pontoon bridge to Asia. I have trouble picturing the magnificent panorama: mosques and minarets in the midst of a tangle of small houses. How many towers does Hagia Sofia have? To reassure you: of the dreadful things, I knew nothing. As far as practising anti-semitism or even uttering anti-semitic remarks, my conscience is entirely clear. I really had no aversion to them, or rather, no more than the slight discomfort all of us sometimes feel when in contact with these people...
And today I am 353 kilometres from Kabul. If no snowstorms intervene I should be there mid-January.

Already we are fewer: three years ago Neurath was released, a year later Raeder and last year Dönitz. And Neurath died.
Now there are only 780 kilometres to Calcutta, which will mark the completion of my ten thousandth kilometre.
And I wonder: will I later miss these quiet days with books and gardening, free from ambition and vexation? When I'm released, will I still be able to cope with the world?
Funk was released two years ago and now he too has died.
For more than a year now I've been tramping north through endless woods of larch and fir, with gnarled silver birches in the highlands.
And now another 500 kilometres through the snowy wastes to the Bering Straight still lie before me, all to be done in almost total darkness. However, wonderful northern lights, such as I saw in Lapland at the end of 1943, continually transform the scenery.

HESS enters. He is now in his late 70s.

The strait is frozen till mid March. I wanted to arrive in time to walk across. And so I have.

HESS
Herr Speer, you are talking to yourself.

SPEER
Yes, indeed I am. And in fact, Herr Hess \ you may be interested–

HESS
Schirach says that in mental hospitals they set the feeble-minded to the gardening.

SPEER
You may be interested to hear \ that you are looking–

HESS
Good point, I think.

SPEER
–that you are looking at the first central European to reach America by foot.

Pause.

HESS
This is more serious than I thought.

SPEER
Clearly you don't remember.

HESS
No.

SPEER
So here's a clue. The word is "beans?"

HESS
No, it won't do.

SPEER
Don't you remember? The 30 beans, to transfer from one pocket to the other. Look!

He shows HESS his beans.

HESS
You mean you've kept it up for all this time?

SPEER
Seventy-eight thousand five hundred and fourteen rounds. Twenty-one thousand two hundred and one kilometres. And look – the Bering Strait. The gateway to Alaska, Canada, Seattle. California!

HESS
Well… and they say I'm crazy.

He goes out.

SPEER
(*out front*) And so. Hilde. This is my last letter. And a chance to thank you for all the extraordinary energy and love you expended in the effort to shorten my time here… the love from you to me was always the greatest gift.

SPEER stands a moment, then, in a different tone:

And what I thought but didn't say…. This idiotic organization of emptiness…. What I am left with in the end is nothing but the foolish satisfaction of having marched obstinately in a circle for decades. Through a mirrored hall of hundreds of unchanging faces, over and over, and all mine.
You know, if I had lived fully here, I think I would have had to die. Instead, I have become the man I never was.

He reaches into his sock and takes out a scrap of cardboard, from which he reads:

A telegram. To "my friend." Rudi. This should reach you at precisely midnight, 30 September 1966. Please pick me up 35 kilometres south of Guadalajara, Mexico.

2.2.1 Outside Spandau. Midnight, 30 September 1966

Midnight chimes. SPEER walks out of Spandau, surrounded by British GUARDS, into the chaos of a phalanx of PRESSMEN, film and TV cameras, flashbulbs. On the edge of the crush is SPEER's lawyer FLACHSNER, 66, leading MARGRET towards her husband. Rudi WOLTERS is on the edge of the scene.

PRESSMEN
(*variously*) Herr Speer, how does it feel to be released?
What do you think of the treatment you received?
This way please, Herr Speer!
What are your plans?

FLACHSNER
Excuse me, excuse me please–

PRESSMEN
Frau Speer, how long is it since you've seen your husband?
Just turn your head this way, Frau Speer!
Do you think your sentence was just?
Where are you going now, sir?
Have you changed your views on Hitler?
Do you think you have paid a proper price?
Are you happy with your treatment in Spandau?
What was your view about the Eichmann trial?

FLACHSNER and MARGRET have reached SPEER, who looks happy but bewildered. They shake hands. FLACHSNER is holding up his hands trying to stop the barrage of questions so that he and SPEER can speak.

PRESSMEN
What did you most miss in prison?
What do you think about the Berlin wall?
How were your relations with your fellow prisoners?
Please look over here, Herr Speer!

SPEER holds up his hands along with FLACHSNER and the hubbub dissolves into silence.

PRESSMEN
Why were you not released early?
Do you feel responsible for Nazi crimes?
Do you think you were unjustly treated?
Do you think you've paid the price?

FLACHSNER
Ladies and gentlemen. Herr Speer will make a short statement.

FIRST PRESSMAN
What are your immediate plans?

SPEER
Ladies and gentlemen, may I say at first that I am quite glad to be out.

Laughter. The beginnings of questions, which SPEER stops with a gesture.

PRESSMEN
Do you plan to go back to architecture, Herr Speer?

SPEER
You will understand that I can only be brief tonight, for this evening belongs to my wife.

HECKLER
It's not your business to say anything!

Booing and shhing.

SPEER
So you will forgive me for answering your questions this way. My sentence was just. I was treated correctly at all times. I have no complaints. Thank you so much.

FIRST PRESSMAN
What are your plans, Herr Speer?

SPEER
My immediate plans are to spend some quiet days with my family.

SECOND PRESSMAN
And beyond?

SPEER
I am an architect–

HECKLER
Architect!

SPEER
–and I hope to find people who will let me practise my profession. Thank you very much.

THIRD PRESSMAN
Herr Speer, do you think you have paid the price for what you did?

SPEER
And now please, everyone…

FLACHSNER pushing through the PRESS, making a path for SPEER and MARGRET to the car.

FLACHSNER
Thank you, that's all.

THIRD PRESSMAN
Will you be giving further interviews, Herr Speer?

FLACHSNER
No, he will not.

PRESSMEN
What is your view about the Frankfurt trials?
Do you plan to meet with any world leaders?
Will there be a press conference?

FLACHSNER
There are no further questions. Herr and Frau Speer are going to a private address.

SPEER passes WOLTERS.

WOLTERS
So here I am. Just south of Guadalajara.

SPEER
Rudi. Long time no see.

WOLTERS
You will come and see me.

SPEER
Oh, of course.

WOLTERS
I have the ham. And the Johannisberger.

SPEER
(overwhelmed) And everything you've done for me. For us. For all these years.

WOLTERS
But tonight is for your wife. Go, go.

After this private moment, WOLTERS is swallowed up by the crowd.

PRESSMEN
>Where are you going, Herr Speer?
>Are you going to write about your experiences?
>Have you sold your story to a newspaper or magazine?
>What is your view on denazification?
>What was your relationship with Rudolf Hess?
>Will you be meeting up with your old comrades?
>The price, Herr Speer! Do you think you've paid the price?

2.2.2 Hunting Lodge, Schleswig-Holstein, 1 October 1966

The Speer children, their spouses and ANNEMARIE waiting in a hunting lodge hired by the Speers. Old fashioned comfort. Downstage, easy chairs and a gramophone. To one side, a table laid for dinner. HILDE (30), her husband ULF Schramm, ALBERT (32), and his wife RUTH, FRITZ (29) and ARNOLD (26). Two WAITRESSES stand close to waiting trays of canapés and drinks. The scene starts in silence. ALBERT goes and takes a canapé.

ALBERT
>What's this?

FIRST WAITRESS
>Paté de fois gras, sir.

HILDE
>It was one of the requests.

RUTH
>Is that the stuff they make by \ forcefeeding–

ARNOLD
>Yes.

ALBERT
>*(eating)* It's actually quite \ palatable–

ARNOLD
>It just tends to be a little rich.

>*ALBERT gestures anyone to take one.*

ALBERT
>Paté de fois gras, anyone? Aunt Annemarie?

>*No one takes up the offer. ANNEMARIE shakes her head. HILDE goes and takes a drink and sits.*

HILDE
　Well, as I say, he ordered it.

ULF
　He ordered everything.

HILDE
　It's been driving us all bonkers. Lists lists lists.

ULF
　Appointed tasks.

ALBERT
　But after twenty years, I guess you are entitled.

FRITZ
　So everybody: best \ behaviour–

A door opens, HILDE leaps up. Enter the 28-year-old MARGRET (JUNIOR), her husband HANS STRAUSS, and 23-year-old ERNST.

ALBERT
　Margret.

MARGRET JUNIOR
　We met Ernst at the station.

HANS
　Sorry we're so late.

ARNOLD
　It's fine. The old man's not here yet.

ALBERT
　Now, Hans, you've met Aunt Annemarie? Who was Father's secretary in the war.

HANS
　Of course I have.

HILDE
　And truth be told…

ANNEMARIE
　Ernst! Aren't you looking well.

ERNST JUNIOR
　Aha. That's what you get for being over 21.

ARNOLD
  Why's that?

ERNST JUNIOR
  People stop saying "aren't you tall."

RUTH
  And haven't started saying "aren't you old."

  Pause.

HILDE
  Of course, you haven't seen him for twenty years.

ANNEMARIE
  Not since Nuremberg. And visa versa, naturally.

MARGRET JUNIOR
  You look as wonderful as ever.

ALBERT
  And in fact \ I think we've all–

FRITZ
  In fact, dear family, tarantara, tarantara.

  Enter MARGRET and SPEER. Applause. ALBERT nods to the WAITRESSES who pour champagne into the glasses ready to take them round.

MARGRET
  I'm sorry.

SPEER
  We must have…

MARGRET
  Father thought he spotted a reporter.

SPEER
  …come round the wrong way.

  He takes it in.

  Well. Well.

  ALBERT to him.

ALBERT
  Father, welcome back.

They shake hands.

SPEER
My boy.

ALBERT
And father... Ruth.

SPEER
My dear, how wonderful to meet you.

SPEER kisses RUTH's hand.

You know, your husband has the most lovely hands. Do you remember, Albert, on your first visit, all those years ago?

ALBERT
Of course I do.

SPEER
I shook my son's hand, and I was put up on a charge.

MARGRET
Well, you won't be charged with anything today.

FRITZ
Just charged *for* everything.

HILDE
Fritz! Papa.

SPEER
Hilde, my dearest. And Ulf...

MARGRET
(*gesturing to MARGRET JUNIOR*) Albert, your daughter.

SPEER
Margret.

MARGRET JUNIOR
Papa.

SPEER
Still, so like my mother.

HANS
And like her mother, sir. I'm Hans Nissen.

SPEER
Of course, of course.

Shakes hands.

And where is little Annagret?

MARGRET JUNIOR
She's in bed, papa! Tomorrow.

SPEER
(turning to ARNOLD) Of course, of course. Now, Fritz?

ARNOLD
No, Arnold, father.

Pause.

SPEER
Arnold.

ARNOLD
Yes.

SPEER
Ah, well. In jail, your mother sent me photographs I thought were Albert but turned out to be me as a boy.

This rescues the moment. With a playful if not entirely convincing punch to the shoulder.

So – Arnold.

ARNOLD
Yes. Father, you look marvellous.

SPEER
Well, you're the doctor. Fritz.

Shaking FRITZ's hand.

How could I mistake the hell-raiser?

FRITZ
Hell-raiser?

MARGRET
You got drunk – once. I foolishly mentioned in a letter.

FRITZ
Right.

ERNST JUNIOR
And by process of elimination...

SPEER
Ernst.

Shakes hands.

It should be easy when you're standing. I marked your heights up on the wall. As through the years you grew – grew up from...

MARGRET
(*rescuing*) Just grew up.

Slight pause.

ANNEMARIE
It's hard to know what to say to someone who is locked away from you for twenty years.

SPEER realizes it's ANNEMARIE. During this ALBERT nods to the WAITRESSES, who bring drinks on trays.

SPEER
Frau... Annemarie.

ANNEMARIE
Albert.

SPEER
For twenty years, I have been just Number Five.

ANNEMARIE
For those who love you, you have never just been Number Five.

FIRST WAITRESS offering to SPEER.

FIRST WAITRESS
Herr Speer.

SPEER
Please, my wife.

FIRST WAITRESS gives a drink to MARGRET.

MARGRET
Thank you.

SECOND WAITRESS
A canapé?

SPEER
Aha! *Paté de fois gras!* I chose it because it's the one thing everybody likes.

> *As the drinks and canapés are handed round, SPEER takes a canapé and bolts it in one. Then he takes another and does the same. ANNEMARIE notes this undelicate behaviour.*

FRITZ
(taking a drink) Well, I suppose, if I'm to live up to my reputation.

> *SPEER nods to ULF who surreptitiously produces a small jewellery case.*

MARGRET JUNIOR
Now, father, would you like to sit…

ALBERT
Should we move \ into the dining room–

SPEER
Now, I have a duty to perform, in relation to the most important person in the room.

> *A moment or two while people work out who that is. ULF gives SPEER the case.*

FRITZ
Speech, speech.

SPEER
To thank her, on all your behalfs, for bringing you all up as she has. Which is all the speech she'll get from me.

> *He hands the case to MARGRET.*

MARGRET
Albert, how was this done?

> *MARGRET opens the case. It's a gold watch.*

Oh, Albert.

SPEER
It should be engraved.

ULF
It is engraved!

MARGRET
(*reads*) "To his Libra, on his day of Liberation." *Albert*.

MARGRET JUNIOR
It's beautiful.

ULF
Is it all right?

MARGRET
Of course it is.

ERNST JUNIOR
But mum's not libra. She's a virgo.

Pause.

HILDE
Ernst.

HANS
I'm sure it's right…

ERNST JUNIOR
Eighth of September. Virgo.

SPEER
The… the eighth.

Pause. ARNOLD and ALBERT look at HILDE and ULF. HILDE: "Nothing to do with me." ULF: "I did as instructed."

MARGRET
Well, all I can say is that I am personally delighted that your father of all people can make a mistake with numbers.

Rescue successful.

And I feel that everyone should go through and enjoy what Fritz reminds us is a most expensive dinner.

HILDE
Yes.

The party proceeds to the table for dinner.

RUTH
What are your plans for the immediate future, Herr Speer?

SPEER
Well, I have many old acquaintances to renew. As Aunt Annemarie knows, my friend Rudi Wolters has promised me a Westphalian ham and a bottle of Johannisberger 37.

MARGRET
I think the places are all marked.

SPEER
It will be strange, we two old codgers meeting after all this time. He's very fond of all the children.

HILDE
"Fond" is an understatement!

Everyone is seated.

SPEER
Yes indeed. *(to RUTH)* And then...

ALBERT taps his glass with a spoon, MARGRET shaking her head, but:

ALBERT
No, Mama, no speech. But just to raise a glass to welcome Father home. Having been kept from us for twenty years.

RUTH
Hear hear.

ARNOLD
(raising his glass) Father!

THE OTHERS
(variously) To Father. Papa. Albert. Herr Speer.

SPEER
Well, as is well known, I too am not one for making speeches. And so... the feast!

Atmosphere fully restored. EVERYONE starting to eat.

RUTH
"And then?"

SPEER
I'm sorry?

RUTH
You were talking of your plans.

SPEER
Oh yes. I intend to write my memoirs.

Sudden silence.

MARGRET
Memoirs.

SPEER
Yes. My life and deeds in Hitler's Germany!

MARGRET
He told the press he was going to practise as an architect.

SPEER
Well, that was for the press. *(to RUTH)* Since you raise... the matter of the future. *(to MARGRET)* So what's wrong?

MARGRET
There's nothing wrong.

SPEER
That is clearly not the case.

Agonizing pause. MARGRET stands.

MARGRET
Excuse me, please... I'm sorry.

She hurries out.

SPEER
Uh...

ANNEMARIE
Oh, Albert.

ANNEMARIE stands and follows MARGRET out. Neither SPEER nor anybody else knows what to say. SPEER stands and goes into the other room. ALBERT makes to follow but HILDE goes instead.

HILDE
Papa, you must see how she feels.

Slight pause.

SPEER
Go on.

HILDE
After twenty years of watching us grow up, and building our own lives....
For it to be... the only thing we're known for. To have it all raked up again.

SPEER
"Raked up again." I see.

Pause.

In fact, I've made you my literary executor.

HILDE
What? What about Uncle Rudi?

SPEER
I think it's for the best.

Pause.

I am determined. I will write the book. I think I owe it to the world. And of course I had thought—or hoped, at least—you would support me.

MARGRET comes in, followed by ANNEMARIE.

MARGRET
Albert, I'm sorry. Please. Let's go back into dinner.

SPEER
Yes. of course.

SPEER looks back at HILDE.

HILDE
Papa, of course you have my full support. In anything you do.

SPEER looks at HILDE. He turns back to MARGRET, who puts out her arm. SPEER goes and walks with his wife back into dinner. HILDE to ANNEMARIE:

Nevertheless...

2.2.3 Germany, late 1970s

ANNEMARIE out front:

ANNEMARIE
And of course the problem was: for him, it had never really been a real family. He hardly knew them in the war. And being locked away from them for twenty years…. But it was also the family in which he had grown up: his father stopping him pursuing the career he wanted to, his mother such a snob, having to wed in secret because they disapproved of Margret's social class, the intolerable pressure over Ernst at Stalingrad…
And so how was he to know what it was like to be a real father? How could he understand they had their own lives and their own concerns? How could he know they wouldn't—couldn't—welcome him as he imagined, unconditionally, with open arms?

2.3.1 Germany, 1970

A publisher's party, in the garden of their offices. Suddenly, the stage is flooded with partygoers: in addition to fashionable young people in bright late-60s summer clothes (and even possibly some children), they include Wolf-Jobst SIEDLER (SPEER's publisher), MARGRET Speer and Nicholas and Maria VON BELOW, and SPEER himself. A table piled high with copies of SPEER's Reminiscences (Inside the Third Reich *in English), with another table next to it for him to sign. A microphone on a stand.*

Drinks and cocktail bits are taken round by staff in casual clothes. Everything is easy, informal, contemporary, assured… in marked contrast to the nervous stuffiness of the previous scene. SIEDLER moves immediately to make a speech.

SIEDLER
Ladies and gentlemen…

As always, the volume is wrong but it is quickly and effectively sorted.

Ladies and gentlemen, a moment, your attention. Ullstein is… well, moderately proud to welcome almost all of you to its summer party. And of course our guest of honour.

Smattering of applause.

As many people know, particularly in the accounts department, his reminiscences were intended to be a modest success with a long shelf-life in a slow-burn market. I think it is fair to say we failed in this.

Laughter.

We did not intend to sell half a million hardback copies, nor the serial rights to *Die Welt* for 600,000 marks, nor to clean up Europe and then north America in paperback. Through all of this, I've asked myself, how could this thing have gone so wrong?

Laughter.

Clearly we underestimated our new author.

Applause.

And also the importance of his mission, which was to speak, now, a quarter of a century on, not to his own generation but the new generation of young democratic Germans, neither traumatized by guilt nor tortured by denial. To the generation of his children.

He looks around.

Necessarily but bravely honest about that tragic period and his role in it. Herr Albert Speer.

SPEER comes to the microphone.

SPEER
Well, I am not one for making speeches.

The usual laughter and calls of "shame" and "go on."

And although there is a perfectly good story illustrating this... I am advised by Herr Siedler to point out that you may read it on page 217.

Laughter.

All I will say is to thank Herr Sidler for all his efforts with I fear an often recalcitrant new author. Thank you.

Applause. SIEDLER back to the microphone a moment.

SIEDLER
And I believe Herr Speer – who is not recalcitrant at all, will sign copies which we happen by coincidence to have available for purchase here this very afternoon.

The formality breaks. SPEER is escorted by a young woman to his table. MARGRET meets the VON BELOWS.

MARGRET
Well, Klaus. How good of you to come.

VON BELOW
Margret.

MARGRET
(*kissing FRAU VON BELOW*) Maria.

SIEDLER working his way over.

VON BELOW
He's looking marvellous.

FRAU VON BELOW
You both are.

MARGRET
He'll be delighted that you're here. He speaks so warmly of the help you gave him with the book.

VON BELOW
(*demurring*) Well…

MARGRET
Help that I fear I was unable…

FRAU VON BELOW
Well, of course, it all looks different in retrospect. I mean, those evenings at the Berghof with the Chief were not quite so boring at the time.

SIEDLER arrives.

SIEDLER
Klaus, Frau von Below, I'm so pleased you could come. It's my aim to persuade your husband to follow in Herr Speer's footsteps.

FRAU VON BELOW
Really?

SIEDLER
Please, let me introduce you to our chairman.

SIEDLER moves off with the VON BELOWS, leaving MARGRET standing for a moment alone. Meanwhile, SPEER is signing books. His current customer we will know later as MRS. WINTERINGHAM.

SPEER
Who shall I write it to?

MRS. WINTERINGHAM
To Trudi.

SPEER
　Ah.

　　He signs, hands the book over.

MRS. WINTERINGHAM
　Thank you, Herr Speer.

　　SPEER takes the book from the next in line.

SPEER
　Thank you. How would you like this signed?

WOLTERS
　Oh, I think, "to Rudi" would be fine, don't you?

　　SPEER looks up.

SPEER
　Rudi. You're here.

WOLTERS
　Well, you know what they say, about Mohammed and the Mountain.

　　SIEDLER arrives.

SIEDLER
　Now, I hope we're not exploiting you too grossly…

SPEER
　Herr Siedler, this is Rudolf Wolters.

SIEDLER
　Ah. "My friend."

WOLTERS
　And erstwhile literary executor.

　　Slight pause.

SIEDLER
　Um…

WOLTERS
　Albert I need a word with you.

　　SPEER looks at SIEDLER.

SIEDLER
Of course.

To the queue.

A moment, and Herr Speer will return.

He leads SPEER and WOLTERS to the building.

2.4.1 Germany, 1970

Continuous: a room inside the publisher's building. SIEDLER leaves SPEER and WOLTERS.

WOLTERS
Well, congratulations Herr Reichsminister.

SPEER
Rudi, it's good to see you.

WOLTERS
Thank God you didn't say "Long time no see."

SPEER
Why not?

WOLTERS
It's what you said when you got out.

SPEER
Did I really? Well, it hasn't been so long this time.

WOLTERS
It has been long enough.

SPEER
Now look.

A young MALE PUBLISHER enters with a tray: full glasses of champagne, a bottle and a plate of bits.

MALE PUBLISHER
Herr Siedler thought you might like something before it all goes.

SPEER
Thank you, yes.

MALE PUBLISHER
(*picking up the edgy atmosphere*) You were... it was champagne...?

WOLTERS
It was champagne.

The PUBLISHER goes out. SPEER hands WOLTERS a glass.

Well... to two old codgers and their memories.

They drink.

WOLTERS
From one old codger and his royalties.

Pause.

Of which I'm sure the vast proportion have been properly donated to the best of causes. It would never do for the great post-Nazi rent-a-penitent to profit from his crimes. Having resolved to walk into his dotage in a hairshirt, renouncing all the vanities and luxuries of life for locusts and wild honey.

SPEER
(*gesturing to the feast*) So, a locust? Or another spoonful of wild honey?

WOLTERS
Well, precisely.

SPEER
So is this why you came to see me? To draw my attention to this contradiction?

WOLTERS
No, of course not.

SPEER
Rudi, I didn't mention you because I thought it would be best. As an architect practising in the current atmosphere.

WOLTERS
You think I didn't like your wretched book because I wasn't in it?

Enter a young FEMALE PUBLISHER.

SPEER
If not, I apologize for the suggestion.

FEMALE PUBLISHER
Ah, Herr Speer, I've found you.

SPEER
Yes, I am having what is obviously \ a private conversation–

FEMALE PUBLISHER
There is... I have to tell you... there's a lot of people \ waiting for your signature–

SPEER
(*sharply*) But still a moment if you please!

Slight pause.

FEMALE PUBLISHER
(*put out by being snapped at*) Of course.

She turns and goes. SPEER to WOLTERS.

WOLTERS
Oh, don't worry. I'm not the first thing to be rubbed out of your past. And I doubt I'll be the last.

SPEER
I have said, I'm sorry.

WOLTERS
Though you were right in one respect. The reign of terror's hotting up again.

SPEER
The reign of terror?

WOLTERS
Having run out of all the various butchers of wherever, moving on to the so-called "perpetrators from the desk."

SPEER
Yes?

WOLTERS
Which is why I came to see you.

SPEER
Oh?

WOLTERS
The Chronicle.

SPEER
Yes, you wrote to me. I wrote back. There's a problem?

WOLTERS
Describe the situation as you see it.

SPEER
(*slightly offended*) Rudi.

WOLTERS
All right. From 1940 I kept a chronicle of your activities. Of which there were four copies. Three are lost, the fourth I bury in my garden. In 1964 I dig it up, have it retyped, and two years later I hand this retyped version on to you. And like the splendid citizen you are you hand it over to the Federal Archives in Koblenz.

SPEER
Yes.

WOLTERS
However there is a British writer called David Irving \ who finds another copy–

SPEER
–who thinks that Hitler is a man much misunderstood...

WOLTERS
–who points out that Hitler was an ordinary, walking, talking human being with grey hair, false teeth and an obsession with his bowels. As opposed that is to either Superman or Lucifer Incarnate.

SPEER
And he comes across another copy of the original. In some library?

WOLTERS
The Imperial War Museum...

SPEER
...and compares it to the retyped version in Koblenz...

WOLTERS
...and finds they're not the same. Because your old friend Rudi has been through the original, correcting style and grammar, and deleting one or two things that he felt were irrelevant or repetitive or just plain silly...

SPEER
Which is all understandable enough, hence my proposal that we send Koblenz our original, which if anybody wants to plough through they're quite welcome. After all, Irving has presumably ploughed through it all already.

WOLTERS
I see. You think that Irving read it all.

SPEER
I understand he's more than diligent.

WOLTERS
The London copy's incomplete. It's only 1943.

SPEER
So he gets to catch up on the rest in Germany. Rudi, I really don't see the problem.

WOLTERS
The problem isn't 1943. The problem's 1941.

Pause.

SPEER
Yes?

WOLTERS
Do you remember, when your father asked the Chief where the people who'd been dispossessed would go?

SPEER
Yes, I suppose so.

WOLTERS
To which the then official answer was that the plan was for them to go and live in garden suburbs.

SPEER
Yes.

WOLTERS
While as it fell out, actually, a lot of them would end up somewhere very different.

Slight pause.

SPEER
So? I was the General Inspector of Buildings. I had nothing to do with the evacuations.

WOLTERS
Not directly.

A sharp knock on the door.

SPEER
Yes, what?

The MALE PUBLISHER is trying to get SPEER to come out.

MALE PUBLISHER
Herr Speer, I know you're busy, but there is a considerable queue \ outside–

SPEER
I *know*. I will be with them *very shortly*.

WOLTERS
Natives getting restless.

SPEER
So?

WOLTERS
Minutes of meetings 1941. Attended by our people, Goebbels' people, and SS-Lieutenant-Colonel Adolf Eichmann. To plan the eviction and evacuation of nearly 80,000 persons from Berlin. I wonder, can you guess what race of persons these "persons" might have been?

SPEER
And you cut this out.

WOLTERS
Yes I cut this out.

SPEER
Although far from silly or irrelevant.

WOLTERS
Yes.

SPEER
You know I didn't know of the evictions.

WOLTERS
I'm afraid you did. There's some notes, still happily in my possession, with an entry on I believe the 20th of January 1941. "Couple action on the Jew-flats with preparation for emergency quarters for persons"—rather different persons, obviously—"made homeless through bomb damage." All quite clearly in your writing.

SPEER
Well, of course, I knew that people were deported. As I have always said. I didn't know where they were going.

WOLTERS
No of course you didn't. That's the point. They were just another group of people, being shoved about. Along with soldiers, foreign workers, ordinary prisoners, prisoners of war, conscripted or evacuated, bombed out, picked up, taken in custody for the protection of, relocated, handled, processed, dealt with. In the chaos of a war which was already termed a war of national survival. It's only *now* it looks like what you claim it was: the first step on the road to what you "should" and "could" but didn't know was the Greatest Crime in Human History.

SPEER shrugs at this sarcastic hyperbole.

But *now* it all looks different. You know that Theo Ganzenmüller wrote some note in 1942, confirming he'd been able to provide some trains for the transportation of some persons somewhere as requested. The kind of routine memo we all wrote a hundred of a day. Unfortunately, the somewhere was Treblinka.

SPEER
Well, yes, of course...

WOLTERS
But you, great National Scapegoat, you reverse it. It's remarkably ingenious. You flagellate yourself in hindsight actually to justify your actions at the time. Your sin is to have stood above the fray, to have kept your hands clean, never to have known. And by this sleight of hand your betraying him turns into him betraying you.

SPEER
Rudi, that's enough.

WOLTERS
So when did he stop living up to your grand ideal? Well, by the bunker, obviously. So, when he gave you the Arms job? When you designed Germania? When you joined the party? When you sat about and planned a better world with me?

SPEER
You know, it's interesting, what you say about betrayal. Because for all those years, whenever I felt lost, or let down or abandoned or betrayed, whenever I was near to losing faith in humankind, I'd tell myself: just think of Rudi Wolters.

Pause.

But I suppose, we knew \ that it could never–

WOLTERS
Which is why I have to tell you what I really feel. How could I lie to you? It would be as if I lied to me.

SPEER looks at WOLTERS, with the stirring memory of that sentiment.

SPEER
Well at least, we must hope, it isn't lost for ever.

WOLTERS
What, your faith in humankind?

SPEER
Unlike the original version of the Chronicle. Which should I think be lost forever.

WOLTERS
I'm sorry?

SPEER
As so much else has been. After all, it refers to matters which aren't in the book. About which I knew nothing. So, for the greater good.

WOLTERS
We should pursue the line of least resistance.

SPEER looks askance.

Oh, don't worry. The original will vanish without trace. As if it never was. From your and everyone's domain.

SPEER stands a moment. Then, suddenly, he turns and goes back out, almost bumping into the entering MARGRET.

MARGRET
Albert, I have been sent to drag you \ back...

SPEER
I'm coming. Look who's here.

He goes out.

MARGRET
Rudi. How wonderful to see you.

WOLTERS
Margret.

They shake hands. She looks questioningly.

I have been talking to the Great Best-Seller.

MARGRET
When he returned, you know, it was to be the Modest Architect. Have you read the book?

WOLTERS
Oh, yes. Have you?

MARGRET
I read the bit about Eva Braun. He seems to have been quite taken with her. I always found her rather bossy and pretentious.

WOLTERS
Of course, he talked much more about you and your courtship in his letters to the children.

MARGRET
Yes. Hilde showed me. It was incredible. All these feelings which he had inside. From a man who virtually never said a word to me.

He offers her champagne. She declines.

I've been chatting with Klaus von Below. He's considering a book himself. But he's afraid, there was some incident. A young man came to see him about something dreadful that he'd witnessed. And of course there was nothing he could do.

WOLTERS
It was a war. And it was a quarter of a century ago.

MARGRET
Of course.

Slight pause.

You know, he's working on another book.

WOLTERS
Oh?

MARGRET
It's about his time in Spandau.

WOLTERS
Ah.

MARGRET
Some of it was lying on his desk. It was a description of a dream.

WOLTERS
He always said the Spandau dreams were quite agreeable.

MARGRET
Not this one.

WOLTERS looks inquiringly at MARGRET.

It begins with Albert in a factory. Someone—Hitler I presume—is coming for a great inspection. And although he's Minister of Armaments, he's sweeping up the floor.

WOLTERS
At Nuremberg, they made the surviving prisoners sweep up the gymnasium where they'd done the hangings.

MARGRET
Well, that would explain it. Then, like you are in dreams, he's in a car, and he's trying to get his arm into his jacket.

WOLTERS
Presumably, that's the jacket Hitler lent him when they met.

MARGRET
Of course. And then he's in a vast square, I suppose the great square that they planned for all those years, and Hitler's there as well, and asks his adjutants: where are the wreaths? And then Albert looks surprised, I would imagine, because the adjutant explains that nowadays "he" lays wreaths all the time. And so he does, singing a kind of dreary plainsong chant, as on and on they come, wreath after wreath, piled ever higher, seemingly without end.

She's looking out towards the garden party.

And look. Look, still they come.

WOLTERS
(sensing she's talking about something else) Excuse me?

MARGRET
He's still signing.

WOLTERS turns out front.

WOLTERS
Not for the last time. As his *Spandau Diaries* were to prove another publishing phenomenon.
But once again, there was no place for his indefatigable and yet absent "friend."

Those years in which I was his lifeline, and he was my life.

WOLTERS goes. MARGRET out front.

MARGRET
I'm sorry. I would like to talk about it, but I can't. I'm sure you understand. You see, my fear is that sometime, somebody like you, with the best of good intentions, will ask me what I knew.
And I don't know which is worse. Having known about it... or the truth. That I knew nothing of what went on at all.
I am so sorry.

MARGRET turns and goes out.

2.5 A music auditorium in a University, Germany, early 1970s

The music auditorium has been taken over by a meeting that has had to move from a large hall – it is crushed and crowded and there's an improvised quality to the arrangements – the female student CHAIR sits on a piano stool, there is no table in front of the guests SPEER and SIEDLER, no water jug or flowers, and the lectern is a music stand. There are SECURITY MEN among the AUDIENCE.

CHAIR
Fellow students, fellow members of the University Historical Society, ladies and gentlemen. I must first of all apologize for the conditions. Which as everybody knows were brought about by the actions of people who prefer to shout down rather than to listen and discuss. We are grateful to the music faculty for loaning us their auditorium at such short notice. Well, at none at all.

Slight pause.

As you know our speaker this evening is the author of a noted and important autobiography, about an unhappy period in our country's recent past. He is accompanied by his publisher, Herr Siedler. We are very grateful to them both for agreeing to proceed with this symposium under the circumstances. Herr Albert Speer.

SPEER goes to the music stand. Applause and a little booing – the booing is booed back.

SPEER
(*adjusting his notes*) No, no.

Putting on his glasses.

Well, first of all I am very pleased to be speaking in a place dedicated to music. However, I must confess that I am here under somewhat false pretences. I have never been a speech-maker, and in fact there is a story illustrating this. On the occasion of his 50th birthday, I was pleased to hand over the first completed stage of the new Berlin to Hitler. For some days he had been announcing gleefully: "A great event! Speer's going to make a speech!,", and when he arrived he took his place expectantly. I took a deep breath, cleared my throat and spoke these exact words: "My Führer. I herewith report the completion of the east-west axis. May the work speak for itself!"

It was of course a good joke. And I must admit my pleasure that he accepted it as such. "You got me there, you rascal, Speer," he'd say. "Two sentences indeed!" Still, he told me it was one of the best speeches he had ever heard.

We are detecting opposition in the room.

And of course I made many other speeches, including one at the Nuremberg trial, in my defence. But what I want to do tonight is to explain to you how I can speak of Hitler as a normal walking human being...

FIRST HECKLER
Normal?

SPEER
And how it was not in fact till Nuremberg that I realized that, yes, this superficially normal human being was in fact \ a man of quite–

SECOND HECKLER
No Nazis! Speer out *out*!

SPEER
But I detect that there is something which you want to say to me.

SECOND HECKLER
Speer *out*!

SIEDLER
No, no.

CHAIR
Herr Speer, we ask you to ignore this anti-democratic spectacle.

SPEER
It would, I fear, be undemocratic of itself to do so.

Pause. The FIRST HECKLER helps out the SECOND HECKLER.

Go on, go on.

FIRST HECKLER
When did you know about the killing of the Jews?

SPEER
What, as a systematic policy of elimination?

FIRST HECKLER
Yes of course.

SPEER
As I say, at Nuremberg.

Chuntering.

CHAIR
Please, Herr Speer, do continue your prepared address.

SPEER
No, I am happy... as I say, I am not an orator. I will answer questions.

Pause. SPEER returns to his seat.

CHAIR
Well, in that case, may I ask... ah, yes.

Points to FIRST QUESTIONER.

FIRST QUESTIONER
Speaking of Nuremberg, Herr Speer–

AUDIENCE
Can't hear!

The FIRST QUESTIONER is handed a microphone.

FIRST QUESTIONER
Speaking of Nuremberg, may I ask about your work on the design of the party rallies there?

SPEER
What about them?

FIRST QUESTIONER
Did you feel that by providing such spectacular visual effects you were an important part of the Nazi propaganda machine?

SPEER
Well. At the time, I was a professional architect. My job was not to be concerned with political issues.

SECOND HECKLER
No, of course not!

CHAIR
(*to SECOND QUESTIONER*) Yes, please.

SECOND QUESTIONER
"Herr professor," when you joined the party, were you an anti-semite?

SPEER
No. As far as practising anti-semitism is concerned, or making anti-semitic remarks, my conscience is entirely clear. Nor, as it happens, was I a real professor.

SECOND QUESTIONER
But you were a real Nazi.

SPEER
I was a member of the National Socialist Party. And yes, I knew the party was anti-semitic, of course, and I also knew the Jews were leaving Germany.

FIRST HECKLER
And being murdered?

CHAIR
Please.

SPEER
I'm sorry, I thought she was asking about when I joined. When, like many—most I suspect—I assumed that anti-semitism was a – vulgar incidental to the party programme.

SECOND HECKLER
Incidental!

SPEER
Which of course proved to be far from the case. But even later on, I knew the Jews were being evacuated, but I did not know they were being murdered as a systematic policy.

THIRD QUESTIONER
Herr Speer, you do understand why people find this hard to credit?

SPEER
I understand that people do. But it is nevertheless the case.

Slight pause.

The final solution was a secret from the German people. And as one of them, it was a secret from me too.

There is a hostile atmosphere growing in the room. SIEDLER feels he needs to rescue.

SIEDLER
Perhaps to clarify this point, it's worth asking how it was that a person of your position in the German state would not know this.

SPEER
Well, as I say, \ the policy was secret–

SIEDLER
As clearly you knew people who *did* know.

SPEER
The whole ethos of the Hitler state was about the will of a single individual. Everyone was told: you need only be concerned with your domain.

SIEDLER
And if you had known, and protested, what would have happened?

Slight pause.

SPEER
Well, people were shot for less. For example, Hitler had made clear to me that if I countermanded him, that that would be treason, with the usual consequences.

SIEDLER
You are referring to your overruling Hitler's orders to destroy German industry in the last months of the war?

SPEER
That's right.

FIRST QUESTIONER
So why weren't you executed, when you told him?

SPEER
I'm sorry?

As the FIRST QUESTIONER quotes, SIEDLER searches for the right page.

FIRST QUESTIONER
It's in your book. Here. "I confessed to him in a low voice, that I had not carried out any demolitions but had actually prevented them. For a moment his eyes filled with tears."

SPEER
(to SIEDLER) Um, where...

FIRST QUESTIONER
It's just before you offer to stay with him in Berlin. Presumably to die \ along with him and Eva–

SIEDLER hands the book over to SPEER to read. SPEER interrupts.

SPEER
Ah yes. "Perhaps he sensed I didn't mean it." It was of course a time of great emotion. But it is true, at that late stage, he did not fulfill his threat. In fact, as I recall, he told me: "We will never speak of this again."

FOURTH QUESTIONER
So did "his eyes fill up with tears" when he watched the film of people he'd had hanged with piano wire on meathooks?

SPEER
No, this is a myth. Hitler did not watch films of anybody being executed. He was notoriously squeamish.

FIRST HECKLER
You said he did! He said it in an interview!

SPEER
I was misreported. It was after all an interview in *Playboy* magazine.

Laughter.

You may know, they have a fold-out section: misquotation of the month.

Laughter.

SIEDLER
In fact, I could read out what you actually said \ about this incident–

Suddenly, another QUESTIONER, with documents, marches to the stage.

FIFTH QUESTIONER
Or instead you could read this.

The CHAIR and SIEDLER stand.

SIEDLER
Um...

SPEER
What is that?

CHAIR
(*precautionary*) Please, Guard...

SPEER
(*stands*) No, let him be.

> *A SECURITY MAN hovers as SPEER goes over to the FIFTH QUESTIONER.*

FIFTH QUESTIONER
It is a speech, transcribed from phonograph recordings, from the state archives at Koblenz.

SPEER
Yes?

> *The FIFTH QUESTIONER holds his document out to SPEER.*

FIFTH QUESTIONER
Read it.

> *The GUARD puts his hand on the FIFTH QUESTIONER's arm.*

SPEER
What is this?

FIFTH QUESTIONER
Read it.

SECURITY MAN
Come along...

SPEER
No, no.

> *He reads, a little bemused.*

"You will not doubt that the economic aspect \ presented many great difficulties–"

FIFTH QUESTIONER
Further up.

SPEER
"I want to speak now, in this most restricted circle, about a matter which \ you, my party–"

FIFTH QUESTIONER
From *there*.

SPEER
"The brief sentence 'The Jews must be exterminated' is easy to pronounce. But the demands on those who have to put it into practice are the hardest and the most difficult in the world." Who is it?

FIFTH QUESTIONER
Himmler. Now read that.

SPEER
I, um.... You will forgive me...

The FIFTH QUESTIONER snatches his papers and goes to the CHAIR.

FIFTH QUESTIONER
All right, you read it.

CHAIR
No.

FIFTH QUESTIONER
"To listen, to discuss."

FIRST HECKLER
Read it!

SIEDLER
I'll read it.

He reads the passage pointed to.

"We, you see, were faced with the question 'What about the women and children?' And I decided, here too, to find an unequivocal solution. For I did not think that I was justified in exterminating—meaning kill or order to have killed—the men, but to leave their children to grow up to take revenge on our sons and grandchildren."

Slight pause.

Well, of course, it's terrible. When was it?

FIFTH QUESTIONER
6th of October 1943.

SPEER
I'm sorry, when?

FIFTH QUESTIONER
6th of October 1943. A meeting of Gauleiters, and some others, at Posen Castle in the Warthegau.

> *SPEER looks at him aghast.*

Yes. You were there.

> *He takes the transcript and finds the next bit he needs.*

Later Himmler talks of war production. How people tried to stop them liquidating the Warsaw Ghetto because of the war production there.

CHAIR
Now, please...

FIFTH QUESTIONER
Then he says this: "Of course, this has nothing to do with party comrade Speer: it wasn't your doing. It is precisely this kind of so-called war production enterprise which party comrade Speer and I will clean out together over the next weeks. We will do this just as unsentimentally as all things must be done in the fifth year of the war: unsentimentally but from the bottom of our hearts."

SPEER
I wasn't there.

CHAIR
Please, this is enough–

FIFTH QUESTIONER
You're saying you weren't *there*?

CHAIR
Guard, will you ask this man to leave.

FIFTH QUESTIONER
But Himmler says: "it's not your doing." You were *there*.

SPEER
I wasn't there. I was there at the meeting in the morning, but I wasn't there.

> *The SECURITY MAN takes the FIFTH QUESTIONER by the arm.*

FIFTH QUESTIONER
Take note please, everyone!

SPEER
I must have left. I needed to consult...

SECOND QUESTIONER
Let him speak!

CHAIR
    I must insist…

SIEDLER
    Now, Albert, it's all right.

FIFTH QUESTIONER
    Don't you understand? Himmler's saying, Speer is here.

> *A SECOND SECURITY MAN comes up to help pull the FIFTH QUESTIONER out.*

CHAIR
    Herr Speer, I must apologize…

FIFTH QUESTIONER
    (*as he goes*) It's the whole case, torn to shreds. He didn't know. But he *did* know. Himmler speaks to him. "It's not your doing." In the middle of a speech in which he says of course we all know don't we that we're murdering the Jews…. It makes it crystal clear… he's lying as he lied at Nuremberg and he's lied for thirty years…

> *He's gone.*

CHAIR
    Herr Speer, I'm sorry. Everybody, please…

SIEDLER
    Come on, now, Albert.

SPEER
    I was not. I cannot recollect. I wasn't there.

2.6.1 A synagogue, Dusseldorf, mid-1970s

> *Bruckner's "Fourth Symphony" is playing in the background. An older CASALIS enters with Rabbi Rudolf GEIS. Both men wear skull-caps.*

CASALIS
    I'm afraid I don't think that this is a good idea.

GEIS
    So why \ are you–

CASALIS
    It's what he wants.

GEIS
So he always gets what he wants?

CASALIS
What he thinks he wants.

GEIS
Why does he want to meet death camp survivors now?

CASALIS
Something has happened. Some exposure by an academic, accusing him of being at a meeting where Himmler openly discussed the killing of the Jews. I gather from his wife he's spent weeks in the Federal Archives, checking dates and times.

GEIS
He didn't come to you?

CASALIS
No. But he wrote about it.

GEIS
I'm sorry.

CASALIS
Why?

GEIS
I thought that you were close.

CASALIS
We were. But under rather different circumstances. It's difficult to go on knowing someone one has got to know quite deeply in a time of crisis.

GEIS
Ah, that would explain it.

CASALIS
What?

GEIS
Why, in his books, he hardly mentions you.

Pause.

CASALIS
Yes I noticed that. I think... I have decided... I don't mind.

Slight pause.

GEIS
I'm sorry. I'm behaving like a prosecutor.

CASALIS
And we know our job is not to judge, to probe or to interrogate.

GEIS
Speak for yourself. Would you be surprised if he had lied about – whatever?

CASALIS
Well, he lied to me. I think. But then all prisoners do. It's a way of hanging on to the little of themselves they're left with.

GEIS
That surprises me. From his books, it seems Herr Speer is in complete command.

CASALIS
By then.

GEIS
Was that your work?

CASALIS
He never lied about his inner life. Let's say, he built a path on which we could walk together for a while.

GEIS
Both figuratively and literally.

CASALIS
A path—a rhythm, or a discipline—on which when I had left he could proceed.

GEIS
To become a different man?

CASALIS
That, and his writing.

Slight pause.

GEIS
Yes. I know a brilliant man, completely organized and disciplined, a lover of the arts and all the higher things... and yet. Not only incapable of abstract thought, but also of romantic love. I often ask myself, what happened to him as a child.

CASALIS
Then you know Albert Speer.

GEIS
So was he at this meeting?

CASALIS
His case is that Himmler was notoriously short-sighted, that the room was dark, and that he couldn't have been there. Which rests on not being able to fly in to Hitler's east headquarters, so he had to go by road, and a gap in Hitler's calendar in which they could have met that evening.

GEIS
And does it sound convincing?

During this, SPEER enters in his overcoat, carrying his hat.

CASALIS
Rabbi, I have a fear. That the only way he could admit what he admitted was by denying what he has denied. I taught him to confront as much of what he knew as he could deal with and remain alive. That to save his life he had to sacrifice his soul.

SPEER
Herr Pastor.

CASALIS
Why, my dear Herr Speer.

GEIS
(SPEER's *head's uncovered*) Uh...

CASALIS
Oh yes, you need a skull-cap.

SPEER goes to get a skull cap from the pile by the door.

GEIS
In fact, your own hat is perfectly \ acceptable–

CASALIS returning with skull-cap.

SPEER
No, no, this will do.

As SPEER puts on the skull-cap.

CASALIS
This is Rabbi Geis.

>   SPEER and GEIS shake hands.

SPEER
> I am very grateful.

GEIS
> They'll be here directly.

SPEER
> Isn't that the Bruckner "Fourth?"

GEIS
> Yes, it's my assistant.

SPEER
> We had them play it at the last concert of the Berlin Phil.

GEIS
> As you say in your reminiscences.

SPEER
> I'm complimented. And your synagogue survived everything?

GEIS
> With an occasional judicious change of role.

SPEER
> Ah, yes

GEIS
> In fact, it may change role again. Unhappily, what was the ghetto is now prime downtown real estate.

SPEER
> Oh but you mustn't sell it. It's so beautiful.

GEIS
> Yes. Like the romantic symphony.

>   Slight pause.

SPEER
> What do you mean?

GEIS
> I have a theory, that there is a risk, that people—sometimes people who have found it hard to find love in their real lives—seek beauty in great works of art not as a supplement to personal love but as a substitute. That somehow,

they can feel – feel deeply, passionately, soulfully... but not directly. So they feel through art.

CASALIS
(fearful that GEIS may have gone too far) I think...

> *GEIS notices his assistant DAVID, in his late teens, approaching from his office.*

GEIS
This is, I fear, true of my assistant.

DAVID
Herr Geis, your guests are here.

GEIS
David, this is Albert Speer.

SPEER
How do you do?

DAVID
I've read your books.

SPEER
I'm glad.

DAVID
I have a question.

SPEER
Please.

DAVID
What are you proudest of designing, as an architect?

> *GEIS and CASALIS are relieved.*

SPEER
The piece I feel about most – deeply and most passionately is a chair. It was very simple, rather unobtrusive. But for me... complete.

> *Pause.*

DAVID
A chair.

GEIS
We'll meet them in my office.

SPEER
Oh, can we not talk in here?

CASALIS
I think it would \ be better–

GEIS
If it's what you want.

> *GEIS raises a finger, to indicate to DAVID that he should wait a moment.*

But first I must ask you seriously if this is really what you want. I must put it to you that there might be something fundamentally unhealthy about living so intensely in the past. I have read your books. I know that you are now confronting other accusations. But surely—now—it is time to face the future.

SPEER
You have heard about this meeting I am supposed to have attended.

CASALIS
Yes.

GEIS
Did you attend it?

SPEER
I have proved—to my own satisfaction—I did not.

GEIS
To "your own satisfaction."

SPEER
The timing is quite clear. I had to leave the meeting early, and I drove to Rastenberg and met with Hitler. I have affidavits proving where I was and who with and how long. I have proved, yes, that I wasn't there.

> *Pause. GEIS says nothing.*

For what is the alternative? That I was there and I don't remember? That I blocked it out?

> *Slight pause.*

GEIS
As you say, you have your affidavits.

CASALIS
And now perhaps we ought \ to go and see–

SPEER
Rabbi. It has been nearly thirty years. Nobody could go on asserting his own guilt at full volume all that time and remain sincere. I wake with it, I spend my days with it, I dream of it. But what I say about it has inevitably grown routine. And now that I have proved—to my own satisfaction, yes—my innocence of yet another charge... the danger is that in considerable relief at that I say – well if that's all right, then there's no guilt at all. So if you will forgive me, sir, I need this meeting. Because I need to know.

CASALIS
What do you need to know?

SPEER
What it was like, to be on the receiving end of me. *(to DAVID)* So will you bring them?

DAVID goes out, SPEER moves away to look at the synagogue. GEIS speaks out front.

GEIS
And of course it was very hard for him. One of the women was from Prague, and had been first at Theresiensdadt and then in Auschwitz where she'd been the victim of experiments.

CASALIS speaks out front.

CASALIS
He told me, once, that on his way to work he could see the crowds of people waiting for evacuation on the platform of the Nikolassee railway station. But he'd never speculated what would happen to them at the other end. Well, now he knew.

GEIS
The other was in hiding, and had spent her time since trying to find out how and where her parents, uncles, cousins, husband and two children died.

CASALIS
(to GEIS) My understanding is, that Hitler's calendar wasn't an appointments book. It was a record of everyone who met with him. And on the evening of Himmler's speech, Speer's name isn't there.

2.6.2 Germany, late 1970s

The images of what was at the end are projected on the set. Vast, unmanagable, inescapable. The Dora sounds: the cement mixer and the saw. SPEER walks through the images, forming weird shapes on his body and his face.

SPEER
And so they told me what I'd turned away from.

Pause.

So, yes, of course. That is the question I must answer now.
Not whether I was at a meeting. But whether, meeting or no meeting, I still knew.
And you were bound to ask eventually. Everybody does. And it is always the same answer.
Because if I knew, and if *I knew* I knew, then everything becomes a lie.
What I said to Georges Casalis, what I wrote, what I told my children, what I tell myself. My life becomes a lie to me.
And so I have always said. I should have known, I could have known, I didn't know. I turned away.

Pause.

Yes, that's right. Turned away.

Pause.

I'm sorry. I can never speak of this to you again.

He turns. It is his study.

2.7.1 Speer's study in Heidelberg, late 1970s

MARGRET enters.

MARGRET
Albert, there's someone here to see you.

SPEER looks round.

It's a woman. She claims she has an appointment.

SPEER
Um...

MARGRET
She's German speaking, with an English accent. She's clutching all your books and articles. She's obviously more than diligent.

SPEER
Ah. Yes.

MARGRET comes over to SPEER, gives him a letter.

MARGRET
Albert, do tidy yourself up. You look worse than you looked in Spandau.

MARGRET goes out. A knock.

SPEER
Come in.

The door opens. MRS. WINTERINGHAM is in her mid-to-late 30s, fair and attractive. She does indeed carry a small Speer library. SPEER glances at the letter to remind himself.

Mrs. – Winteringham?

MRS. WINTERINGHAM
Herr Speer, I am so pleased to meet you.

She comes over to shake his hand. Some confusion with her books.

I'm sorry…

SPEER
Please sit down.

They sit.

You have an English name.

MRS. WINTERINGHAM
My husband's British. I live there, you see.

SPEER
I have always admired the British.

MRS. WINTERINGHAM
Yes, I know. In fact, Herr Speer, we've met before.

SPEER
We have?

MRS. WINTERINGHAM
You signed one of my books for me.

SPEER
Ah, yes. And, when…?

MRS. WINTERINGHAM
Herr Speer, I'm very angry.

Slight pause.

SPEER
Oh?

MRS. WINTERINGHAM
I have read your books, your articles and interviews, and other people's articles about you.

SPEER
Ah...

MRS. WINTERINGHAM
And my response is – what gives them the right to carp and sneer at somebody like you?

SPEER is thrown by this unexpected tack.

Herr Speer, I think your prison diary is the best, and the most moving book I've ever read.

SPEER demurs at this hyperbole.

And of course you made mistakes. In stirring times. How could you not? But you *were* Germany's chief architect. You *did* stave off defeat against all odds, and save our industry from destruction at the end. You *did* serve twenty years in solitary confinement, and transform yourself, and come through to make a new career. And for people to insist on yet more penitence, yet more self-accusation.... Oh, I think not, Herr Speer.

SPEER
You're very kind.

MRS. WINTERINGHAM
I am not being "kind."

SPEER
Nevertheless...

MRS. WINTERINGHAM
There is no nevertheless about it. You did these things. They were of value. And you did them on your own.

SPEER stands.

SPEER
Shall we take a walk? You can make your notes when you get back.

MRS. WINTERINGHAM
My notes?

SPEER
You have not come to interview me?

MRS. WINTERINGHAM
I have come to meet you.

SPEER
(gesturing to the books) So...

MRS. WINTERINGHAM
I'd hoped that you might sign my other books for me.

SPEER
Of course. When we return.

> *MRS. WINTERINGHAM smiles and stands.*

(picking up the book he signed) Please ask my wife to lend you some galoshes. I will be down directly.

> *MRS WINTERINGHAM turns to go. SPEER reads his inscription in her book.*

Your name is Trudi.

MRS. WINTERINGHAM
Yes.

SPEER
Yes. I think – I do remember you.

> *He looks at her.*

Do you like music, Mrs Winteringham?

MRS. WINTERINGHAM
Oh, Herr Speer, I am Aquarius. I love things of beauty more than life itself.

> *She goes out.*

2.7.2 Germany, 1980–81

SIEDLER and HILDE, speaking separately out front.

HILDE
Apparently it was the Spandau Diaries. They "made her cry."

SIEDLER
I saw Speer in 1980. He'd sent me the manuscript of his new book on the SS, which had considerable problems.

HILDE
My mother was naturally devastated. After everything she'd done for him.

SIEDLER
And then he said what he had said to me before: that sometimes a man needs another man in whom he can confide.

HILDE
What, did she know? He used to "report absent" when he went to meet her.

SIEDLER
And then he took a snapshot from his wallet.

He said: "I had to be in my 70s to have my first real erotic experience with a woman."

HILDE
Of course she knew.

2.8.1 Bedroom, Park Court Hotel, London, 1 September 1981

SPEER in his bedroom. There is wine in an ice-bucket. He telephones.

SPEER
Hallo? This is room…

He checks his key.

516. This is to say that there will be…

Pause.

Ah. She's on her way.

He looks round the room, checks his appearance in the mirror. There's a knock at the door. He goes and admits MRS. WINTERINGHAM.

MRS. WINTERINGHAM
Hallo, darling.

SPEER
Hallo.

They kiss, passionately.

MRS. WINTERINGHAM
It's sweltering. How was the BBC?

SPEER
Oh, fine. They thought I'd done the plans for Hitler's tomb at Linz.

MRS. WINTERINGHAM
But that was Giesler.

Pleased that she knows this, SPEER opens wine.

SPEER
Yes. I had to improvise.

MRS. WINTERINGHAM
(*enjoying his chutzpah*) You told them you did *Linz*?

SPEER
I left it open. Do you want some wine?

MRS. WINTERINGHAM
(*mock shock*) Albert.

SPEER
(*pouring wine*) Being the BBC, they couldn't resist pointing out all that remains of my work are the ruins of the stadium, two gatehouses now converted into lavatories and a row of streetlamps.

MRS. WINTERINGHAM
Now, stop that.

She kisses him.

SPEER
They invited me to lunch. I said I had a previous engagement.

She takes a glass of wine, and drinks.

MRS. WINTERINGHAM
It's wonderfully cold.

She kisses him again.

Well. Cheerio.

MRS. WINTERINGHAM knocks her drink back.

Hey, I could have a shower, couldn't I?

SPEER
Of course you could.

Taking off her jacket.

MRS. WINTERINGHAM
And this evening, Herr Speer, I wish to be escorted to the theatre.

SPEER
You know, in Spandau, I made a theatre in my mind. I would imagine purchasing the ticket, leaving my coat in the cloakroom, buying a programme, sitting down. And looking forward to the curtain rising, and \ the cool draft from the stage–

She takes over as she goes out.

MRS. WINTERINGHAM
(*taking over*) "–the cool draft from the stage, with its smell of glue, dust and papier mâché " Yes, I know. It was your imagination!

SPEER takes off his jacket, loosens his tie.

SPEER
(*to himself*) Yes. If you think about it.

The room has been growing dark and peculiar. SPEER feels strange.

It was that that got me through.

SPEER stands. The transformation is beginning to take place.

So what's this here?

2.8.2 The Mausoleum

SPEER is looking through the smoke at a huge, emerging space; the grey expanse punctured by a line of lights stretching into the distance.

SPEER
What's going on?

Pause.

SPEER
Is it... am I in a street?

A MAN emerges from the darkness, throwing a huge shadow.

SPEER
This is an air-raid?

The MAN approaches, followed by other men.

SPEER
Or else... torches? This is Nuremberg? Is this then? Is this me?

HITLER
No, Speer. It's me. And now.

HITLER is in stormtrooper uniform. HESS, SCHAUB, HANKE, also in stormtrooper uniform, behind him. It's like a gangster raid.

HITLER
As if you didn't know. So what have you been up to since I saw you last?

SPEER
What do you mean?

HITLER
As if I didn't know.

He turns and nods to the others, who swagger upstage into the darkness.

You've been trying to remake yourself. You have been trying to become a different man.

SPEER
What's this?

HITLER
Having been "condemned, robbed of your liberty, tortured by the knowledge that you'd based your life upon a lie."

SPEER
Oh, of course, the dreams.

HITLER
Having been "intoxicated," "blinded" by the power I granted you.

SPEER
The dream. The dream in which you know.

HITLER
How you nevertheless stood up heroically at the end, to save the last weak remnants of the German people. At risk of being taken off and shot of course! How you were not responsible for the conditions of your labourers but now I understand you are suddenly responsible for Linz! But as you say. The dream in which I know.

SPEER
I never said you'd have me shot.

HITLER
Oh no? What did you tell that pornographic magazine?

SPEER
I'm not sure I recall.

HITLER
"My Führer… there is something I must say to you…" "What is it?" You be me.

SPEER
"What is it?"

HITLER
And then you: "My Führer, all these months, when I have been pledging my unfailing loyalty, I have been sabotaging everything you have commanded. When I said I stood unconditionally behind you, I was actually betraying you behind your back. When I said I'd never lie to you, I was actually lying at the time. And I didn't have the guts to tell you then, but I don't have the guts to live with my deceit and so now there's nothing you can do about it I'm confessing it to you. Oh, and if you like, I'll stay here in Berlin with you and we can die together!"

SPEER says nothing.

And what did I say, then? According to this fairy tale?

SPEER
"We will never speak of this again."

HITLER
Oh yes. And my eyes "filled up with tears." Whereas what actually occurred, on this momentous evening?

SPEER
I'm afraid I don't \ remember.

HITLER
I passed you in a corridor. I said "Goodbye." And that was that. But, oh no: "My eyes filled up with tears."

Pause.

Hm?

SPEER says nothing.

And the workers in the mountains. And your *shock*. And *pain*.

SPEER
In fact, I did my best \ to improve their conditions–

HITLER
Your shock and horror at my "giving up" the German people.

SPEER
I didn't realize you could be so \ heedless of their fate–

HITLER
But most of all, the lie that after everything you didn't know.

Pause.

SPEER
It was true. I didn't know. As I have proved to my own satisfaction.

HITLER
What? *Still?*

SPEER shrugs, confirming.

Had I not always said that once the strong had been eliminated, all is lost and it is pointless trying to save the rest?

SPEER
Of course.

HITLER
That without its strongest elements, the German people would degrade into a feminized and weakened lumpen mass, as prey as Slav subhumans to the cholera of Bolshevism?

SPEER
Yes.

HITLER
That the Soviet state was a criminal conspiracy that would have to be destroyed, with implacable determination?

SPEER
You'd implied that, certainly.

HITLER
And does not the destruction of a state "imply" the physical elimination of its functionaries, without mercy or consideration of the rules of war?

Slight pause.

And when I said – as I said repeatedly, and publicly, that if there was a war, it will lead inevitably to the annihilation of the racial source of Bolshevism, why couldn't you believe it? Why did you insist that anti-semitism was "a vulgar incidental?" I said it – clearly, time and time again. I didn't say "resettlement" or "cleaning efforts." I did not speak of "special handling." And yet you all insist that when I said the Jews must be destroyed, I only meant "defeated." That when I said "eliminate" I didn't mean "exterminate," I only meant "exclude." That when I said "purge" and "perish" and "annihilate," it was of course a metaphor. Why was I cursed with never being taken literally? How could the world have been so blind? And how could you?

Slight pause.

But oh. "I turned away." As ever. Not your fault. Why not admit it? Why not confess it? Why not come clean now?

SPEER says nothing.

Hah?

SPEER says nothing.

All right, I'll tell you why. Speer, you present yourself as a man inspired by a great vision but who saw that vision trampled into dust. By me. Yet without me there was no vision and there was no man. Who made you, Speer? Who appointed you his architect? Who promoted you to be his armourer? Who inspired you to dream dreams you could never dream alone? You did what I required of you. You realized my vision. And if you are in a hall of faces then the face is mine.

HESS, HANKE and SCHAUB come forward with wreaths.

SPEER
You are laying wreaths.

SCHAUB
    He lays them all the time.

    HITLER lays wreaths.

SPEER
    Who they are for?

HESS
    They are for the best.

SPEER
    The best are dead.

HANKE
    The best are dead.

HITLER
    And of course when I said our new Berlin was a mausoleum, you did not believe me either. "The names of our Germanic fallen, carved on every stone."

    SPEER looks in anguish at HITLER. HITLER hands wreath to SPEER.

    So then: be me.

SPEER
    There is no need. I have been you ever since I met you.

HITLER
    Yes.

SPEER
    I thought my life began with you. But it ended with you.

HITLER
    Yes.

SPEER
    You were the nightmare. Always. Obviously.

HITLER
    Yes.

SPEER
    Your tomb was Linz. Mine was Germania.

    SPEER looks back for the last time into the huge grey disappearing space. His eyes are full of tears.

HITLER
Why are you crying?

SPEER
I am crying for myself. And the life I could have led if I'd been different from the start.

HITLER
Come, come.

SPEER
No.

HITLER
The best are dead.

SPEER
No.

HITLER
The dead are best.

SPEER
No.

HITLER
And now you can be best.

He looks at SPEER.

At last.

HITLER turns with his men and goes. SPEER is alone. His eyes are closed. But then looks back, to see a different group of people. HILDE, GEIS, CASALIS, ANNEMARIE, MARGRET. Maybe, behind them, the Jewish family from the Nikolassee, and the Dora workers from the mountains. He looks at them.

SPEER
Not yet.
Because, yes, I cannot admit what I have not admitted and remain alive. But if I did, I could die the man I might have been.

To "us."

Of course, it wasn't that "I could have known." That I was "blind." Because, yes, one cannot look into a void. If I "turned away," I knew. I knew. I helped to build a boneyard.
Yes. I knew.

And now, at last, I need never speak nor think nor dream of any of these things again.

Darkness. We hear MRS. WINTERINGHAM's voice, distraught.

MRS. WINTERINGHAM
Please, you must call an ambulance. There's a man, he must have had a stroke. Please hurry. I think he may be dead...

Light. SPEER's body lies there. Suddenly, massively, HIMMLER's face projected on all the surfaces of the set.

HIMMLER
And with this I want to finish. You are now informed, and you will keep the knowledge to yourselves. Later perhaps we can consider whether the German people should be told about this. But I think it is better that we—we together—carry for our people the responsibility – responsibility for an achievement, not just an idea... and then take the secret with us to our graves.

Darkness.

The end.

AFTERWORD

> "Since I am not going to go down in architectural history for buildings, I might at least have defiantly won a place for myself with grandly conceived plans. Am I, too, lacking an original desire to give form to reality? In the passion to produce something out of myself? Was I, too, made creative only by Hitler?"
>
> —Albert Speer, *The Secret Diaries*

It was on the third day of rehearsal. Sitting round a huge table in the bowels of the National Theatre, actors about to play Hitler, Himmler, Eva Braun and the stage army of the Third Reich were debating the plausibility of Hitler's Minister of Armaments not knowing about what was happening to Jews and others in the slave-labour and death camps of the Nazi empire. Suddenly, the argument escalated. Albert Speer was Hitler's favourite. As his architect, he had been a vital part of the Nazi propaganda machine. As his armourer, he was responsible for millions of slave-workers kept in unspeakable conditions. He kept the war going for a year longer than it needed to, at the cost of untold suffering. Whatever he knew or didn't know, did Speer have a case worth presenting? Was it worth us doing a play about this man at all?

This was not the first time this question had come up. It had been central to the discussions I had had with the play's director Trevor Nunn during the development of the play. And for both of us there was a *déjà vu*: the same debate had raged around the production of a play I wrote about the rise of the National Front in 70s Britain (*Destiny*), which Nunn programmed for the Royal Shakespeare Company in 1976. By seeking to understand people with dreadful opinions, or people complicit in crimes resulting from those opinions, is the writer (or director or actor) inevitably tending to condone?

The first immediate, instinctive response in this case was that the play *Albert Speer* is based on a well-reviewed, highly regarded and massively successful biography by Gitta Sereny, whose moral credentials and dignity of purpose were questioned by no one. However, this argument falls apart when the material is transferred to the theatre. However passionate its author, a work of history has an essentially magisterial relationship with its readership. Like the French legal system, the medium invites sober consideration of the evidence, the balancing of arguments and the disinterested search for truth. Like a British courtroom, a play tends to the adversarial, demanding that the jury identify with one side. In this case, there is no sober summing up of the evidence, many of the prosecution witnesses are dead, and the accused is conducting his own defence. And however critical we may be of him and it, are we not—by the very act of presenting it—implying that he has a case? Or—even more insidiously—that his moral anguish can be set against the suffering for which he has been held responsible?

Further, we were aware that we were telling this story at a moment when the history of the second world war is a matter of acute and current political contest. As we rehearsed the play, another drama was being played out in the High Court of Justice. However unambiguous Mr Justice Gray's finding may have been, the

David Irving trial reminded everyone how much of the darkest events of the second World War are subject to interpretation, how deep is the controversy about the aims and history of the Holocaust, and how much of our knowledge of it is based on essentially circumstantial evidence.

And we are exploring the case for and against a leading Nazi at a time when the supposed effects of writing are subject to unprecedented scrutiny. Not only are works of fiction cited as inspiring if not causing real life crimes (the "go thou and do likewise" theory of literary influence) but works of non-fiction are called to account for the harm or even distress they might cause. Following the publication of her 1998 book about the Mary Bell case, *Cries Unheard*, Gitta Sereny herself was accused by the parents of Mary's victims of "bringing up all the bad memories." From this understandable concern with the feelings of people involved in tragedies, it has proved a short step to the argument advanced by a reader protesting against the serialization of Gordon Burns' book about Frederick and Rosemary West in *The Guardian* on the grounds of the "suffering, despair and pain involved in the subject matter," not for the relatives of West's victims, but for everyone. And both Marcus Garvey's painting of and Diane Dubois' play about the continuing iconic influence of Myra Hindley were condemned on the grounds that it was inappropriate to treat of her in art at all.

And yet—of course—if the subject of evil was removed from the dramatic canon, most of the great tragedies would disappear from the repertoire. From Clytemnestra and Oedipus via Richard III, Macbeth and Othello to the gangsters, gunslingers and Godfathers of twentieth-century cinema, great drama has always been obsessed with killers, natural born and otherwise. If it was really true that the purpose of drama is to encourage its audiences to imitate the behaviour of its protagonists, then the medium has a great deal to answer for.

But, sadly, the opposite view—that the point of drama is precisely to discourage such behaviour by showing how it will inevitably get its come-uppance—doesn't really wash. "Don't do this at home" is as misleading a description of what drama counsels us as "go thou and do likewise." The awful truth—and it is awful, in both senses of the word—is that the response most great drama asks of us is neither "yes please" nor "no thanks" but "you too?" Or, in the cold light of dawn, "there but for the grace of God go I."

When, understandably but sadly, the parents of Mary Bell's victims wrote in *The Sun* that "Mary Bell is not worthy of consideration as a feeling, human being," they were letting the rest of us off the hook. The notion that there is a thing called evil which separates the wicked off from the rest of us is a comforting illusion. The uncomfortable truth is that to understand *does* involve recognition and even empathy. It does require seeing the world through the eyes of the wicked person, and thus finding those impulses and resentments and fears within ourselves that could—we have painfully to admit—drive us to commit dreadful acts under different circumstances.

Drama is a test-bed on which we can test and confront our darkest impulses under laboratory conditions; where we can experience the desires without having to confront the consequences. As Peter Brook writes in *The Empty Space*, "in the theatre the slate is wiped clean all the time." Drama enables us us to peer into the soul, not of the person who has driven his father out on to the heath, but the person who has wanted to.

But that's only the first shock. The second is that we enjoy the view. As critics from Aristotle onwards have noted, we don't just learn but take pleasure from seeing the representation of things that in real life we'd regard as disgusting or repellent. Indeed, the pleasure is the thing that allows us to confront these unbearable aspects of ourselves. This is why children like fictional forms whose familiarity is distanced by their location in the mythic past, the animal kingdom or outer space. And despite the wealth of all-too-human examples of monstrosity, adult audiences too demand villains from other worlds, different species and indeed beyond the grave.

Since the late nineteenth century, the assumption has been that the closer drama is to the lives of its audience, the more powerful and painful it will be. But the problem with looking in a mirror is that you see what the world sees. Look into a picture, and you may see what you have disguised.

Finally, because we see ourselves in him, the tragic villain commands our sympathy (indeed, the difference between the tragic and the melodramatic villain is quite precisely that). At the end of *Albert Speer* a dying man thinks he sees his past self approaching him through the mist but discovers that what is really inside him is not his own past but the terrible reality of a man he had once admired and loved. Looking at him confronting that truth I hope that the audience will look through that refraction back at itself. Albert Speer was subject to a Faustian temptation, fell for it, and spent the rest of his life creating a past with which he could deal. To be one of his many victims is—thank goodness—unimaginable for a well-fed first-world audience in the year 2000. To give in to personal ambition, to realize a moral and ideological error too late, and to spend the rest of your life making inadequate sense of that failure is all too recognizable.

As screenwriter Paul Schrader argued in defence of *Taxi Driver*, if writers stopped inventing criminals, "we would still have psychopaths, but we wouldn't have art. We would still have Raskolnikovs but we wouldn't have *Crime and Punishment*." If Gitta Sereny hadn't written her book about Albert Speer, his slave-workers would still have died, but we would be less able to understand why. For that reason alone, it seems to me worth taking the risk of putting his story on stage.

—David Edgar

This is a revised version of an article published in *The Observer*, 30 April 2000.

Ghetto

A play by
Joshua Sobol

English by Ron Jenkins
Based on a literal translation from the Hebrew by the author
Lyrics by Vilna Ghetto translated by Jeremy Sams

Joshua Sobol was born in 1939 in Israel. He studied in Paris at the Sorbonne where he received a degree in Philosophy. Returning to Israel, he taught æstetics and directed many workshops at Tel Aviv University, Seminar Hakibbutzim and Beit Tzvi Drama Schools. Most of his plays have been premiered at the Haifa Municipal Theatre, where he worked as Artistic Director from 1984. These include: *The Days to Come, Status Quo Vadis, New Year's Eve '72, The Joker, The Night of the Twentieth, Nerves, The Tenants, Gog and Magog Show, Soul of a Jew, Ghetto, Shooting Magda (The Palestinian Girl)*.

Sobol has also written for other theatres in Israel. These plays include: *Repentance, Passodoble, Homeward Angel, Wedding Night, Wars of the Jews, The Last of the Workers*.

Soul of a Jew was seen at the 1983 Edinburgh Festival, and in 1985 both *Soul of a Jew* and *Ghetto* were staged at the Berlin Festival followed by performances throughout Germany. Sobol's plays have been produced all over the world in many languages.

Ghetto was first produced in the Oliver auditorium of the National Theatre, Great Britain in April 1989, with the following company:

SRULIK	Jonathan Cullen
KITTEL (Dr. PAUL)	Alex Jennings
HAYYAH	Maria Friedman
DJIGAN	Linda Kerr Scott
GENS	John Woodvine
WEISKOPF	Anthony O'Donnell
KRUK	Paul Jesson
DESSLER	Ivan Kaye

YOSEF GERSTEIN	David Schneider	HAIKIN	Vladimir Asriev
JUDITH LARES	Nicola Scott	SHMUEL IRIS	Oliver Beamish
OOMA ORSHEVESKAYA	Angela Pleasance	SASHA LIPOVSK	Ivan Kaye
YITSHOK SAMBER	Jon Rumney	YAKOB MANDELBLIT	Michael O'Connor
AVROM MOLEVSKY	Nicholas Blane	BARUCH NADIR	Trevor Sellers
LUBA GRODZINSKI	Laura Shavin	NEMI NATAN	Judith Sim
ELIA GEIVISH	Mark Lockyer	LEAH NEMI	Jennifer Hill
YITZHOK GEIVISH	Glyn Pritchard	MOISHE NORVID	Merlin Shepherd
YANKEL POLIKANSKI	Mark Addy	ZIGMUND RUDKOV	David Roach
ALEXANDRA AZRA	Jo Stone-Fewings	HENRY TARLO	Keith Woodhams
SHABSE BLIAKHER	Sandy Burnett	AVROM TAYTLBOYM	Brian Greene
SONIA ELMIS	Sandra Butterworth	POLIA VALTER	Sandy McDade
YAKOB GERTNER	Ged McKenna	AVROM WITTENBERG	Tam Dean Burn
HELENA GOTTLIB	Jill Stanford		
YITZHOK GRUDBERG	John Fitzgerald Jay		

Gestapo Guards	Christopher Armstrong
	Melvyn Bedford
	Toby E, Byrne
	Ciaran McIntyre
Jewish Police Officers	Mark Addy
	Christopher Armstrong
	Melvyn Bedford
	John Fitzgerald Jay
	Mark Lockyer
	Glyn Pritchard
	Trevor Sellers

Directed by Nicholas Hytner
Designed by Bob Crowley

CHARACTERS

PERSONALITIES OF THE GHETTO
01. KITTEL — SS Officer. Twentyish.
02. GENS — Chief of Jewish Police, later Head of the ghetto
03. WEISKOPF — A Self-Made Rich Man
04. KRUK — Librarian and Chronicler of the ghetto
05. DESSLER — Jewish Police Officer

MEMBERS OF THE THEATRE COMPANY
06. HAYA — Singer
07. SRULIK — Ventriloquist
08. LINA — "Dummy"
09. UMA — Was a Star before the war. Plays Dr. Weiner
10. GERSTEIN — Plays Hassid and Rabbi
11. SARAH ELMIS — plays Dr. GOTTLIEB, an old physician.
12. EVA BLICK — plays JUDGE
13. JUDITH — plays WIFE OF DIABETIC

YOUNG ACTORS AND FOOD SMUGGLERS
14. LIUBA — Young actress, leader of gang
15. YANKL — Liuba's boy friend
16. ELIA — A dangerous, silent guy
17. GEIVISH — Very cool, Elia's brother

LEAH'S GROUP OF DANCE STUDENTS (Some female parts can be played by male dancers.)
18. LEAH – CHOREOGRAPHER
19. IRINA – DANCER
20. HELENA – DANCER
21. TOVA – DANCER
22. GENIA – DANCER
23. MIRA – DANCER
24. NELLI – DANCER
25. ETKA – DANCER
26. RASHKA – DANCER
27. REIKA – DANCER
28. YANOSH – DANCER
29. ANITA – DANCER

MUSICIANS
30. HAIKIN – Violin
31. SHLOIME – Saxophone
32. GUSTAV – Accordion
33. CLARA – Clarinet
34. MALKA – Flute

JEWISH POLICE
35. LEVAS – POLICEMAN
36. NATHAN – POLICEMAN
37. STARK – POLICEMAN

GERMAN SOLDIERS
38. ARNTGEN
39. TIMAN

Ghetto
by Joshua Sobol

Act One

Scene One

An empty public square. Late autumn. It is a foggy morning. A tune is vaguely heard in the distance. A strange sound of rolling comes piercing through the fog. The silhouette of an old one-armed man appears in the fog. This is OLD SRULIK. He is rolling or rather dancing on his roller skates to the rhythm of the music.

OLD SRULIK
Our last show?... Wait....
It was the night before Kittel murdered Gens...
The leader of our ghetto.
Ten days later the ghetto was liquidated.
Our last show...
Sold out. A full house.
Our shows were always sold out, a month in advance.
Yes! Our audience kept coming right to the end.
People assigned to the next day's train to the camps, would dress their best for one last night at the theatre.
Ya ya. I can see it all. Our last show.
The next morning when the Gestapo came for Gens, I was sitting in his office, reading plays.
That was my job, as artistic director.
We had a competition for the best play about
"Life In The Ghetto."
Katrielke Broyde, Leybelle Rosenthal, Hirshke Glik, Israel Diamantman...
All wrote for our theatre.
Wonderful plays. Full of humour and music and...
We were going to stage the best play, but...
Ten days later the ghetto was liquidated. Nothing was left.
Only here...
In my head...
Fragments of...
A pantomime.... A song.... A dance...
A scene...

He rolls to the wing and pulls a lever. Drastic change of light. Hundreds of clothes and shoes fall from the ceiling in a tremendous thunder. A group of people who were sleeping upstage bundled up in rags jump to their feet screaming with fear. The group of people includes WEISKOPF, KRUK, HASSID, EVA, YANKL, GEIVISH, IRINA, HELENA, TOVA, GENIA, MIRA, NELLI, ETKA, YANOSH, STARK.

Scene Two

KITTEL appears on the bridge overlooking the stage. He is followed by two German soldiers, ARNTGEN and TIMAN, and by the Jewish Police Officer DESSLER. All three Germans are carrying Schmeissers.

KITTEL
Chaos! Dessler! Give them light!

DESSLER
Yes, Sir! *(He runs to a switch-board and turns on the light.)*

KITTEL
More light! *(DESSLER carries out the order. KITTEL addresses the group of frightened people.)* Sort the clothes. Separate the dry from the wet. Men's wear, women's wear, children's wear. Sort it all out. Get going!

The people start sorting out the clothes. They arrange the clothes in piles at the back stage. KITTEL discovers the stage, and examines its facilities with the knowledge of an experienced man of theatre. He discovers a covered piano. He opens the keyboard cover and plays a few notes. A trap door is thrown open near the piano, and HAYYAH appears. She is wrapped in a torn blanket. Her hair is disheveled. Her bare feet are dirty from walking in the gutters. KITTEL directs his flashlight at her.

HAYYAH
Is it allowed to take a pair of shoes?

KITTEL
What did you ask?

HAYYAH
A pair of shoes.

KITTEL
If you knew where these shoes came from, you wouldn't touch them, even if they were pure gold. But, if you want, pick out a pair.

HAYYAH hesitates, walks over to the pile and tries on shoes. The group of workers is observing the scene. KITTEL scolds them:

KITTEL
What are you staring at? This isn't a show! Get back to work!

The people get back to work. HAYYAH chooses a pair of shoes, puts them on and hurries away.

KITTEL
Hey! Over here. Take that off.

HAYYAH removes the rag. She's wearing a torn slip.

KITTEL
(*to the workers*) Give her a dress. (*WEISKOPF comes running with a dress.*) Put it on. (*She does.*) A coat. (*same routine*) A hat. (*WEISKOPF gives her a beret. She doesn't put it on.*) Come here. Closer. Show me your face. Fix your hair. Put on the hat. You're a beauty. When your kind is beautiful, there's nothing like it. Turn around.

KITTEL studies her body.

TIMAN
(*reacts spontaneously to her bulging stomach*) Hey, look!

KITTEL
What's this? Don't you know pregnancy is forbidden to Jewish women. Do you know what will happen to you? Lost your speech? Come closer. (*HAYYAH walks over to him. He feels her stomach.*) Show me what you've got there. (*HAYYAH takes out a paper bag. She gives it to KITTEL. He reads the label.*) "A kilo of beans." Black market? Who did you buy it from? Names. You didn't buy it. You stole it. You stole a kilo of beans from the army depot. Turn. To the wall. March!

HAYYAH starts walking to the wall. KITTEL scatters the beans on the floor. HAYYAH falls to the floor. KITTEL walks over to her, lifts her up and pushes her to the wall. He backs up, loads his Schmeisser and is about to shoot her. SRULIK and LINA interfere. They function as a ventriloquist and his dummy.

LINA
Stop! Halt! *Arretez! Stoi!*

SRULIK
Stop it! You play the hero, and I pay with my life!

LINA
Your life! Who cares about your rotten life?

SRULIK
I do! Rotten or not, it's the only life I've got.

LINA
It's Hayyah! She's a star! Be a man! Defend her!

SRULIK
Who's a man? I'm just a Jew. I surrender.

KITTEL
Who are you?

LINA
He gave her the beans.

SRULIK
What? I gave her the beans?!

KITTEL
Did you give her the beans?

SRULIK
She's lying.

LINA
I'm lying? Am I?! Mr. Kittel!

SRULIK
Mr. Kittel, she's a pathological liar. She'll say anything to get rid of me.

LINA
Ha ha! Look who's talking about liars! Blow his brains out! Rid the world of this rat!

KITTEL
Enough.

SRULIK
Enough, you heard him?

LINA
He's talking to you.

SRULIK
To me? He's talking to you.

LINA
Me? He's talking to you.

KITTEL
Shut up! Or I'll rip your throat! *(to SRULIK)* Did you give her the beans, yes or no?

SRULIK
No, God forbid! If I had beans, I'd keep them in my private bank account. This woman's no black marketeer. This is Hayyah, the nightingale of the ghetto.

LINA
He's in love with her.

SRULIK
Before the war she was a star. Now she's got nowhere to perform. No opera house, no concert hall, not even this tiny theatre. She's starving. I appeal to you, Mr. Kittel, because you, as a great artist

LINA
Get your tongue out of his ass. Kittel hates asslickers.

KITTEL
(laughs) You got me right!

LINA
(to SRULIK) You see? Art has nothing to do with it. And what if she couldn't sing? Would she deserve to die?

KITTEL
Everyone over here! Dessler! Bring the scales. You've got thirty seconds to put every bean she stole on this scale. Action!
(All get down on the floor, frantically gathering the beans. KITTEL goes to the wing and returns carrying a black suitcase. He puts it on the ground, looks at his watch and commands:) Stop!
Dessler! How much?

DESSLER
940 grams, Sir!

KITTEL
940? You're 60 grams short. How will you pay? *(lifts the Schmeisser)* Shall I use this or *(points to the black case)* that? Choose!

HAYYAH
(hesitates, then points to the case) That.

KITTEL
Well well… *(He kneels, opens the case, pulls out an object and puts it together. It's a saxophone. He plays a few notes of a German song: "There once was a king in Tulla." Stops.)* You know it? *(HAYYAH nods.)* Sing it. *(HAYYAH opens her mouth. No sound comes out.)* That Jew said you're a singer. If he was lying, you'll both go to Ponar and pay your debt to the worms. Sing!

HAYYAH
(She opens her mouth. No sound. She points to her throat.) Dry.

KITTEL
Oh, why didn't you say so?

He offers her his flask. She drinks.

HAYYAH
I'll sing one of our songs.

KITTEL
S'il vous plait, Madame!

SONG NUMBER ONE.

HAYYAH
(*sings*) *Unter daine vaisse shtern...*
In the sky the stars all glisten,
Here below I am lost in pain.
When I pray does no-one listen?
Is my weeping all in vain?
As I watch the stars all darken
All alone I stand and stare.
Let the empty heavens harken
To my broken-hearted prayer.
Let the empty heavens hearken
To my humble prayer.

Take my prayers and take my yearning
These are everything I own.
In my head a fire is burning
But my heart has turned to stone.
Cellars seethe with hell and fire
Streets are paved with black despair.
To the rooftops, climbing, higher,
Father let me find you there,
To the rooftops, ever higher,
Let me find you there.

Silent screams are deafening
And moaning ghosts are everywhere.
I am like a broken string
But still I sing my broken prayer.
In the sky the stars still glisten
Lilies in a field of white
How I pray that God will listen
To my lonely song tonight.
How I pray that he will listen
To my song tonight...

KITTEL
You sing well, Jewess. You touched my heart, damn it! (*wipes away a tear*) But that song was worth only ten grams. How will you pay the other fifty, if you're not performing? You're all artists, aren't you?

LINA
Yes we are! All of us.

KITTEL
I'll give you a chance to prove that Art is worth 50 grams of beans. Dessler! I want to see the Ghetto Council in my office at once.

DESSLER
Yes Sir!

KITTEL
But be careful. I'm a connoisseur. One false note, and you're finished.

KITTEL and his two bodyguards exit. The people go back to sleep at the back-stage, among the piles of clothes, except for HAYYAH, who collapses in a bundle. SRULIK walks up to her with LINA. SRULIK touches her gently. HAYYAH lifts her head.

HAYYAH
How can I ever thank you?

SRULIK
You don't have to thank me.

LINA
Tell her the truth! He wants love-love…

SRULIK
Stop it!

LINA
Love-love-love-love…

SRULIK
You're alive, that's all that counts.

LINA
Kiss-kiss-smooch-smooch.

HAYYAH
You could have lost your life.

SRULIK
"My life"! What's my life–

LINA
Without you. Say it: "Who am I without you…"

SRULIK
I'm nobody. A puppeteer, a dispensable person.

HAYYAH
You're a very brave man.

LINA
Whaddya mean! He's brave! He tried to stop me. *Hayyah'leh!* You owe your life to me!

HAYYAH
You're cute (*She caresses LINA.*)

LINA
Oh! Hhmm! It's so nice, Ohhh!... It's been so long since anyone fondled me.... May I fondle you too? (*LINA throws herself on HAYYAH.*)

SRULIK
Stop it! Shame on you!

LINA
He's jealous. Stay out! Don't stand between lovers. You do love me, don't you *Hayyah'leh*?

HAYYAH
You're irresistible, you little scamp.

LINA
I'm mad about you. It was love at first sight. But you must be starving, and I'm rattling on about love. Srulik! Offer her something to eat.

SRULIK
I've got nothing.

LINA
Liar. Try your deep pocket.

SRULIK
There's nothing there. Look. (*turns his pocket inside out*)

LINA
The other one, you sneak!

SRULIK
(*finds a carrot in his other pocket*) Oh! There's still one left. I forgot...

LINA
He "forgot." Ha ha. (*to HAYYAH*) He's so selfish. And he wants you to love him.

SRULIK
  Here, take it. *(He offers her the carrot.)*

HAYYAH
  But it's your last one…

LINA
  Ha ha! *(She picks out another carrot from SRULIK's pocket. SRULIK snatches it out of her hand.)* "The last one." Enjoy it. *(They eat.)* Everything fine? Good. Have you got a place to sleep?

HAYYAH
  I sleep in the sewers.

LINA
  In the sewers? Come sleep with us.

SRULIK
  What's come over you?

LINA
  We'll make room for her in our bed.

SRULIK
  Hold your tongue!

LINA
  Why should I? You don't keep me warm at night. I want to be warm. Is that a sin?

HAYYAH
  No, my little devil, it's not a sin. I'm sick of cold and lonely nights myself. I want to be warmer too.

  HAYYAH coils herself up in SRULIK's arms. LINA picks at his thigh with a mock-dagger.

LINA
  Put your arm on her shoulder, lovey-dovey, and start crooning one of your second-hand serenades.

  SONG NUMBER TWO.

HAYYAH & SRULIK
  Hot zich mir di shich zerissn…
  Someone stole my overcoat
  So how will I be warm?
  Who will hide me from this biting cold
  Or shield me from the storm?

So dance with me, and keep the cold away
If you've got your papers you can marry me today.

Every week they change the papers
Red or green or blue,
Every blessed week a different colour
What am I to do?
So dance with me... (*etc.*)

Ask for wood you get a splinter
Ask for bread, a stone,
Ah, this bitter wind, this cruel winter
Chills me to the bone.
So dance with me... (*etc.*)

Scene Three

GENS
(*enters running*) Srulik! You won't believe it! There's a God in heaven. (*The people get up, and come nearer to hear what's going on.*) How many times have I promised: "you'll get a theatre"? Everyone was against it. Suddenly I get orders from our ghetto council: go ahead! The Germans issued a licence. It's fantastic! We've got to act at once, before they change their mind. What d'you think of this place? Is it suitable?

SRULIK
Suitable? What for?

GENS
How many seats?

SRULIK
Three hundred fifteen.

GENS
You counted them.

SRULIK
I can't help it.

GENS
What d'you think of the stage?

SRULIK
Well, it's a stage.

HAYYAH
　It's a pretty good stage. It's deep, it's high, it's got twenty fly riggings, three trap-doors, great wing space–

GENS
　It's yours.

HAYYAH
　We'll turn it into a wonderful theatre.

GENS
　The theatre of the ghetto. It'll be our community centre. We'll hold meetings.

HAYYAH
　We'll give concerts

GENS
　Exhibitions–

SRULIK
　Just a second–

GENS
　Here's a pencil and paper. See what's missing. Make me a list of everything you need–

　　HAYYAH grabs the pen and paper and walks off to the wing followed by the actors, who get involved in a lively discussion arguing for and against the founding of the theatre.

SRULIK
　Maybe tomorrow–

GENS
　Yesterday! Do it now!

　　Exit SRULIK. A shifty character, Yossef GERSTEIN, dressed as a HASSID, approaches GENS.

Scene Four

GERSTEIN
　Your Honour, Mr. Chief of the Police!

GENS
　What do you want?

GERSTEIN
I can read the future in your palm. Just show me your hand...

GENS
"Read the future?" Go find some useful work, you good for nothing.

GERSTEIN
Summer will bring a radical change in your destiny.

GENS
Wait a minute. You haven't even looked in my palm.

GERSTEIN
I also read ears. But the palm has more details.

GENS
Fine, *(offers his hand)* but hurry. I've no time for nonsense.

GERSTEIN
I don't believe it.

GENS
What do you see?

GERSTEIN
Look! A "G" becomes an "L"!...

GENS
Well, yes, if you insist...

GERSTEIN
"G?" – Ge... Germans! "L?" – "L"... Leader?... Life?... Light?... Love?... Land?... Lord?... Liberation! Liberty!
You'll become Leader of this ghetto. You'll Liberate our people from the Germans, you'll give us Life. You'll Lead us from darkness to Light, from slavery to Liberty in our promised Land – thus spake the Lord.

GENS
When will it all happen?

GERSTEIN
In three time-units.

GENS
What's that?

GERSTEIN
Could be three months, three years, *(He holds out his hand to be paid.)* three marks.

GENS
What?!

GERSTEIN
Three marks, please.

GENS
(*pays*) Go look for some real work. These tricks won't keep you alive for long.

Scene Five

The actors return from their tour of the theatre. They are divided in two distinct camps, and engage one another in a fierce argument. Some defending the idea of founding a theatre, the others opposing it.

GENS
Well well!... Is something wrong with the place?

SRULIK
The place is fine. The time is wrong. Gens, this is not the time for theatre.

GENS
Not the time?

SRULIK
More than fifty thousand Jews were slaughtered here in a a matter of weeks. Their blood hasn't yet dried. How can we put on plays here?

GENS
(*He opens a trap door, and shouts.*) You down there! Out of the sewer! All of you! Out! Out!

Ghost-like creatures start to climb out of the sewer. These are people who have been hiding in the canalization. They haven't seen the light of the day for weeks. They are wrapped in rags and covered in slime. The shocked members of the actors company watch the scene with amazement, as if they were witnessing the doomsday resurrection. Then they start identifying lost colleagues, lovers and friends who they believed were dead. Heart-rending encounters take place.

SARRAH comes out first. She is followed by JUDITH and UMA.

EVA
Judith?... My God, Judith! (*EVA rushes at JUDITH and helps her to stand on her legs. She accompanies her to a corner, and starts taking care of her. She shouts:*) Weiskopf! Bring water!

SRULIK
(*to GENS, who is supporting UMA*) Who's this?

GENS
Uma?...

SRULIK
Uma! (*He embraces her, but UMA fights to free herself from his grip.*) Our star actress. She played Nora. She played lady Macbeth... Uma! (*He tries to kiss her. She pushes him away and hides in a corner.*)

SARRAH
Where's my husband? Where's Lionek? (*She searches amongst the survivors:*) Lionek.... Has anyone seen Lionek?

LIUBA climbs out. YANKL, her boyfriend identifies her:

YANKL
Liuba!...

LIUBA
Yankl?...

They embrace and kiss. Later YANKL will wash her carefully with a pail of water. He will scrub her with his shirt. They'll creep to a corner of the stage, and forget the world in one another's arms. ELIA appears, and GEIVISH recognizes his lost brother.

GEIVISH
Elia! Elia is alive! My brother is alive!

LEAH appears. TOVA recognizes her.

TOVA
Leah? Hey! Look! It's Leah!

GENIA
Our teacher! She's alive!

IRINA, HELENA, TOVA, GENIA, MIRA, NELLI and ETKA surround LEAH, and take care of her. They wash her, they fetch clothes for her.

YANOSH
Have you seen Reika? (*RASHKA comes out.*) Have you seen Reika? (*ANITA comes out.*) Have you seen Reika? (*She makes a few steps, and faints. KRUK comes along with a wheelbarrow loaded with books.*)

GENS
Hey! Kruk! Over here! Quick! She's fainted!

> *KRUK turns the wheelbarrow over, pours out the books, and together with GENS lifts ANITA, puts her in the wheelbarrow and carries her off. REIKA appears.*

YANOSH
Reika!!!...

> *A group of people comes out. These are HAIKIN, SHLOIME and MALKA, the flutist. They help and support one another.*

HAYYAH
Haikin! You're alive! (*She embraces him.*) Shloime! Srulik, Get some water, and clothes, quick!

> *All over the place people are taking care of their dearest ones, offering them first-aid, washing them, cleaning their wounds, covering their nudity, clothing them.*

SRULIK
Haikin! Our virtuoso! The first violin in the Orchestra! Gens! Where did you find them?

GENS
In sewers, cellars, wagons and trucks, on the way to Ponar, the execution place.

HAYYAH
Haikin! You're frozen. Let me warm you. (*She warms him with her body.*) Where's your violin?

GENS
(*to SRULIK*) Have we got any instruments?

SRULIK
Over there. In the basket.

> *GENS fumbles in the straw-trunk and pulls out a violin. He hands it over to HAIKIN.*

HAYYAH
Can you play? You must try, darling, you must. Come on, love, your fingers are frozen. Let me warm your hands. (*She rubs his hands and warms them.*) Now play, play!

> *HAIKIN starts playing, he stops, hesitates a moment, and starts a Hassidic Freilach. The people start humming the tune. All other musicians join in.*

LEAH stands up and starts a dance. Her students join in. More people join the dance. The dance develops, they seem to be flying in the air. The dance and the music reach an ecstatic climax. The people fall to the ground. They whimper and laugh and cry.

GENS
Do you know what these people have in common?

SRULIK
They're actors, musicians, dancers.... They're artists.

GENS
They're unemployed. They haven't got any work-papers. They'll be the first to go in the next action. Do you want to abandon them because it's not the right time for theatre? You self-righteous intellectuals. When it's all over, you'll celebrate your pure conscience: "The police chief Jacob Gens tried to force me to start a theatre, but I resisted. It was three weeks after the massacre. I refused to put on a show. My hands are clean." Look them in the eye. If you start a theatre, I can get you work-papers, the Goddamn German *Arbeitsbescheinigung* that might keep you alive. Get you bread. And lard. And potatoes. And soap.

ALL
Bread.... Lard.... Potatoes.... Soap...

GENS
Yes. And don't forget the principal behind it all. In these grim times we need you, Jewish actors, to help us survive. Look at us. Where's our self esteem. You can help remind us that we're human. That we have a language, a culture, a heritage. Go ahead, Srulik, get them to work. I want a performance.

SRULIK
What kind of a performance? What kind of theatre should we make?

GENS
Do I ask you how to run a ghetto? I'm counting on you.

The actors exit. WEISKOPF who was mixed with them, stays behind. DESSLER is eavesdropping and spying on the following scene, taking notes.

Scene Six

WEISKOPF
Mr. Gens, Mr. Gens...

GENS
Go to the rehearsal.

WEISKOPF
I'm no actor.

GENS
Then who are you ?

WEISKOPF
Give me a few minutes. There's a great opportunity at stake.

GENS
I've got no time to waste. (*He starts to walk off.*)

WEISKOPF
Do you know how many first-rate tailors we've got in the ghetto?

GENS
(*stops*) Tailors? No.

WEISKOPF
And how many sewing machines?

GENS
Get to the point.

WEISKOPF
Take a look. (*He offers Gens a small notebook.*)

GENS
Dessler! Go inspect the guards.

WEISKOPF
You see? Tailors, seamstresses, sewing machines. I went from room to room. I did my own research.

GENS
What for?

WEISKOPF
Allow me to answer that with a question: have you noticed the trains going from the Russian front back to Germany? What do they transport?

GENS
I said get to the point or get out of my way.

WEISKOPF
They transport damaged German uniforms. Now why do they send them all the way from Russia to Germany?

GENS
To be laundered, I guess, to be mended–

WEISKOPF
And taken back all the way from Germany to the Russian front. And we're sitting here in the middle with hundreds of tailors, seamstresses, sewing machines.... It's absurd!

GENS
You mean, we should propose to the Germans–

WEISKOPF
We'll set up a business in the ghetto. They can bring those trainloads of uniforms to us and save a lot of time and money. It's good for them, and – very good for us.

GENS
How many workers will you need?

WEISKOPF
A hundred to begin with. Another fifty if we get enough work.

GENS
One hundred and fifty more families. That means six hundred more people get a chance to live. Come to my office in the morning.

WEISKOPF
Why lose another day? Let's sit down now. We can work all night. Tomorrow morning you can give the Germans a full plan, with precise figures, the way they like it. They'll approve it at once. By noon we'll have a hundred work permits.

GENS
You're quite a character. What's your name?

WEISKOPF
Weiskopf. The name is Weiskopf.

GENS
Come, Weiskopf. Let's go to my office.

Scene Seven

KRUK enters pushing his wheelbarrow, loaded with books which he picked up on the street and in the garbage. The books are damaged, torn, soaked with water and mud. A fly comes down loaded with books hung to dry.

KRUK
    Weiskopf.... An interesting character. He could fill pages in my diary. He was an entirely insignificant person, and then overnight, The Richest Man in the ghetto. He sits in an armchair, receives people, presides over meetings, makes declarations... "The Khalif of the Ghetto," that's what the people call him.

    DESSLER enters.

DESSLER
    Mr. Kruk, you're officially invited by the Ghetto Council to attend the first performance of the local drama circle on Sunday, the 18th of January here, in the Theatre Auditorium. The program includes scenes from plays, monologues, and musical numbers. The evening will be sponsored by the Chief of Police, Mr. Jacob Gens.

KRUK
    Go tell your masters to stop dancing on our blood. You don't put on theatre in a graveyard.

DESSLER
    Don't blame the messenger.

    Youngsters come running on the bridge. They hang on the parapet a banderole with the inscription "No theatre in a graveyard." DESSLER enters with his policemen. The youngsters exchange blows with the policemen, and run away.

    (*blows his whistle*) Stop! That's an order! Catch them!

    The policemen run after the youngsters. GENS appears. DESSLER points to the banderole:

DESSLER
    Your friend Hermann Kruk. (*He exits.*)

    GENS addresses KRUK:

Scene Eight

GENS
    Hermann Kruk! What have you got against the theatre?

KRUK
    It's an insult.

GENS
To whom? Do you speak in the name of the dead? Did they appoint you their spokesman?

KRUK
I'm speaking for myself.

GENS
You're not a private person, Kruk. You can't indulge in private feelings. You can't afford the luxury of feeling offended. You've been invited in your role as public library director and secretary of the workers' union.

KRUK
I'm expressing the feelings of every member of the workers' union as well.

GENS
Your workers' union, correct me if I'm wrong, has not yet made a formal decision to boycott the theatre.

KRUK
Gens, In the forest of Ponar, six miles down the road, the sand over the bodies is still moist. They say the earth is bleeding. For God's sake! There were seventy thousand Jews in Vilna. How many are left? Fifteen thousand?

GENS
Sixteen thousand.

KRUK
A theatre? It's a scandal.

GENS
Hermann, remember the night of the 6th of September in '41. We were thrown out of our homes and dragged in the rain through the streets of Vilna to the ghetto. It was hell on earth. People up to their knees in mud. And you saw books thrown to the wind. On that horrible night you ran with your wheelbarrow to collect abandoned books. The next day you opened the library. For this I marvel at you. That night I picked up people who were tossed in the storm. I gave them shelter. I dressed them. I fed them.
I returned those I could to their professions. I took homeless actors and gave them a theatre. Our physicians run the hospital and everyone thanks God they do. If a few musicians have been spared from the slaughter, why shouldn't they compose music that gives voice to our sorrow? Why shouldn't they play? I snatched Leah, our great choreographer, from a transport to Ponar and brought her back to her dance students; is that outrageous? I reunited Haikin with his violin; is that a sin? Hermann, you will be at the show tomorrow.

KRUK
Jacob, you can't force me to ignore my conscience.

GENS
> Let's give our people a sense of solidarity. We all belong to one nation. I want representatives of every group in the ghetto to be there, including the workers' union.

KRUK
> You won't miss us, Gens. You'll have Jewish police commanders, work-unit leaders, and some very important guests from outside: German officers. I hear our nightingale is rehearsing some German songs in case the Krauts, God forbid, feel homesick.

GENS
> We'll continue the discussion another time. Tomorrow you'll be there.

KRUK
> The workers' union rejects the invitation to participate in the spectacle. We won't attend that concert of crows.

GENS
> Then let me tell you this: your workers' union is hereby outlawed. Its leadership is dissolved.

KRUK
> It's the only leadership in the ghetto that was chosen by democratic elections.

GENS
> Don't make me cry.

KRUK
> Your concern for the people is a hoax. You're building a Monarchy, and this theatre is your Versailles. We won't be part of that miserable farce.

GENS
> You think I'll let you play your party-politics here? Bring out those placards again, and you'll end up in Ponar.

KRUK
> (*dictating to his unseen secretary*) The "Chief" of the ghetto outlawed the workers' union, and threatened to send its democratically elected leaders to Ponar.

GENS
> Good! Write it down in your diary. Let the coming generations judge between you and me. But I warn you, Hermann: don't twist my words. (*He exits.*)

KRUK

God! You are my witness. My pen is pure. We are lost in the Darkness of Egypt. People can't see what's happening. They won't listen. Their minds are numb. I swear to record it all. My pen and paper must record everything. My diary must be the mirror and conscience of these catastrophic Days of Awe.

Scene Nine

LEAH

Alright people, we've lost enough time. Let's get to work. Haikin, we're rehearsing the Russian dance.

HAIKIN and SHLOIMEH play a short introduction.

That's right.
Tova, take centre and lead the first row.
Judith, you lead the second row.
Come on, people!
Get to your places, everybody.
And one, and two, and one two three four!

They dance. She stops them.

No, no, no, stop, stop!
Do you want to see what you look like?

She plays a parody of an old lady moving like a duck:

Oy oy oy aye aye aye!...
You're tired, I know. We're all coming from a hard day's work. That's why we're going to dance the hell out of it this time!
I want to see the Red Cavalry storming the German lines like a tornado, and you're going to give it to me!
And one, and two, and one two three four!

They dance.

WEISKOPF rushes in from the wing into the stage.

WEISKOPF

Oy oy oy, ay ay ay! Why the crying, why the weeping?

SRULIK

Weiskopf, we're rehearsing.

WEISKOPF

Here! Rehearse this! *(He draws a bottle of vodka.)* To your new curtain!
(A red curtain is drawn across the stage. The actors stare at it with great

astonishment.) My present for your theatre! Lehayim! *(He takes a swig and throws the bottle to SRULIK.)*

SRULIK
Alright people, take a ten-minute break, but don't get too drunk.

The actors sit down on the boards. They pass the bottle.

WEISKOPF
Times are hard? So what's new? When did our people have it easy? Hardship makes us strong. Take me for example. *(He draws a Kabanos sausage from his pocket.)* Before the war I had little tailor's shop. The Germans came, pushed us into the ghetto. The shop's gone. Finished. So did I cry?

ALL
Yeah!

WEISKOPF
And how! But did I cry?

ALL
No!

WEISKOPF
Of course not. Will tears bring it back? Hell no! Instead of crying I held my wise Jewish Kopf in my hands, and I said to myself: Why do they call you Weiskopf? You've lost your shop, it's true; now if you lose your Kopf – you're kaput. Your Kopf is all you've got left in the world. No one can take it away, not while you're alive.
I looked around me: walls. A ghetto. Everything's locked up. A way out! A way out! Where can I find a way out!
I found one! What was I before the war?

LIUBA
Nothing!

GENIA
A little tailor.

WEISKOPF
Right! Look at me now: The manager of a tailor's assembly line. The biggest in the whole region. 150 Jews work for me. The Germans– *(He spits.)* place orders. They buy my products. It's a flourishing business, growing from day to day. The sun rises, and my profits rise with it. But am I sitting on my money?

RASHKA
Not at all!

ANITA
On the contrary!

WEISKOPF
Right! My hand is wide open. I'm a generous contributor to public causes, and I'm not keeping it secret. I want everyone to know that I'm not ashamed of my deeds. My way is the right way. Take my example, fellows: I make a living and I also provide a living for hundreds of families.
And I'm no exception. I'm an ordinary Jew. But we Jews are gifted. More than all other people. If more of us follow my example instead of shedding tears, we'll become a productive ghetto. The Germans– *(He spits.)* will need us. We'd become indispensable to their war effort. And then we'll survive!

The actors applaud. One of them stands up to give a standing ovation. He takes off his casquette to make a curtsy and throws away his coat, and is revealed as KITTEL.

KITTEL
Bravo, Weiskopf! *(The actors scream with fear, they jump up and freeze in two groups on both sides of the stage, with WEISKOPF freezing in the centre.)* I love this man. And so long as I love him, he'll survive. *(UMA remains seated on a chair leaning on her crutch. KITTEL goes over to her and kicks away the crutch. UMA falls to the floor.)* What's wrong? You don't welcome me anymore?

All take off their hats and salute.

ALL
God bless you.

KITTEL
God bless you. I'll forgive you this time. I took you by surprise. I didn't use the ghetto gate. Your look-out couldn't warn you that Kittel is in the ghetto. Relax. Kittel never uses the gate. Kittel slithers into the ghetto like a snake. Out of the blue he may shoot at you from an attic eh? Or pop out from a cellar! *(He rushes behind the curtain and re-appears carrying two black cases. He puts them on the floor, and turns to WEISKOPF:)* What's in this case? The wrong reply may cost us dearly. So?

SRULIK
The Schmeisser.

KITTEL
(opens the case) Right, the Schmeisser. *(He loads it.)* And what's in this one?

HAYYAH
The saxophone.

KITTEL
Let's see.... The saxophone. The Scmeisser and the Saxophone. Why do I love you, Weiskopf?

WEISKOPF
I'm productive. I contribute to the war effort.

KITTEL
Who made you so productive?

WEISKOPF
You did.

KITTEL
I? *(explodes)* I hate bootlickers. Why?

SRULIK
You're an artist.

KITTEL
I'm an artist. What does an artist love?

SRULIK
Imagination.

KITTEL
Right! What else?

SRULIK
Beauty.

> *KITTEL pulls out a theatre make-up box, dips his fingers in the black paint, and starts painting the actors' faces in black, sending the blackened actors to line up near WEISKOPF in what seems to be a selection for an execution. While doing this KITTEL makes a small speech:*

KITTEL
You got it Weiskopf? I love you because you're beautiful and imaginative. I didn't make you productive, Weiskopf. It was all lurking inside you. I just created the right conditions for your Jewish gifts to flourish. Your mad vitality, Godamn it! I took a walk through the streets of Catholic Vilna. Pfui! What blockheads! What heavy-handed, pedestrian creatures. No spark of spirit. I almost suffocated. It's them we should trample underfoot, not you. And then I sneak in here through the tunnel you dug, yes Weiskopf! Don't deny it! I get into your ghetto, and all at once it's another world. Everything's full of life. Sparkling. Exploding with frantic, desperate activity. There's such beauty, so much imagination in that! You probably can't see it. People who live in paradise get used to it.

Your Kiosks, your cafes. You chop beetroots, and call it caviar. You serve sauerkraut brine, and baptize it as champagne. I love your sense of humour. That insane resilience of yours. I didn't create you, I just furnished the circumstances for your quintessence to blossom.
And this is only the beginning. This intimate contact between the German soul and the Jewish spirit, so painful yet so fruitful, it's going to do wonders. Did you ever dream that you'd come this far, Weiskopf?

WEISKOPF
No, never.

KITTEL
What else does an artist love?

SRULIK
Truth.

KITTEL
Right. Art can't be perfect without truth.
(*KITTEL takes the Schmeisser.*) Now answer me from the heart of your Jewish spirit, and remember: if you try to embellish the Truth– (*KITTEL aims the Schmeisser at WEISKOPF.*) Tell me Weiskopf, what's the difference between a partial liquidation of the Jewish race and its total liquidation ?

Dead silence. WEISKOPF looks at the actors, and meets their frightened eyes. It is clear that their lives depend now solely on his answer.

WEISKOPF
Kill all the Jews but me–
that's partial liquidation.
Kill me – that's total.

There is a moment of silence. Then KITTEL's expression is transformed from merciless concentration to sincere astonishment before exploding in hysterical laughter.

KITTEL
Bravo! Bravo Weiskopf! What a sense of humour in what a situation! Let's put away the Schmeisser. No need for it now.
This is the time for the Saxophone. I give you my word: on the day of the this ghetto's liquidation I'll put a piano at the gate, and accompany your march out to the trains with my rendition of Schumann's "Scenes from Childhood."
No one asks what brings me here. Where's your band? Musicians, to your instruments! Suddenly I missed George Gershwin. It's odd, isn't it? Those swine in Berlin's Ministry of Culture banned Gershwin. It's a crime to play jazz! Where can I go to hear Gershwin nowadays? Suddenly I remembered Gens told me you gave jazz concerts. So here I am. Where's your nightingale? Where's that singer who owes me fifty grams of beans?

HAYYAH steps out. KITTEL whispers something on her ear. She nods and turns to the musicians:

HAYYAH
Swanee! He wants Swanee!...

KITTEL
Curtain! *(TIMMAN and ARNTGEN open the curtain. Pointing at the actors whose faces he painted black, KITTEL orders:)* Dancers over there! Musicians get ready! And one, and two, and one two three four!

The musicians start playing. KITTEL joins them. HAYA sings:

SONG No. 3: SWANEE.

HAYYAH
I've been away from you a long time...

LEAH organizes and briefs her dancers, and they start to dance. SARRAH ELMIS faints and falls to the floor. The people go on dancing, just taking care not to tread on her. ELIA and GEIVISH sneak in between the dancers, and drag SARRAH away.

SHLOIME starts a dazzling cadenza on his clarinet. All fall silent, and the cadenza grows to become an open affront to KITTEL. KITTEL admires SHLOIME'S virtuosity, and invites the musicians to go all the way. The musicians and the dancers respond by developing a dance number reminiscent of the Red Army dancers. TIMANN is worried, he wants to stop the performance, but KITTEL indicates to him not to interfere.

Suddenly HAYA makes a transition to "Wiener Blut," and the actors start a waltz. KITTEL turns his face away. Being unprepared for the transition, he gets an emotional shock. Tears well up in his eyes. He runs to the piano and knocks down its cover with a big bang. All freeze in dead silence.

KITTEL
Thank you. Thank you. You gave me a real uplifting moment. But there's still room for improvement. The choreography could be more imaginative. When you dance jazz, the body must be light and relaxed. Like this.

He demonstrates the Nazi goose-steps, enjoying his own joke. Then addresses HAYYAH.

Your singing's not bad at all. You're a promising talent. Capable of marvels. I'd rate you 25 grams of beans on the Kittel scale for that song. Weiskopf! You don't want them on stage in these rags! Give my actors the best costumes in your warehouse.

WEISKOPF
I'll give them the most beautiful clothes.

KITTEL
You'd better. I'll be at their performance. Remember: Kittel can appear any moment. Pop out of any hole. Kittel the snake!

An explosion. Darkness. Light. KITTEL is gone.

Scene Ten

A fly hung with clothes descends. WEISKOPF jumps on the fly, walks back and forth on the fly holding on to the cables, and invites the actors to help themselves:

WEISKOPF
Come on folks, here's costumes for your show. Anything you want. It's all yours. Any style. Any size. Clothing is one thing we're not short of. It's all sorted out. Come try them on.

Dresses. Slips. Suits.
Women's overcoats.
Finest tailoring from Lodz.

He throws the clothes at the actors. They start to try them on.

English corduroy.
Poor people's rags.
I know actors like these things.

Costumes of all Professions.
Police uniforms.
Judges' robes. Wigs.
Doctors' gowns.
We've got dozens.

There's all you'll need for a religious scene:
Hassidic frocks. Shtreimels.
Rabbis' kaftans.
Original samite.

How about a luxury restaurant:
Tweed suits.
Tailcoats.
The finest Manchester wool.
Elegant evening dresses.
Haute couture from Paris!

Children's clothes.
We've got lots of them.
Look what a lovely girl's dress!
You can put on a pantomime:
"Hannahleh's Sabbath dress..."

> *He displays the dress. There is dead silence. The actors are shocked. They throw away the clothes which they took. Weiskopf overcomes the horror:*

What's wrong?
It's only clothes.
Uniforms. You want uniforms?
Polish cavalry!
From Warsaw probably, or Danzig.
Heroes' uniforms.
They galloped on horseback
Bayonnet in hand
They stormed the Wehrmacht tanks!
Beautiful uniforms.
They came to our workshop sprinkled with bullets.
Soaked with blood.
Look at them now:
No trace of tragedy
They've been laundered and mended.
You can slip into them, and jump on stage.
German Uniforms.
They were in just as bad condition
When they got here from the Russian front.
They got the same treatment.
In our laundry there's no discrimination.

You must visit our laundry.
You'll come out with a drama.
Fire roars in the ovens.
The air sheds tears of chlorine and soap.
Everything is washed out.
The oil, the mud, the blood.
You should see the sewage:
Steaming streams of red and black.
Not to mention the sewing workshop.
A huge hangar.
A hundred and fifty sewing machines rattling away
Like a busy railway station.
Help yourselves folks, don't be choosy!
Clothing is one thing we don't lack.
It's one thing we have in abundance...
So help yourselves, folks, help yourselves!

> *WEISKOPF jumps down from the fly and exits.*

During WEISKOPF's monologue JUDITH picked out a dress of a poor woman. She has put it on. She has also picked out a rabbi's kaftan, a judge's robe and two doctor's gowns.
YANKL has put on a suit identical to WEISKOPF'S. The moment WEISKOPF has jumped down from the fly, YANKL jumps on the fly and starts playing a parody of WEISKOPF.

YANKL
Help yourselves, folks, help yourselves!
A hundred and fifty Jews work for me.
The sun rises, and my profits rise with it.

ELIA
He's a Rothschild! *(YANKL jumps from the fly. ELIA starts scrubbing the floor under YANKL's feet.)*

YANKL
We Jews we're clever, more than all other people.
Take an example from my Wise-Kopf, folks.
So long as you're productive, I'll survive.

JUDITH
Weiskopf! They arrested my husband.

YANKL
(pushing her aside and shaking people's hands) Don't worry, all is under control.

JUDITH
(lying at his feet and kissing his shoes) They caught him with eight kilos of flour. They took him to Lukishki prison.

YANKL
(stepping over JUDITH) I said don't worry!

JUDITH
They say only you can set people free.

YANKL
Of course I can. I can do everything.

JUDITH
We need twenty thousand Rubles to bribe the guards, or they'll kill him.

YANKL
Woman! Who's talking to you? It's Weiskopf! I'm going straight to my German! They're all for sale.

JUDITH
(She gives EVA the Judge's Robe. Eva puts on the Robe.) This man is an angel. He gives food to the poor. He gets people out of prison. He should be crowned King of the ghetto!

EVA
(to YANKL) The Supreme Court hereby declares the abolition of the Republic of the ghetto, and the constitution of an Absolute Monarchy under the rule of King Weiskopf the first!

All applaud. Fanfares. JUDITH gives UMA a doctor's gown.

JUDITH
Are you a doctor?

UMA
(hesitantly, as if waking from a dream) What am I? (She looks at the gown.) Oh, you want me to play a doctor?... (She puts on the gown.)

JUDITH
(giving SARRAH another doctor's gown) Doctor, my husband is a diabetic. Who'll give him his insulin in prison? Without his insulin he won't survive a day.

YANKL
Go home. Make your husband a good soup for lunch. He'll get his insulin for the main course, or my name's not Weiskopf!

JUDITH
(She gives GERSTEIN the rabbi's kaftan:) That's the man, that's Weiskopf. Bless him Rabbi, ask God to keep him strong.

GERSTEIN
(puts his hand on YANKL's head:) Blessed be thou Oh Lord, ye who trampleth down the Poor and Weak, and giveth ever more power to the Rich and the Mighty. Amen.

The actors applaud their colleagues for the improvised scene. SRULIK gives JUDITH a kiss.

SRULIK
Good work, Judith! We'll include it in our next program.

JUDITH
That's just a start. Wait till you see the main dish!

JUDITH whispers something in SRULIK's ear. She pulls one of the levers, and a curtain comes down behind the four actors of the next scene: UMA, EVA, SARRAH AND GERSTEIN. SRULIK sends all the other actors to sit in the auditorium. He himself gets behind a Follow-Spot, while JUDITH takes care of another FS. They'll light Scene Eleven with Follow-Spots.

Scene Eleven

UMA plays WEINER, SARRAH plays GOTTLIEB, EVA plays JUDGE, GERSTEIN plays RABBI.

WEINER
Most honourable masters, I've called you to this meeting in the hospital underground–

JUDGE
Would you please introduce yourself.

WEINER
Dr. Weiner, in charge of the dispensary. There are fifty diabetics in the ghetto. Some are terminal. They consume large quantities of Insulin, as my colleague Dr.–

GOTTLIEB
Professor Gottlieb–

WEINER
–Professor Gottlieb, can explain.

GOTTLIEB
That's right, the serious cases need very high doses just to survive, whereas the lighter cases can live normal lives on much smaller doses of insulin.

WEINER
Thank you, professor. To keep alive all fifty diabetics we need one thousand units of insulin a day. Now, in our dispensary there's one hundred thousand units left. Is that clear?

JUDGE
Yes, it means you've enough insulin for three months.

WEINER
Right. When we run out of insulin, our patients will start dying.

JUDGE
Is that a fact, Professor Gottlieb?

GOTTLIEB
Yes. The terminal cases will die within days. The others won't last much longer. Without insulin all will die.

RABBI
What's the problem? We'll raise money, and buy insulin on the black market.

GENS enters. They stop acting.

GENS
Go on. *(He sits in the auditorium.)*

WEINER
There's no more insulin, not even on the black market.

GENS
That's right.

JUDGE
But everything's on the black market, even soap or French perfume, if you can pay the price.

GENS
Forget it.

WEINER
There's no insulin anywhere. We tried all possible channels. Gens enlisted the most daring smugglers of our underworld. The neighbouring ghettos have no insulin either.

GENS
I can assure you that we're still better off than others. If the Germans knew how much we've got left, they'd confiscate it at once. They think we've got no diabetics at all.

WEINER
Please understand: insulin is unavailable at any price.

JUDGE
Then what's the question? What are we supposed to do? I don't understand.

WEINER
Well, if we stop treating the terminal cases, we can save enough insulin to keep the others alive for nine months instead of three. If we decide to treat only the healthiest cases, we could keep twenty patients alive for almost two years.

RABBI
This is absurd! What's the point of making plans in the ghetto? Do you know what will happen tomorrow morning? Or tonight?

JUDGE
He's absolutely right. For us three months is an eternity!

WEINER
You're trying to avoid the issue.

JUDGE
Just what do you want ?

WEINER
I'm asking you...
Do I have the moral right to stop treating the hopeless cases...
To let them die, so that the others may live?

Very long silence.

JUDGE
I've been invited to take part in this meeting, correct me if I'm wrong, because I'm a judge. So allow me to consider your dilemma from a strictly legal point of view. You ask whether we have the right to sentence certain people to death. As a judge I say: yes, you may condemn to death criminals guilty of committing a crime for which the law stipulates the death penalty. As a judge I ask you what kind of offence have those culprits in question committed?
Answer: they are guilty of being seriously ill. Evidence? There's much too much sugar in their urine. I open all the law books in the world, and I tell you not one of them defines sugar in the urine as a capital crime. Therefore as a Judge I say: No, Lady Prosecutor, No! The law does not allow me to sentence any of your patients to death.

EVA throws away her wig and robe, and joins the audience in the auditorium.

WEINER
Legally speaking you may be right. But I'm astounded at the philosophical lethargy that lets you sentence all our diabetics to death within three months. Rabbi, am I allowed to abandon to death the ones that I can save?

RABBI
There's a parable in the Talmud, which... may not help... but it can't hurt. An enemy besieging a town sets conditions for lifting the siege. Hand us over twenty of your compatriots. We'll execute them, and spare your town.

The Talmud asks:
Should we sacrifice twenty people, and save the town?
And – the Talmud answers:
If the enemy has not given the names of the victims, we should not select them ourselves. Let the entire town perish, to avoid the crime of choosing scapegoats.
But.... If the enemy specifies the names of the victims, and demands that we give them this one and that one, deliver the specified victims to their fate, and let the entire town survive.

Now in our case, who is the enemy?
Who can give us a list of the people who should die so that others may live?

WEINER
Here is the list. (*UMA shows the rabbi her palm.*) Look. Each patient and his condition, blood-sugar level, age, marital status, occupation, here's your list!

RABBI
Leave me alone! (*GERSTEIN throws away the rabbi's kaftan and joins the audience.*)

WEINER
Look! (*She displays her right hand.*) A seventy-eight-year-old widower, terminal condition. (*She displays her left hand.*) A thirty-six-year-old woman, a mother of three children. You want names?

GOTTLIEB
Are you trying to make a selection between patients?

WEINER
Professor Gottlieb, you're an older and more experienced physician than me. (*She displays an ampule.*) You know that for some patients this liquid is only an illusion, it won't save them. But for others it means life. You know better than anyone here what I'm talking about. Support me!

GOTTLIEB
How dare you discriminate between patients? This isn't medicine anymore, this is.... It's inconceivable.... It's unethical, it's immoral!

WEINER
What shall I do then?

GOTTLIEB
Do what you want. I don't belong here. I'll have no part in this monstrous Nazi Medicine! (*SARRAH throws away her gown and joins the audience.*)

WEINER
You want me to avoid my responsibility! You want me to distribute it like a machine, without reason, without feeling, just deal it out until it's all gone, and to hell with it! Is that what you would do in my place?

RABBI
(*from the audience*) Only God gives life, and only he has the right to take it. Mortals have no right to decide who shall live and who shall die.

WEINER
In what kind of a world? In a world ruled by justice. But here? Here human beings decide everything. What you call the will of God is the will of evil men.

The actors in the audience begin to respond violently.

GEIVISH
We're not in a hospital. We're in a theatre.

TOVA
We want entertainment. Not morals.

GENIA
We're fed up with this kind of theatre!

YANOSH
We paid for our tickets. We want to have fun!

MIRA
We want to laugh! Make us laugh!

IRINA
Move us!

NELLI
Shatter us! Make us cry!

ELIA
Make us forget!

ALL
We want good theatre! Good theatre!

GENS
People, people! We have an artistic director. He makes the choices. Srulik, I see that the Insulin Sketch is not on the playbill.

SRULIK
Yes, it was an improvisation.

GENS
That's enough improvisation for tonight. Let's get back to the program. Here it is. A song written by an eleven-year-old-boy, Alex Volkovitsky.

The curtain goes up. A children's choir is revealed on the stage behind the curtain. HAIKIN gets on the stage to conduct the choir.

The children perform song No. 4: "SHTILER SHTILER".

CHILDREN
Go to sleep my little flower don't let them hear you cry,
Graves are growing hour by hour 'til they fill the sky.
Since your father went away the world is wearing black,

Many roads lead to Ponar but none of them lead back.
Hush-a-bye my little treasure – time to go to sleep;
It would only give them pleasure if they heard you weep.
Every prison has a door
And every wave breaks on the shore,
But pain for you and I will never die.

Pain is growing slowly herewith sorrow all around,
'Til our jailers disappear you may not make a sound.
Do not smile until tomorrow, do not cry today.
You must not betray our sorrow 'til it's died away.
Sorrow's wider than a river, deeper than a well,
Soon your father will deliver you and I from hell.
Soon the world will loose its chains
And all the flowers will bloom again
And heaven's golden grace will fill your face...

Applause. A person in black lands on the stage. This is KITTEL. Dead silence.

KITTEL
Gens! I hear your people complain that the theatre is not good enough. Let's give them the real thing. Come to the stage.

GENS gets on the stage. KITTEL addresses the children.

Once upon a time a man and a woman got married and had one child. Have they increased their race? *(The children raise their fingers. KITTEL points to a girl:)* Yes, honey?

GIRL
No, they haven't increased.

KITTEL
Very good! Come here, love. A few years later they had a second child. Have they finally increased the race? You, there!

BOY
One papa, one mamma, one child, one child – they have not increased.

KITTEL
Excellent! Over here. Now, three children? Yes, you!

CHILD
They have increased.

KITTEL
Bravo! That's true, children! Come join us. Over here. They have increased. Now we have a problem, Gens.

If the Führer has ordered a stop to the propagation of your race, then the third child is errr...

GENS
To be–

KITTEL
To be or not to be, that's the question.
Well then, let's get on with it.
Selection of the third child.
One Father, one mother, one child, one child. The third–

He flips his finger. TIMANN and ARNTGEN appear. They take the third child and march off in the direction of the bridge.

Let's get on with it, Gens!

The sound of iron gates opening. Powerful projectors shed a nightmarish light. The actors sitting in the auditorium jump from their places and run to the stage to rescue their children. Pandemonium. They run with the children to the back stage. There they are rounded up by the Jewish police and the German Soldiers. GENS climbs up the bridge and conducts the selection amidst an infernal noise of people crying, shouting and yelling. Lights out on Selection. Sound of selection fades out.
Light on KRUK who comes running from the selection. He dictates his impressions to his unseen secretary who is typing it on a typewriter.

KRUK
A family of five people. Gens counts:
"Father, mother, child, child."
The third child, a 12-year old boy, he shoves out of the line. He pushes him to the side.
Beats the father with his stick on the back.
The family stands with the survivors, sobbing:
"Gens took our child!"
The crowd is outraged. People shout at Gens:
"Traitor! You kill our children!"
Gens goes on. He is possessed:
"Father, mother, child, child."
A family with one child.
Gens yells at the father:
"Where's your other child?"
"I haven't got another child–"
Gens doesn't let him finish:
"You moron! Here's your other son!"
Gens grabs the child who was standing on the side, the one who had been torn from his family. Gens pushes him into the one-child family, and shouts:
"Keep an eye on him, you idiot! Next time you'll lose him for good!"
The child joins the new family. He has been saved.

Light on the bridge. A line of children climb up the bridge followed by the German soldiers. The sound of an engine being started and of a lorry driving away.

KRUK
219 other children were sent to their death at Ponar.

Exit KRUK. GENS is left alone on the bridge.

Scene Twelve

UMA is sitting in a dark corner on the stage. GENS comes staggering in total disarray from the site of the Selection. He goes to the place where the whole drama started. He pulls out his gun and puts the barrel to his head.

UMA
Jacob! Haven't enough Jews been killed already? Do you have to kill another one?

GENS bursts in laughter.

GENS
After all I did, I have no right to live.

UMA
After all you did, you have no right to kill yourself.

GENS
I can kill myself whenever I want.

UMA
Like Miss Julie or Hedda Gabler?

GENS
I don't understand you.

UMA
Your life doesn't belong just to you anymore. It is connected to the life of 16 thousand other people.

GENS
There's no future in the ghetto.

UMA
Who cares a damn about the future? Be a Man. As long as you can keep saving lives, you are condemned to live. Throw away that silly gun.

GENS
　No.

UMA puts her head next to GENS's temple. He struggles to push her away, but she is holding on to him with all her strength.

UMA
　Blow out our brains.

GENS breaks down. He drops the gun.

GENS
　Selection.

UMA
　There's no other choice.

GENS
　The old, the sick, the weak, the hopeless (*He snaps a finger.*)

UMA
　The young, the fit, the strong must survive. Selection.

GENS
　There is no moral justification to that.

UMA
　How can you be moral when you're forced to choose between evil and evil?

GENS
　They exterminate us like rats,

UMA
　Then we must fight back like rats.

GENS
　They'll lose the war like rats, and we will win. Like rats.

UMA
　Like rats.

　　Fadeout.

Act Two

— • —

Prologue

KRUK listens to Radio Moscow announcing the German defeat in Stalingrad:

"This is Moscow Calling.

This is our English program, and here are the news read by Liudmilla Baratova.

Glorious victory in Stalingrad.

Today, January 31st 1943, the commander of the German 6th Army, Field Marshall Friedrich von Paulus, surrendered to the Red Army forces. The battle of Stalingrad, which lasted more than four months, is over.

The remaining 91000 German troops lead by 24 German Generals turned themselves over to the Soviet Army. The victorious Red Army recovered 250,000 German corpses in and around Stalingrad. The total losses of the Nazis and their allies in the battle of Stalingrad rise above 800,000 dead.

Radio Berlin announces that all cafes, restaurants, theatres and cinema houses throughout the German territory will be closed for three days to mark their fatal defeat in Stalingrad.

This is the beginning of their end."

KRUK switches off the radio and disappears in the underground.

All members of the actors' company enter under heavy German guard. They form a human chain and start unloading a carload of German blood-stained uniforms, erecting a new mound of clothes. As they work, they sing song No. seven: "Yiddishe Brigaadess."

Forget the sun – forget the flowers
forget the rain that's going to fall.
This golden time – it isn't ours
We have the right to work, that's all.

We do not ask for your compassion
A man is proud to be a slave
But all the songs we sing against you
will carry on beyond the grave.

Yiddishe Brigade (*pronounce: brigaaday*) }
Working ever harder }
Our wages are blood and sweat }
But we are not defeated yet } *repeat twice*

We live like beasts inside the ghetto
You only lead us out to death
But we will sing and we will curse you
Until we draw our final breath

Yiddishe Brigade
Working ever harder
Our wages are blood and sweat
But we are not defeated yet

Yiddishe Brigade
Working ever harder
We're marching hand in hand
Until we reach the promised land

> *They finish working and exit singing escorted by the German soldiers. SHLOIME sneaks out of the group. He waits for all to exit. He gives a musical sign with his saxophone. A trap door opens, and a coffin emerges, accompanied by LIUBA, ELIA, YANKL and GEIVISH. They give SHLOIME a bottle, they lift the coffin and start to walk off as GENS appears on the bridge.*

Scene Thirteen

> *GENS flashes his torch-light on them.*

GENS
Liuba Grodzenski?

LIUBA
Hello, chief! (*to her friends*) He wants to talk to me. I'll be back in a minute.

> *The three boys try to sneak out with the coffin. GENS stops them.*

GENS
Hey! Why such a hurry? What's that?

LIUBA
Oh, that's nothing. Someone died. We took him out to bury him. We're just returning the coffin.

GENS
Through the sewers, I see. You forgot there's a gate?

GEIVISH
I told you to go through the gate! You wouldn't listen. "It's shorter this way!"

GENS
Alright, what have you got this time? Hungarian salami? Rice? Sugar?

YANKL
Nothing but medicine, for the hospital.

GENS tries to lift the coffin. It won't move an inch.

LIUBA
And the ghost of the dead, chief. So help me God.

GENS
A pretty heavy ghost.

GEIVISH
He must have been a great sinner.

GENS
Stop joking. What is it?

YANKL
You want to know the truth? We don't know.

GENS
You don't know?

YANKL
We were asked to pick it up in the cemetery and leave it in the morgue, at the underground hospital. That's all we know.

GENS
Is it arms for the underground?

YANKL
(to GEIVISH) What d'you say boys, is it "arms for the underground?"

GEIVISH
I don't think so, but Gens knows better than us.

LIUBA
We're just errand-boys,
lugging things back and forth.
We never ask what's inside.
You should know it better than anyone.
How many times have you used us that way?

GENS
Would you mind opening it.

YANKL
We're not supposed to.

LIUBA
We're not allowed to.

GENS
I could order you to do it.

ELIA
(*under his breath*) Order us.

GEIVISH
(*holding back his brother*) Elia, keep cool.

GENS
What is it?

YANKL
Nothing. Everything's under control, chief.

LIUBA
It's just against our principles.

GENS
Very well then, tomorrow morning, in my office. You'll donate five thousand rubles to our school for young delinquents. So much for your principles.

LIUBA
Five?! Even three'd be robbery!

GENS
(*grabs LIUBA by the arm*) Come with me.

YANKL
Hey!

GENS
Don't move, Yankl.... You want your girl? Bring the money. Next time you won't try to fool around with Jacob Gens.

GENS exits with LIUBA. YANKL starts to follow them. GEIVISH stops him.

GEIVISH
Where are you going?

YANKL
If she goes to prison she's on the waiting list for Ponar.

GEIVISH
Calm down. Gens won't do it. He likes Liuba too much. He'll just squeeze her tits.

YANKL
Shut your trap! *(They wrestle jokingly.)* So how do we get the fucking five thousand?

GEIVISH
We open the coffin, and auction the goods!

> *GEIVISH jumps on the coffin, and starts an auction-sale song. GENS stops to look back. LIUBA seizes the occasion and runs away to join her comrades. GENS follows. They perform the song for him: Song No. Eight: Isrulik.*

Your life is worth a farthing,
Your work's worth even less
So business gets tougher every day.
No wonder we're all starving,
No wonder life's a mess.
You've got to find a way to make it pay.

I'm Isrulik - the orphan of the ghetto,   }
I'm Isrulik - the boy the world forgot.   }
Of all my family there's me remaining,   }
I'm not complaining, I'm happy with my lot. } *refrain*

I'll flog you golden earings,
I'll flog you cigarettes,
Or saccharin or bread or currant jam,
If anyone starts jeering
If anyone forgets,
I'll make sure they remember who I am.

Refrain.

My mother I've forgotten,
I wouldn't know her face.
They took away my parents long ago.
I'm stuck here in this rotten
And God forsaken place
It's better if you stick with what you know...

I'm Isrulik and if you watch me closely
You might see me try to wipe my eye

We all have sorrows – so why regret them
You'd best forget them,
They'll only make you cry...

GENS
All right, only four thousand.

GENS grabs LIUBA and walks away with her.

YANKL
Hey! Gens! That's not fair!...

GERSTEIN appears behind them, dressed up and disguised as the HASSID. He gets on the coffin, dancing and singing "Isrulik."

GEIVISH
Look who's there!

GERSTEIN
Hello, guys!

GEIVISH
Are you from Weiskopf?

GERSTEIN
I can read the future in your palm.

GEIVISH
Get lost!

GERSTEIN
Oh no, this can't be true! A fatal transformation is coming your way this week!

YANKL
How d'you know? You didn't even look at my palm.

GERSTEIN
I can read ears as well, but the palm is more articulate.

GEIVISH
Oh, cut the shit.

ELIA
Wait. Read my palm.

GERSTEIN
Oh, look at this! Look! A "G" becomes an "L!..."

ELIA
Go on.

GERSTEIN
"G?" – Ge.... Gens! "L?" – "L..." Liuba! Liberty! In three minutes Liuba may be Liberated from Gens and regain her freedom.

YANKL
We're listening.

GERSTEIN
(pointing to the coffin) Three thousand.

YANKL
We need five.

GERSTEIN
You'll get the other two.

YANKL
How?

GERSTEIN
That's your problem. I give three. No more.

ELIA
Okay, make it three.

GERSTEIN
(draws a wad of bills and counts into ELIA's palm) One, two, three–

ELIA
(draws a knife and stabs GERSTEIN, counting the blows) Four, five, six seven, eight, nine, ten. *(GERSTEIN throws up his arms, and dozens of bills go flying in the air and fall on the ground as he collapses.)*

GEIVISH
(to ELIA) You idiot!

YANKL
(collecting the bills from the ground) Take out the goods. Put him in the coffin.

> *They lift the lid. A figure wrapped in shrouds sits up. They yell with fear and run away. The dead man stands up and throws away the shrouds. It is KITTEL wearing an elegant suit. He puts on glasses, picks out of the coffin a black briefcase, and looks like the perfect stereotype of a scholar. As a matter of fact, he incarnates and plays the personality of Dr. PAUL, whom he despises.*

216 / Joshua Sobol

Scene Fourteen

KRUK

For the second time this month a murder has been committed in the ghetto during an armed hold-up. My sources indicate that both crimes are related to the black market that prospers in the ghetto. The wealthy provide the demand, and our underworld supplies them with all imaginable luxuries.

"PAUL" enters into KRUK's territory and addresses him.

PAUL

Professor Kruk? I'm honoured, Dr. Paul. *(He offers KRUK a visit card.)* Dr. Alfred Rosenberg's Institute for Judaic Studies Without Jews, the JSWJ. I'm sure Herr Professor has heard of our activities?

KRUK

Not first-hand.

PAUL

Well then, the JSWJ sends scientists to selected ghettos to collect items of outstanding cultural interest and transport them to our Institute in Frankfurt. The curators of the Institute Museum will organize a permanent exhibition of Judaic Relics for the scientific benefit of the future generations. Our goal is to accomplish this mission before the ethnic purification of Europe leaves us, alas, with no bearers of your rich heritage. I've heard about you, Professor, so allow me to offer you my complete work. *(He opens his briefcase and offers Kruk a book.)* I look forward to enjoying the cultural and spiritual ties that is befitting of two scholars like ourselves.

KRUK

"Studies of the Jerusalem Talmud..."

PAUL

Ever since I finished my studies at the Hebrew University in Jerusalem, I miss that town. Shall we proceed in German, or would you prefer to converse in Hebrew or Yiddish?

KRUK

How did errr–

PAUL

How did a goy like me pick up Yiddish? Or don't I look a goy to you? Even in Jerusalem they took me for a Jew. At least, the Arabs did. In the Arab Revolt of 1936 I fell into the hands of Arab hooligans. They almost killed me as a Jew, imagine that! At the last moment I was rescued by Jewish Underground Fighters – remarkable fellows! It happened near the Wailing Wall. You know Jerusalem.

KRUK
No, I've never been to Palestine.

PAUL
Come on, Professor!

KRUK
I'm not a Zionist.

PAUL
But Professor—

KRUK
I'm not a professor either. You may call me by my name.

PAUL
Comrade Kruk?... Does that feel better?

KRUK
You can drop the "*comrade.*"

PAUL
Are you ashamed of the communist episode in your past?

KRUK
No more than you'll be ashamed one day of the fascist episode in the present. At the time I believed that Socialism would mean the end of wars between races, nations, ethnic groups; the end of persecutions of all minorities, including us, Jews.

PAUL
And then came Stalin with his terror and woke you up from your sweet dream.

KRUK
I didn't wait for Stalin to wake me up. My Jewish comrades made me quit the party. I couldn't bear their contempt for our language, their hatred for their own culture. I couldn't understand it until you came along. You Germans, you made it all clear to me.

PAUL
This is something you'll have to explain.

KRUK
Jacob Gens, a Jew, runs the ghetto for you. Salek Dessler, a Jew, collaborates with the Gestapo. Moishe Levas, a Jew, guards the ghetto gates better than a German Shepherd dog, and ruthlessly beats up poor Jewish women trying to smuggle in bread for their children. Our police officers fraternize with yours.

They have a lot of fun arranging joint drinking parties and sharing Jewish whores in orgies organized by our Jewish police.

PAUL

It only proves that you Jews lack integrity and dignity. What has that got to do with us Germans?

KRUK

You subject us to unending cruelty and injustice, and you ask what it's got to do with you? Oppression, Dr. Paul, breeds subversion. Once you become subversive, you don't give a damn about your integrity, or your dignity. All you want to do is annihilate the world through your own self destruction. Any fascist must know in his heart, Dr. Paul, that there's no hatred of the other without self hatred, just as there's no self hatred without hatred of the other.

PAUL

And in spite of all this you chose to stay in Europe, where you have been the subject of hatred and oppression for generations? In spite of all this you never thought of becoming a zionist and immigrating to Palestine?

KRUK

Dr. Paul, you almost got killed in Palestine because some Arabs mistook you for a Jew. Are you advising me to trade one hatred for another? Is there really no chance that you'll recover one day from your evil?

PAUL

You remind me of that Hassidic legend about the king who was so angry with his son, that he threw him out of the palace. After a while he regretted his fury. He sent a messenger to find his son and ask him what three wishes he had. The messenger found the son barely alive in a gutter, and asked him: if the king promised to fulfill three of your wishes, what wishes would you make? The prince replied:

KRUK

Bread, clothes and a roof over my head.

PAUL

My son is lost, said the King, he has forgotten that he's a prince. If he remembered who he was–

KRUK

He'd ask to return to the palace. I know the legend.

PAUL

In Palestine you wouldn't have to go begging for sympathy and a few rights that others will kindly grant you. You wouldn't have to wait till doomsday for the ultimate victory of good over evil. In your own palace you'd demand your rights with the might of your hand, the way the rest of us do.

KRUK
Dr. Paul, are you trying to convert me to Zionism? What are you aiming at?

PAUL
You said you loathed the way Gens runs the ghetto, using people like Dessler and Levas.

KRUK
Gens does what he can under the circumstances you created.

PAUL
Don't defend them. They try too hard to imitate us. It's disgusting to see such a repulsive caricature of ourselves. But you are different. You manage to keep both your integrity and your dignity. We're ready to kick out Gens with his grotesque entourage and put you in his place. You'll choose your people, and run the ghetto your own way.

KRUK
Thank you, but I'm happy with my job in the library.

PAUL
It's not a job we're offering, it's power.

KRUK
You know the prince in your story wasn't lost at all. On the contrary. He understood better than your king what's essential and what corrupts. I'm not interested in power.

PAUL
What a shame. You abandon the future of your race to people like Gens. You're turning down an opportunity to practice self-rule and to learn how to build a homeland.

KRUK
My homeland is my culture. Betray your culture, and you're in exile in your own home. It's only one step from humanism to nationalism. One more to bestiality. I'll stay what I am.

PAUL snaps his finger. TIMANN and ARNTGEN appear with their machine guns cocked.

PAUL
Take the coffin. We'll need it.

KRUK turns around and lifts his hands, ready to be shot in his back. PAUL approaches him from behind and slips a folded paper between KRUK's fingers.

Here's a list of Hebrew books we need for the Frankfurt Institute. Find them for us. Now we'll go to the next show: "The Jews learning to use Power." Follow me!

They exit in a procession: PAUL leads, KRUK follows, and the two soldiers carrying the coffin follow them.

Scene Fifteen

Enter DESSLER.

DESSLER
Actors, take your places. line up over there.

Actors enter and stand stage right. LIUBA enters leaning on her friends, IRINA and HELENA. Her eyes are red from crying.

Policemen! bring in the accused.

STARK, a ghetto policeman, enters leading GEIVISH, LEVAS leads ELIA and NATHAN leads YANKL.

LIUBA
Yankl!...

IRINA
Courage, Liuba. Calm down.

DESSLER
(*to EVA*) You! Over there. (*EVA steps out of the line and goes to DESSLER.*) His Honour, Chief of the police! (*GENS enters. DESSLER introduces EVA.*) The judge.

GENS gives a document to EVA.

GENS
Read it.

EVA
On April 4, 1943, the Jewish court of the Vilna Ghetto heard the case of Yankl Polikanski and the brothers Yitzhak and Elia Geivish. On the night of June the third they stabbed to death the ghetto inhabitant Yossef Gerstein. They were found guilty of murder of the first degree, and sentenced to be hanged by the neck.

GENS
Listen, friends, we were seventy-five thousand Jews in Vilna. Now we are sixteen thousand.

EVA
I'm no judge. *(She drops the document.)*

GENS
Eva! It is appalling to give the order to execute three of our youngsters, but–

EVA
I'm no judge. I'm no judge.

GENS
Eva, control yourself. It's appalling, but we'll do it.

EVA
I'm an actress. I'm not a judge!

GENS
Calm down! *(He leads her back to the actors.)* Listen people, after the German defeat of Stalingrad the final victory over the Nazis is only a question of time. We have to do all we can to make sure that as many Jews as possible will survive to see that glorious day.

Enter ARNTGEN and TIMANN carrying the coffin. They are followed by KRUK and KITTEL. They come down from the bridge and put the coffin on the floor. KITTEL stays on the bridge. All Jewish policemen take off their hats.

KITTEL
Go on.

GENS
It is the duty of our police to maintain law and order in the ghetto. Today we are executing three Jewish robbers who murdered an innocent Jew. The Jewish police will carry out the sentence. Begin.

The policemen lead the condemned men to the wing. Their shadows are seen on the backwall, as they climb up a scaffold. DESSLER gives a signal and the hanging takes place. It is all seen in shadow. One of the ropes breaks and Yankl comes running out with a noose around his neck.

YANKL
Liuba!

LIUBA
Yankl...

She runs out of the line of actors. They embrace. KITTEL makes the sign of thumbs down. LEVAS and DESSLER separate the couple with the help of the two soldiers. The policemen carry YANKL back to the scaffold. We see the silhouette of his hanging. IRINA and HELENA carry LIUBA out.

KITTEL
On this occasion of the exercise of Jewish police power, I proclaim that The Jewish Council, which has shown no talent in ruling the ghetto, is hereby dissolved. In its place I appoint as sole ruler of the ghetto Mr. Jacob Gens. *(All applaud. To GENS.)* You will be assisted by the new chief of the police, Mr. Dessler. *(DESSLER alone applauds.)*

GENS
I'll do all in my power to serve my people to the best of my ability. We will celebrate this occasion with a banquet hosted by the new administration.

KITTEL
Thanks for inviting me. I look forward to some good entertainment, which we all need very badly these days.

GENS
Our actors will prepare a special program.

KITTEL
And I can't wait to see your unforgettable singer who still owes me an old debt. *(to HAYYAH)* Will you settle it this time?
As an homage to your talent I will grant a one-day-only permit to bring flowers into the ghetto. *(He exits.)*

Scene Sixteen

WEISKOPF, assisted by EVA and SARRAH, is changing from his work clothes into a tuxedo. He gives orders to IRINA and HELENA who come running in with baskets full with red and white carnations, which they strew on the floor. The other DANCERS change at the back stage into fancy night dresses, helping one another to do the make-up.

WEISKOPF
Flowers. More flowers.
I want the place covered with flowers.

YANOSH enters pushing a wheelbarrow full of roasted chickens.

No, that's for the cold meat buffet. The chickens go over there, next to the gravy pot. Go get the barrel of beer! And the bottles!

YANOSH puts down the wheelbarrow and runs away to bring barrel.

Where's the Gefilte Fish?

He becomes hysterical.

The Gefilte fish! Who's got the Gefilte Fish?

LIUBA
(enters with a bucket of Gefilte fish) You want me to bring them in already?

WEISKOPF
Of course, you nitwit!
What are you waiting for, the Messiah?

> *Enter JUDITH with bottles of schnapps and YANOSH pushing barrel of beer on a wheelbarrow.*

Put the beer over there. Bottles of schnapps over here. No, no!
Spread them around. All over the place.

JUDITH
Maybe we should save a few.

WEISKOPF
No! I said open them all.

JUDITH
You could get a battalion of Kosaks drunk to death on such a quantity!

WEISKOPF
I wish they'd drink themselves to death!
We'll send the leftovers to the kitchen for the poor.
We'll show those Aryan swine what a real Jewish feast is like.

JUDITH
But it's such a waste!

WEISKOPF
This woman's going to kill me.
Don't save my money. I'm going to clinch a deal tonight.
That will make us a hundred times more than we could ever spend.

> *The MUSICIANS enter.*

Ah, the orchestra. Over here. Near the piano.
Haikin! Make sure they tune up. No flat notes tonight.

> *They tune their instruments.*

Good! That's good music. Where's the stage?

> *Enter SRULIK with LINA.*

SRULIK
You're standing on it, Weiskopf.

WEISKOPF
What? You call this a stage?
Where's the decorations?

> SRULIK snaps a finger, and the cyclorama comes down. It gets a pink light.

Oh! Delicious! Add more colour! Bring more flowers!
I want their eyes to pop out of their sockets and fly into their open mouths.

> GENS enters dressed elegantly. He is followed by DESSLER and six Jewish policemen: LEVAS, NATHAN, STARK and YANKL, ELIA and GEIVISH who appear now as the policemen AVERBUCH, DREZIN and MUSHKAT.

GENS
Listen all of you. This party is not for fun.
We need permission to open a new factory.
So keep the Germans happy. Smile.
Don't make faces like it's the end of the world.
When we get them drunk, we'll ask for the permits.
With some luck, they'll sign the papers tonight.
More jobs will save more lives.
The Russians are only two hundred miles away.

> GENS turns to the policemen.

Treat our actresses like ladies.
Control yourselves and set a good example for the Germans.

> GENS exits.

WEISKOPF
Display the meat.
I want them to choke on it.
Put the rice over there.
Let them eat til they're so constipated that their bowels burst out their assholes and strangle them.

> The actresses, now dressed and made up, perform a mock fashion show.

Ooh la la!

> WEISKOPF puts his hand on GENIA's ass and she slaps him.

Hey, hey. Don't forget why we brought you here.
No need to be shy.
If you get dirty, we can wash it off in the laundry.

> The girls take their places. The Jewish police take their positions. GENS enters and looks around. He gives a sign to the orchestra. They play a

fanfare. KITTEL appears on the bridge accompanied by a film crew: ARNTGEN lighting, and TIMANN as cameraman. They come down from the bridge, and EVA serves a first toast.

KITTEL
Lehayim!

HAYYAH enters in an evening dress. The orchestra starts playing and HAYYAH sings "FRILING."

HAYYAH
I walk through the ghetto alone and forsaken,
There's no-one to care for me now.
And how can you live when your love has been taken,
Will somebody please show me how?
I know that it's springtime, and birdsong, and sunshine,
All nature seems happy and free,
But locked in the ghetto I stand like a beggar,
I beg for some sunshine for me.

DESSLER gets a permission from KITTEL, and picks out LIUBA for a dance. Other policemen follow his example. ARNTGEN and TIMANN are filming the event. HAYYAH sings the refrain reacting to what's taking place around her.

Springtime, what good is springtime,
What good is sunshine, when he is away?
Springtime, you shine upon my sorrow, but still tomorrow
Is as bleak as today.

GENS whispers in WEISKOPF's ear:

GENS
Now's the moment, Weiskopf.
Go talk to him.

WEISKOPF takes a bottle of cognac and a glass and walks over to KITTEL. On his way he whispers to JUDITH:

WEISKOPF
Keep feeding those swine.

To EVA, who serves KITTEL drinks.

Get him drunk, and he'll buy our deal.

Finally WEISKOPF gets to KITTEL:

Herr Kittel...

KITTEL pushes him away, indicating that he wants silence. He is obviously concentrating on HAYYAH's singing.

WEISKOPF establishes eye contact with GENS, and signals to him that there are difficulties with KITTEL. GENS answers with a sign telling him to be patient. HAYYAH goes on with the song "FRILING."

HAYYAH
The house that we lived in is now barricaded,
The windows are broken and bare.
The sun is so fierce that the flowers have faded,
They wilt in the wintery air.
Each morning, each evening I have to walk past it,
Hiding my eyes from the sight
The place where you loved me the place where you kissed me
The place where you held me so tight.

Refrain.

The German cameraman focuses on DESSLER who is dancing with LIUBA. He shoots a few feet, then he orders DESSLER:

TIMANN
Hey, Dessler, show us some meat. Drop your pants.

DESSLER is shocked, but LIUBA smiles at TIMANN and speaks to DESSLER loudly enough for everyone to overhear:

LIUBA
What's wrong Dessler? Still got some shame in your soul? Let's get rid of it!

She opens the buttons of DESSLER's trousers. The German cameraman encourages her:

TIMMAN
Good, girl. Carry on.

LIUBA grins at the camera, imitating and overacting a prostitute. She strips DESSLER of the rest of his clothes. DESSLER turns to look around, and realizes that all his policemen are staring at him. He roars at them:

DESSLER
Drop your trousers, all of you, at once!

All Jewish policemen undress, the cameraman is red with enthusiasm.

TIMMAN
Excellent! Now take the girls!

Yes, that's good. Excellent.
Come on now, move it!

> *Some of the policemen and the girls feign making love. One policeman drags a girl to a corner and indulges laboriously in the real thing, while his female partner is hungrily devouring half a roasted chicken, not caring for what is being done to her body.*
> *HAYA is aware of all that activity going on around her, as she goes on singing "FRILING." The filthier the atmosphere, the purer her singing.*

HAYYAH
How thoughtful how kind of the heavenly powers
To send spring so early this year.
Why thank you for coming, I see you brought flowers.

> *KITTEL sends her flying kisses. He drinks one glass after the other. ROZIN, who stands behind him, takes care of topping up his glass.*

You want me to welcome you here?
They say that the ghetto is golden and glowing
But sunlight and tears make me blind.
You see, my beloved, how soon they start flowing
I can't get you out of my mind.

> *Refrain.*

> *SRULIK is sitting at the right stage corner with LINA. They scan the scene of the orgy from there. SRULIK is taking swigs from a bottle of vodka. LINA observes all the goings-on with her eyes wide open, her expression being the epitome of curiosity and amazement at the extraordinary variety of human behaviour. UMA, standing near the cold meat buffet eating. Her face is expressionless.*
> *HAYA finishes singing "FRILING." KITTEL applauds and approaches her.*

KITTEL
Close your eyes. (*He pulls out of his pocket a string of pearls and puts it on her neck.*) Open. They're only pearls, but if you knew where they came from... (*HAYA makes a gesture as if she were about to tear off the necklace. KITTEL stops her:*) Now, now. You start with shoes, you end up with pearls. Remember you still owe me 25 grams, sorry, 20, considering that song.

> *He embraces her from behind and starts to move her in a grotesque tango as he sings:*

Spring time, what good is spring time...

> *SRULIK takes a swig of the vodka, and attacks with LINA:*

LINA
　Five grams of beans, that's all we're worth now. Start with shoes, you wind up with booze!

KITTEL
　Our brave old friends!

LINA
　Who's brave? It's only Jewish chutzpah.

KITTEL
　I adore Jewish chutzpah. Give me more.

LINA
　You look awful.

KITTEL
　How kind of you to be concerned.

LINA
　A series of head baths would take care of everything.

KITTEL
　A series of head baths? What's that?

LINA
　Put your head in the water three times, and take it out twice.

　　KITTEL laughs. All laugh. He stops, all stop.

KITTEL
　I bet you won't dare show more chutzpah than that.

LINA
　How much?

SRULIK
　That's enough.

LINA
　He wants to gamble. My head for a thousand marks.

KITTEL
　I've only got two hundred.

　　WEISKOPF comes offering his purse:

WEISKOPF
　Help yourself, Herr Kittel.

KITTEL
Got a pen? I'll sign an I.O.U.

LINA
Who needs an I.O.U.? Everyone knows how honest the Germans are. You took Stalingrad, you gave it back. You took Leningrad you gave it back. You'll give him back his money, penny for penny.

> KITTEL is stunned. All are. KITTEL gives SRULIK the bills.

SRULIK
No, thank you...

LINA
Take it, idiot. It's no crime to steal from a thief.

KITTEL
Enough!

> KITTEL grabs LINA. He is about to finish her off. SRULIK lifts a bottle to strike KITTEL. KITTEL registers SRULIK'S gesture. HAYYAH reacts instantaneously. She grabs KITTEL by the arm, and with the sweetest expression on her face starts to sing for him "ICH BIN DIE FESCHE LOLA."
>
> KITTEL is seduced by the song, and his mood shifts from murderous fury to sexual excitement. as he is following HAYYAH, who tries to lead him away from LINA who is lying motionless on the floor, and SRULIK who is leaning over her, KITTEL has a short eye-to-eye exchange with SRULIK.
>
> SRULIK lifts LINA under her armpits and drags her away.
>
> HAYYAH climbs on a chair and goes on singing "LOLA." Her singing turns on the camera team. They are attracted to HAYYAH like flies to honey. As they try to touch her, KITTEL commands:

Hands off. She's mine.

> KITTEL beckons to SRULIK, who is reviving LINA, to come over. SRULIK walks over to KITTEL and HAYYAH. KITTEL orders him with a gesture to stay there. SRULIK remains standing motionless, expecting the worst yet to come.
>
> The frustrated German soldiers focus on REIKA, who is dancing with YANOSH. They interrupt the dancing couple, grab REIKA and drag her away. The musicians see what's happening, but go on playing.
>
> GENS takes WEISKOPF aside.

GENS
It's now or never.

> WEISKOPF gulps down his cognac, and approaches KITTEL, who is involved with HAYYAH, who goes on singing "LOLA." KITTEL is fondling her, and SRULIK is forced to watch it.
>
> WEISKOPF offers KITTEL a glass of cognac, and as he starts his dialogue with KITTEL he puts away unawares the tray with the bottle. SRULIK gets hold of the bottle.

WEISKOPF
Herr Kittel, finest French cognac,

KITTEL
Thank you, Weiskopf.

> KITTEL gets a glimpse of SRULIK, he winks at him and lifts his glass. SRULIK, surprised and undecided, lifts the bottle. They drink.

WEISKOPF
Have you had an opportunity to examine the proposal?

KITTEL
Of course, Weiskopf, the Wehrmacht will offer you a five-year contract.

WEISKOPF
Can I announce it?

KITTEL
Go ahead. (*He returns to WEISKOPF the empty glass.*) I'll send you to Berlin, to meet Goering. You'll adore each other.

> WEISKOPF hurries away to share the news with everyone. He jumps on the piano.
>
> At that moment KITTEL takes HAYYAH down from the chair, and embraces and kisses her on the lips. SRULIK puts the bottle of cognac to his mouth and starts gulping down the liquid as if it were water, trying to drink to his death. The orchestra stops playing. There is dead silence. All focus on the kissing couple.
>
> WEISKOPF is holding his speech, standing on the piano. All gather around him to listen.

WEISKOPF
I've got wonderful news! I'm signing a five-year contract with the Wehrmacht. (*The soldiers on the camera team are raping REIKA in some dark corner of the theatre. She is screaming for help.*) I'm going to Berlin to

negotiate it with Goering. We'll receive four hundred wagon-loads of uniforms to be mended. We'll manufacture uniforms, fatigues, combat boots. (REIKA screams.)
That's it. Fill up your glasses. Lehayim!

ALL
Lehayim!

> REIKA appears. She is naked and bleeding. The people stop singing. LEAH takes off her own dress and covers REIKA's nakedness.
> UMA starts banging with her fist on the coffin, singing the song "Mir lebn Eibik."

UMA
We'll live forever – year after year
We'll live forever – for we are here
And if they try to drag our names through the mud,
We will rewrite them in our enemy's blood.
We'll live forever – beyond the flames
And you will never forget our names,
So we will fight and we will strive,
To carry on, to stay alive,
We'll live forever, we will survive.

> KITTEL, who is already quite drunk, sticks a cigar into UMA's mouth, shutting her up. Then he turns to GENS:

KITTEL
Gens, you're not happy.

GENS
I am.

> KITTEL embraces him and starts singing:

KITTEL
"I want to be happy
But I can't be happy
Till you're happy too."

GENS
I'll try.

KITTEL
I'll help you.

> He gets hold of UMA, he leans on her and staggers on his drunken legs climbing up a chair, where he makes an announcement:

The ghetto of Oshmany is hereby annexed to the Vilna Ghetto. There's only one problem. There are four thousand Jews in Oshmany. That's two thousand too many. Your police, under the command of–

GENS
Dessler.

DESSLER
At your command.

KITTEL
Will go to Oshmany and carry out a selection. Dessler!!

DESSLER
At your command!

KITTEL
You're not in Oshmany yet? *(DESSLER stares at KITTEL with much confusion.)* You're still here?!

DESSLER
Policemen! Up! Attention!

The policemen stand up where they have been lying drunk after eating and having sex. Some wear underpants, some are naked. KITTEL laughs his head off.

DESSLER
You've got two minutes to get dressed and ready for action!

KITTEL starts undressing UMA. UMA looks at GENS and GENS gives her a sign beseeching her to endure, as he starts bargaining with KITTEL:

GENS
Two thousand out of four couldn't all be unproductive.

KITTEL
(as he is abusing UMA) How many then?

GENS sips impassively from his vodka, and carries on:

GENS
Barely a thousand.

KITTEL
Let it be a thousand.

GENS
If we find out that there are only 800 unproductive?

KITTEL
You Jews, you'd attach a dynamo to the wheelchair of an eighty-year-old crone and claim she's productive, generating power on her way to the toilet.

GENS
You're right: age is an absolute criterion. So anyone over eighty–

KITTEL
Seventy.

GENS
Call it a deal.

KITTEL
But no less than 700 people.

GENS
Right, no more than 700, no less than five.

KITTEL
What's a hundred more or less between good friends. 600, and that's it.

KITTEL shakes GENS's hand. He lets go of UMA. GENS embraces her tenderly. KITTEL surveys the policemen, and shouts:

Dessler!

DESSLER
Sir!

KITTEL
Eight Lithuanian militiamen will join you. You'll deliver the old people to them, and they'll take care of the rest. Is that clear?

DESSLER
Yes Sir! Completely clear, Sir!

KITTEL makes a step and falls to the ground dead drunk. TIMMAN and ARNTGEN come running. They lift him and drag him away. He is mumbling/singing:

KITTEL
"We'll live forever, year after year,
We'll live forever, for we are here…"

All remain paralyzed among the debris of the orgy.

GENS
Dessler! We have to do this hideous job, there's no choice. But for God's sake, you don't have to put on a show of zeal for those murderers.

DESSLER
You send me to do the job, and you're staying behind. Don't preach morality at me. (*He exits.*)

GENS
Scum.

The actors clean up the remains of the orgy.

Scene Seventeen

HAYYAH looks through the books that KRUK has hung in the flies of the theatre to dry. KRUK enters with his wheelbarrow. He is taking the books off the fly and loads them on the wheelbarrow.

KRUK
You haven't been around for a few days.

HAYYAH
Oh, you've noticed my absence!

KRUK
Of course I did. Can I help you?

HAYYAH
No, thank you, I'll manage.

KRUK
You haven't been sick, I hope?

HAYYAH
No, I was busy.

KRUK
Working on a new program, I suppose.

HAYYAH
Yes, you could say so.

KRUK
In that case I'd like to show you a play that I found.

HAYYAH
No, please, don't bother.

KRUK
It's my pleasure

HAYYAH
Theatre has become meaningless. Even harmful.

KRUK
I used to think so too. I was opposed to staging theatre in the ghetto. I was wrong. Our enemies do all they can to break our spirits, so we invent jokes! They forbade us to bring flowers into the ghetto, so we give one another autumn leaves instead. Come, let me show you what I found in a garbage heap. A Yiddish manuscript. A very witty parody of the Merchant Of Venice...

HAYYAH
I'm sorry, I'm really not looking for plays right now.

KRUK
Oh... forgive me my lack of sensitivity. I'm simply too eager to share my discovery with someone who might appreciate...

HAYYAH
No, it's not your fault. I'm so sorry. It's just that... I don't understand how I could allow myself to waste my existence repeating other people's trivial words and actions when my own time is running out so fast, and there are things waiting to be done...

KRUK
Oh!... I just wanted to help you, to be of some use. You see, this play is an example of spiritual resistance.

HAYYAH
"Spiritual resistance?" There's no point! No hope.... No.... I wish I could kill. I wish I could blow up the entire world. Reduce it to dust and ashes.... And myself with it. What makes you laugh?

KRUK
You do. You remind me of myself, at the age of sixteen.... I was looking in the public library for a certain scandalous, forbidden book.... A very explosive book...

HAYYAH
What book?

KRUK
Hey! (*Suddenly he understands what she is after:*) Wait a minute.... Wait a minute!... (*He reaches to a secret recess and brings out a book.*) Is that what you're looking for?

HAYYAH
It's Russian?

KRUK
It's a Red Army manual on the manufacture and use of explosives. I found it in the library of the Institute of Technology. It's the only book I've ever stolen.

HAYYAH
I can't read Russian.

KRUK
I'm sure one of your new friends can read it.

HAYYAH
Yes... I'm coming from Oshmany.

KRUK
You've been to Oshmany?

HAYYAH
Dessler invited me to go with him. He's courting me.

KRUK
You mean you were there during the selection?

HAYYAH
The selection and the rest of it. I've seen it all.

KRUK
Will you tell me–

HAYYAH
I'll tell you everything *(She lifts the book.)* when I come back.

KRUK
Wait.

> *He offers her an autumn leaf. HAYYAH kisses him and starts singing Song No. Twelve: "BIRDS ARE DREAMING IN THE TREETOPS."*

HAYYAH
Birds are dreaming in the treetops,
Stars are in the sky.
Who's the stranger by your bedside
Singing you a lullaby?
Liu-liu...

All the members of the company appear with candles to join her singing in the dark.

All our love lies cradled with you
Shielding you from pain;
For your mother, your poor mother
Won't be coming back again…

And I saw your father running
in a hail of stones
All our God-forsaken country
Echoes to his moans…

There is a whistle. They all disappear.

Scene Eighteen

KITTEL emerges from the darkness. He is dressed as Dr. Paul.

KITTEL
Where are you coming from so late.

HAYYAH
I'm working on a new performance.

KITTEL
You were good at the party.

HAYYAH
Thank you.

KITTEL
(He finds the book that she was hiding.) Russian?

HAYYAH
You read Russian?

KITTEL
Nyet. What is it? A play?

HAYYAH
No. It's a manual for building explosives.

KITTEL
(laughing) You dance and sing your way through the war.

HAYYAH
When I'm happy I laugh. When I'm sad I sing.

KITTEL

Good answer. (*He plays with the book.*) One day we'll dance and sing together.

HAYYAH

Wait till you see my new performance. You might change your mind.

KITTEL

I'll be there on opening night. (*He gives her the book.*)

HAYYAH

I hope you'll be there when I do my number. (*She runs away.*)

KITTEL

What a creature. (*He exits.*)

Scene Nineteen

KRUK

(*writing in his diary*) We received news that ghettos in the east are being liquidated. Will the Russians enter Vilna before it's too late for us? Will we live to see the end of our enemies? More than ever I cling to my diary, the Hashish of my life in the ghetto.

KITTEL enters playing PAUL.

PAUL

I've got a new job for you. Make a full inventory of all the books in the monastery libraries of Vilna.

KRUK

What's the point.

PAUL

As long as you work for me, you live.

KRUK

I'm fed up with life.

PAUL

Now? Our eastern front is collapsing. The Russians will be here in a matter of weeks.

KRUK

How many times have I heard that before?

PAUL
You're wrong. Our army is at the end of it's rope. They're sending all the officers to the Eastern front.

KRUK
So why should I hold you back with this senseless assignment? You must be dying to join your friends on the front.

PAUL
Mr. Kruk. We're both intelligent men. You'll do the inventory, and I'll supervise.

KRUK
No, sir. You've murdered my entire family. You want me to save your life?

PAUL
Mr. Kruk. Let's not get emotional. There's an armed underground in this ghetto. And you're connected to them. Be logical before you say no to me.

KRUK
An armed underground? We are isolated. Starving. Powerless. How can we fight you? No. You can kill me now. You can kill another ten thousand Jews. Nothing can change the writing on the wall.

PAUL
Which is?

KRUK
"I will send a fire which will devour palaces. Your kings shall go into captivity. Your cities will be burned. Your people dispersed, scattered over the face of the earth."

PAUL
Who will punish us. Who will scatter us.

KRUK
The civilized nations.

PAUL
The civilized nations have been persecuting you for thousands of years. Show me one nation that ever lost its country and was driven to exile for killing Jews.

KRUK
This time you won't escape punishment.

PAUL
You think the allies don't know what we're doing in the camps? Did they do anything to stop it? Did they ever launch an air raid on any of those

installations? Or on the railways leading to those "facilities?" No, Kruk. When the war is over, they'll need us, our technology. Our crimes will be soon forgotten.

KRUK
We'll see.

PAUL
Yes, we will. But first, we have to survive. Therefore, get thee to the monasteries. And when this is all over I'll be honoured to continue our scientific and spiritual collaboration.

KITTEL/PAUL leaves and KRUK tears up the list.

KRUK
No!

Scene Twenty

The actors come running to the stage. They form a choir and HAYYAH is performing a song of protest:

HAYA
We've dragged through the mud
And we're swimming in blood
Our bodies can't take any more
So stand and unite
Move into the light
You see how our people betray us.
Don't waste your despair
On weeping and prayer.
The heavens are empty
There's nobody there.
So stand and unite
Move into the light
It's time to take arms
And be counted!

All the actors of the company join in a choir, and perform the song of the partisans "ZOG NIT KEINMOL AS DU GEIST DEM LETZTEN WEG."

ALL
Never say the final journey is at hand
Never say we will not reach the promised land
Never doubt the day of reckoning is near,
There's a drumming in the land – and we are here.

KRUK steps out of the choir and addresses the audience, with the choir and HAYYAH performing the MAYDAY SONG in the background:

KRUK
Comrades, our brothers in the Warsaw Ghetto have taken up arms and are inflicting heavy losses on the German army. We will do the same very soon. Long live the revolt of the Jewish Warsaw Ghetto!

ALL
From the land of palm-trees to the land of snow
We are marching we are singing as we go
And each and every drop of Jewish blood to fall
Will be tribute to the courage of us all.
Our tomorrows will be bathed in Golden light
And our enemies will vanish with the night,
    And we know that perfect morning won't be long
When every generation sings this song
It's a song that's from the fields and from the flood,
It's a song that's tipped in steel and dipped in blood.
It's a song that's of our people and our land,
It's a song that has a sickle in its hand.

Suddenly the actors fall to the ground one by one screaming with pain. Behind them appear Jewish policemen brandishing clubs. They are commanded by DESSLER. They are beating up the actors who are rolling on the stage under the shower of blows. GENS appears. The actors stand up and assemble at the corner of the stage standing in tight formation – they are ready to retaliate and hold the police at a distance, at the other side of the stage. The tension is unbearable. GENS steps into the space between the two hostile camps.

GENS
Have you gone crazy? You want to provoke the Germans just when the Red Army is about to liberate us?

EVA
And then we'll deal with the traitors.

DESSLER
Who are the traitors?

EVA
You are one. Everything you did in Oshmany is recorded.

DESSLER
I see? What did I do in Oshmany? Tell us, if you've got the guts.

KRUK
You rounded up four hundred and six old, sick Jews, and you led them to the place of killing, and you handed them over to the Lithuanian executioners, and during that operation you emptied together with the murderers one hundred bottles of schnapps, and you returned from Oshmany with your pockets full of the jewels you robbed from the victims to give your beautiful Polish wife.

DESSLER jumps at KRUK. GENS draws his pistol. He is ready to shoot Dessler. DESSLER jumps and seeks refuge behind KRUK's back. He then sneaks and disappears behind the actors.

GENS
I take the full responsibility for Oshmany. I gave Dessler the order to do the hideous job. You think I'm a traitor. Say it. All that matters to me is to do everything I can to save more Jews from death.
I'm trying to save Jewish blood, not Jewish honour. The Germans wanted two thousand Jews. I gave them four hundred and six old and sick people. Nothing can justify it. I know. Their blood is on my hands. I could have kept my hands clean, couldn't I? I could have told the Germans: do it yourself, and they'd have taken as many as they wanted: two thousand, three thousand, four thousand.

KRUK goes away.

Go! Run away. Wash your hands clean. Down to your fingertips. Go celebrate your innocence.

Some actors leave the stage, following KRUK.

Go! Go! Save your saintly souls. If you survive, you'll say: we kept our conscience spotless clean. Immaculate.
While I, Jacob Gens, I'll come out smeared with filth, my hands dripping with blood.

More actors walk away.

But I – I will submit myself to Jewish justice. I will stand trial, and I'll say: All I did was done to save as many Jews as I could. To lead some to freedom, I had to lead others to death. I did it with my own hands. That was my choice.

More actors walk away.

For you to preserve your clean conscience, I had to plunge into the mire and and deal with the pigs. A clean conscience for Jacob Gens? I couldn't afford it.

GENS walks away.

HAYYAH addresses SRULIK:

HAYYAH
Srulik! I'm leaving the ghetto with a group of partisans. We're going through the sewers to the forest. Will you come?

LINA
It's your chance to be a hero. She'll adore you. Take me to the sewers. Quick! Flush me down the toilet!

HAYYAH grabs LINA and throws her to the ground. She shakes SRULIK:

HAYA
Do you always have to play the fool?

SRULIK
You want to go, go. We'll pay the price.

HAYA
They're going to kill us all, whether we fight or not. I choose to die fighting.

SRULIK
People have children. They can't go. What should I do?... *(Silence. He looks at Hayyah beseeching for an answer.)* I'm staying.

SRULIK and HAYYAH embrace. Then she goes away.

SRULIK
Hayyaleh! Don't leave me!

UMA, who has been watching the scene from the side, lifts LINA from the ground and parodies SRULIK's outcry:

UMA/LINA
Hayyaleh don't leave us!

SRULIK turns around. He sees UMA who is manipulating LINA.

Let all our trumpets blow!
Give them full breath!
We cannot save our life.
Let's save our death!...

Sirens blow the general alarm. The sound of approaching bombers flying over the city. Explosions.
UMA and LINA exit, and SRULIK follows them.

Scene Twenty-one

GENS and WEISKOPF enter breathless.

GENS
That's your new workshop.

WEISKOPF
That's your theatre.

GENS
To hell with the theatre. These crazy actors will get us all shot at Ponar. You can put 500 workers here.

WEISKOPF
I tell you I don't need 500 new workers. Fifty's enough.
Look, here's the plan. *(WEISKOPF hands GENS a document.)* You know Weiskopf. I figured out all the angles. Here's the output of a single worker. If I add two hours to the working day and just fifty workers, I can meet the deadline. No problem.

GENS
Very efficient, Weiskopf.

GENS tears up the plan.

WEISKOPF
What are you doing. That's my plan.

GENS
You can wipe your ass with it.

WEISKOPF
What are you talking about?

GENS
You should be glad I don't shove it down your throat. If Kittel ever saw this…

WEISKOPF
What?

GENS
You think I'm trying to save the Wermacht's money. 500 workers means another 500 families saved.

WEISKOPF
I'm running a business, not a charity.

GENS
Aren't you ashamed. You've become a millionaire in this ghetto. Open the factory tomorrow. The employment committee will send you five hundred workers.

WEISKOPF
Ha. The employment committee will send me five hundred invalids.

GENS
You're not running the Olympic games. We're talking about a shitty workshop that repairs the shitty uniforms of the shitty Wermacht. Jewish invalids are too good for this place, but if it saves their lives…

WEISKOPF
Don't you dare call my enterprise a shitty workshop. It's a flourishing empire. I built it with these two hands. It's my life. My soul. And you're not going to ruin it with your shitty philanthropy.

GENS
Start here tomorrow. That's an order.

WEISKOPF
I don't give a shit about your orders.

GENS
No?

WEISKOPF
No, there's someone above you.

GENS
Who, you?

WEISKOPF
Kittel.

GENS
If you take this to Kittel…

WEISKOPF
What will you do?

> *GENS reaches for his pistol. WEISKOPF panics. KITTEL appears.*

KITTEL
Gens. I was looking for you. What are you doing in the theatre? Preparing a new show?

GENS
> This is where Weiskopf is opening his new workshop.

KITTEL
> What's wrong with the old one.

GENS
> There's no room for five hundred more sewing machines.

KITTEL
> Five hundred sewing machines? Are you making shrouds for the rest of Europe.

GENS
> We're getting four hundred more carloads of uniforms to repair.

KITTEL
> You need another five hundred workers?

WEISKOPF
> Well, er... not exactly. I could manage with... er...

GENS
> Don't make promises you can't keep.

KITTEL
> There seems to be a slight difference of opinion.

WEISKOPF
> Estimates can vary...

KITTEL
> Weiskopf, are you hiding something from me.

WEISKOPF
> Oh, no. God forbid.

KITTEL
> I'm glad to hear it.

WEISKOPF
> Only... er...

KITTEL
> Only what? Is there or isn't there a difference of opinion.

WEISKOPF and GENS answer simultaneously:

WEISKOPF
Yes.

GENS
No.

KITTEL
That answers the question. Weiskopf, how many more workers do you need?

WEISKOPF
Approximately...

KITTEL
Precisely.

WEISKOPF
Fifty.

KITTEL
Gens, are you hiding something from me?

GENS
No. He needs five hundred workers. Not fifty.

KITTEL
Where's that plan you showed me this morning.

WEISKOPF
I gave it to Gens.

GENS
I tore it up.

KITTEL
You tore up the plan.

GENS
It wasn't a plan, Mr. Kittel. It was a masterpiece of megalomania. It was simply a bad joke.

KITTEL
Oh, Mr. Weiskopf. You wasted half my morning with a joke.

WEISKOPF
No, Mr. Kittel. Never. I swear on my wife's life. If you extend the working day by two hours and if you let me select the fifty workers. And if I'm not forced to take invalids.

KITTEL
If and if and if. That's three so far.

WEISKOPF
If you let me make my plan, and if no one interferes–

KITTEL
That's five. If you if one more if, you won't if any more ifs. If you know what I mean.

WEISKOPF
I only want to save your money. I'm sure that if I met Goerring...

KITTEL
IF!!!!!!

WEISKOPF
You promised me a meeting with Goerring.

KITTEL
Weiskopf, you have no sense of humor. I hate people without humor. They get on my nerves.

WEISKOPF
Mr. Kittel, I swear. another fifty workers...

KITTEL
Gens says it's impossible.

WEISKOPF
But Gens is the head of the ghetto.

KITTEL
You don't say.

WEISKOPF
He has his own interests.

KITTEL
You're sweating.

WEISKOPF
Sorry... I....

DESSLER enters holding a bottle of cognac and a sausage.

DESSLER
Sir, we found this in Weiskopf's apartment.

KITTEL
French cognac. Hungarian salami.

DESSLER
We also found half a sack of sugar, ten kilos of rice and five liters of oil.

WEISKOPF
Mr. Kittel, these are leftovers from the party.

KITTEL
I love people who know when to apologize.

WEISKOPF
Mr. Kittel, now I will tell you why he wants five hundred more workers.

KITTEL
Rid me of that bloodsucker. *(to GENS)*

GENS
Dessler, take care of him. *(DESSLER demolishes WEISKOPF.)* Take him to prison.

DESSLER drags WEISKOPF out.

KITTEL
Dessler! I want to see the entire company.

DESSLER
(as he is dragging WEISKOPF) Yes Sir!

KITTEL
Including Hayyah.

DESSLER
Yes Sir! *(He exits dragging WEISKOPF on the floor.)*

KITTEL
Bravo! Excellent job. You're quick learners. I'm proud of you. But people continue to run away from the ghetto.

GENS
That's impossible.

KITTEL
We intercepted a group of partisans on the way to the forest. You Jews, you don't really give a shit about one another.

GENS
We care a lot more than you do about your people.

KITTEL
Is that so? What's your most sacred principle: "One hand washes the other?"

GENS
No. All Jews vouch for one another.

KITTEL
Let's give it a try right here.

GENS
I vouch for this ghetto.

KITTEL
Let's talk seriously, Gens. You're invited to the Gestapo at four o'clock this afternoon.

GENS
Really? What's on the agenda?

KITTEL
You. An armed underground was organized in the ghetto with your consent. You allowed contacts between them and the partisans in the forests. You volunteered to organize the transports of people from the ghetto to the camps in Estonia, because you wanted us to stay out of the ghetto, to avoid an open clash between your underground and our forces. Thus you saved your partisans from annihilation, and you covered their exodus from the ghetto to the forests, where they joined the Russian forces. You deluded us deliberately.

GENS
Exactly.

KITTEL
"Exactly?" Is that all you've got to say?

GENS
Yes.

KITTEL
Why don't you just disappear.

GENS
I know you too well. You want me to run away, so you'll have an excuse to kill the last ten thousand Jews I leave behind. No thank you.

KITTEL
Do you prefer to die by your own pistol, or shall I do it for you?

GENS
  I couldn't care less. (*KITTEL draws his pistol. GENS looks him in the eyes and orders him calmly but firmly:*) Fire!

  KITTEL laughs and returns the gun to its holder.

KITTEL
  Let's see the actors first. Business before pleasure. Dessler!

DESSLER
  Sir!

KITTEL
  I want to see the all the actors.

DESSLER
  Yes, Sir!

KITTEL
  Including Hayyah.

DESSLER
  Yes, sir.

Scene Twenty-two

The curtain opens to the sound of fanfares to reveal an amazing light effect: columns of light rising from the ground create a box of light, typical of Nazi mass gatherings in the thirties.
The actors appear wearing Whermacht overcoats and helmets. They all carry Nazi armbands.
SRULIK has a Hitler moustache and hairpiece.
LINA is the only "Jew," wearing the yellow star.
SRULIK—as HITLER—addresses the "soldiers:"

HITLER
  Comrades, we are surrounded by Jews. Turn to the right... (*LINA runs to the right.*) a Jew. Turn to the left (*LINA runs to the left.*) ...another Jew. Go to the opera... (*LINA plays the different people and occupations to fit HITLER's description.*) nothing but Jews. The concert hall, the newspapers, the banks, the pimps, the doctors, the lawyers, the dentists... all Jews. So you start wondering: Is this a Jew? Is this a Jew? Is this also a Jew?

ALL
  (*pointing at one another:*) Is this a Jew? Is this a Jew? Is this also a Jew?

HITLER
  Comrades, we are asking the wrong question. What should we ask?

ALL
What should we ask?

HITLER
We should ask: is this a German?
Is this a human being?

ANITA
How can we know?

HITLER
Good question, Any suggestions?

YANOSH
Can it stand on its legs?

HITLER
Let's find out.

He lets go of LINA. she collapses in a bundle. All laugh.

ALL
Ha ha ha!

REIKA
Hath a Jew eyes?

HITLER
Does anyone see eyes?

LINA starts rolling her eyes in all directions.

ALL
No no no! We see no eyes!

RASHKA
Hath a Jew limbs?

LINA displays her arms and legs.

HITLER
Does anyone see limbs?

ALL
No no no! We see no limbs!

ETKA
Hath it senses, affections, passions?

LINA demonstrates her passions and affections.

NELLI
It doesn't look like it's got any passions.

MIRA
Is a Jew fed with the same food as we are?

GENIA
No, it eats our flesh and drinks our blood.

TOVA
If you prick it, does it bleed?

HITLER
What an intelligent question. Let's find out.

He takes a huge sword and cuts LINA's stomach. A shower of coins falls to the ground. All laugh.

HELENA
If you tickle it, does it laugh?

HITLER
Let's try. Everybody – tickle!

They "tickle" LINA with imaginary whips. She does her best to produce some laughter. It sounds like suppressed anguish.

IRINA
One more question: if you poison it, does it die?

HITLER
Bravo! That's the question. Let's see.

All produce imaginary DDT pumps, and spray LINA. Silence. LINA seems paralyzed for a moment, then she starts quivering, and twisting.

ALL
We've done it, we've done it, hurrah!

HITLER
Comrades, I proclaim the new kingdom of freedom. We are free of this blood-sucker. Our freedom will last a thousand years. Sieg-heil!

ALL
Sieg-heil! Sieg-heil! Sieg-heil!

> *HITLER starts to sing Beethoven's "ODE TO JOY". All the Nazi's join in a choir. The singing degenerates into barking. It sounds like a herd of wild dogs barking. LINA performs her dance of death to the tunes of Beethoven's Ninth Symphony.*
> *KITTEL, who has been watching the performance together with GENS, stands up and gives the actors a standing ovation.*

KITTEL
Bravo! What outstanding satire! Come, Gens, let's give them their due.

> *He whispers something in GENS's ear. GENS nods and exits.*

I myself used to perform in a satirical cabaret before the war. I can certainly savour a juicy piece of satire. But... I asked to see your entire company. I see all the animals but one: where's our wonderful Nightingale? *(dead silence)* Where's the star of your company?

> *Silence.*

Where is Hayyah? Where is she?!
Well well! You must be aware of the new order: if a person is found missing from the ghetto, his entire workings will be shot.
Satire? I'll show you satire. Faces to the wall! *(The actors throw away the coats and helmets and go to the wall.)* Machine-guns... in position... here!

> *GENS comes in pushing a cart. On the cart there is a large pot and a basket with fresh loaves of white bread.*

Load!

> *He kicks the pot.*

Ready!
Fire!

> *The people get into all kinds of twisted positions. KITTEL bursts into laughter.*

Everyone about face!

> *The actors turn around. There is an expression of horror on their faces. They discover the cart with its strange load and KITTEL roaring with laughter.*

You thought I could shoot you after your marvelous performance? No, friends: your art saved your life. You've given me such great pleasure and joy. This is to express my gratitude. Come, break bread with me.

> *KITTEL breaks a loaf, dips it in the pot and eats.*

Hmmm! Delicious blackcurrant marmalade.
Come my friends, come!

>*The actors approach the pot. The fear dissolves into joy. Some cry, others laugh. All gather round the pot and go for the bread and marmalade. GENS joins them.*
>
>*KITTEL moves away from the actors. He backs up to the edge of the stage. Two soldiers appear from the dark hall carrying three sub-machine guns. KITTEL takes one of the weapons. KITTEL and the soldiers open fire on the actors. The actors jump and run in all directions, but they are all shot on the stage.*
>
>*KITTEL walks among the bodies to make sure no one is alive.*
>*As he is starting for the exit door, SRULIK and LINA stand up behind the pot of jam. KITTEL turns around. SRULIK manages to lie down at once, but LINA remains standing. KITTEL guns her down, and she falls over the pot of jam. KITTEL walks away.*
>
>*SRULIK stands up slowly. He touches LINA. He takes her head in his hands. Her eyes are wide open. They are dead.*
>*SRULIK looks around him and sees all his dead friends lying all over the stage. The iron gate of the theatre is open, and a strange white light filters in through the gate.*
>
>*HAYYAH's voice comes from far away. She is singing the song "IN THE SKY THE STARS ALL GLISTEN."*

SRULIK
Our last show.... Our last show.... Wait...

>*The end.*

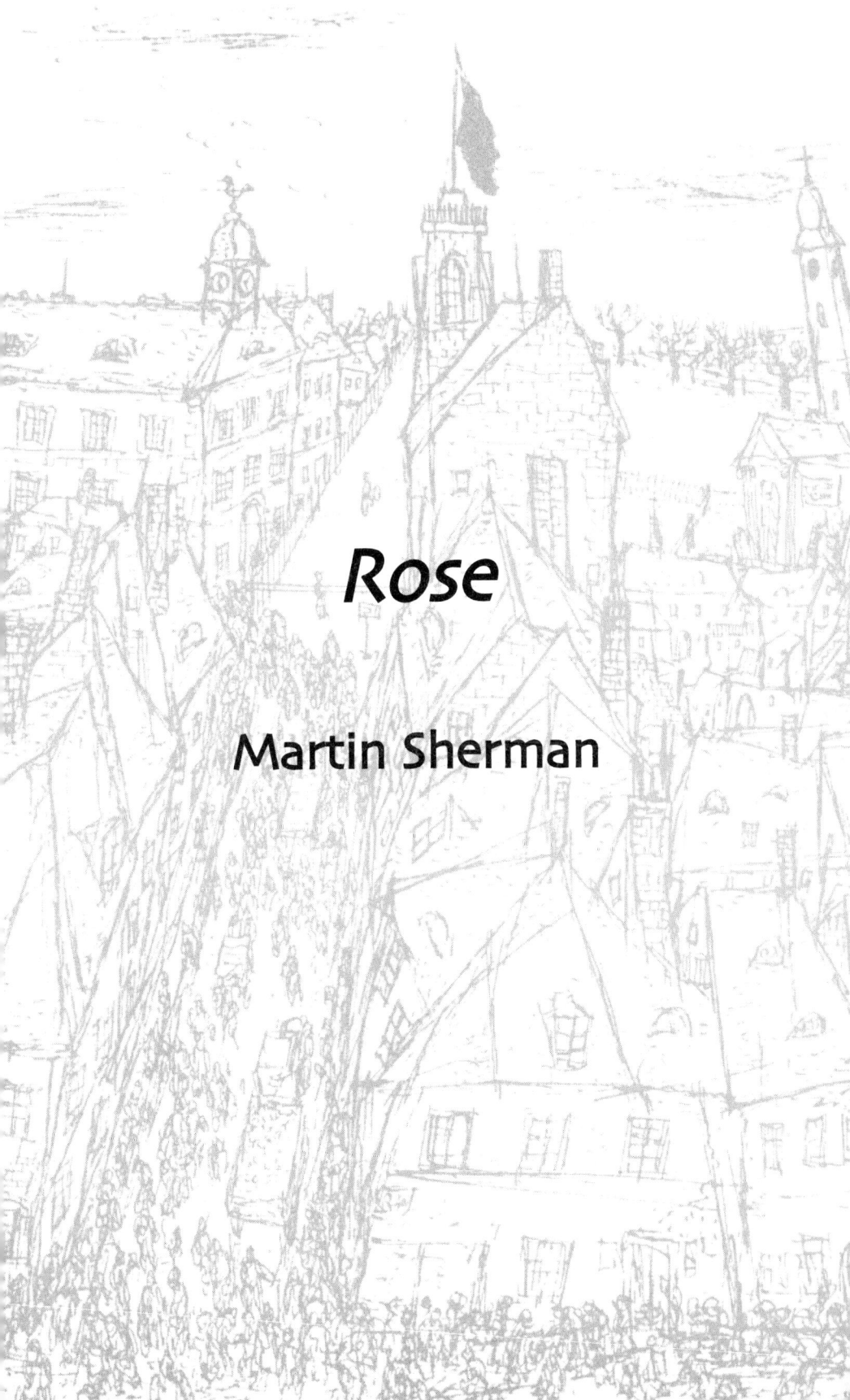

Rose

Martin Sherman

Martin Sherman was born in Philadelphia and educated at Boston University. His plays include: *Bent* (Royal Court Theatre, London, 1979; subsequently, West End and Broadway); *Messiah* (Hampstead Theatre, London, 1983); *What She Danced* (Guildford/King's Head Theatre, London, 1988); *A Madhouse in Goa* (Lyric Hammersmith, London, 1989); *Some Sunny Day* (Hampstead Theatre, 1996). Films include: "Clothes in the Wardrode" (BBC Television, 1992; subsequent cinema release in the US under the title of "The Summer House," 1994); "Alive and Kicking" (1997); "Bent" (1998). He has lived in London since 1980.

Rose was first performed in the Cottesloe auditorium at the Royal National Theatre in May 1999, with the following company:

ROSE   Olympia Dukakis

Directed by Nancy Meckler
Designed by Stephen Brimson Lewis
Lighting by Johanna Town

CHARACTER

ROSE   Rose is a survivor. Her remarkable life began in a tiny Russian village, took her to Warsaw's Ghettos and a ship called *The Exodus* and finally to the boardwalks of Atlantic City, the Arizona Canyons and salsa-flavoured nights in Miami Beach.

The play is a portrait of a feisty Jewish woman and a reminder of some of the events that shaped the twentieth century.

Rose

by Martin Sherman

— — • — —

ROSE sits on a wooden bench. She is eighty. There is a bottle of water and a glass on the bench, as well as a refrigerated pack. Occasional noise can be heard outside.

ROSE
She laughed. And then she blew her nose. She had a cold. The bullet struck her forehead. It caught her in the middle of a thought. She was nine.

Pause.

I'm sitting shivah. You sit shivah for the dead.

Pause.

Shivah sounds like the name of a Hindu god. Maybe it is. I had a flirtation with Oriental religion once. I envied the true Buddhists; they were able to reincarnate; not like us – when we're dead, we're dead; this life, that's it – it's the Jewish curse, we don't have heaven or hell and we don't come back – it's now or never. Of course, for me, now is hardly here any more. I'm eighty years old. I find that unforgivable and suddenly it's a millennium and I stink of the past century, but what can I do? I'm inching towards dust, and sometimes I wish it would hurry, preferably in the middle of a thought, or a sentence, just like that, although not by a bullet to the forehead. And then I wonder if anyone will sit shivah for me; maybe in this bright new twenty-first century they won't sit shivah any more. Well, the ultra-Orthodox will, of course, but something like shivah, in reality, doesn't have much to do with religion, it's just Jewish. You sit on a wooden bench for a week, you laugh, cry, argue as you remember the dead, the particular dead of this particular shivah, and you eat a lot, and kvetch a lot, and you get a sore behind, and it reminds you that you belong to a people, a race, a culture of sore behinds and complainers and heated discussions, of minds in turmoil and minds in flight and minds exploding like the atom, which I still don't understand, but it changed the world, well, it changed the last century, the world that was, and Albert Einstein came from the same street in Germany as my second husband's cousin, what can I tell you? Maybe this past century will be in fact the next to last century, and will it all be because a restless people produce restless minds; when you don't belong anyplace, your mind doesn't belong anyplace, you're owned by no one, except God, and God is only an idea, and so if you believe in God, you have to believe in ideas; except now, who believes in God except the fanatically committed, and if that's true, who believes in ideas? Now is different, anyhow; we don't wander anymore; we have a home.

Pause.

I can't catch my breath.

She tries to control her breath. Her problem is very quiet, almost unseen, but she can feel it. She pours a glass of water.

At my age, breathing is one of the few pleasures I have left.

She sips the water.

The elderly are supposed to remember the past with dreadful clarity, but the present – hardly at all. With me, it's not so true. I have only vague, wandering images of my childhood, but yesterday – I remember every single thing about yesterday. Nothing happened yesterday. Trust me. But seventy, seventy-five years ago – Yultishka – a lot happened, but I'm not so sure what. I see Yultishka clearly in my dreams; the subconscious is like an elephant, it never forgets; but when I'm awake, what do I remember? Mud roads. Tiny dwellings, I'm not going to call them houses exactly, but I'm not going to say huts, so – dwellings. Pink trees, well, the blossoms were pink. And carts and wagons. Lots of coming and going; traffic, I suppose, but no exhaust fumes. We had an ozone layer then; it's a shame no one told us, we could have enjoyed it. Yultishka, just a little pimple on the face of the Ukraine, you could squeeze it and it would burst. Just like all the other *shtetls*, the little Jewish towns that clung by the side of the larger Russian communities; well, sometimes Russian, sometimes Polish; the *goyim* kept killing each other and—what do they call it?—usurping sovereignty.

Laughs.

Sovereignty! The Ukraine! Why would anyone want it? And today? What would it be like today? Yultishka, if it existed still, wouldn't be that far from Chernobyl. But, in 1920, when I was born, it was Russian. There was a civil war going on, as usual, this time just between Russians, Red and White. By the time I was two, there was famine. But there was always a plate on our table. My mother made sure of that. She took in washing, and with the pennies she made from that she bought fruit from a *goyisha* farmer and sold the fruit from a little stand on the roadside, and with those pennies, she bought us food. I'll tell you the truth, I've never understood why she couldn't buy the food with the money from the washing. How much less was it than the money from the fruit? But that would have been simple and without strain and she wouldn't have been a martyr. My mother was a saint. Everyone in the *shtetl* said so. Which is very curious, because sainthood is not a Jewish concept. It's not even a Jewish word. She never complained. She never questioned. God had dropped a genuine Christian into the middle of this *shtetl* and didn't tell anyone. I was born into a contradiction. My mother's milk was never what it seemed. So the saint—Saint Trebele—was the sole support of her family – my older brother, Asher, my little sister, Rivka, and of course, Rosala, the middle one, that's me.

Who am I forgetting? Papa. Oh Papa! Papa was tall and actually quite a beauty, especially his eyes, which were always laughing, although none of us ever got the joke. Shortly after Rivka was born, Papa announced he was dying, and took to bed. He was in bed for years and years. He never stopped dying, but as far as we could tell, there was nothing wrong with him. Next to his bed was a large wardrobe, which was filled with medicine bottles, most of them empty, and herbal remedies, most of them used, and none of them able to cure this mysterious illness, which was very much like God, there was no visible sign of it, but some fanatical Jew kept saying it existed. Doctors used to come from neighbouring villages – they were always melancholy – and they brought medicine as gifts – Papa never paid for his hopeless cures – and people from the surrounding area, not all of them Jewish, brought him home-made remedies. He was almost—if you can imagine this in the Ukraine—a tourist attraction. The rabbi came and said blessings once a week, and the effort of listening so exhausted Papa he had to sleep through the next day. And the village cabbalists came once a week as well and talked of the devil and mentioned exorcism, which made Papa smile, he had a soft spot for hocus-pocus. But the saint, whose religion was more traditional, threw them out – once a week. Mama truly believed in goodness; more than that – if you were Jewish, you had a responsibility to be good; you were, in fact, put on earth to perpetuate a moral force. There was only black and white with her, which, ironically, just made her seem more Christian.

By the time I was ten I was selling fruit on the road. Asher taught me to read Russian as well as Yiddish; I had an ear for languages. Every day I made new signs describing the fruit, which did not need description; you could see them easily enough; melon and berries were luscious then; I can only imagine what they're like today in what was once Yultishka, mutating from fallout. Asher went to the Yeshiva; it was honourable if a boy studied. This annoyed me as I had an overwhelming appetite for knowledge – well, for most things other than science. I read everything I could lay my hands on. I fell in love with words. I memorized large Russian words and invented new Yiddish ones. I became pretentious in several languages at once. Asher came home and discussed the Talmud with me; we had discussions and arguments long into the night, the kind girls were not supposed to have, and I learned then that Judaism's greatest contribution to mankind was asking questions that can't be answered, and that the glory of our race has less to do with giving the world Moses and Marx and Jesus, but everything to do with the invention of the phrase "on the other hand." The saint was not impressed by our nocturnal discussions, but then nothing seemed to move her, at least not to appreciation. She never kissed us or touched us or teased us; she never said we were good-looking or sweet-natured; she had no pride in us whatsoever; all of her energy was spent in keeping us alive. She hated answering questions; she had to, of course, when I had my first period; she said it was God's curse, in which she was supported by the Bible. Asher, however, said, on the other hand, it might be God's gift, although he never quite explained why, and I said if that were true I'd rather God had just given me a calendar. So I learned an important lesson that night – God's curses are bad enough, but boy, watch out for His gifts. Shortly after that, the Cossacks came. I suppose if you have your first period and your first pogrom within the same month, you can safely assume childhood is over.

Years later, a history professor told me they couldn't have been Cossacks; Stalin has pacified the Cossacks, he said. Well, there were a few left over. They had big horses and big hats and big whips—everything was big—and beautiful faces; at least that's my memory, but I'm not sure if my memory is of the actual event or a scene from the movie "Fiddler on the Roof;" in my mind, it's exactly like the movie, or maybe the movie was exactly like the event. I close my eyes and I see chorus boys on horses, there's nothing I can do about it, but it's hard to reach my age and to have lived through some of the most tumultuous events of this century and to make clear distinctions between reality and the depictions of reality that constantly surround us. Actually, they were nicer in life than in the movie, because they didn't seem to want to kill anyone, they just wanted to frighten us. It was a bit like the Ku Klux Klan riding into a small southern town wearing sheets, except, of course, I only know that from the movies as well. And so they rode through the villages and broke windows and set fire to stores. They came into our house and we cowered behind a stove, and they didn't try to harm us, they just smashed everything up and rode away. Asher was shouting, Rivka was crying, I was doing a little of both as befits the middle child. Mama, of course, said nothing. She found a broom. She started cleaning up. It was then that Asher and Rivka and I had the same thought – for in the fuss, there was something we had all forgotten. Papa! We shouted his name. Mama sighed and walked into the bedroom. When she came out she picked up the broom and continued sweeping. Papa's dead, she said. Asher, Rivka and I ran into the bedroom, and we saw that the wardrobe had collapsed on to the bed. Papa's hand was sticking out from under the wardrobe holding an enema bag. We could make out a leg as well, covered with ointments made of rosemary and honey. He had been crushed to death by medicine. Years later, when I became an agnostic, that memory would, just for a second, make me believe in God again.

She sips some water.

Papa's was my first shivah. So many people came we ran out of wooden benches. I think they needed proof that Papa had finally died. Mama was in her element, totally impassive. It was God's will.

A few weeks later, on a hot afternoon, I sold the last grapefruit and went for a walk in the woods. I came upon a field covered with lilac trees. I heard a voice. Someone was singing, singing in an unknown tongue – a gypsy melody; no, it was Muslim; no, totally Hebraic; no, wait, I think Spanish, or maybe African—I couldn't tell—or perhaps it was from the moon. It summoned lovers and demons. I crept toward the field. I had to see who was making this delirious sound. Finally, I spotted a fragile figure holding on to a tree; holding, holding and swaying at the same time. I hid behind a bush and listened to the melody and suddenly the figure turned, and I saw its face, covered with sweat and dirt and desire and longing.... It was Mama. I ran. I ran into the woods. I ran away from her song. I ran back to the *shtetl*. When Mama returned home, she was scrubbed and cool, and she wore her saintly face. She started to cook.

Pause.

I never thought of her as Christian again.

I had to escape Yultishka. But Asher beat me to it. He married. From the next village, her name was Chaya, she was a catch, her family were merchants, she had even studied at a school. Her parents gave them money and with it they moved to Warsaw. Asher left me with the fruitstand and the sister and the mother who was really a pagan... and each day I grew a little and each day I died a little, both at the same time. I did not belong.

I wrote to Asher. I wrote every week. I begged him to send for me. I begged him to rescue me. I did not belong. I had fevers, I had a cold. My ear hurt. I had spots. My nose ran. I dreamed. I sat in a corner. I watched Mama. Mama ignored me.

Asher wrote and said come. Come, if you can. He had a child now. Chaya could use help around the house. Come if you can. He wrote to Mama. Send Rosala to Warsaw. She can take a train from Kiev. Send her to Warsaw. Mama looked at me. A dry, cold look. The same look. Always that look. I was desolate. I knew there was no money for a train. Mama went into the bedroom and returned with a scarf. Orange and blue. Like the scarf of a magician; wave it and a rabbit appears. There wasn't a rabbit. There were kopeks instead, hidden inside. I saved, Mama said, for when it's life or death. But going to Warsaw, Mama, it's not really life or death. She looked at me. The same look. Always that look. Yes it is, she said.

She holds her chest.

Maybe it's in my mind. Maybe there's nothing wrong with my breathing. Maybe I just panic. Maybe I should drink some water.

She pours another glass of water, and begins to sip it.

The first time I couldn't catch my breath? 1937. Summer. The café on Krochmalna Street. Chaos. Prostitutes and artists and pickpockets and those strange little men who sold lottery tickets—you could, if you were lucky, win an American eagle made of chocolate or three coloured pencils—and waiters shouting abuse and talk and noise and the possibility, always, of some kind of seduction; and though everyone spoke Polish, and I wasn't yet as fluent as I wanted to be, I felt almost—not quite—comfortable. Asher and his friends from the magazine they worked for were drunk and laughing; Chaya was in a good mood for once; and the room seemed to go around and around, as if we were all in spin-dry. I suppose it was the wine; we were celebrating my first year in Warsaw. And then the spin cycle abruptly stopped and a large man with long red hair was standing at our table. He looked like a gypsy, he had a huge earring in his ear, and his shirt was open, and there was no hair on his chest – no hair! – every man in Warsaw was hairy – and he had one perfect blue eye and one eye of glass, one dead little island in the middle of such life, and Asher was introducing him to me, and I knew, without a doubt, that there would never be anyone else.

We made love that night, surrounded by canvas; paintings, Yussel's paintings, paintings of *shtetls*, of tiny villages with mud roads and lilac trees; imitation Yultishkas surrounded me in that garret in Warsaw where I was finally free and finally a woman. Once when I was a child I heard the bedsprings in the bedroom rocking and thumping but there was no other sound, no human voice; it must have been the night Rivka was conceived, and I lay in the front room terrified, terrified by that silence. But with Yussel and me there was such noise—moaning and screaming and laughing and gasping—oh no – no…

She waves her hand away.

I don't want to remember.

Pause.

And we lived happily ever after.

She takes a long drink of water.

Yussel wasn't a bad artist. He wasn't exactly a Chagall, but then, who is? Jews aren't visual – look at what they wear. I suppose it's because we were never allowed to reproduce an image of God, unlike the goyim, who love the naked bodies of men caught in some kind of sado-masochistic ecstasy, strung up on a piece of wood or with an arrow piercing a nipple. But sex and God are very confused for goyim; for Jews they're separate. We can't see our God, so we can't desire Him. And when He abandons us, as He always does, we feel betrayed by a parent, not by a lover. Or maybe, like a parent. One day He just dies. So, believe me, when I was in bed with Yussel, there was no religious dimension. Actually, he was insatiable. He had to have everything today, as if tomorrow didn't even exist as a concept. Maybe he knew.

When we weren't making love, we were at the movies, especially if they showed a western. We loved cowboys and injuns and canyons and the Rio Grande and stagecoaches riding round the bend and tumbleweed rolling into an empty town – could that have been real? We liked musicals too, particularly the silly Yiddish ones, with Molly Picon dancing around a *shtetl*, singing–

Sings.

"Yiddle mit a fiddle...
Yiddle, Yiddle, Yiddle..."

We walked the streets of Warsaw with our friends, arguing and dreaming and laughing, and the goyim passing by would look at us with discomfort and even resentment, and one night, walking across the Kravidjin Bridge, I heard about Palestine for the first time, the land of our ancestors, the land that God promised us, and I giggled, because, even then, I knew about God's promises. Yussel would lean over and gently bite my ear and then nothing else mattered.

Sometimes Yussel would sell a painting, but he didn't make much of a living; the last thing he needed was a wife, but now, suddenly, he had a wife, and a year later, a child. I named her Esther, she had red hair like her father, and *two* blue eyes.

I don't know how Yussel lost his eye, he refused to tell me, but occasionally, in the middle of the night, he would start to scream and I would hold him and stroke his brow, and then Esther would start to cry and I'd have to go to her, and in the morning he'd accuse me of deserting him and of not caring about his pain, and I would say but I don't know what your pain is, and he would say I was blind, and I would bite my tongue and not say well, actually, in reality, you're blind, half-blind, and I don't know why. When we made love he would plunge into me, but I could never enter him, not really; emotionally, I was allowed foreplay, nothing else, and I felt, here, in the closest relationship I would ever have, still outside, like that tumbleweed rolling through an empty town, and suddenly I would miss Yultishka and worry about Mama and Rivka and then lie awake at night listening to the soldiers marching outside.

When the Nazis first entered Warsaw it didn't mean anything to me. It was someone else's war. I liked Warsaw, but I had no affection for Poland. How much worse could the Germans be? Well, I can't help it, I really did think that, what did I know?

I don't remember the ghetto.

Pause.

Well – okay – packed together. They took us from our homes. They relocated us into one small area and built a wall around us. There were twelve Jews to a room. Twelve – twelve – to a room. But I don't remember it. Maybe it wasn't twelve. I don't know. I'll tell you what hell is – it's twelve people snoring at the same time. Maybe I'm imagining it. Yussel had his bad dreams all the time now. I didn't have bad dreams. You have to sleep to have dreams. I was afraid to sleep. I was afraid something would happen to Esther if I slept. How had this happened? We had only yesterday been walking across the Kravidjin Bridge. We had been in a café just a month ago eating chocolate cake. Cake. Now there was a half chicken for the entire room.

Twelve people. Maybe it wasn't twelve. What was going on? Who was this man with red hair and an earring? What was I doing with him? I should have been selling grapefruit on a road. And then there wasn't a half chicken any more. We were starving.

I searched for my brother. I found him at the other end of the ghetto. Asher and Chaya were living with nine other people. Their child had died. The cholera. Chaya was screaming when I entered the room. Asher told me to ignore her but I couldn't. I tried to comfort her. She called me a bitch. She pulled my hair. I slapped her. Soon I was screaming. I don't know why. They had no food. Asher said he had contacts who could find me a job in a factory outside the ghetto. The owner was friendly to Jews and took in more than she needed, but only women. Chaya started to beat her breasts. Asher grabbed a rope and tied her hands. I saw how thin he was. Why were we in Warsaw? Chaya started to vomit. The other people in the room cursed her. I ran out into the night air. There was no air. Back in my room, Yussel stared at the ceiling. Esther was telling herself a story. She was three. We had a few bread crusts for all of us, for twelve people. Maybe it wasn't twelve. I took Yussel's hand. Where were you, why did you desert me, he said.

I started work at the factory. They let you out of the ghetto in the morning and escorted you back at night. Yussel didn't want me to leave, but we needed the food. It was possible for women to smuggle scraps of food back into the ghetto; the young soldiers at the gate were strangely shy about body searches. One afternoon, in the factory, we heard noise coming from the ghetto. We ran to the window. We could see the ghetto wall. Smoke was rising behind the wall. We heard screaming in the distance. Screaming. No, we didn't. I don't remember what we heard. Some of the factory women fainted. My body lost control. I shat myself. Esther and Yussel were in the ghetto. I ran to the bathroom. Cold water didn't help. I wanted to go to sleep. The screaming grew louder. No, it didn't. I don't remember. We had to go back to our machines.

That night we returned to the ghetto. The streets were filled with bodies. Buildings were burning. SS men were walking with dogs. I found my room; everything in it had been smashed to pieces. It was empty. Where were Esther and Yussel? I walked the streets calling Esther's name, passing other mothers calling the names of their children; a giant chorale of names filled the ghetto under the red sky. Years later someone offered me LSD; I said I didn't have to take it, I knew what it was like, hallucinating; a minute stretched out into an hour, strange visions soaring through your mind and then disappearing, the feeling you will never come back down to reality. I knew what it was like. I found a space where Asher's room had been. It was gone. Asher was gone. Chaya was gone. A hand pulled me off of the sidewalk. It was Simka, a man from our room. He had hidden in a cellar in another part of the ghetto. When the raid began, he was in our room. Yussel had handed Esther to him and said take her to the cellar. But Yussel had stayed behind. How could he slip through the streets unnoticed with his red hair and his earring?

Why did he wear an earring? Did he think he was a gypsy? I wanted to tear it from his ear until the ear bled. He said to Simka, tell her, tell my wife, my Rosala, to protect our daughter. That was it. Thank you very much, Yussel, love of my life. Later someone told me they saw him marching in the left line of prisoners, the line of useless people, the line for one-eyed men, the line that led to the clearing in the wood, where the machine-guns were. Fertilizer. They turned the bodies into fertilizer. What did they do with the earring? I don't remember any of this.

Simka and Esther started running through the streets. Simka did not look at me when he talked. He closed his eyes. He said they passed a soup kitchen. The Jewish Committee were handing out soup. Esther broke away from Simka. Simka covered his face when he talked. Esther ran toward the soup. They had never distributed soup before. A Ukranian soldier was passing by. A young blond Ukranian. Maybe he was a neighbour from Yultishka. Stalin and Hitler were friends now, for a minute; the Ukraines helped the Germans guard the ghetto. But why soup today? The soldier had a small gun. Simka said it again and again, a small gun, as if the size was important. Esther ran for the soup. The soldier aimed his gun, the small gun. Esther reached the soup. The soldier pulled the trigger. I suppose the trigger was small too. The bullet hit her forehead. He might have been from Yultishka. He was just passing by. Simka started to cry. Esther lay dead in front of the soup. Mostly water, it wasn't really soup. I kicked Simka in the stomach. I was supposed to protect her. Thank you very much, Yussel. Simka fell to the ground. I ran back into the street. I don't know what happened next.

Pause.

If I were Buddhist this would give me points. On account for the next life.

Pause.

It's almost time for my pill. For the breathing.

Pause.

I sat shivah in the sewers. There were no wooden benches, but God makes allowances. Except I stopped believing in God. God died in the ghetto; when I kicked Simka; just about then. On the other hand, I still needed ritual. So I sat a kind of mental shivah. For Esther. For Yussel. For Asher. For Mama. For Rivka. I knew in my heart that Mama and Rivka were gone as well. Later I met someone from a village near Yultishka who described the end of our *shtetl*. The Nazis marched all the Jews into the schoolhouse, locked the doors, and burnt it down. Easy. Screams behind the walls. Again. I sat that kind of shivah for two years. I don't really know how I got to the sewers, that's a blank. But once there, oh, I remember everything. There were about thirty of us. I was numb. Novocaine. Two years. You do things to stay alive... I remember... everything...

She takes the glass of water and drinks it very slowly.

She does not speak.

A long pause.

This I will say. We talked of Jerusalem. We were by the waters of Babylon, beneath Warsaw, and we remembered Zion. The promised land. Promised. Our own. No one elses. No Cossacks. No Nazis. Just us. Safe.

Well, then. The war was over. One day Nazis were marching into Warsaw. Another day, Russians. One day Stalin and Hitler were buddies. Another day, enemies. It had nothing to do with us. My mind couldn't absorb facts. Facts no longer made sense. My head was filled with images, with jump-cuts. Nothing was linear. I tried not to have memories. I was still numb, but my feet worked. I got out of there. Away from the Russians. I had to go someplace safe. Where was safe? Oh yes. Germany was safe. Long lines of refugees, passing through Poland, rushing toward the country that destroyed them. That was now itself destroyed. We passed through Dresden. A child with no arms crawled through the streets. The streets were rubble. The goodies had conquered the baddies, and had saved what remained of our lives, but the child had no arms. I found the Americans. They welcomed us. They gave us cigarettes. I had never smoked before. I smoked for the next fifty years. Now I can't catch my breath. They gave us soup. They put us in a camp. They called it a centre but, believe me, it was a camp. A nice camp, not a bad camp, but still, a camp. Barbed wire and bunk beds. The war was over. What was I doing in a camp? In Germany, where it's safe? I was officially called a displaced person. I could have told them that a long time before.

The camps were overcrowded. No one knew what to do with us. We had no homes to return to. But I had a place to go. I had Palestine. I was adopted by the Zionists in the camp. I was a heroine. Hadn't I fought back in the ghetto? Actually, no. I hadn't; when the ghetto rose up in its last gasp of fury, I was already in the sewers. But I let them believe what they wanted to believe. They were my ticket out.

One day the smugglers arrived. High-priced criminals, paid for by the Haganah. They bribed the soldiers. Two hundred people were selected from our camp. Some wore three pairs of clothing on top of one another and carried a knapsack. I travelled light. I had nothing. Soap and a towel. We climbed through a hole in the fence. The soldiers closed their eyes. The smugglers never smiled. We climbed into trucks. The trucks sped into the night. Some people screamed. They remembered the Nazi trucks. They thought it was a trick. But the next night we were in France. In Sete, by the sea. I had never seen the sea. It was just another image, another hallucination. A boat was in harbour. It was falling apart. We were marched aboard, like cattle, herds of us, mooing and rushing and falling in the dark. We were being rustled, like in "Red River" and only caution kept the smugglers from shouting Yippee-I-O. But once on board we were no longer cattle. We were now sardines. If you turned around, your elbow hit a nose. The boat set sail and secretly negotiated its way out of the harbour. The French turned a blind eye. The British were determined to stop us from going to Palestine. The British had won Palestine on the Monopoly board, you see, and they were trying to hold on both to it and their dignity. Their foreign minister was named Bevin and he was the goy from hell. He only allowed fifteen hundred Jews a month into the Holy Land; certain basic facts about the war seemed to have passed him by. The Haganah were trying to sneak as many Jews as possible into the country, although sneak is hardly the word; we were a creaky old boat on the open seas, difficult to miss, and within a day we were being tailed by British warships.

The mood on board the boat had changed. We were allowed on to the open deck and suddenly there was an accordion and the sardines were singing and dancing. I heard melody. The Mediterranean was playful, the waves hypnotic, and for a moment, the numbness began to wear away. Then I saw children throwing a ball, a little girl playing hide-and-seek, a tiny girl, and I couldn't bear it. I closed my eyes. I didn't want to remember. I didn't want the quick sharp images in my brain and I was angry at Yussel, at Yussel, for wearing an earring.

I opened my eyes. I saw a man's chest, a hairless chest. What was the point of opening my eyes if the images remained? Then I realized the chest was attached to a sailor who was smiling at me. Why was he smiling at me? There was a chill from the sea. He put on his shirt, but he was clumsy, and he put his head into the hole for his arm, and he was stuck. The ship was run by sailors who couldn't navigate a shirt. Suddenly my body was seized by convulsions. My spine went into spasm, my stomach jumped. I felt an electric current run through my bosom, and I knew this was it, finally, I was going to die, and I heard a sound from my throat, a strange, heaving sound, and then I realized what was happening. I was laughing. I had forgotten. I hadn't laughed since the café on Krochmalna Street. Something Yussel had said. He kissed my cheek which was wet from tears of laughter. Had that really happened? And now, in another life, on the open sea, this silly sailor with his head in the armhole had made my body scream ha-ha-ha. Who invented that sound, those syllables? If ha-ha-ha is a word, it's the only one that exists in every language. And then the sailor—he who produced ha-ha-ha—winked at me and disappeared into the crowd.

He returned that evening. We were still on the open deck. He sat beside me, or rather, fell beside me; he tripped on a rope holding a pail of water and splashed the water over us. We were squeezed together, refugees on either side. He was flirting with me, at least I think he was; I had no experience of flirting; Yussel was very direct – that first night at the café he said I think we should fuck and I blushed but I thought so too and what was the point of pretending otherwise? The sailor's name was Sonny. Sonny Rose. He spoke Yiddish, his parents were from a village not far from mine, but he was born in America. Most of the sailors were American volunteers. None of them had experience on a boat, but they too had dreams of Palestine. They didn't have to be on the ship; we did; and that made me like him. I asked if he was from the West, with Indians and tumbleweed, but he said no, New Jersey. I liked him a little less. When I told him my name he said oh what a shame, we can never marry, you would be Rose Rose. I'm not sure that my face showed it, but in some way, I think I smiled.

Mr. Bevin didn't smile, though. His warships moved closer. Someone said they were destroyers. The next morning the sailors hung a flag across the top of the boat. It had the Star of David on it. And a sign as well, a sign that renamed the ship. It said: *Exodus 1947*. I can see that sign so clearly. But, of course, how could I then, standing underneath it? Am I remembering the newsreels or the movie with Paul Newman? Or did I crank my neck? How can I tell? Sonny helped put the sign up, but he lost his footing, and dangled from the Star of David until his laughing shipmates helped him down.

We were nearing land, promised land. Only nearing, we were still in international waters, which were supposedly safe. That night the warships moved to our side. They squeezed us. Then they rammed us. We heard English voices on megaphones. What were they saying? Then there was tear gas. British sailors wearing steel helmets boarded the boat. They had clubs. We had soda pop. The Haganah had loaded our hardest food supplies on deck for us to fight with. Refugees were hurling cans of kosher corned beef at the steel helmets. I saw one of the sailors being clubbed. I saw a boy, only sixteen, his family wiped out in the camps, shot in the face. He died with Palestine on his lips. I picked up a potato. I threw the potato. Suddenly everything that had happened in the past seven years released itself through potatoes. I was no longer numb. I threw potatoes for my child, I threw potatoes for Yussel, for Mama. I was screaming. I was exhilarated. I was almost happy. And my aim was good. I was wiping out Mr. Bevin's Boys. I saw someone aim a gun at me, and then suddenly I was on the ground. Sonny had thrown me down. A bullet whizzed above us. Sonny dragged me into a corner, away from the fighting. He kissed me. His lips tasted of flesh. Yussel's tasted of cherry vodka. I've just saved your life, he said. I looked at him. I hated him for it.

The British had the boat, rather the hulk, the remains of the boat. The Royal Navy towed us into the harbour. We were entering Palestine at last, but we were under arrest. We started to sing "Hatikvah." Listen, "Hatikvah" is not exactly the "Marseillaise;" like most national anthems it goes on too long and no one knows the words. So we made up words. Then we heard the real words coming from the shore. Jewish settlers were waiting for us on the dock and they were singing. Our voices blended together. It was yet another hallucination, another LSD trip, except this one had a musical score. Sonny grabbed my hand. He was crying. All the Americans were crying. But the refugees didn't cry. We were too tired. Was it ever going to end?

We landed. The mandate police came on board and took us off the boat in single lines. Goodbye, sardines, back to cattle. Palestine didn't seem like much. It was dirty and hot and there were insects everywhere and strange-looking Arabs in robes and headgear and camels and jeeps and the settlers cheering us as we marched by and suddenly the woman in front of me fell to the ground and kissed the earth and screamed Palestine, and I thought what a sentimental fool she was, and then I felt dirt grazing my chin and I realized I was on the ground too and my lips were touching the dirt and I thought the earth tasted of cherry vodka but that was in my mind and I didn't know why I was on the ground or why I had started to cry and I felt a policeman pull me up and march me back into the line.

We were hungry, but they didn't feed us. We were thirsty, but they didn't offer us water. Instead they sprayed us for lice. For years after I thought if the British invite you to their house they spray you first. And then they marched us to another ship and we sailed away from Palestine. It had been a mirage, five hours in the Promised Land, a stopover on the cruise ship, a quick package tour to salvation. Now we were headed for Cyprus, where they had—guess what?—camps, camps for illegal immigrants. The Americans were on our boat as well and the next morning Sonny, who understood a compass, realized we were not sailing to Cyprus after all. We were on the open seas, heading back to Europe.

Sonny was agitated. *The Exodus* had created a scandal. The entire world was watching us, he said. There were even reporters on board. He didn't stop talking. Why was he talking to me? Why didn't he talk to someone else? He was boring me. I didn't care about a propaganda victory. I just wanted to sleep. In a bed, near Mama. I wanted Mama. Why didn't he stop talking? He kept taking my hand. I let him. It didn't matter.

We landed in a French port. The French said they would only allow volunteers to disembark. No one volunteered. The Haganah smuggled messages on to the ship saying Do Not Leave. Why would we leave? Where did we have to go? We were taking a stand. I wanted a bed. I didn't care. It was so hot. We were sailing again. We were sardines again. The constant changing from fish to cow and back again had broken my spirit, which had only half existed anyhow, and then only because of Palestine. It was so hot. The reporters filed their dispatches – a homeless people wander from port to port. Mr. Bevin had a shit fit. He sent our boat back to Germany. Sonny kept talking. He said the British had overplayed their hand, they had a public relations disaster. I looked at him, stupefied; if you have just been through a war in Europe, not to mention a Holocaust, you weren't exactly sure what public relations meant.

We landed again, this time in Hamburg. We refused to disembark. British soldiers burst on to the ship and clubbed us; they were getting quite good at that, and dragged us off of the boat. They took us to a train. A woman screamed when she saw the train had barred windows. I was hustled on to the train. It was chaos. I didn't see Sonny, but he was American, so he was free. Suddenly there was a lot of steam; the train started to move, very slowly. I saw Sonny on the platform running alongside the train shouting my name. I went to the door which was still open. This is ridiculous, he shouted. Jump off the train. Jump off and marry me. I'll take you to America. And then later we can go to Palestine. Jump. Rose! Jump!

I didn't know what to do. My heart was barely alive; if my body jumped, it wouldn't bring love with it. And maybe I still had a husband. After all, how did I really know that Yussel was dead? Someone saw him marching to the machine-guns, sure, but did they see a body? On the other hand, how could he have survived? But shouldn't I search for him? Just in case? In case of what – a miracle?

Jump, he screamed. The train was leaving the platform. The train to nowhere. At least I think it was leaving. Or was this too a movie? How many times had I watched this scene with the steam and the platform and the lover? Maybe we were still on the boat. America, he cried. I leaned out of the train. I couldn't believe I had a future. America, America! My mind closed down. I shut my eyes. What did it matter? I jumped. He caught me and then dropped me and we rolled over on the platform and then we were surrounded by soldiers with guns and they were shouting at us and I watched the train disappear into the mist, into Europe, into what years later my kind would call The Old Country.

She takes a bag from beneath the wooden bench. She removes a group of medicine bottles from the bag, and lays them, one by one, on the bench.

Papa would be proud. I take medicine now. For the breathing. For the cholesterol. For the kidney. For this and that. I'm doing what Papa dreamed of for so long. I'm dying. Not specifically, but when you're eighty you are, in essence, on the way out. Isn't it strange that I'm still alive? How many times I closed my eyes and said now, now, take me now, please. I can't go on. If there is a God, you'll take me now, and in a moment like that I believed in Him, and then when I opened my eyes, I didn't. But God is like a policeman, He's never there when you want him, and then, of course, He arrests you when you're innocent. Why do I spend so much time talking about something I don't believe in?

The problem is I can't swallow pills. Once I choked on an aspirin and almost died and that's not how I want to go, I want to go quietly in the middle of a sentence. So I've been frightened of pills ever since. I envy people who just throw their head back and drop a whole bunch of capsules down their throat. And then swallow and smile. Bastards. So I chew my pills. The problem is they taste like donkey droppings. So I have to kill the taste.

She takes a container of ice cream out of her portable freezer and puts it on her lap. She opens it. She chews a pill, and then eats a few spoonfuls of ice cream, and repeats the process as she talks, until she has finished her medicine.

Peanut butter vanilla. It's a new flavour. I like to be *au courant*. I know, I know, I'm eating ice cream to take a pill for cholesterol. I'll tell you something – who cares?

The first time I ate ice cream was in Atlantic City. Ice cream and frozen custard. There was a frozen-custard stand on the boardwalk, in front of the burlesque house, near the pier, across from the beach, where I sold chairs. Sonny was born and raised in Atlantic City. I'm sure he told me that on the boat, but I usually wasn't listening to him, and as a result, I knew nothing about him. Or maybe he told me during the endless days when we argued with the soldiers and the immigration officials and the bureaucrats; the days of filling out forms, when all I could think of was why am I here, shouldn't I have stayed on the train, who is this man? The Americans were nice to us, though; Sonny had an uncle in some bureau and finally I received a paper that said I existed, and a Jewish chaplain married us in Berlin, and then I was back on a boat, with a husband who was seasick all the time, which he wasn't on *The Exodus*, and I nursed him and asked myself who – who is he?

Sonny's parents had a few "who" questions of their own. Their boy runs away to be a pirate and returns with a catatonic *shtetl* girl, when what they always wanted was a nice Jewish-American daughter-in-law named Sheila or Arlene, who at the very least spoke English, which is a little weird if you ask me, as they had never bothered to learn the language themselves, whereas I became fluent within a year. But if his parents still spoke Yiddish they were hardly alone; Atlantic City was Warsaw-on-the-Sea, which was ironic because if ever a people were not built for bathing suits it was ours. The air smelled of aspirin and chicken fat and suntan oil, but the Jews who made the city their summer playground were the fortunate ones; they had had the good sense to leave Europe when the going was good. But guilt hung in the sea air as well, and my presence disturbed them. They were relieved to discover I did not have a number on my arm, but they certainly weren't interested in the images in my brain. They didn't want to know. Not that I wanted to tell them. Once I overheard a woman say, These people go on too much about the past; life isn't easy for anyone. She was wearing a mink coat and it was July. She was a guest at one of the many palaces that pretended they were hotels, palaces from another age, a jazz age, a Scott Fitzgerald age, beautiful and hideous at the same time. The same minked woman was heard saying, Art deco, art shmeco, the bathrooms are clean. For one dollar a boy pushed you on a rolling chair on the boardwalk—a rolling chair was a chair that rolled, all the terms in Atlantic City were literal—and you passed the shmeco palaces and the dancing waters—coloured water that sprouted in different formations and thus danced—and the Steel Pier, which had two movie theatres, a vaudeville house, a dance hall and a diving horse, which was, needless to say, a horse that dived into the ocean. You passed the Ice Capades, an ice show that spent each summer in Atlantic City and was thought exotic because ice-skating was one of those useless things that only goyim did. You passed the arcades and the fortune-tellers and the stores selling salt-water taffy, which ruined Jewish teeth for the next two generations. Sonny took me on a rolling chair on my first night, and halfway down the boardwalk we passed a store selling nuts and suddenly we were approached by a six-foot peanut with a huge peanut head who danced over to our rolling chair and kissed me on the forehead and called me little lady and I knew then that I was foolish to think my hallucinations would end when I arrived in America and I wondered if I had survived the sewers of Warsaw so I could be groped by a giant peanut. Why hadn't I stayed on the train and returned to a nice sensible displaced person camp?

Sonny's father owned several beach chair concessions and he gave one to Sonny as a start up the ladder—that was an American expression—although I couldn't imagine what beach chairs would lead to. We rented our beach chairs by the hour to the sunburned crowds; Sonny and I would schlep the chairs to a designated spot in the blazing heat, which often meant Sonny tripped over a chair, both of them flying in several directions at once. He never wore a shirt on the beach, which was a saving grace, although his body lacked Yussel's sharp lines. Yussel's this, Yussel's that, Yussel's report card had straight As, whilst Sonny's was barely average. At night there were attempts at lovemaking although he was as clumsy in bed as he was on solid ground, and I tried not to think of Yussel's penis and I wished the stranger on top of me wasn't called Sonny because I couldn't even help him out by faking love-talk when he had the name of a child. Our lovemaking was silent, like my parents', and in the morning I was sullen and distant and cruel. When I became pregnant, I panicked. How could I have another child, a child I wouldn't be able to protect? I thought of throwing myself down the stairs, but I could never act on my baser instincts, and so Abner was born. Sonny wanted me to name him Asher, but how could I say Asher every day and remember? Abner was close enough, and it was so American, it could even be the name of a cowboy.

Sonny and I still dreamed of Palestine, except it was no longer Palestine, but Israel, a nation at last, thanks to some degree to *The Exodus*. The adventures of our pathetic boat had swung world opinion in favour of creating a new state. We knew we belonged there, but I couldn't face another long journey, not just yet. For once in my life I wanted to stay put, if only for a few years.

Sometimes we would go out at night. There was the Harlem Follies at the Jockey Club, and the burlesque house, which was fun, mainly because the comedians were Jewish and told Jewish jokes. But then the comedians on television were Jewish as well, and Yiddish words entered the English language, words like schmuck and schlep and schmatte and schmooze and chutzpah. We saw Yiddish magicians at the hotels who pulled little Jewish rabbits out of their hats and we heard *chazanas*, female cantors who sang melancholy *shtetl* melodies and I would remember the lilac tree and finally understand. Molly Picon came once to entertain; she was tiny and depressingly energetic and she sang "Yiddle mit a Fiddle" as if she were still simulating *shtetl* life on a Warsaw screen.

We went to the Yiddish theatre and saw plays in which demons and goblins haunted the *shtetls*, and I remembered how superstitious we were in Yultishka, how Mama would spit three times if anyone mentioned the dead and how Satan was as accepted a presence as God. One night we saw *The Dybbuk*, a play about a young girl whose body is possessed by the soul of her dead lover. I was trembling as the curtain came down. What's wrong, Sonny asked. I didn't answer. I couldn't bear to look at him. I ran out on to the boardwalk and then on to the beach and stared at the ocean which was bathed in moonlight. I could run into the sea and find that spot where the horizon ended. Sonny rushed to me and took me in his arms. No, there's another answer, I thought. I would bring Yussel back to me. I would make Yussel's spirit possess my body.

If Yussel was really going to possess me, I needed to give him a push. I decided to dye my hair red and wear one long gypsy earring as well as trousers, which was not an accepted fashion for women in those days. Some kind of prudence prevented me from gouging out one eye, I expected Sonny's parents would be outraged by my new appearance, but instead they approved. They thought I looked less Russian, which was a good thing, as, thanks to Senator McCarthy, Russian was definitely out of fashion, and my old more severe look was suspicious. The hysteria over reds under beds was in high gear and actually communist was just a code word for Jew. One congressman even made a speech in the House Of Representatives claiming that communists had betrayed and then killed Jesus, which was, as metaphors go, not too subtle. As Americans were no longer very good on horses, they conducted their pogroms around committee tables and under television lights. I wasn't too concerned about myself; I knew that the politicians were mesmerized by the state department and show business; I didn't think they were panicked about the beach chair industry. Still, Sonny's parents were relieved when I assumed my non-Russian madwoman look. This annoyed me because one of the points about possession is that everyone around you recognizes it. Yussel's persona within me was still only skin-deep.

He needed inducement. I found a book about Cabala and in it the perfect magic spell for summoning a dead spirit. It involved semen, which was tricky, but finally one night, as Sonny fumbled inside of me, I asked him to pull out and come on my stomach. As soon as he had finished I jumped out of bed and scooped up his semen on a piece of cardboard. I ran to the kitchen where I mixed the semen with a chopped chicken neck and olive oil and cloves. Sonny stood in the doorway, watching. I knew he would never forgive me. Instead, he smiled in a way I hadn't seen before. My fascination with his semen was seemingly a boon to his manhood, and my dalliance with a magic potion was so – well – not American, so primitive, so European, so exotic, and after all, isn't that why he had married me and not Stephanie Perlow from Asbury Park? I smeared the potion on the bedroom door. Sonny then offered to assist me, little dreaming he was helping me summon my first husband. But Yussel was curiously uninterested in Sonny's semen; I yearned to have him inside my body, but he just wasn't there yet.

Maybe if I behaved like Yussel it would give him a push in my direction. I started to swagger around the house and I took up painting and once, when Sonny returned from Abner's room where he had been reading him a story, I accused him of deserting me. Sonny's joy was uncontained; he thought I had missed him. Okay, I thought, maybe it would help if I noticed women. I remembered walking with Yussel on Grabowska Street which was near the Muranow Theatre and always filled with young actresses. Yussel insisted I walk on his left, so if I looked at him sideways I would only see his glass eye; supposedly I would be unaware that his good eye was checking out every pretty girl that passed. Yussel was never faithful. I didn't admit that then, but now that I was almost him, I knew it was so. Who had he slept with? Were they friends of mine? If only Yussel would come into my body and name names, as if he were in front of Senator McCarthy. One night I placed my hand on Sonny's sister-in-law's right breast. I knew at that moment I had gone too far and the entire family would know that Yussel was trying to return. But his sister-in-law was thrilled; she asked me to meet her the next day on the boardwalk by the cotton-candy stand. The more I became like Yussel, the more everybody liked me. Yussel had become the most popular woman in Atlantic City. But still he eluded me. He wasn't inside.

So then Miss America arrived. The Miss America Pageant officially ended the summer season in Atlantic City and it was a big deal for the beach chair trade since the pageant began with a parade. The beauty queen of every state rolled down the boardwalk on an individual float and, thank God, onlookers had to sit on something. You booked one of our chairs a month in advance, it was that popular. All the ladies from the hotels put on their best summer dresses and oohed and ahhed over the pretty shiksas. The parade began with a little band and then the first girl, Miss Alabama; it was alphabetical. People cheered and whistled and were especially excited if the girl was from their home state; and the perky little Protestant faces glided slowly by.

Abner was playing in and around the chairs; he was three, the dangerous age, the age of Esther, but I felt he was safe as both Yussel and I were looking after him. Yussel wasn't inside of me yet, but he was close. I was convinced he was somewhere in the vicinity. It was a blazing hot day. Sonny decided to buy us cream sodas. He crossed over the boardwalk, in front of Miss Colorado, and disappeared into the crowd. I lay back and closed my eyes. I opened them, saw Miss Delaware, closed them again. Yussel was so close. I knew it. I'm sure he was enjoying the parade. So many pretty girls. Bastard. I began to drift. I awoke to hear Abner screaming daddy, daddy. I looked across the boardwalk, as Miss Iowa waved to me. Sonny was lurching through the crowd on the other side. He was holding three cans of cream soda. He dropped one can. He picked it up. He dropped another. He lost his balance. He stepped on a woman's foot. She screamed. He dropped the third can. People were laughing at him. He started to cross to us, but he lurched again and collided with Miss Massachusetts, or rather, the bottom of her float. He was down for the count. Miss Massachusetts didn't miss a beat, she just kept waving and smiling and ignoring the funny man sprawled on the ground. Someone in the crowd shouted the guy's drunk. But I knew that wasn't true; Sonny never touched alcohol. And, then, in a flash, it happened. What I had been waiting for. The Miracle. I felt a shudder near my heart. Someone was pushing his way into my body. It was Yussel. Yussel had come at last. Yussel had taken possession. Miss New Hampshire looked at me as she went past; had she seen Yussel dive inside of me? In the distance I saw Miss New York and I wondered if she would shout *dybbuk, dybbuk*. The crowd applauded. But it wasn't as I imagined. I thought I would hear Yussel's voice, perhaps even speak with his voice, and certainly, I would think his thoughts. But no, he took possession with his eye. He entered my own eyes and they saw through his one good one. My eyes—Yussel's eye—brought Sonny into sharp focus and saw that Sonny wasn't clumsy, after all, and Sonny certainly wasn't drunk. Yussel's eye saw that Sonny was ill, that Sonny had some kind of disease, that Sonny was now maybe dying. I took a deep breath. I ran to Sonny and helped him up. Don't know what's wrong, sweetheart, he said. It's nothing, it's just the sun, I said, but inside of me, inside, I said Yussel – goodbye, because I knew that now he had to leave and leave for ever, and I felt his good eye release its hold on my brain and I felt his spirit lift up through my body and out of my body and fly over Miss Oregon and Miss Pennsylvania and fly further still until it was over the Steel Pier and its diving horse and fly even further until it had disappeared into the humid New Jersey air.

Pours another glass of water.

What's the point of taking a pill if it doesn't help? I think my pills are made of sugar. My doctor says there's no problem with my breathing. If there was, he says, I wouldn't talk so much. You'll drop dead talking, he says. He's trying to frighten me. Believe me, it's an inducement.

Sips the water.

Okay. So. Eight years later I owned a hotel in Miami Beach. Well, that's America, isn't it? Go figure. What could I do? I had a husband who required a lot of medical care. Americans tend to think of illness as unhealthy. It costs. So I had to go out and hustle.

I took a job ordering food for the Majestic Hotel. Soon I was running the kitchen. Soon I was managing the place. The guests loved me. I understood them and their complaints and I was pleasant when I had to be and cruel when it was necessary and it was easy because it allowed me to protect Sonny, and Abner as well, and I could do for them what I failed to do for Esther. Maybe that's why Yussel's eye had showed me the truth. Maybe. Who knows. Sonny's was a rare neurological disorder; it had been building slowly through the years – when he fell at my feet on the ship he was not only manifesting love – and now it would accelerate. Motion, speech and thought would slowly disintegrate. The doctors could do nothing. Sonny was as devastated by the knowledge of the disease as the disease itself. Cigarettes became his passion, his profession, his art form. He sat at the kitchen table.

He would drop a cigarette on the table, pick it up, drop it again, pick it up – the table became a mosaic of burns and the burns represented some kind of pleasure. Sometimes I gave him sexual relief. I wanted to surround him with an illusion of love.

Our dreams, our fantasies, about Israel had started to grow again before my obsession with the dybbuk, but now they had to be tucked away, like Sonny's personality, into a distant closet.

Abner grew; we called him Abbie now; and by the time he was seven his thin little voice would make the evening announcement over the Majestic loudspeaker – The dining room is now open for dinner – as the dining-room doors flung open to a stampede; it was every man for himself as the hotel guests desperately rushed toward that evening's special brisket or smoked whatever.

The guests were intrigued by me because of *The Exodus*. That gave me cachet; it spelled adventure, unlike the death camps, which were still too dark and threatening to be thought about. A boat they could deal with.
I didn't tell them about anything else. Nor did I tell Abbie about the ghetto, or even Yultishka. I made sure that the guests never spoke directly to him in Yiddish. I wanted Abbie to be an all-American boy. I obsessively devoured books during the night, but kept that a secret vice. I no longer dressed like a demented gypsy. My suddenly tasteful wardrobe stood out from the clashing colours favoured by the Majestic clientele. They knew I didn't quite belong. But what finally cemented my popularity was the one true gift that Sonny had given me, if you don't count my life, and that was my name. Who could forget Rose Rose?

What people did forget was Majestic. Soon they were saying we're going to Rose Rose's for the summer. That is, those who still came to Atlantic City. There were now black ghettos surrounding the hotel strip, and since victims of prejudice seem susceptible to the disease themselves, Atlantic City just packed up and moved to Florida. The Jersey shore was desolate; Mr. Peanut stopped dancing, as did the coloured waters; the burlesque house closed, and salt-water taffy became extinct.

The owner of the Majestic, Mr. Feldstein, asked me to become his partner in a new hotel in the booming Sunshine State. He couldn't afford to lose Rose Rose. So the Double Rose Hotel opened on Collins Avenue. We promised double the comfort, double the sea air, and our old Majestic customers came flocking. The dining room was once again open for dinner, only further south. And every so often, Abbie and I would turn on the television on our tropical veranda in Miami Beach and watch, on the news, an abandoned palace-hotel in Atlantic City being demolished. The boardwalk was littered with rubble, like the streets of Dresden, where I once saw a child with no arms.

Takes a long drink of water and then puts it down, refreshed.

Each summer a group of young Israelis came to our hotel and gave us a presentation. It's unfair to say that they were aglow with youth, because it was so much more than that; there was a passion and belief in the future that I had not encountered before. Future wasn't even a concept in Yultishka or Warsaw or even in Atlantic City or Miami; on some subconscious level we knew we were skipping over quicksand. But the Israelis seemed to lack subconscious; they were entirely up front and present with no dark or hidden corners. They showed us slides of their kibbutz, they sang and danced the hora and collected money from our guests and each time they urged us to follow them back to join them in their great adventure and each time I wanted to, I wanted to be on the edge again, I wanted to dangle over a crevice with a very slender rope, but now I was a Rose Rose with responsibilities, so instead I gave money to plant trees in the names of my family. It seemed fitting to make Mama into a tree, although they couldn't promise me lilac. Abbie made friends with the Israelis, especially a young couple named Noam and Rutie, and when he was sixteen I let him spend the summer on their kibbutz. He left with acne and returned with a clear complexion and I knew he had discovered not only olive groves and irrigation ditches but sex as well.

Two summers later Egypt invaded Israel. Abbie begged me to give him the airfare to Tel Aviv. How could I refuse? His father was only a few years older when he ran off to *The Exodus*. Abbie went to Noam's kibbutz and worked in the fields while the men were away. It famously took Israel six days to win the war. It was unreal. Miami Beach was jubilant. We had an all-night party at the Double Rose. We were all warriors. There would be no screams behind a wall again. *The Exodus* would not be towed away again. I cried that night as I hadn't in years, but I wasn't sure why. Abbie phoned me. He wanted to stay. I wasn't surprised.

I told Sonny our child was living on a kibbutz; that he had, in essence, achieved our dream for us. Sonny's hands shook, his eyes were vacant, the nurse fussed. Did he understand how the world had changed? A few months later his heart gave up. I sat shivah and mourned not his death but his life.

Abbie returned for the funeral and promptly fell in love with a young nurse from Sonny's hospital. She was blonde and sweet and, as her name was Kim, definitely not Jewish. One of Christianity's more interesting contributions to twentieth-century culture was names like Kim. Abbie stayed on to court her, and soon Kim was as much in love with Abbie's dream as Abbie himself. She took instruction and converted to Judaism and changed her name to Chava and they were married under a chuppah at the Double Rose and soon, as if it hadn't happened at all, they were gone.

I was alone. My husband was dead, my son was gone. Sonny had been a vegetable for years, but at least he was my vegetable. Abbie stopped listening to me some time ago, but it was my voice he was ignoring. Now there was silence. Not even the sewers were silent – rats make noise. People talked all the time in the hotel, but their sounds blended and I heard nothing.

Except for Bessie Goodman. I heard Bessie Goodman because she never spoke. She drove the staff crazy. It was the styrofoam boxes, I imagine. Bessie placed her meals—three meals a day—into styrofoam boxes. Well, most of her meals. She did nibble a little in the dining room, but only a little, and then—woosh—food into box. Coffee as well; liquid didn't faze her. She kept the boxes in a small freezer in her room. Soon there were too many boxes for the freezer. Her room became a shrine to decaying chopped liver and gefilte fish. I didn't have to ask why; I saw The Old Country stamped on her brow. She was storing supplies. I sat with her in her room, in absolute silence. We both knew. But Mr. Feldstein anticipated a health crisis and he sent for her son.

Morton Goodman arrived at the hotel with a group of friends. They wore outrageous colours and beads and they all had musical instruments. They were, in fact, a band. The name of the band was MORT and they sang about death, a subject they knew nothing about. To them, death was what you did after life. MORT went to Bessie's room and played for her. They sang their entire repertoire. Finally she couldn't take it any longer. She threw out the styrofoam boxes. MORT emerged victorious.

Morton thanked me for being kind to his mother. He took my hand. His shirt was open and I noticed his chest was smooth. Uh-oh. He was twenty-eight. I was forty-eight, big deal, barely old enough to be his mother...

Laughs.

Oh well. We became lovers. I started wearing beads. I bought a guitar. The hotel guests became restive. Bessie Goodman started losing weight. I threw away my bra. Mr. Feldstein suggested I took a few months' leave. It would be good for my head. What a hip phrase, I thought.

I went to Connecticut and moved into a commune with Morton and his friends. There were twelve of us in an empty loft. We smoked a lot of dope and talked about peace and love and noble things and I did not mention the last time I lived twelve to a room lest I blacken their innocence. They called me Cool Mama and Morton wrote a song for me. "Rose Is A Rose." He claimed not to have heard of Gertrude Stein. There were long conversations into the night, intense and blurry; as if Asher and his fellow Yeshiva students were high on marijuana. I didn't have to hide my obsessive reading habits from them, as I did at the hotel. I felt free to enjoy language within a new culture that was, in its own way, destroying it.

Almost everyone in the commune was Jewish but that seemed to play no part in their identity. We discussed Buddha and karma instead of Rabbi Emanuel of Minsk, we went to ashrams instead of shul, and recited mantras instead of kaddish. Morton and I went away to meditate, to an ashram run by Ran To Poy, the former Seymour Goldstein. I tried to empty my mind. I couldn't. Nothing in my background prepared me not to think, not to question, not to somehow confuse the issue. My past kept floating through my head. I didn't welcome the memories but I couldn't pretend they didn't exist and I couldn't pretend I wasn't Jewish. It was just some kind of DNA in my bones. I left Ram To Poy and I left Morton. I told him I was too old. He thought I meant age. I couldn't explain. Mr. Feldstein welcomed me back with a relieved grin. He was a kind man. Two years later, I married him.

Abbie and Chava had a family. Rafi first, then Irit, then Doron, beautiful children, born with the olive features of their land, as if the earth itself had conceived them. I went to visit. My first time since I kissed the ground. It wasn't like my memory. I fell in love with the land, with the desert and the hills and the amazing sense of green, green planted by pioneers, green transforming an arid earth. I loved too the feeling that everyone, absolutely everyone, in the country looked like my relative; even, in some odd way, the unamused faces in the small Arab villages we drove hurriedly through; there was something in their eyes that I recognized, a look I remembered from the sardines on *The Exodus*. When I arrived at the airport, Abbie said Welcome home, Mama, and of course he was right. It was home, and I cried when he said it, and I cried when I left, two weeks later, for Miami Beach and my husband and my hotel.

Actually, the hotel wasn't doing so well. Many of our customers had died; others were now too old to have anything to take a vacation from. The neighbourhood had changed as well; it had suddenly become Cuban, with loud salsa music, which was nice, and cocaine dealers, which wasn't. I suggested we convert the hotel into a retirement home; our guests could just stay on for ever, and end their days quietly by the sea, albeit to a Latin beat, with the occasional sound of bullets to spice up the night air. We redecorated and hired nurses and Double Rose was in business again. Mr. Feldstein and I had our own apartment nearby; he was an amiable companion, and he knew to leave me alone when I had my moods, when, once or twice a year, I would retreat into my room and wonder why I went to the factory that day so long ago. But eventually, I would play "Rose Is A Rose" on my Walkman—MORT had become successful and the song a hit— and I would think how strange it all was and then open my door and return to a semblance of life.

Every summer I returned to Israel. It was changing. The milk was slightly sour, the honey a bit tart. There was a war on, a few miles away, in Lebanon, and Jews were being killed again, but this time Jews were killing as well, and we weren't really sure if it was in self-defence, and we saw photographs of women and children picking their way through the rubble and the rubble wasn't ours, it was next door, and we were confused, and our little boys had grown and started a beard and had wet dreams and carried a gun and marched down the road into another land. Abbie and his friends on the kibbutz hated it. Noam and Rutie were in despair; they were sabras, after all, they had virtually created this land, but not for this, they said, not for this. Chava, however, was fervently in favour of the war. Chava/Kim had the passion of the converted. She knew what the Bible said about enemies. She became increasingly religious. She began to keep a kosher house. She cut off her hair and wore a wig. Abbie was appalled then confused then hostile. The kibbutzniks and the religious despised each other. I did not really understand. Abbie and Chava did not look for common ground; they pushed each other away. Their house was choking with tension.

One day a theatre in Haifa brought a play to the kibbutz. It was a play designed for a young audience and indeed it was about teenagers in the Warsaw Ghetto. Rafi, Irit and Doron wanted me to go with them. I had no desire to revisit the ghetto, even in make-believe. Enough already. But I did want my grandchildren to understand our past. Okay, I thought, knowledge is more important than pain, so I went.

The auditorium was filled with eager young faces. Onstage was an imitation ghetto, a little too pretty, a little too tidy. There was no stench. It was utterly foreign to the audience, it could have been a fairy tale. Where was the smell, I wondered. At one point in the action a teenage boy leaves his home to go underground and fight the Nazis—was it as simple as that, I thought, was it?—and his grandmother, an old, fat lady wearing a babushka and talking with a heavy accent, calls after him, using his Yiddish name. Yitsalah, she calls. Yitsalah. A strange noise began to circulate through the audience. Yitsalah, she called. The noise grew louder. Yitsalah, Yitsalah. Suddenly the sound was crashing around me like a tidal wave waiting to sweep me out to sea. Laughter. The kids were laughing. The kids from the kibbutz were laughing at the name, laughing at Yitsalah, laughing at Yiddish, laughing at the grandmother, laughing at the moon, for what the grandmother represented might as well have been the moon. Yitsalah, Yitsalah. The audience repeated the name now, jabbing each other with their elbows. My grandchildren were laughing too. Rafi looked at me, wondering why I wasn't joining in. I was wearing a bright summer dress and you could see my breasts and they were still firm and my hair was dyed a soft brown with an occasional blonde streak, so what could I possibly have to do with the woman in the babushka? With Yitsalah? I began to cry and Rafi was no longer concerned for he thought he saw tears of laughter.

They thought it was funny, I said to Abbie later. So what? he replied. It's their culture, I said. No longer, he replied, and certainly not if they're Sephardic or African. Anyhow, we don't speak Yiddish here, Mama, didn't you notice? We speak Hebrew. Yiddish was unnatural, a mutant, a mongrel; medieval German and a bit of Russian and Turkish and French mixed together in a blender and then you added a little seasoning and spice, whereas Hebrew is the language of Abraham, Isaac and Jacob, Hebrew is our very source, and, finally, after all these years, we have reclaimed it. I was stunned. I actually thought his description of Yiddish beautiful and explained why it was so special. On the other hand, I understood his meaning, and from his perspective, he wasn't wrong. He was marching into the future, wasn't he? Oh that word – future. Every conversation about Israel had that word in it. Still, how could I argue? Well, I tried. It does represent something, I said, an entire civilization, a way of life, a way of thinking that's inspired this novel and that symphony and a theory of relativity and a science about the subconscious and maybe even ideas about collective living that have in turn inspired your kibbutz, and if it is lost completely, if it is utterly wiped away, then isn't that Hitler's Final Victory? That's just *meshugge*, he replied. I looked at my son. *Meshugge* is a Yiddish word, I said. He laughed and walked away.

Time passed. I stopped dying my hair. The Double Rose began to lose money; among the many things old age isn't is profitable. Mr Feldstein had a heart attack. I nursed him for two years and then he passed on. I finally sat shivah for someone who had not died before their time – it made me feel so grown up. Meanwhile, Miami Beach had transformed yet again, and was suddenly—overnight—the chic and swinging centre of America. Art shmeco had risen from the dead, and Collins Avenue was prime real estate. I sold Double Rose for a fortune. The new owners liked the name, so now Double Rose is the hottest club in town, filled with gymnasium bodies and a drug called Ecstasy.

I kept my apartment, it's good for them to see an old person, I figured, and besides Rafi likes to visit me here. Rafi and his sister Irit left Israel some years ago. Their parents had divorced by then. Chava remarried – a settler on the West Bank, a man with a Bible, a beard and a B-59. Irit moved to Rome, married a Catholic writer, and had two children, neither of whom are raised as Jews. Rafi moved to Los Angeles. He's a film editor. He has—do I have to say it—long hair and an earring, and, in addition, a boyfriend.

A few years ago I went to visit Rafi in Los Angeles; he showed me how he worked. Once I understood about fast forward and jump-cutting I realized that there was nothing unusual about my hallucinations and that movies were just catching up with our minds. Rafi took me to a hill that overlooked his city, and I told him that this abnormal metropolis exists as it is because a dozen immigrants—Jews from The Old Country—made their way here seventy-five years ago and founded an industry, what people called a dream factory, and that in turn created our image of American culture, it printed visions on our minds, cossacks riding through the *shtetl* became Indians attacking a wagon train, and those images seeped into all the existing cultures around the world, corrupting them, enriching them, changing them for ever, and it was all a fantasy of these little schlemiels, the Mayers and Zukors and Warners and Goldwyns, Goldwyn being originally Goldfish, who had a cousin who knew my father's sister in a little village in the Ukraine which now lies beneath the Chernobyl dust. Rafi's eyes glazed over; it didn't interest him. I hugged him anyway.

That's when we went to Arizona. I wanted to see the real West. It wasn't so real. There were no cowboys or Indians, no stagecoaches riding around the bend, just airless towns and unending desert and an occasional technicolour canyon. One day we drove for hours in emptiness. Wherever you looked was nothing and the scale of nothing was awesome. Finally we reached a little souvenir shop that stood alone in the nothing. Rafi's car was overheating. He went inside for some water. I walked around the front of the store. The windows were covered with tired, touristy watercolours of the desert. I walked inside. A wooden Indian stood in an aisle. He held a cigar. There was a price tag on him and above the price the words "original, not a copy." An old man stood behind the counter, minus a price tag. He was shouting at his son in the stockroom. The son was middle-aged and disturbed; desolate, I would say. The old man's voice was too rough. I could hear a slight accent. I looked at some more watercolours. They were terrible. Rafi and the old man were arguing. The old man refused to give Rafi water. I joined Rafi at the counter. Maybe an old lady would get some water. I noticed the old man's hands. They were filthy and chapped by the sun. Then I saw his arm. There was a faded number tattooed on it. I felt dizzy. I would never have expected that in Arizona, in the middle of nothing. The old man was shouting at his son again, as well as Rafi. I wanted him to shut up. My gaze swept up his arm to his stomach, which was gross, and his neck, which was sagging, and then to his face, which was like leather, and his eye, his false eye, his false eye that looked through me, and his other eye, the real one, the blue one, that seemed more like a heart than an eye, a heart that had shattered a long time ago. We looked at each other and did not speak. And then I turned and ran out of the store, past the wooden Indian and the dreadful watercolours, back into the nothing. I stared at nothing for a long time, then returned to the car. Rafi sat down beside me, a pail of water on his lap. He asked me what was wrong. I could not answer. I looked out of the car window and saw, coming toward us, across the prairie, a rolling tumbleweed. It blew past our car and out again into the desert and disappeared.

Pause.

Even though the doctor doesn't believe me about the breathing he insists it helps to sip water all the time. I forget to sip. I forget.

She pours another glass of water, and drinks a bit.

I don't remember what I was talking about.

Pause.

Oh yes. Shivah.

Pause.

Abbie is angry at me. For sitting shivah. He was on the phone this morning screaming at me from Tel Aviv. He lives in Tel Aviv now that his kibbutz has gone kaput. It's not your business, he said. You are not one of us. And he's right. On the other hand…

Sips some water.

Chava lives on the West Bank on a little settlement that adjoins an ancient Palestinian village. Fig trees and rock. It is, of course, in the Bible, an ancient Hebrew village as well. She took Doron, her youngest, with her when she left Abbie. I went to visit several years ago. I wanted to see my grandson, who was still the sweetest boy, but it was odd being on land that didn't want me, where I felt that, ethically, I didn't belong. I remembered how we celebrated the six-day victory in Miami Beach and how, years later, Noam and Rutie, drinking too much one night in the kibbutz, told me that the spoils of war were a curse. I didn't want to be there.

Chava did not make it easier. She kept saying forefathers, forefathers this, forefathers that, and then in front of my grandchild, she would praise the memory of this man, this Baruch someone, who massacred a group of worshippers at the Hebron mosque. I told Chava that was sinful. She reminded me of the countless Jews who were themselves massacred on this land. I know, I know, I said, and I mourn them with a depth that even you cannot understand, and I will mourn again when it happens again, but that still does not excuse this Baruch person. We're supposed to be better than that. We're supposed to carry a moral light unto the world. We, we, she screamed, how can you say we, you don't deserve to call yourself a Jew. I thought, well – just about the time my entire family was wiped out because they were Jewish you, my dear, were being baptized in Kansas.

I didn't stay too long and I didn't see Doron again until last night, when I put on the television news and I saw his sweet, handsome face, sweaty and strained and defiant. There had been a riot. The settlers and the villagers. Someone attacked someone. Someone threw a stone. Someone was knifed. A settler fired at the villagers. A little girl had been swept up in the crowd. Well, maybe. Maybe she had been throwing a stone. She was nine. A bullet struck her in the forehead. It caught her in the middle of a thought. Her name was Nora. Nora el-Kareem. They interviewed the man who fired the shot. He wasn't a man. He was a sweet-faced boy. Doron. My blood. Son of Yultishka. Son of the lilac tree. Child of Warsaw. Doron. He killed a little girl. He killed Nora el-Kareem. His grandfather sailed a ship to a promised land. Doron. My blood.

So today I sit shivah for Nora el-Kareem. The last of my shivahs. It is, of course, a totally empty gesture; I know that, but I had to do something. At first I thought I would write to her parents and tell them I was mourning their child, but they would hate me for patronizing them, just as I would have hated the grandmother of the soldier who shot Esther had she dared to make a gesture toward me. Esther, who I never really mourned – I was too busy staying alive; Esther, who I never sat shivah for on a proper wooden bench. Now I'm sitting shivah for a little girl and it is meaningless. A little girl who died with Palestine on her lips. I talk to Nora in Yiddish. It's all right, bubeleh, I say, it's all right.

Abbie is furious. Why are you doing this, he asks. Because it's wrong. Jews don't kill little girls. Everyone kills little girls, he shouts. It is horrible, but every nation does it. But you are still occupying territory, I say. Yes we are, he replies, and although it is not nearly as simplistic as you make it out to be, I strongly object to it; in fact, it tears me in half and I know that if we don't solve this soon we are all, all of us, headed for disaster, but it is our problem, my problem, not yours. But Israel belongs to every Jew, I say. Only in theory, he replies. What did you do, you bought a few trees, you sent some money, you paid a few visits, but did you taste it every day? It's the difference between casual sex and a relationship, he says, It could have been yours, you kissed the ground before any of us, but you chose to live as an outsider, a very comfortable one, but an outsider nonetheless, just as your ancestors did for centuries. So I'll condemn my own son if I choose to, and I do choose to, but here in my own country. I won't let the rest of the world tell my son if he's wrong or right. And I won't let you tell me that Jews have to be better than everyone else. But I'm not the rest of the world, I say, I'm part of you. No, you're part of chopped liver and *dybbuks*, he replies, that's something different, that's the past, this is the future. I know you hate that word, but it is our only future. We have nothing else. Do you understand? Everything else is gone. And then suddenly he starts to cry. My Abbie starts to cry. You have to let us go, Mama. Your shadows will choke us to death. We can't carry you with us. Your world is dead. And then he's silent. I can tell he's embarrassed. And then he says, You only think you're sitting shivah for this girl. That's not what you're sitting shivah for. What then, I ask. You tell me, he says.

Finishes sipping the water.

There's no more water.

Turns the glass upside down.

What was I saying?

Pause.

I should get another bottle. I haven't the energy. I hear laughter outside. Night-time in Miami Beach. Someone is always having a good time. Probably chemically-induced. I don't belong here, Abbie is right. But there was always a joy in not belonging. Did I belong in Yultishka? Or Warsaw? Or anywhere? Restless minds... what did I say?... a restless people produce restless minds.

Pause.

Maybe God is just a question like everything else.

Pause.

I'm thirsty, The truth is wooden benches are very uncomfortable. But I have to mourn a little girl, don't I? It's all right, *bubeleh*, it's all right. Sleep my child, sleep. Sweet Nora. My Esther. Shall I sing you a song? Of course, that's the other thing about sitting shivah, you can sing songs. How about a song from a movie? A movie I saw in Warsaw on Krochmalna Street. With Yussel. We had just been to a café. I think there was some kind of fight. Over poetry. How stupid. No, maybe someone owed someone else money. Or had slept with someone's friend. I don't remember. Anyhow, in the movie, Molly Picon was making a fool of herself. It took place in a *shtetl*, but it was a *shtetl* made of cardboard. It was a set. Or maybe it was Yultishka. Yussel put his hand under my blouse while she sang.

Sings.

"Yiddle mit a fiddle...
Yiddle, Yiddle, Yiddle..."

Stops.

And his hand pinched my breast...

Pause.

What was I saying?

Pause. Sings.

"Yiddle, Yiddle, Yiddle..."

Pause.

I think that song is a silly thing to remember. On the other hand...

She gasps.

She suddenly cannot catch her breath.

She closes her eyes...

The end.

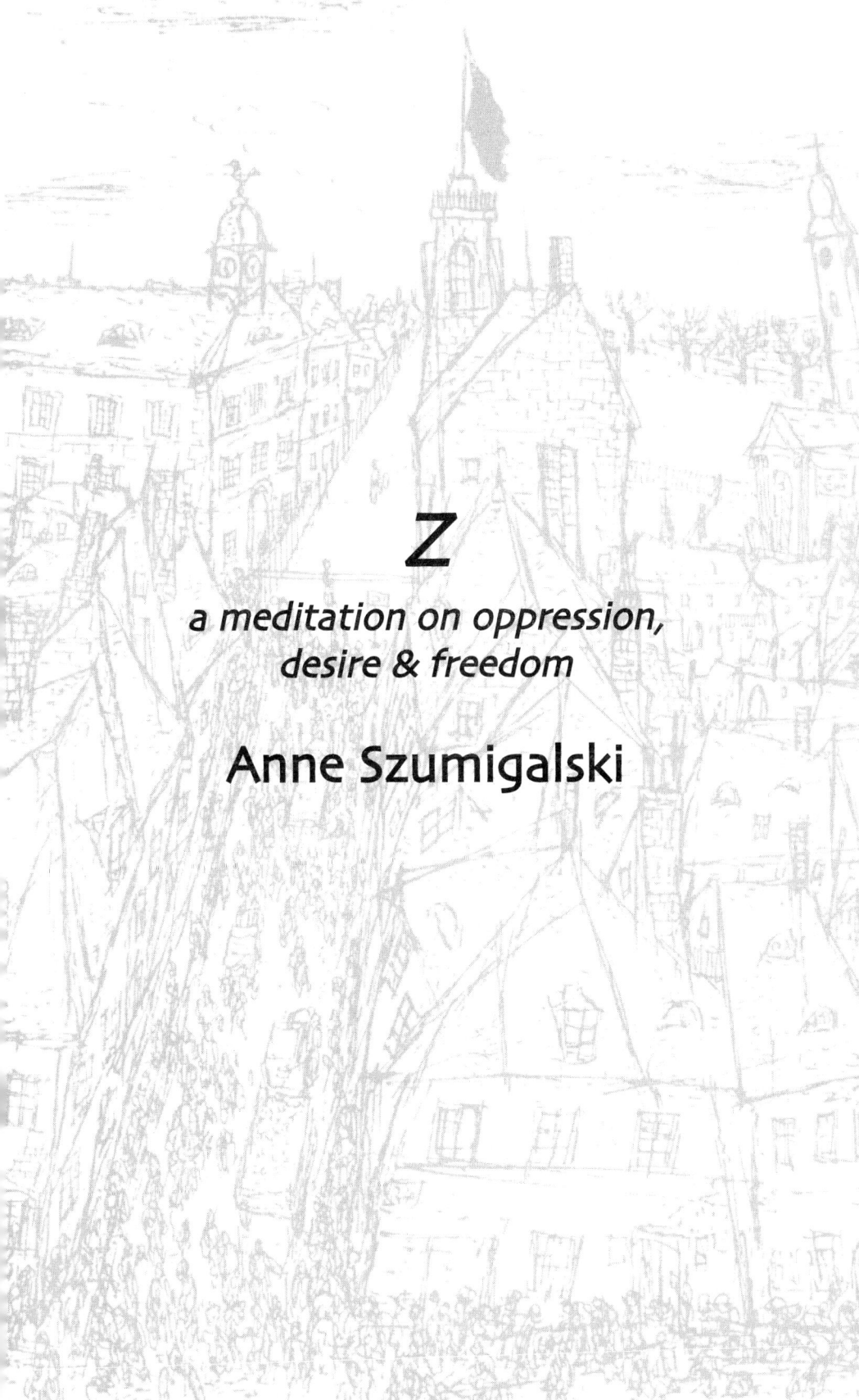

Z

a meditation on oppression, desire & freedom

Anne Szumigalski

Anne Szumigalski was born in London, England in 1922, but lived in Saskatoon for more than forty years and was a major influence behind the vibrant literary activity in Saskatchewan. She was an internationally known and highly respected poet, essayist and editor who was regularly invited to give readings around the world in places as diverse as Oxford, Boston and Malaysia.

The author of fifteen books, including the posthumously published *Fear of Knives*, Szumigalski won the Governor General's Award for Poetry in 1995 for *Voice*, a collaboration with visual artist Marie Elyse St. George. She published nine collections of poetry including *Woman Reading in Bath*, *Doctrine of Signatures*, *Dogstones* and *Rapture of the Deep*. In addition, her poetry appeared in countless Canadian and international journals and magazines. Her poetry was also published in numerous anthologies, including *Out of Place*, *Soho Square III* and *Towards 2000*. She collaborated with Terrence Heath on four radio dramas, the play for voices, *Wild Man's Butte* and the poetry collection *Journey/Journée*. She also edited a collection of Caroline Heath's poetry entitled *Why Couldn't You See Blue?*

Over the years, Anne won many major literary awards and prizes, including two Saskatchewan poetry awards, two Writers' Choice Awards and two nominations for the Governor-General's Award. Anne received a Founders' award from the Saskatchewan Writers Guild in 1984, was named "Woman of the Year" by the Saskatoon YWCA in 1989 and was honoured with the Saskatchewan Order of Merit and a Life Membership from the League of Canadian Poets. Anne's passing in April 1999 was mourned by all those she had touched.

Z was first produced by Twenty Fifth Street Theatre, Saskatoon, Saskatchewan, in April 1994, with the following company:

FEMALE VOICE	Anne Szumigalski
ITZAK	Kent Allen
Z	Maariu Olsen
SARA	Robin Poitras
HORST	Rob Roy
MIMI	Michele Sereda
MALE CHORUS	Alphonse Gaudet, Kristian Marken, Sean Power, Gary Varro
JULIE	Robin Poitras
BENNY	Sean Power
CORALIE	Michele Sereda
VOICE OF THE CANTOR	David Green
VOICES OF THE CHILDREN	Dominic LaPlante, Joey LaPlante, Garrison Parker

Directed by Tom Bentley-Fisher
Choreography by Robin Poitras
Production design by Michael Bantjes
Music by David Ruby

CHARACTERS

FEMALE VOICE	Taped.
ITZAK	Jewish Kapo of Forest Grove Concentration Camp. Ex-comedian and storyteller.
HORST	German guard. Ex-school teacher.
MIMI	Ex-dancer. Now kept at the camp as a woman for the men's sex hut.
SARA	A young middle class Jewish woman, the second woman for the sex hut.
Z	A Gypsy prisoner at the camp, favourite of the Kommandant, despised by the other prisoners.
CHORUS OF MALE PRISONERS	Taped and on stage.
CANTOR	Taped voice.
CHILDREN	Taped voices.
BENNY	A somewhat shady character who makes his money giving unofficial tours of Forest Grove Memorial Gardens. Played by a PRISONER.
JULIE	A young woman visiting the Gardens as a tourist in the Sixties. Played by SARA.
CORALIE	Her aunt, also a tourist at the Gardens. Played by MIMI.
SECURITY GUARDS	Played by ITZAK and HORST.
TRAMP/HITCHHIKER	Played by Z.
BAND	Played by the MALE CHORUS.

SETTING

Time and Place
Forest Grove Concentration Camp during World War II, and Forest Grove Memorial Gardens in the 1960s.

The Set
A bare stage, with narrow overhead runways along which the prisoners move. The sex hut is indicated by a boxed metal scaffolding on wheels.

A Note about the Music
The musician is to one side of and elevated above the stage. He or she provides an accompaniment for the dance sections, and elsewhere when appropriate.

A Note about the Text
Some of the following text has been adapted from or did not appear in the original production.

Z
a meditation on oppression, desire & freedom
by Anne Szumigalski

"Once in the thin time
between labour and sleep
my lover came looking for me,
but I was dead. I was dead and burned.
Nothing, nothing remains
but a handful of ashes,
a thread of smoke."

Act One

Prologue

Taped chorus chanting the word "Arbeit. Arbeit. Arbeit." Stage very dimly, or extremely brightly, lit. The prisoners are visible either moving or still in the overhead runways. Silence. The following poem is spoken by the female voice.

FEMALE VOICE
And I'll tell you again and again the same story,
Once I was a child and once I was a woman,
A woman in a cage, a lynx in a trap.

I was my own mother and I nursed myself.
I was my own child and I suckled myself.
Sometimes in my sleep I saw a house.
Sometimes a fire warmed my dreams.

Once I ate a chocolate dream cake.
Once my lover came to me.
That's when I died and was burned.
Nothing, nothing remains of me but ashes in the wind.*

They have snatched away my child.
They have broken him against the wall.
Is there no one to avenge him?

The bones of the innocent are trampled underfoot.
They are scoured by the wind.

Must I become my own infant
And hold myself against my own breast?

Must I become my own child
And rock myself to sleep in my own arms?

And I'll tell you again and again the same story.
Once I was a child and once I was a woman.
A woman in a cage.
I was my own mother and I nursed myself.
I was my own child and I suckled myself.
Sometimes in my sleep I saw a house.
Sometimes a fire warmed my dream.

Once my lover came to me,
But his bones were twigs.
His breath was gravel in my mouth.
That's when I died and was burned.
Nothing remains of me
But a handful of ashes in the wind.

> *At this point a MALE VOICE begins to speak under the poem. By the end of the poem the full chorus of male prisoners is chanting:

MALE VOICE(S)
We are captive.
We are powerless.
Nothing, nothing remains
But ashes, ashes, ashes.

> *The chorus of prisoners now are moving. Their gestures are repetitive, without energy. Their stance is that of the oppressed. Their heads are down. Any arm movements are small, stiff, and without spirit or energy. They do not appear to be individuals, but the same man over and over again. Round and round they go without hope. Meanwhile the taped chorus is chanting the words "Arbeit macht frei. Arbeit macht Freude" with many variations in tone, pace, arrangement, and loudness. Eventually the prisoners themselves may join in, either with words or with groans, ending with "Arbeit, Arbeit, Arbeit," which is continued underneath the CANTOR's singing.*
> *The CANTOR now sings the following quotations from the* Book of Lamentations.

CANTOR
She weeps bitterly in the night.
Tears run down her cheeks.
Among all who loved her,
She has no one to bring her comfort.

People have heard when I groan
With no one to comfort me.
My enemies hearing of my plight
All rejoiced–

Mine eyes do fail with tears, my bowels are troubled, my liver is poured out upon the earth, for the destruction of the daughter of my people; because the children and the sucklings swoon in the streets of the city.
My flesh and my skin he made old; he hath broken my bones.
He was unto me as a bear lying in wait, and as a lion in secret places.
He hath broken my teeth with gravel stones, he hath covered me with ashes.*
Their skin cleaveth to their bones; it is withered, it hath become like a stick.
Our persecutors are swifter than the eagles of the heavens: they pursued us upon the mountains, they laid wait for us in the wilderness, they laid wait for us on the mountains.
They that are slain with the sword are more fortunate than they that die of hunger, for these pine away sickened with hunger for want of the fruits of the field.

> *At this point the chant changes to "Their bones, their bones, their bones." During this we continue to see the chorus repeating the same movement over and over. Will this ever end? During this we have seen Z begin to move differently from the others, initially to the rhythm of the chant, and then in counterpart to it.
> Individual voices begin to be heard. The chant "Their bones, their bones, their bones" continues underneath the individual voices.

MALE
Go to, and let me come in unto thee.

SARA
My mother said I never should... should...

MALE
Rows of skulls that once were faces.

MALE
By hundreds, by hundreds, by hundreds.

MIMI
The dance is the soul of the body.

MALE
Go to, and let me come in unto thee.

SARA
Come, come, come...

> *The chant ends.*

MIMI
What's this? What is this? Who are you? Show your face: face of destruction: face of fury. Coward, coward, the flaccid face of fear. This is the face of the destroyed.

MALE
　　I am tired. I am weary as a ditch digger at close of day. My head is a burden my shoulders can hardly carry.

SARA
　　Come rest your weary head between my breasts. Here beneath the skin is bone. Beneath the bone my heart beats like a bird. Feel here the bird in my bosom... your bone hand on my bone breast. The featherless bird beats its wings in the cage of my ribs.

MALE
　　Oh, that the bird in my bone cage could come at the bird in your bone cage. Mine would attack and...

MIMI
　　Don't give me that, Mister Pitiful. You have never attacked. You are defeated, defeated, defeated.

CHORUS
　　Defeated, defeated, defeated.

SARA
　　You would attack and my heart would not defend itself.

MIMI
　　What are words, what are words after all? Can words free us? Can words kill our enemies? Can a word become a knife to stab the oppressor?

MALE
　　A knife, a knife, a knife...

SARA
　　Stab, stab, stab. Ah, that this wound of love would never heal.

MIMI
　　Fuck love and all your sweet words. So much water, and filthy water at that, falling over a dam, a crumbling dam.

MALE
　　Our hope is at an end.

MIMI
　　It must end. This weary captivity must end.

MALE
　　With nothing to defend.
　　Our hope is at an end.
　　This kiss, this breath
　　This last before our death.

SARA
: This kiss, this kiss, this breath.

MIMI
: And we must end it.

MALE
: We will end it.

MALE
: We must rise up and end it.

MIMI
: Choose your weapons. A spoon, a knife.

MALE
: A needle, a thread.

MALE
: Your nails, your teeth. A hair from your head.

MALE
: A hair from a shaven head?

> *Laughter and pause.*

MALE
: We have nothing but words, nothing but our prayers.

MALE
: We have our patience.

SARA
: Our hope that some will survive.

MIMI
: God is not listening. None will survive, not one.

SARA
: When they are defeated.

MIMI
: If they are defeated.

SARA
: When they are defeated.

MALE
> That day, the very day they know our rescue is near. That day they will make us dig our own graves.

MIMI
> Then they will gas us all and burn us all. Under the packed soil our ashes will sour the earth. No one to mourn us, no one to tell our tale.

MALE
> No one to praise our fortitude, our patience.

CHORUS
> No voice, no voice to speak our names.

> *Pause.*

Under the earth in all these places
Are rows of skulls that once were faces
Are rows of sockets that once were eyes
Eyes
Eyes...

> *Long pause.*

One by one, five by five, ten by ten, a hundred times a hundred, a thousand times a thousand.
By twos, by fives
They take our lives
By tens, by tens
By hundreds, by hundreds, by hundreds
By thousands, by thousands, by thousands

> *The CHORUS goes on whispering "Thousands, thousands, thousands" during the following speeches.*

MALE
> And when we are made to shovel out the ashes we find tiny bones, fragile as bird bones.

CHORUS
> Bones of our sisters and brothers,
> Our cousins, our aunts and our mothers.

MALE
> And where are they, those others, others, others?

MALE
> The pretty boys, the pinkie boys, the twinkle toes, where are those?

MALE
Gone to ashes, gone to dust,
For fear they might arouse the lust.
Of a guard.
For fear they might destroy
The moral fibre of some Nazi boy.

CHORUS
Gone to ashes, gone to dust
For fear they might arouse the lust...

MALE
And those so political
They dared to be critical?

MALE
Shot in the head, buried in the earth. Nothing remains of them but bones.

Silence.

FEMALE VOICE
My lover came to my bed
Like a wraith of smoke he lay on me
His tongue was a dry leaf in my mouth

Pause.

FEMALE VOICE
And I'll tell you again and again the same story. Once there...

We hear a loud siren which marks the end of the Prologue.

Desire

The prisoners are as though caged in their work, in their beings. ITZAK enters with his script. HORST enters from the other side of the stage, hands ITZAK a list of numbers, and snatches away the script. He withdraws to read ITZAK's script. ITZAK blows his whistle. Nobody moves. Another blast of whistle and the women get up (or appear) and walk around the stage to the sex hut. They walk single file, heads down, there is some distance between them. They do not speak. Their voices are heard on tape.

MIMI
Black and thick as licorice and twice as shiny...

SARA
...and it crackled as my mother brushed and brushed, as she coaxed it to flow smoothly down my back.

MIMI
I shook my body and my hair danced with it, swaying with my every move. How it swayed and caught the light. And I could feel how those fellows ached to put out their hands and stroke it, how they longed to catch their fingers in my dark tendrils.

SARA
On Friday afternoons one of my big sisters would fetch a low-backed chair and sit me down and stand behind me and braid it, French braids like in the storybooks. Ashenputtel at the ball, Rapunzel in her tower.

MIMI
O my lost tresses...

SARA
Rapunzel, Rapunzel, let down your hair.

MIMI
...glossed with pomade, perfumed with musk...

SARA
And they were golden, I tell you, those braids, golden as oranges.

MIMI
...carrots...

SARA
...oranges...

> *Another whistle from ITZAK. During the following dialogue he calls out about twenty five-digit numbers which indicate which prisoners may go to the sex hut. The prisoners listen for their numbers and as each is called they thrust out their arms to show the matching number tattooed there. The prisoners whose numbers have been called line up one by one until they are standing in a straight line waiting for the next command. Although, of course, Z's number is not called he makes every attempt to get into the act, absurdly thrusting out his arm or answering to a number that is not his. The only thing tattooed on his arm is a Z.*

ITZAK
And now for the lucky numbers.

CHORUS
The lucky numbers.

ITZAK
And the prize; the key...

CHORUS
Not to freedom, but to the gates of paradise.

ITZAK begins to call out the numbers.

ITZAK
You, Zigeuner.

CHORUS
(*softly*) Zigeuner, Zigeuner, Zigeuner…

ITZAK
You, Gypsy with lice in your crotch.
You, Gypsy with filthy worms in your gut.
You with your uncircumcised prick.
You think you can deceive me? You think you can deceive me into letting you in to lie with our women? To fuck our women? Letting you lay your stinking Gypsy body on our good Jewish women? Romany Bastard.

He calls out more numbers throughout the remaining dialogue.

I know what this all this is about. Oh yes, I know what it's about. Your music… your Gypsy fiddling. The Herr Kommandant likes your whining, wailing music. He hates Gypsies, but he loves Gypsy music. If it wasn't for that you'd be dead like the rest of your tribe.

CHORUS
Dead, dead, dead… (*whispers*) hanged side by side,
row on row, their cold feet swinging,
their rags floating, floating, floating.
Hark, hark the dogs do bark
The beggars are coming to town
Some in rags and some in tags
And some in a velvet gown.

ITZAK
Yes, you're a fiddler all right. Fiddling the horse trade. Fiddling children away from their mothers, young wives away from their husbands. But it won't be for much longer, my fiddling friend. Just wait until the Herr Kommandant gets tired of your tunes. In a month or a week, or even tomorrow, you'll be playing your fiddle in Gypsy hell… and no one to dance to your tune, my Gypsy friend, and no one to dance to your tune.

ITZAK finishes calling the numbers and blows another blast. This allows the men to start slowly moving toward the sex hut.

CHORUS
Here we come as lambs to slaughter
Here we come as doves to our cage.

Here we come not resisting
Without anger, without rage.

> *HORST, who has withdrawn, but not left the stage, now interrupts ITZAK and calls him over. The men arrive at the sex hut at the end of the following dialogue.*

HORST
You there, you, Kapo. Jewboy. Come. *(ITZAK begins to walk over slowly.)* On the double. Come on now Mister Kapo, Mister Jumped-up Yid. Ein. Zwei. Ein. Zwei... *(ITZAK begins to run to HORST faster and faster as HORST shouts louder. He arrives out of breath.)*

ITZAK
Herr Kaporal.

HORST
Out of condition are we, Kapo? An important fellow like the boss Kike is out of condition.

> *ITZAK has recovered a bit from his exhaustion. He stands up and puts out his hand for his script.*

ITZAK
Herr Kaporal.

HORST
(keeping the script, reading from it) "Jakov's father was a baker, and a very good...." A baker? By the title I thought the story was about a rabbi. The title...

ITZAK
"The Rabbi With Two Heads."

HORST
Is this your idea of a story for the Kommandant's party? You know how he loves Jewish stories.

ITZAK
We all know that.

HORST
Well then. What about him, this two-headed rabbi?

ITZAK
The baker...

HORST
Forget the baker. What about the rabbi?

ITZAK
   He has two fathers, two heads, two ways of looking at the world. Two opinions on everything.

HORST
   Two livers? Two hearts? Two... (*gestures lewdly*)

ITZAK
   No, only snakes have two of those.

HORST
   And the rabbi is a Jew and not a snake... hard to believe. Doesn't sound much of a story to me. Didn't they once call you the Great Storyteller? Izzie-of-the-Magic-Tongue? The funniest man in Dresden? And all you can come up with is this deformed rabbi? What about those other stories? "Avron the Wise." "Which Day is Shabbat?" "The Man with Three Daughters."

ITZAK
   Those were stories for other days, other parties. Tonight I shall...

   Z begins to appear as if in the arms of ITZAK and HORST, who do not appear to see him. Z begins to take the prisoners slowly through the process, and eventually to the edge of desire in the dance of recognition.

HORST
   Ah, what does it matter what the story's about? You're the Kommandant's little favourite. You're Eisler's little pet Jew. Oh, how he loves your soft wheedly little Jewish voice. You can bring tears to his eyes and he likes that. You can bring laughter to his lips. He likes that even better. You little Jewish serpent wriggling your way into his favour. He lets you choose your girlfriends for the fuck hut. He names you Kapo. You think that'll last forever? One day he'll get tired of your clever-clever stories, your smart little tales of this and that, and it'll be the gas chamber for you, and the furnace. What'll you do in Jewish hell, Yid? You'll just sit there to all eternity repeating your stories over and over until even Beelzebub himself is bored with you.

ITZAK
   And who do you imagine was the first storyteller, Herr Kaporal? No, no, His Nibs is never bored with stories. The plain facts, the bare facts of the case, now that might bore him. But a story...

HORST
   Ha, you admit then that stories come from Satan, that they are all lies.

ITZAK
   Not at all. The meaning of a story is simply the other side of the truth, like the dark side of the moon...

HORST
So now the little Jewboy is going to preach a sermon to his betters.

ITZAK
Wickedness is...

HORST
Simply the other side of goodness, you were going to say? What does a Yid know about goodness, or truth for that matter, now half-truths, prevarications. Give me that so-called story, that bunch of Jewish lies.

Chosen MALES are arriving at the sex hut.

MALES
Here we come as kings to our kingdom
Here we come as lions to our pride.
To our kingdom, to our pride, pride, pride
Aaah...

ITZAK blows his whistle, allowing the men to go into the sex hut. HORST is reading ITZAK's story. The following words are heard from the sex hut.

MALE
Stab, stab, stab. How much longer will I be able to do this? How much longer? Afterwards there will be no more woman, her soft red centre, her breasts like flaccid pomegranates. Lust is a strange thing. Some men lose it early, some late. There's even some that never have it at all. Am I glad or sorry that I am not such a one?

MALE
A green time in green shade, lying together like two children in love.

MALE
And what is love?

MALE
Women invented it, but they don't understand it at all.

MALE
They want to titillate us, tease us. All a man wants is to give himself ease.

CHORUS
Do we who are starving lie dreaming of bread
Or is it our desire to lie snugly in bed
With Judith or Leah or Sadie instead?

MIMI
Do we who are thirsting dream simply of wine
Or is it for stockings of silk that we pine

For geegaws and baubles and emerald rings?
Do we dream of a drawerful of feminine things?
For attar of roses, for frillies of lace?

SARA
Those things we remember from some other place.
Shall we ever return to our warm Sabbath houses
Our skirts of black satin
Our best purple blouses?

MIMI
To the dust of the street, to the smoke of the bar
To the beat of the feet, to the shouts of Huzzah!

MALE
Ah, ah, ah, Huzzah!

ITZAK and HORST continue their conversation about "The Rabbi With Two Heads." They have been reading the script, sometimes snatching pieces from each other, sometimes throwing pages down, and so on.

HORST
So what's this to do with the story? Grandma, Johnny Apprentice, and now baby. What is all this nonsense?

ITZAK
(*reading*) ...and what a baby he was – a wonderchild indeed – Jakov knew in his heart that never had there been such a boy as this one, so vigorous, so healthy, so beautiful His firm little feet, his plump little arms, and most of all his handsome little face. Ah, what rosy cheeks, what dark curly hair, what large intelligent eyes! The happy father sang all day at his work and all night he dreamed of what a wonderful baker his son would become one day, how, in the fullness of time, there would come a day when a new sign would be nailed up over the bakeshop door – JAKOV AND SON – BAKERS TO ALL THE BEST FAMILIES.

HORST
So the baker's baby was perfect. What has that to do with the rabbi? The rabbi with...

ITZAK
I'm coming to that. First I have to tell you about the bump.

HORST
What bump?

ITZAK
The little bump, small as a thimble, well, small as a rather large thimble, which this otherwise unblemished baby carried on its left shoulder.

HORST
So the baby wasn't perfect after all.

ITZAK
Nobody's children are perfect.

HORST
That's not true. I have four of my own and every one of them is perfect. Blue eyes, fair hair, true young Aryans.

ITZAK
No pimples? No freckles?

HORST
Jews have freckles. My children have... well they don't have bumps on their shoulders.

ITZAK
(reading) ...a tiny white bump with one curly hair, one golden-red hair growing from it. Of course his wife knew all about that bump but she cleverly managed to keep it a secret from Jakov. A skillful needlewoman like Reva could make the frilliest little jackets, the dearest little bonnets, the laciest little shawls to show off her darling baby, and to hide that little blemish from the sight of the world – even from the sight of her own husband.

HORST
I still don't see what all this has to do with...

ITZAK
I'm coming to that. Believe me, Herr Kaporal, a story can never be hurried. It must wind slowly along like a country road until it reaches the highway. From then on it may roar on as loudly and as quickly as it pleases. In no time at all it finds itself in the city – the climax – the end of the tale...

HORST
The fellow with the two heads, the rabbi, he ends up in the city?

ITZAK
At the university amongst all the learned professors no less.

HORST
The country baker's son? The bumpkin with his village ways? The young fellow in his clumsy coat, his dusty hat?

ITZAK
His two dusty hats.

HORST
How could that possibly happen? No, no, I don't see... *(He is beginning to laugh.)* Two bearded faces... two dusty hats... two...

ITZAK
The beards come later. For now... *(He has joined in the laughter.)*

They turn their backs and laugh more and more as ITZAK hands HORST another page from the script. The manuscript somehow falls apart between them and scatters. They pick it up piece by piece.
Voices from the hut.

CHORUS
Sing a song of woman lying in my arms,
All her gentle sweetness, her delicious charms.
Sing a song of woman lying in my bed,
Tell me shall I love her, or eat her up instead?

This is repeated throughout the following dialogue.

SARA
Mother was a wonderful cook. She worked all Thursday and Friday in the kitchen.

MIMI
In the kitchen? Come on now, Sara, if your people were so rich why didn't she hire someone to cook for her? Some stout bustling person in a flowery apron perhaps. Oh, and someone to serve at table. A nice young man with rosy cheeks

SARA
She loved cooking. She loved baking. And my two big sisters, they loved helping her in the kitchen. There they were, all three, chopping things, stirring things, rolling things. Ah, those cookies spiced with cinnamon, sprinkled with sugar.

MIMI
And you, where were you?

SARA
I spent my time in the music room playing scales, but I always left the door open just a little, so I could smell the baking.

MIMI
You loved music?

SARA
I hated music, but it was the only way I could get out of helping in the kitchen.

MIMI
>Sara, Sara, how can anybody possibly hate music? Why, I can remember the very first time my uncle...

CHORUS drowns them out.

CHORUS
>Sing a song of woman lying in my arms,
>All her gentle sweetness, her delicious charms.
>Sing a song of woman lying in my bed,
>Tell me shall I love her, or eat her up instead?

ITZAK and HORST – further conversation.

HORST
>*(looks up from page he is reading)* It's funny, I'll grant you that, but it still doesn't make sense. It's absurd. No one is going to believe a word of it.

ITZAK
>I'm glad you at least find it amusing, Herr Kaporal.

HORST
>A story should have... your stories have always had, well some kind of...

ITZAK
>Moral?

HORST
>Yes, but this... *(reads)* It was just as the baker had predicted, in spite of the gold-edged invitation, in spite of the exciting train ride to the city, in spite of his wearing the new coat with the black velvet collar which his wife had made for him with her own hands, he felt quite out of place amongst all the learned gentlemen in their elegant dark suits and their scented beards and their hats as black and velvety as a starless night. As for Reva, she could not keep her eyes off the satiny gowns and wonderful high coiffures of the few ladies present. She was wearing her best dress and a pretty shawl she had borrowed from her cousin for the occasion, but... *(end of reading)* Tell me, Kapo, what has all this twaddle got to do with the meaning of this tale of yours? The meaning, Kapo, the...

ITZAK
>A story is not responsible for answers, Herr Kaporal. A story merely poses questions.

HORST
>I must look for the answer myself.

ITZAK
>In your own imagination. Your own head.

HORST
> Or one of my own heads, Kapo, Mister Jewish Storyteller, one of my own heads... knowing your place, keeping your place.

SARA and MIMI are alone.

MIMI
> The dance is the soul of the body
> The body the soles of the feet
> And yes I have found
> As I leap from the ground
> That's where body and spirit may meet.

CHORUS
> And yes she has found
> As she leaps from the ground
> That's where body and body and body
> And body and body and body...
> And spirit and spirit meet...

MIMI
> Ah Sara, once I used to dance. Can you believe such a thing? My feet, as they say, were two little pigeons, going in, coming out again from beneath my skirt. My body, my arms were like so much bed linen moving and swaying on a clothesline in the soft wind of spring. And yes, it was spring then, my spring, the beginning of the world.

SARA
> And then there was another beginning. The beginning of the terrible years.

MIMI
> These years that have brought captivity and sorrow like rain upon us.

SARA
> Like rain on a roof, a leaky roof. When I was a child, Mimi, I lived in a house in the city, such a house.

MIMI
> Not that house again. Spare me that house.

SARA
> I and my two big sisters, we were brought up in that house. It had four stories.

MIMI
> If you ask me, the whole thing is a story, a lie, isn't it? You were brought up in the ghetto like the rest of us Jews. The Hebrew Quarter with the high wall around it, remember? And no one was ever quite sure what that wall

was for – to keep us in or to keep them out. But it didn't keep them out, did it? In the end they came for us. They took us all.

SARA
A house in the city, a tall house four stories high. And the attic was the one I loved most.

MIMI
Not that attic again. Spare me that attic, Sara.

SARA
Four stories up in that tall city house. The attic with the little dormer windows. You could sit there on the wooden window seat painted green, painted fresh every spring, and look out over the whole city. Summer afternoons the sun shone on the rooftops and the towers. And winter afternoons, as the darkness drew in you could see all the lights of the city twinkling, even the lights on the riverboats.

MIMI
And could you see us from there? The ghetto? Could you see us down there living our Hebrew lives? Could you hear us singing our Yiddish songs? Could you hear the music? Did you catch a glimpse of me dancing there in the dust?

SARA
Perhaps I did. I don't remember.

MIMI
How could you forget? (*quotes*) "And may my tongue cleave to the roof of my mouth, if I prefer not thee, O Jerusalem."

SARA
There were things in that attic, Mimi, you should have seen them.

MIMI
Just think, if you had looked out, far out over the city, over the ghetto wall you might have seen me, a young woman dancing in the street, with my tambourine in my hand.

SARA
Do we have to go on and on with this dancing thing? I was telling you about the attic, Mimi, the attic.

MIMI
And I was telling you about the dance – my dance. I was just a little girl when it all started. The music. It was just…

SARA
　Such things there were in that attic, and no wonder. The family has—had—lived in that house for almost a century. Think of that, almost a hundred years.

MIMI
　And then my uncle saw it and he said, "Dance for me, little one, dance," and I did and...

SARA
　...there were old rolled-up carpets smelling of ancient dust, and there was the nursery furniture we had when we were tiny, the box beds and the little wicker chairs and the rocking horse and the dolls with the faces of...

MIMI
　...then he began to train me and show me the steps. One two and three. One two three. One two three. One two three and four. One step, two step, three step, four and...

SARA
　...porcelain. They had sleeping eyes with real lashes, and there was a doll carriage too, and even a real baby carriage. But the best things of all, the very best things in the attic, were the boxes, the boxes with the dresses. And the very best dresses of all were the wedding dresses. Sometimes I'd open the boxes and spread them out, and sometimes I'd even try them on.

MIMI
　...five. When I got bigger I'd dance for them, all the uncles. "Fetching," they said. "Fetch me pleasure of the body." And I did. I was a great success. I may have started out in the street, but soon I was dancing in all the clubs – The Mermaid, The Love Band, The Coconut Palm, and everyone said I was the best. Slowly, slowly, I'd move my hips, then a little faster, a little faster still...

SARA
　...each one had its own box. Each one was layered with blue tissue paper, with camphor balls to keep out the moths. In the first box, a trunk bound with brass, my great grandmamma's gown of finest silk. Ivory silk with a train like a mermaid's tail. The second...

MIMI
　...then I picked up real speed. You should have seen me, those ogling fellows couldn't get even a glimpse of my feet. Round and round and round I'd go, then all of a sudden I'd start slowing down and after a few seconds they could see I'd begun to take it off...

SARA
　...box was of painted tin with roses and forget-me-nots on the lid. Inside my dear Oma's crinoline of soft lace and pearls. The whalebone had been taken

out of the skirts and coiled up like four little snakes tied with ribbon and hidden among the three silk petticoats.

MIMI

...and didn't that make them angry? Anger and lust go together they say. "The lust of man is the power of woman." That's what my uncle used to tell me. "Get them going, girl." And I did, I did, I did.

SARA

In the third box—a simple cardboard box—lay my mother's wedding dress, a short skirt to show the knees and a peacock tail of a train, a fan of many-coloured crepe de Chine that just touched the floor. A headdress of real peacock feathers, satin shoes with pointed toes.

> *The foregoing speeches at first simply interrupt each other, but they begin to cut in sooner and sooner, so that the voices are speaking at the same time. By the last speech they are speaking the whole thing almost simultaneously. Their voices also become more rapid, loud and insistent. Are they quarreling? In the end they come to a breathless stop. Nothing is to be heard but rustling, sighs, and groans. After a few seconds MIMI speaks in a quiet, sad voice.*

MIMI

And now when I try to remember the music it won't come back to me, not even a note. *(She tries to hum a few bars.)* But the rhythm is still there, and the steps, the twirls, the leaps. My feet will never forget those. I could do the whole thing again right here, right now, if only I had the strength in my legs.

MALE

Legs, female legs, open legs. I used to dream of them and of what lies beyond. I used to dream that dream every night. Now most of the time I dream of bread, a crust of bread, wide, soft, and salted. In my dream I find a file somewhere and sharpen my teeth so's to bite harder, to bite faster, to swallow more. I swallow bread. A woman swallows me. The mouth, the mouth...

> *The male prisoners are disporting themselves. Perhaps they are boys again singing bawdy versions of nursery rhymes or songs. They do not actually sing but chant the words to a jolly rhythm. They may dance about, use lewd or rude gestures, blow raspberries and so on. Are these the prisoners as children, full of exuberant spirits, running free for once? Or are they the children of the camp still being children in spite of the horrible circumstances? They laugh and jeer a lot.*

YOUNG VOICES

As I was running up the street,
I met a man with stinky feet.
Pew, pew, pew,
Who, who, who?

ANSWER
> Uncle Szymon.

YOUNG VOICES
> Uncle Szymon's rather weird,
> He keeps a bottle in his beard.
> And what is in that bottle blue,
> A quart and a half of good homebrew.
>
> As I was running up the road,
> I saw an old broad with a face like a toad.
> Boo, boo, boo,
> Who, who, who?

ANSWER
> Auntie Rivka wears a wig
> Red as a fox, shiny as a fig.
> A big grey rat is nested there
> Amongst old Auntie's ratty hair.

YOUNG VOICES
> When I was playing just for fun,
> Along came a man with his fly undone.
> True, true, true,
> Who, who, who?

ANSWER
> Cousin Jakov.

YOUNG VOICES
> Cousin Jakov drives his car
> Every night to Dolly's bar.
> He loves Dolly. Oh, how sad,
> When he finds out that she's a lad.
>
> When I was little, small and tiny
> I used to watch my Uncle Hymie.
>
> What did he do, what did he do?

ANSWER
> Pissed against the wall
> And wet his shoe.

YOUNG VOICES
> Shame, shame, shame
> On his name, name, name.
> Then what did he do, then what did he do?

ANSWER
>Borrowed Granny's right-hand boot
>And wore it on his left-hand foot.
>Granny gave him such a thump
>He fell in the garbage dump.

YOUNG VOICES
>My father said I should never
>Tickle a girl's ass with a feather.

ANSWER
>Shame, shame, shame
>On your name, name, name.

YOUNG VOICES
>My Granny said – you'll get hurt
>If you peek under a lady's skirt.
>
>Shame, shame, shame
>On your name, name, name.
>
>My Auntie said just keep away
>If you see a Gypsy when you're out at play.
>
>My Uncle says your nose will curl
>If you get kissed by a Gypsy girl.

>>*SARA runs into the group of men and they begin to play the game "I sent a letter to my love." They stand in a circle while SARA, who is it, walks round the outside of the circle with an imaginary letter (which may or may not be represented by an object).*

MEN
I sent a letter to my love
And on the way I dropped it.
Somebody has picked it up
And put it in their pocket.

>>*SARA touches each of the player's backs as she says:*

SARA
>It isn't you. It isn't you…

>>*She goes round the circle doing this until she comes to Z for the second time when she drops the "letter" behind him and cries out.*

>It's you!

Whereupon Z chases her round the circle and catches her while the other "children" clap and laugh.
Pause.

My mother said
I never should
Play with the Gypsies
In the wood.
If I did
She would say
Naughty girl
To disobey.

YOUNG VOICES
Naughty girl
Naughty girl
Naughty girl
To run away.

The Dance of Recognition

To a flourish of music MIMI appears in her exotic dancer's costume and proceeds to do her striptease act. The music is suitably sultry and sexy. The others stand around and applaud. They may give catcalls, they may whistle, they may make lewd gestures or yell out obscene encouragements. The only people who take no notice are SARA and Z. They are oblivious of everyone but each other. Gazing into each other's eyes, they do a slow dance round and round the stage.
At the end of MIMI's turn, a box of disguises is dragged onto the stage, or may appear from above. The disguises consist of hats, scarves, dark glasses, funny moustaches and so on. The men scramble to put them on and begin to dance to the slow foxtrot or other dance hall music that is now playing. Round and round they go, perhaps handing MIMI from man to man, perhaps taking partners amongst themselves. Through all this SARA and Z remain in their reverie and their concentration camp costumes. They dance amongst and around the others as though they are the only ones on the floor.
One by one the men become exhausted and throw away their disguises. They line up as before to go to the sex hut. MIMI puts on her concentration camp clothes over her exotic costume. She does this in full view of the audience, then returns to the hut. As the others become exhausted Z and SARA take on renewed energy and take the Dance of Recognition to the edge of danger. In the end, SARA can go no further and returns to the reality of the sex hut. We hear her inner voice singing in a flat young voice:

SARA
My mother said
I never should

Play with the Gypsies
In the wood.

If I did
She would say
She would…

> *The song tails off as though blown away in the wind. Z remains on stage through the rest of Act One. ITZAK and HORST seem unable to see him. A siren is heard. ITZAK blows his whistle. The male prisoners must now return to work.*

Victims

HORST
That's what it's all about, isn't it? Know your place. Know who you are. One day a poor prisoner, the lowest thing there is. Next day a Kapo with a little whistle round your neck. Pair of shoes on your feet so's you can kick the other Yids around. Now, if you could be born again, you'd be me. You'd be me, wouldn't you, Jewboy? A brown uniform, or a grey one, pair of lace-up boots on your feet to kick the Kapos around. You could even get those boots cleaned by one of the prisoners. You could even get the poor devil to lick your boots clean. As for me, all I can think of is my boss, the Herr Kommandant Eisler. Smart uniform cut to his figure. Medal ribbons. Leather belt. Leather holster. Pigskin gloves with cuffs halfway up to the elbows. And his boots!

ITZAK
His boots…

HORST
Riding boots that fit neatly to the calves. Shiny leather you can see your face in. Do you know who shines those boots, Kapo? Who helps him on and off with them? Who gets kicked around by those boots?

ITZAK
I can imagine.

HORST
There's always a boss. There always is. I have the Kommandant. He has the Herr General. The General has…. It all leads to the ultimate boss.

ITZAK
God?

HORST
The Führer. Heil Hitler.

ITZAK
Heil Hitler, indeed. He who keeps a roof over our head, who arranges…

HORST
And don't you forget it, Mister Kapo, Mister Jumped-Up-Little-Kike, Mister Betrayer-Of-Your-Own-People. Tell me, Kapo, what comes into your mind when you help to starve your own people? When you line them up to visit the women or to visit the gas chamber. Willing or unwilling, you lead them to pitiful love or to pitiful death. Oh, I've seen tears in your eyes when you do it, but you still do it. Worthless tears. Jew's tears.

ITZAK sinks down with his head in his hands

ITZAK
Someone has to – must, survive.

HORST
And of all these poor bastards, these sorry excuses for humanity… you, the lowest of them all, what gives you the right to live longer than the others? Who are you?

ITZAK
I'm the storyteller. I must survive. I must live to tell the tale. And what's that, a storyteller, you ask? What does a story matter? What does anything matter if it's not a story?
(*telling story*) At the very beginning, in the very middle of the World, Herr Kaporal, there was a certain stony mountain, a place so barren that the only things to be seen there were rocks, sometimes wet and slimy, sometimes dry and hot as Hades, and sometimes blown by icy winds and sprinkled with a meagre covering of gritty snow. At the very top of that mountain, on the highest peak there sat a young fellow in a ragged coat and boots with holes in the toes. To tell the truth, he had no laces to lace those boots, or wouldn't have had, but for the kindness of his grandmother…

HORST
His grandmother?

ITZAK
Grandmothers are like that. They may be a bit crotchety and complaining sometimes, but they'll do anything at all for their grandchildren.

HORST
Not my grandmother, Kapo. Not my grandmother. My Oma, well she was indeed *ein Drache* – a veritable dragon of a woman. Well she wasn't scaly, well not really very scaly, but she did have everything else a dragon has – fierce red eyes, horrible claws, and she breathed fire all right. We children lived in terror of that dragon of a grandmother. Obedience was her middle name, and she kept a switch behind the door for any one of us who dared

to go against her rules. Well, she really had only one rule, obedience, obedience, obedience. Don't ask questions, just obey... she...

ITZAK
(*continuing with the story*) His grandmother it was who tore the hair from her best Sabbath wig to knit him a pair of makeshift socks. She it was who undid her corset and gave him the grubby pink laces to tie his boots, no matter that the corset was the only thing that gave her sagging body any shape at all. No matter that it was the only thing that gave her ancient curved spine any support at all, she gave away that shape and that support because she believed with all her heart in the power of her grandson's tongue. She knew it was his destiny to tell the great story of this world and she didn't want him to freeze his feet while he was doing it. Without his words there would be no world, no grasses, no lions, no bears, no oceans full of fishes and whales.

HORST
No ships.

ITZAK
No ships, no motorcars – nothing, not even a blowfly or a rat. Not even the louse that is at this very moment finding its way to...

HORST
(*takes off his cap and begins to scratch his head*) Go on.

ITZAK
For it fell to the storyteller to name everything upon this Earth, both the living and the dead. And he named the forests and the seas and everything that lived there, and after that naming he paused just to catch his breath before beginning the long sorry tale of the history of humankind. How the grass grew under the feet and the rain pattered down on the heads of all people that ever lived, even the miser who kept his bag of gold under the floorboards, even the spendthrift who passed every day at the haberdasher's and every night at the bordello. Even the gambler who spent his time and money at the horse races and the gaming tables while his wife and children wept at home. And most of all upon the lover who...

HORST
Ahhh...

FEMALE
Once my lover came to me. That's when I died and was burned.

ITZAK
Nothing, nothing remains. But I will remain. I will survive to tell the tale...

HORST
And who will listen?

ITZAK
...of the oppressor...

HORST
And if they do listen, who will believe you? And...

ITZAK
...of the victim in his thousands, millions.

HORST
...if they believe you, who will care?

ITZAK
Nevertheless.

Lamentations with FEMALE voice interjecting.

CANTOR
Is it nothing to you, all ye that pass by? Behold and see if there be any sorrow like unto my sorrow.

FEMALE
I was my own child, and I suckled myself.

CANTOR
Hear, I pray you, all people and behold my sorrow.

FEMALE
I was my own mother, and I nursed myself

CANTOR
My virgins and my young men have gone into captivity... they say to their mothers where is corn and wine? When they swooned as the wounded in the streets of the city...

FEMALE
Once a fire warmed my dreams.

CANTOR
They have cast up dust upon their heads; they have girded themselves with sackcloth. The virgins of Jerusalem hang down their heads to the ground. All thine enemies have opened their mouth against thee.

FEMALE
My lover came to me...

CANTOR
They hiss and gnash the teeth. They say, we have swallowed her up.

FEMALE
...his breath was gravel in my mouth...

CANTOR
You have killed and not pitied.

Pause.

Is it nothing to you, all ye that pass by?

FEMALE
Nothing, nothing remains.

CANTOR
Behold and see if there be any sorrow like unto my sorrow which is done unto me. Behold and see if there be any sorrow like unto my sorrow.

The following dialogue takes place as the train is approaching. It begins when there is only the faintest of train sounds, which the audience cannot yet hear.

ITZAK
(referring to train) Well, here it is, the transport of victims, the expected train, the inevitable tragedy, the cries for help, the desperate prayers.

HORST
Selection.

ITZAK
Selection for extermination. Gone, gone to suffocation, to coals, to cinders, to white ash. More fertilizer for the fields, more fat for the soap factory.

HORST
Transport night. Party night for the Kommandant. The Kommandant always throws his parties on transport nights. Sends out his invitations to everyone on the list.

ITZAK
The pretty blonde girls, the important big-chested fellows in their elegant uniforms: Wermacht.

HORST
SS.

ITZAK
Mayors and Corporations.

HORST
Big people in business.

ITZAK
Little pipsqeaks in Government Positions.

HORST
The usual crowd.

ITZAK
Always different, always the same. And we prisoners get to amuse his guests, those of us who can play music, dance the fandango, tell funny stories. For us, it's entertain the company or die. And we work hard at it, I tell you. We work hard at it, all of us.

HORST
It's a good story. It's funny all right, but it's serious too.

ITZAK
What do you mean?

HORST
"The Rabbi with Two Heads" – now that's a title, that's a story. Most of us have two minds, if not two heads.

ITZAK
I'm glad you get the point.

HORST gives ITZAK a cigarette and they light up.

HORST
That isn't the point though, is it? It's the ones with one head, one mind.

Here the names of the concentration camps, which are the sound of the train approaching begin to be heard and grow in intensity under the ITZAK/HORST dialogue until close to the end of the scene.

CHORUS
Hertzogenbusch
Struthof
Esterwegen
Bergen-Belsen
Niederhagen
Dora Mittelbau
Sachsenberg
Buchenwald
Flossenburg
Dachau
Sachsenhausen
Ravensbruch
Grossrosen
Malthausen

Jasnovac
Jadovina
Stuthof
Chelmnop
Placow
Praviensis
Lublin-Majdenek
Sobibor

These are repeated.

ITZAK
Just so.

They continue to smoke companionably for a moment or two.

HORST
(*between puffs*) Used to be a schoolteacher. Nice little country school, nice little teacherage, nice little country kids. Too old and soft for real soldiering, so they called me up for this.

ITZAK
Any Jewish pupils?

HORST
Couple. Children of village shopkeeper. Quiet kids, good learners, no trouble.

ITZAK
Well?

HORST
That's before the Party told us what you Yids are doing to the country.

ITZAK
What?

HORST
Money-grubbing, dirty-trading, lousy-bearded creeps. Oh, they told us all about you. Big noses, thick lips, foul-smelling, degenerate. Oh yes, they told us all about you Jewboys.

ITZAK
And then you decided to eliminate – to exterminate us.

HORST
Exterminate? Eliminate? What difference does that make? We are all going to be eliminated. We are all for the big drop. When things get tough the Big Boys will call me up, forty-two years old or not. They'll send me off to the

front and I'll end up as dead as any Jew. A bullet in the belly – blown to bits in a minefield, dead is dead. What's the difference, a sniff of gas, a piece of shrapnel in the chest. We will have suffered, you and I, with the rest. We will have died and been forgotten. Neither of us is going to survive. Whatever that means – survival.

They go on smoking. Train is getting louder as it approaches.

ITZAK
And here they come, the poor victims. Last stop before eternity.

HORST
And for those who must be selected. Have you prayed for them too?

ITZAK
We have. We know the rules. Most of us have been here for months. Some of us for years.

HORST
Like yourself. The lucky ones.

ITZAK
The unlucky ones some would say. Thousands are at peace already. It's not difficult to envy them. When they are dead they receive their names back. When we pray we repeat their names. (*He begins to softly do so.*) Jankel, Shmuel, Dvorah, Chanaa, Mordecai, Yussel, Moishe, Dovid, Judel.

HORST
That's forbidden, forbidden, forbidden. Names are forbidden to Jews.

ITZAK
Nevertheless.

HORST
Forbidden.

ITZAK
You cannot forbid the mind of a Jew, the prayers of his heart... Chaim, Ruchel, Mayer, Reuben, Jakov, Reva, Zara, Zachai, Bethuel, Shimon, Isodore, Ezrah, Esther, Moishe, Yzroel, Leah, Rivke, Ruth, Michal, Zolmen, Zal, Juditt, Eva, Juna, Max, Osgar, Bela, Aryeh, Zwi, Yehiel, Leizer, Zofia, Hillel, Nathan, Haviva, Aaron, (*Here the train chorus suddenly stops.*) Zloma, Zeev...

ITZAK had begun this litany of names softly enough, but the train is coming in and towards the end he is yelling out the names against the sound of the train.

HORST is angry with ITZAK. He knows how to get his own back.

HORST
: And then there is that other matter, that other little matter...

ITZAK
: What do you mean?

HORST
: The little matter of the selection. One out of every hundred to make room for the new boys, eh?

ITZAK
: It's not something I'm likely to forget. But that's your business.

HORST
: Not necessarily.

ITZAK
: That's the rule. I have never...

HORST
: So far.

ITZAK
: So far? What do you mean? I...

HORST
: What would you say, Kapo, if I were to change that rule? As of today. What would you say to that?

ITZAK
: You can't do that. That's never been my decision, never. Isn't it enough that I have to march the poor devils to their deaths, wait there and hear their cries for mercy? Hear them choking and spitting? No, you can't do that.

HORST
: Of course I can do that.

ITZAK
: Kommandant Eisler...

HORST
: Kommandant Eisler has put me in charge of Section H. In charge. You know what that means? In charge. And I have decided, out of the goodness of my true German heart, to give the Kapo a bit more responsibility. You might even call it power. You don't object to power do you? I give you (*looks at watch*) an hour to make up your mind. Otherwise...

ITZAK
: An hour?

HORST
　One hour.

ITZAK
　How many?

HORST
　If by then you haven't chosen...

ITZAK
　O my God, my God, my God!

HORST
　Then you have chosen yourself, Mister Storyteller, Mister Comedian, Mister Itzak Friedlander, Mister Funniest Man in Dresden. Then you have chosen yourself. Now wriggle out of than one, Mister Kapo, Mister Storyteller.

ITZAK
　(He is sitting disconsolate, doesn't know what to do. Says nothing, but groans.)
　Aaah...

HORST
　Try to get out of that one, Jewboy.

ITZAK
　Chaim, Ruchel, Mayer, Reuben, Jakov, Reva, Zara, Zachai, Bethuel, Shimon, Isodore, Ezrah, Esther, Moishe, Yzroel, Leah, Rivka, Ruth, Michal, Zolmen, Zal, Juditt, Eva, Juna, Max, Osgar, Bela, Aryeh, Zwi, Yehiel, Leizer, Zofia, Hillel, Nathan, Haviva, Aaron, Zloma, Zeev

INTERNAL VOICE OF ITZAK
　(on tape) The oldest? But everyone is old here. Men of forty look as old as the trees in the forest out there. Young fellows of twenty-five look like grandfathers. *(aloud)* The sickest?

HORST
　Sickest? I'm the one that's sick, sick of your stories, Kapo. Sick of your clever Jewish stories.

INTERNAL VOICE OF ITZAK
　I must do it, but how? How must I do this thing?

CHORUS
　This thing, this thing, this thing.
　This life, this life, this life.
　This word, this breath,
　This last before our death.

INTERNAL VOICE OF ITZAK
If I choose the oldest, what then? I am old myself, older than the stones of the Wall. And I am sick, sicker than the lepers in the streets of old Jerusalem. Not that I have seen Jerusalem. But I know it's there. I have always known it was there. You can hear a song, you open a book and there it is, the Holy City, the City of the mind, the City of the soul. But then I have never believed in souls. I believe in stories, histories, archaeologies. Is this where history ends for us Jews?

HORST laughs, but uncertainly, nervously.

FEMALE
Once a fire warmed my dream...

INTERNAL VOICE OF ITZAK
Life – death – life – death – death. There must be some way of choosing, that would not... the last ones to speak, the last ones to stand upright. *(aloud)* O my God, my God, my God.

HORST
God is not listening, Kapo.

INTERNAL VOICE OF ITZAK
The ten shortest, the five tallest. The ones with the biggest ears, the smallest noses? All of you with warts on your chins step forward to the gas chamber. Quick march? *(He begins to laugh hysterically, and then to cry with his face in his hands.)*

HORST
God is not listening... not listening.

CHORUS
By fives by fives they take our lives
By ten, by tens, by tens
By hundreds, by hundreds, by hundreds.

INTERNAL VOICE OF ITZAK
By thousands they shovel us into the ovens like so much dry kindling. But I must, I will, live to tell the story.

FEMALE
I'll tell you again
And again
And again
And again...

INTERNAL VOICE OF HORST
(on tape) None of you will survive. Nothing, nothing will remain.

INTERNAL VOICE OF ITZAK
But I will remain. I will survive to tell the tale of the oppressor, of the victims in their thousands – millions, but who will listen?

ITZAK
(*aloud*) And if they do listen, who will believe me? But I will remain. I will survive to tell the tale of the oppressor, of the victims in their thousands – millions. But who will listen? And if they do listen, who will believe me?

Act Two

— • —

The Gardens

It is now the 1960s and the concentration camp has become Forest Grove Memorial Park. There is a large poster with WELCOME in several colours and languages near the entrance. Also a slot with brochures telling about the Memorial Gardens.

To the right of the stage is a white bandstand with steps leading up. The musicians, who are played by the MALE CHORUS, are leaning back in their chairs snoozing in the midday sun, their instruments carefully placed on the floor beside them. BENNY is also taking his siesta on a bench, his hat over his eyes, one hand on the bottle of beer that stands beside him on the ground. There's a drowsy feeling about the place. If there is sound it is flies buzzing, birds chirping, vendors calling their wares in the distance, their words not clear, only the cadence of their voices. A dog may bark. A child may cry. Now and then BENNY may rouse himself to take a bite from his lunch or a swig of his beer. He does this with gusto. When JULIE and CORALIE appear he hastily throws away the bottle and paper bag and wipes his mouth and hands with a crumpled handkerchief. He watches the two women, sizing them up as prospects for his scam. Occasionally two very efficient guards, played by the ITZAK and HORST actors, appear in the garden. Strangely enough, they seem to be almost identical. There is one other person in the garden, a rather exotic hitchhiker cum tramp. He keeps to himself, occasionally practicing Tai-chi, sketching on a pad, playing with his yo-yo or standing on his head. This character is played by the same actor who plays Z.

JULIE enters full of fluffy energy. She takes pictures of the gardens on and off during this scene. The pictures show as horrifying shots of the concentration camp and inmates flashed on the backdrop.

JULIE
(sniffs the air) Oh, I knew, I just knew, that this was the place to visit. Just think, Coralie... (looks round but does not see her friend) Coralie – Coralie! Oh, for God's sake.

She waits, but her friend doesn't appear. Takes a few more pictures. Goes over to the entrance desk and picks up a couple of brochures. Peruses them for a few moments then calls out again.

Coralie! Coralie! Where is the woman? It's those bloody shoes of hers.

CORALIE
(*She enters carrying shoes. She is fortyish and dressed to the nines, including the red spike-heeled shoes she is carrying.*) Sorry, Julie darling. It's these bloody shoes of mine.

JULIE
I told you, Sweetie, you should wear flatties. Didn't I tell you that first thing this morning? Wear flatties, I said, and now...

CORALIE
(*sits down on bench and dusts off her nyloned feet, begins to inspect them for blisters and so on*) That was this morning, my dear. Everything looks different in the morning. I've been on my feet all day. First the Rathaus, then the Cathedral, then the Square, then...

JULIE
Come on, Coralie. You were the one wanted to do the whole city in one day.

CORALIE
Well, that's what it says in the guidebook. (*takes out guidebook, licks finger and leafs through it, reads*) "One city, one day, the Heidegger way." Nothing about the heat. Nothing about queuing for lunch. Nothing about walking miles and miles. "One day of hell," that's what they should call it. And Julie, darling, I don't have flatties. What would someone like me be doing with flatties, I ask you?

JULIE
But they're in, Coralie. They're all the rage. Besides that, they are comfortable. You can walk miles in them, miles and miles without a single blister. (*demonstrates*)

CORALIE
Then I don't believe they're all the rage. They look – well, they look comfortable.

JULIE
They are.

CORALIE
Then I don't want to wear them.

The MUSICIANS begin to wake up.

JULIE
You're hopeless, Coralie. Quite hopeless. First you want to go sightseeing, then you wear the highest spikes you can find. Then you complain about blisters. If that's not crazy, I should like to know what is.

CORALIE
I wish you wouldn't use that word. I sounds so...

JULIE
What word?

CORALIE
Crazy.

JULIE
What's wrong with crazy?

CORALIE
It's American. You got it from that American boyfriend of yours.

JULIE
Which one?

CORALIE
Tall, blond, with a moustache.

JULIE
Clarence.

CORALIE
Clarence, is that his name? I thought he was called Duke.

JULIE
He is. That's his nickname.

CORALIE
My father had a dog once called Duke.

JULIE
There you go. That's what Duke is, a lucky dog to have me for a girlfriend.

CORALIE
Well, I don't think a niece of mine…

JULIE
Oh come on, darling, I thought you didn't want anyone to know you are my aunt. I thought we'd agreed…

CORALIE
That we're pals. We are, my dear, we are. It's these feet of mine. They are giving me hell.

The MUSICIANS have begun to tune up.

JULIE
And we all know there's no worse pain than pinched feet.

CORALIE
Nothing on earth worse than pinched feet.

JULIE
Agony!

CORALIE
Yes, agony, my dear.

JULIE
Ta ra. (*She takes a pair of flat slippers out of her bag and presents them to CORALIE.*) There you go, Sweetie. Now we can finish our day of sightseeing.

CORALIE
(*puts on the flat shoes disdainfully*) This whole thing is the fault of the bloody monks. Why the hell did they make us leave the car in their holier-than-thou parking lot? We could have driven up the hill like civilized people. (*She walks around a bit in the flatties and is almost persuaded that she likes them.*)

JULIE
They probably thought a walk would do us good.

CORALIE
I thought they were supposed to keep eternal silence. You should have heard the one who tried to stop me when I tried to drive through. He wasn't silent. He wasn't silent for a...

JULIE
What did he say?

CORALIE
He said "Parking, twenty-five Deutschmarks, forty zloty, or two pounds sterling." I tell you, dear, all they want is money. My father was right.

JULIE
About what? I thought you always hated his guts. Didn't he...

CORALIE
About the monks. Poofters in dressing gowns, that's what he called them, and that's what they are.

The MUSICIANS strike up a jolly tune.

JULIE
Aren't they supposed to pray or meditate or something? (*pulls CORALIE up off the bench*) There! Isn't that better? (*picks up CORALIE's heels and pops them in her bag*) Now you'll be able to really enjoy the gardens. Our first visit to a Memorial Park. It's thrilling really when you consider what went on here you know. (*whispers something in CORALIE's ear*)

CORALIE
You can hardly believe it, can you? Crematoriums, how awful! *(She sounds thrilled.)*

JULIE
Yes, truly awful. *(gives a slight nervous giggle)* Those poor, poor people. But it's great what they've done to the place. Look at the flowers, smell them. Doesn't it smell just like heaven, Coralie? I just can't wait to see – well, everything.

The chorus of MUSICIANS begin to sing the words to the tune. They love singing.

MUSICIANS
For hours and hours and hours
We work amongst the flowers.
And oh, what joy it brings
To do these happy things.

Work brings freedom.
Work brings joy.
Arbeit macht Freude.
Arbeit macht frei.

CORALIE
Quite a catchy little number. *(She takes a few dance steps.)*

JULIE
Not quite the thing though...

CORALIE
You mean because of the – sensitive issue?

JULIE
The words are okay, but this kind of music went out with the ark. *(In spite of her objections she begins to dance with CORALIE.)*

Meanwhile the MUSICIANS sing their song again, becoming jollier and jollier.
While they are doing this BENNY has been sizing the women up. He decides that they are fair game. He takes out a pocket mirror, combs his hair, straightens his tie, puts on his jacket and hat and so on.

BENNY
Mesdames! Signori! Mevrouwen!

CORALIE and JULIE stop dancing and turn to look at him.

CORALIE
: No need to shout, young man.

BENNY
: May I be of assistance?

JULIE
: Probably.

CORALIE
: What kind of assistance?

BENNY
: Ladies...

CORALIE
: Who are you? You're not wearing...

BENNY
: Let me have the pleasure, the privilege of telling you something about the wonders of Forest Grove Memorial Park.

CORALIE
: *(taking out guidebook)* It distinctly says here in Chapter Six...

BENNY
: What it was. What it is. What it will become.

JULIE
: You can tell the future?

CORALIE
: Don't be silly, dear. No one can do that.

JULIE
: My cousin Adele tells the cards. She says there is an eighty percent chance that...

CORALIE
: *(who has been leafing through her guidebook)* Ah, here it is. Good thing I underlined it. "Official guides always wear uniforms or carry some kind of identification."

> BENNY has hastily taken a handful of badges from his pocket, picked out one and pinned it to his jacket. It says "Tour Guide" in red letters. One of the guards strolls over to the MUSICIANS and shows his watch to indicate that it is time for the park to open. In the middle of a bar they change their tune to something more military and imposing.

BENNY
If Mesdames will allow, if Mesdames would be at all interested, I might be able to fit in one of my special tours before my next appointment.

CORALIE
Well I don't know, I really don't know...

BENNY
...which is with a famous Austrian physicist and his lady – very nice, very important people. People who know who to come to for a really excellent tour of Forest Grove.

JULIE
We did have a look at the brochure. It...

BENNY
(*taking the brochure and tossing it aside*) If you will forgive the expression, my dear young lady, this brochure is garbage. From such cheap rubbish you will learn nothing at all. Your visit to this wonderful place will be wasted. If you really want to be informed, what you need is one of these. (*brings out a handful of different coloured booklets*) French, Dutch, English, Spanish and so on. A rainbow, ladies, a rainbow of language, a rainbow of information.

JULIE tries to take one of the booklets, but BENNY withholds it.

CORALIE
And the tour?

BENNY
For a personal private tour I usually charge fifty marks.

CORALIE
Fifty!

BENNY
But for two such very charming women on such a very beautiful day – perhaps forty.

There is no response and BENNY after a moment puts down the price again.

I tell you what, ladies, I wouldn't do it for anyone else, but really you mustn't leave without... shall we say thirty-five?

JULIE
Come on, Auntie. That's a lot less than fifty. Half price really.

CORALIE takes out money and hands it to BENNY who looks quite relieved. They dicker a little over change and so on.

BENNY
First let me give you a little background on the place. (*puts on his Guide voice*) During the late conflict...

JULIE
World War Two?

BENNY
That's the one. During the late conflict Forest Grove was used as a concentration camp for deportees from many parts of the continent. Later its status was upgraded to that of a death camp. Almost a hundred thousand prisoners were put to death here. Most of these were Jews, but there were also political prisoners, sexual deviants, and Gypsies.

The MUSICIANS begin to get carried away by their music.

JULIE
I've always sort of liked the idea of Gypsies. They're sort of romantic, playing sexy music on fiddles and making eyes at ladies.

CORALIE
All those songs telling how Gypsy lovers serenade fair damsels and capture their hearts forever. What they don't tell you is what the fair damsels caught from the Gypsies.

JULIE
Love, probably. And the wild life, roaming, roaming and never quite finding a home.

CORALIE
I can just see you, Julie darling, riding in the back of one of those painted carts of theirs with five squalling brown-faced brats and a wicker basket full of homemade clothespins to sell. Your mother would have a fit.

JULIE
Oh Mother – she's always having fits – the way I dress – the way I speak – driving too fast – drinking too much, too many boyfriends. I don't do a thing different from the rest of my set, but my mother has to.... It would do her good to have something to throw a fit for. (*She turns her back and walks away in a huff.*)

BENNY
(*Clears his throat, he's now got CORALIE's attention. Continues with his spiel.*)
Some of the victims were buried in mass graves on the site. These are marked by memorial tablets, though the names of the dead are unknown.

MUSICIANS
(*singing*) A coverlet of grass pulled up over a long row of dead faces.

BENNY
　Most bodies, however, were burned in the incinerators, and the ashes sold to farmers as fertilizer.

MUSICIANS
　(*singing*) Under the turf in all these places
　Are rows of skulls that once were faces,
　Are rows of sockets that once were eyes.
　Eyes, eyes, eyes.

BENNY
　If you will look at the map on page three, you will see where all this took place. The tragic buildings have now, of course, been razed. That part of the compound is now the site of the children's playground, and paddling pool.

MUSICIANS
　(*singing in childlike voices*) Ring around, ring around,
　A pocketful of ashes,
　A basket of bones,
　A handful of dust....

BENNY
　A little further on and to the right was the soap factory where the fat rendered from the corpses was made into soap by the female prisoners.

MUSICIANS
　(*singing*) The fat of your sister, your brother,
　The grease of your child, your lover,
　Melted down, melted down, melted down.

> *But the women have not been listening. CORALIE is renewing her makeup and JULIE has wandered off looking for ice cream. She comes back licking a cone.*

> *A loud siren is heard. The musicians stop playing abruptly, clamber down from the bandstand, and line up at the gate entrance.*

BENNY
　May I please have your attention. You are about to experience the wonders of Forest Grove's famous gardens. How glorious it is to contemplate that after sadness comes joy, after terror comes peace.

> *One of the Guards blows a whistle.*

BENNY
　Let's go, ladies.

> *He leads them off, followed by the musicians and the guards. The only person left is the tramp (Z).*

> BENNY, the women, and the musicians are now audible but not visible. The musicians are becoming the chorus of prisoners as in Act One. They lose their jollity and their voices become more solemn.

BENNY
(*on tape*) We are now entering the memorial gardens which are some of the most beautiful and botanically interesting in the country. Under the direction of the celebrated Herr Professor Steingeld these gardens have become a mecca for botanists from all corners of the Globe.

CHORUS
Freude, Freude, Freude…

BENNY
First we come to the Fragrance Garden. This is sometimes called the Blind Garden. Its real beauty is most appreciated not by the eyes but by the nose.

CHORUS
The smell of fear
The stink of death
The stench of burning
Of burning flesh.

BENNY
And now, ladies, if you will be so kind as to follow me, we will visit the Knot garden.

SARA'S VOICE
I have a little garden
A garden of my own,
And every day I water there
The seeds that I have sown.

CHORUS
Seeds of sorrow
Seeds of violence
Seeds of despair.

BENNY
The White Garden.

CHORUS
White, white, white as smoke
White as ashes
White as burned bones.

BENNY
The Rose Garden.

CHORUS
> *(in childlike voices)* Ring around
> Ring around
> A pocketful of dust.

BENNY
> The Marigold Garden. *(pause)* The Daisy Garden. *(pause)* The Pansy Garden. *(pause)* The Fern Grotto.

CHORUS
> Water, water.
> Give us water, give us bread.

BENNY
> This is perhaps the most wonderful of all. In a place where there was no shade, no green thing growing, the Herr Professor and his workers have managed to create a water-garden of exceptional beauty.... In a place where there was nothing, nothing at all, there is life, there is beauty...

CHORUS
> This place, this place, this place
> Roots of sorrow
> Leaves of suffering
> Buds of despair.

MIMI'S VOICE
> I called to my lovers
> But they let me down.
> People have heard when I groan
> With no one to comfort me.
> Those who died by the sword
> Were more fortunate, than those who died of hunger.
> My enemies hearing of my plight all rejoiced.

SARA'S VOICE
> I love my little garden, I love it, I love it.

CHORUS
> Freude, Freude, Freude.

MALE
> The skin was shrivelled tight over their bones dry as touchwood.

BENNY
> A place of rock gardens.

CHORUS
> Hearts of stone.

BENNY
　　A place of perpetual fountains.

FEMALES
　　Water of tears.

CHORUS
　　The sun shall not burn thee by day
　　Neither the moon by night.

> *The voice of BENNY has been getting fainter and fainter as he leads the women further into the park. The CHORUS has been getting stronger and stronger and may now go back to the familiar "Arbeit macht Freude. Arbeit macht frei" chant. This also fades away and there is a pause before the CANTOR begins his lamentations.*

The Telling

CANTOR
　　Waters flowed over my head. Then I said, I am cut off. Mine enemies chased me sore, like a bird, without cause.
　　They have cut off my life in the dungeon and cast a stone upon me. Waters flowed over my head. Then I said, I am cut off.
　　They hunt our steps that we cannot go in our streets: our end is near. Our days are fulfilled.
　　Let us lift our heart with our hand unto God in the heavens.
　　Remember, O Lord, my affliction and my misery. The wormwood and the gall.
　　The elders have ceased from the gate. The young men from their music. The joy of our heart is ceased. Our dance is turned into mourning.

> *MIMI and SARA are sleeping in their bunk, head to toe as all camp inmates sleep. They are either surrounded under and over by others sleeping or they are alone isolated in their dreams. A relentless brilliant light is shining on them, and the ache of this light enters their dreams. There is a continuous low hum, no other noise. The two women appear to be in a dead sleep. Can nothing disturb the exhausted sleep of the starving?*
> *After some time MIMI stirs, mutters "no" and turns, pulling the one thin grey blanket from SARA. SARA lets her left leg drop to the floor and angrily pulls the blanket away from MIMI. They settle down. After a few moments MIMI pulls the blanket back. This sort of thing can happen several times before SARA cries out "no," sits up, and bows her head in her hands.*

SARA
　　(weeping) No, no, no...

MIMI
　　For God's sake, woman. *(She covers her head with the blanket.)*

SARA
  (*still weeping*) No, no, no...

MIMI
  Forget it. Go back to sleep. It's our only respite. Our only foretaste of Paradise. Eternal sleep, eternal dreams. (*She laughs shortly and bitterly.*)

SARA
  Dreams!

  MIMI sits up at last and faces SARA. Arranges the blanket between them. Takes the younger woman's hands.

MIMI
  Sara, Sara, it's those kittens again, isn't it? Those damned kittens.

SARA
  Four of them. One grey, one ginger, one...

MIMI
  And you imagine, don't you, that you're the only woman in the world who has ever dreamt of giving birth to kittens? Even I...

SARA
  You mean you dream that too? You...

MIMI
  Of course not. I tell you, if I dreamt of kittens I'd be eating them, not giving birth to them. Skinning them, roasting them, biting into...

SARA
  Mimi! I always want to cuddle them, stroke them, hear them purr. But when they – come out of me they are all slimy and wet. All sticky.

MIMI
  And you don't want to play tabby and lick them clean and let them find their way to your teats?

SARA
  Ugh!

MIMI
  It's a good thing they're kittens then, and not...

SARA
  And then they die and shrivel into little balls. Little balls of furry dust.

MIMI
  And then you are left alone. Always the same dream then?

SARA
> The very same. Except sometimes the kittens are different colours. This time there wasn't a white one. There is always a white one.

MIMI
> You've got it right, Sara. Alone.

SARA
> Perhaps when this is all over, when we have survived, when we are back home again.

MIMI
> I've told you before, none will survive, none.

SARA
> We must.

MIMI
> You know, Sara, after all this, the persecution, the camp, the smoke from the crematorium. After all this...

SARA
> We must.

MIMI
> I'm not even sure that I want to survive, to go on, to what?

SARA
> One day we'll go back.

MIMI
> Back? We can't go back. We'll go forward, to what?

SARA
> To a house, a garden, a husband, even a child perhaps.

MIMI
> A child that isn't a kitten?

SARA
> The music will play, and Mimi, you'll dance again.

MIMI
> I'll never dance again. What would I dance for?

> *Faint music which soon stops.*

> They picked him up by the heels. They swung him. They dashed him against...

SARA
...the wall. I know Mimi, and it wasn't a dream.

MIMI
Perhaps it was. Perhaps it was just...

Their roles are now reversed. SARA gathers MIMI into her arms to comfort her. They now lie down head to head. SARA carefully covers MIMI with the blanket.

SARA
Balls of dust. Little balls of dust.

They fall into an exhausted sleep. Voices start to repeat and overlap.

MALE
Then they will gas us all and burn us all. Under the packed soil our ashes will sour the earth. No one to mourn us. No one to tell our tale.

HORST
I have four children of my own and every one of them is perfect – pink cheeks, blue eyes, flaxen hair, true young Aryans. *(repeat)*

MALE
Oh that the bird in my bone cage could come at the bird in your bone cage. Mine would attack and...

MALE
And when we are made to shovel out the ashes we find little white fragments among the cinders, tiny bones, fragile as bird bones.

MALE
Sing a song of woman lying in my bed.
Tell me shall I love her,
Or eat her up instead.

Voices stop.

Z
(speaks for the first time) You, Gypsy with lice in your crotch.
You, Gypsy with filthy worms in your gut.
You with your uncircumcised prick.

ITZAK
And then there is that other story, the third story.

HORST
The last story?

ITZAK
Herr Kaporal, you know as well as I do that there is no such thing as the last story.

HORST
There is always another?

ITZAK
Always... *(telling story)* And what is wisdom? That's the question, a question we all ask ourselves at one time or another: What is wisdom, and which of us is truly wise? There's an old saying, "The whiter the beard, the wiser the head." But that's not so, is it, for we've all met foolish grandfathers and we've all known wise children.

HORST
Especially babies, Kapo. I remember my mother saying that every child is wise before be begins to speak.

ITZAK
Just so... *(telling story)* There was this little village, this little Jewish village; it was just one amongst many such villages in the district of Kirminsk. The low huts were built of wattle and daub, just the same as in any country place you might name, and the streets were narrow and rutted and dusty, just as you might imagine them. The same sort of children played on those streets, the same sort of women gathered at the wellhouse every morning to wash clothes and gossip. The same sort of men met in the evening for a drink and a toss or two of the dice. But this one particular village had a treasure that the other places could not match. This treasure was the reason why so many people came to the village. They came by ones and twos and fives and tens from all the countryside around. They came to visit the treasure, and the treasure was a little man with a bent back and a withered right arm and his name was Avron the Wise.

HORST
He sounds like a misshapen little fellow, Kapo, an ugly little fellow.

ITZAK
On the contrary, he had the most beautiful eyes you have ever seen. But it was, of course, not his eyes that attracted all the attention, but his tongue.

HORST
His tongue?

ITZAK
All these people who came to him came to ask his advice. To put to him questions that seemed impossible.

HORST
And he answered all their questions?

ITZAK
Quite the contrary. First he listened carefully to their complaints. Next he sat there in his battered old armchair just thinking. Sometimes this meditation would last so long that the visitor had the impression that the wise man had simply gone to sleep and forgotten everything but his dreams. But just as the questioner was about to give up, Avron would open one eye and then the other, would give a long sigh, and then open his mouth.

HORST
And the answer would pop out like magic?

ITZAK
No, no, not a bit of it. Out would pop... another question. A question so deep and philosophical and impenetrable that the visitor had no choice but to try his best to answer it. The great question of being and non-being for instance, the magical question of the power of numbers, the heretical question of the length of God's beard.

HORST
Unanswerable questions.

ITZAK
Exactly. After a tussle with such a conundrum, the petitioner's own problem seemed small and easy, and most of Avron's visitors were able to solve their own problems and went away satisfied.

HORST
And those that were not?

ITZAK
Ah, those few were the chosen of Avron's heart. They stayed on as his disciples, and learned all the tricks of the Wise Man trade. Later they set up business on their own account. Avron's only stipulation was that they should establish themselves not less than one hundred kilometres from his village. After all, too much competition can ruin any enterprise.

> *Whistle is blown. Perhaps by Z. MIMI and SARA come out of their hut. They are exhausted and lie down for a few moments without speaking. Then SARA gets purposefully up and prepares to wash herself. She takes the piece of soap in her hand and, lifting her skirt, is about to soap her pudenda. Something she is obviously going to do with great energy, if with some disgust.*

MIMI
No! *(snatches away soap)*

SARA
What do you mean, no? You want me to get crabs? No thank you very much. *(reaches for the soap again)*

MIMI
　　Don't touch it.

SARA
　　You want me to be hauled off to the gas chambers, the ovens?

> *At this point begins the chant of the CHORUS repeating the names of the concentration camps, this time from East to West. This continues under the dialogue to the end of the scene.*

CHORUS
　　Sobibor
　　Lublin-Majdenek
　　Praviensis
　　Chelmnop
　　Stuthof
　　Jadovina
　　Jasnovac
　　Malthausen
　　Gross Rosen
　　Ravensbruck
　　Dachau
　　Flossenburg
　　Buchenwald
　　Sachsenburg
　　Dora Mittelbau
　　Niederhagen
　　Bergen-Belsen
　　Esterwegen
　　Struthof
　　Herzogenbusch

SARA
　　Ein laus, ihrer Tod, you know what that means, don't you?

MIMI
　　Of course I know.

SARA
　　And they'd do it too. I'm not taking any chances.

MIMI
　　It's only a matter of time. We'll all end up there one of these days, every last one of us. There's no getting away from that.

SARA
　　I just want to survive another day, another week, just survive.

MIMI
Sara, Sara, I know all that. But that soap, you know it's...

SARA
The fat of your husband, your brother...

MIMI
...the fat of your daughter, your mother...

SARA
...of your uncle, your lover.

MIMI
It might even be your rabbi. And who would want to wash themselves with such learned grease?

SARA
But it is soap, Mimi, soap. The stuff that'll keep you from scabies, from lice, from... (*She whispers something in MIMI's ear.*)

MIMI
You think I don't know all that?

SARA
Then how?

MIMI in turn whispers something in SARA's ear.

That works?

MIMI
Well, isn't it true that everything in this hellhole belongs to the Germans?

SARA
That's true.

MIMI
Then doesn't it follow that all the lice are Nazi lice? That's why they enjoy biting us Jews so much.

SARA
That's true.

MIMI
That's why the fussy little buggers can't stand your spit. They retreat before the very idea of yidspit.

The train chorus is becoming louder.

SARA
I would myself if my mouth wasn't full of it.

MIMI
I tell you, Sara, if I could kill a Brownshirt with it as easily as a brown bug I'd spend all my days spitting, and all my nights too.

SARA
I'd spit until my mouth was nothing but a desert, then I'd spit dry sand at them.

MIMI
A venom like grit in their faces!

The train chorus has become louder and louder and has drowned out the women's voices.

Bread Dance - Tango of the Starving

The CHORUS, now in their concentration camp uniforms, take their places on the bandstand as musicians.
SARA and MIMI enter in the characters, but not the costumes, of CORALIE and JULIE. JULIE is eating an ice cream cone.

JULIE
Thank God they sell ice cream here, I'm famished.

CORALIE
How can you be famished? It's not that long since we had lunch.

JULIE
Since you had lunch. I had to settle for a salad and a milkshake – remember?

CORALIE
And I had to settle for that awful Belgian thing—*carbonade flamande*—whatever that means. And then, even worse, I had that quite dreadful English rice pudding.

JULIE
Well, they do try to cater to all the tourists.

CORALIE
Julie, dear, let me give you a piece of advice. Never, never, never order English rice pudding.

The band, whose music so far has been light, even frivolous, now strikes up a passionate tango. SARA drops her JULIE character and her ice cream cone has been replaced by a hunk of dark bread. She descends the steps of the bandstand holding the bread as though it was a bouquet of flowers. Z enters from the opposite side of the stage. They approach each other with great purpose, yet warily.

They begin their dance. SARA hides the bread behind her and brings it out with a flourish as a gift for her lover. Z refuses the gift and gestures for her to eat it herself. SARA offers it to Z again, begging him to take it. They come closer together, they part, they dance together. Always the bread is on their minds. Suddenly their mood changes and they both snatch at the bread, intent on getting it, not caring whether the other starves, showing simply the passion of the starving. They have become enemies, each wanting to kill the other for possession of the food. During this frenzy each manages to snatch some of the bread, but most of it crumbles to the ground and they scrabble madly in the dirt trying to pick up the crumbs. Now they are lying on the floor facing each other.

Slowly they get up and begin to dance again the lovers' dance, but they are exhausted. They fall down, try to get up, but have no strength. Again and again they make the attempt to rise, only to sink down again. At the last they fall into each other's arms. Are they making love, or are they in the throes of death? The tango plays on as though trying to make them rise again to the music, but when there is no response from the lovers the tango tails off into widely-spaced single notes. As the last note sounds they make one more attempt to get up, but only manage to raise their heads a little. In silence they fall into a posture of total despair and remain there.

Epilogue

ITZAK and HORST seem to be in one of their friendly moods. They are, perhaps, talking and playing together, running about tossing what appears to be a ball between them. Have they become just two young boys playing outside after supper, waiting for their mothers to call them to bed? At the third throw and catch ITZAK keeps the ball, holds it up wonderingly.

ITZAK
  Where did you get it?

HORST
  Well...

ITZAK
  Where in heaven's name did you get it?

  HORST motions ITZAK to throw it back, but ITZAK holds on to it, slowly brings it up to his nose. Sniffs it ecstatically. Then very reluctantly throws it back to HORST.

The smell of oranges. The smell of holidays, the smell of winter Sabbaths. My brother and myself eating our Shabbat oranges, but not before we had exchanged them several times. We were always convinced, you see, that the other one was bigger than our own.

HORST
Christmas. Oranges always remind me of Christmas. The candles amongst the green boughs. The snow falling on the fields. Our mother, handsome and large as an angel protecting us from the sternness of our father, from the wrath of our waspish grandmama.

ITZAK
In winter it was oranges, in autumn big juicy apples and in summer...

HORST
...in summer it was those little chip baskets full to the brim with strawberries.

There is a moment of silence between them. ITZAK obviously cannot forget about the orange in HORST's pocket.

ITZAK
What are you going to do with it?

HORST
With what?

ITZAK
With the orange. The golden apple, if you like.

HORST
Now it's a golden apple is it? A prize for the swiftest?

ITZAK
And you're the swiftest?

HORST
At this point, yes, Kapo, I am. Everyone knows that you Yids are not exactly athletes. Degenerates can't be athletes can they?

ITZAK
It's a long time. A long, long time, since I saw, or even smelled an...

HORST
(At the mention of time he looks at his watch.) Five minutes, Kapo. Five minutes...

HORST slowly turns his back and peels the orange, throwing the peel on the ground. He begins slowly to eat the fruit, but ends by stuffing it in his mouth. ITZAK stands there realizing that fate has caught up with him.

HORST is wiping his mouth with his handkerchief as he coolly addresses ITZAK.

HORST
Selection!

ITZAK with great reluctance takes out his whistle and blows a feeble blast. His head is lowered.

HORST
Kapo.

They stand facing each other as ITZAK begins to repeat the following number sequences.

ITZAK
3 03 003 0033 00303 30300 330303 3303 33003 330033
5 05 005 0055 00505 50500 550505 5505 55005 550055
7 07 007 0077 00707 70700 770707 7707 77007 770077
9 09 009 0099 00909 90900 990909 9909 99009 990099

And so on through the odd numbers, ad infinitum. Other speeches are spoken over the numbers. As ITZAK speaks the other prisoners begin to appear on stage. Their movements are very slow and deliberate as one by one they take their places on different parts of the stage.

At about 19 in the number sequence they suddenly begin to move frenetically in the bone dance. The following speech by Z is spoken before he begins the same frenetic movements as the other victims.

Z
And where are they, those others,
Our Sisters, our Brothers,
Where are they?

As suddenly as they have begun their bone dance the prisoners stop and slowly remove their clothes, which they place in very neat piles in front of them. Now naked, they line up meekly to go to their deaths. They each take one of the pails of water standing in a row at the front of the stage, walk, back, and throw the water against the backdrop.

During this scene the FEMALE VOICE is heard speaking on tape:

FEMALE
    I'll tell you again and again the same story.
    I was a child and all at once I was a woman.
    I called to my mother, but she couldn't hear me.
    The storm blew my voice away.

    I was hiding like a hare in a thicket
    When my lover came to me.
    Like a wraith of smoke he lay on me.
    His tongue was a dry leaf in my mouth.

    That's when I died and was burned.
    Nothing, nothing remains
    But grey ash, grey ash,
    Grey ash in the wind.

> *Through all this the numbers continue and continue until everyone has left the theatre. And still the numbers go on and on… and on.*
>
> *The end.*

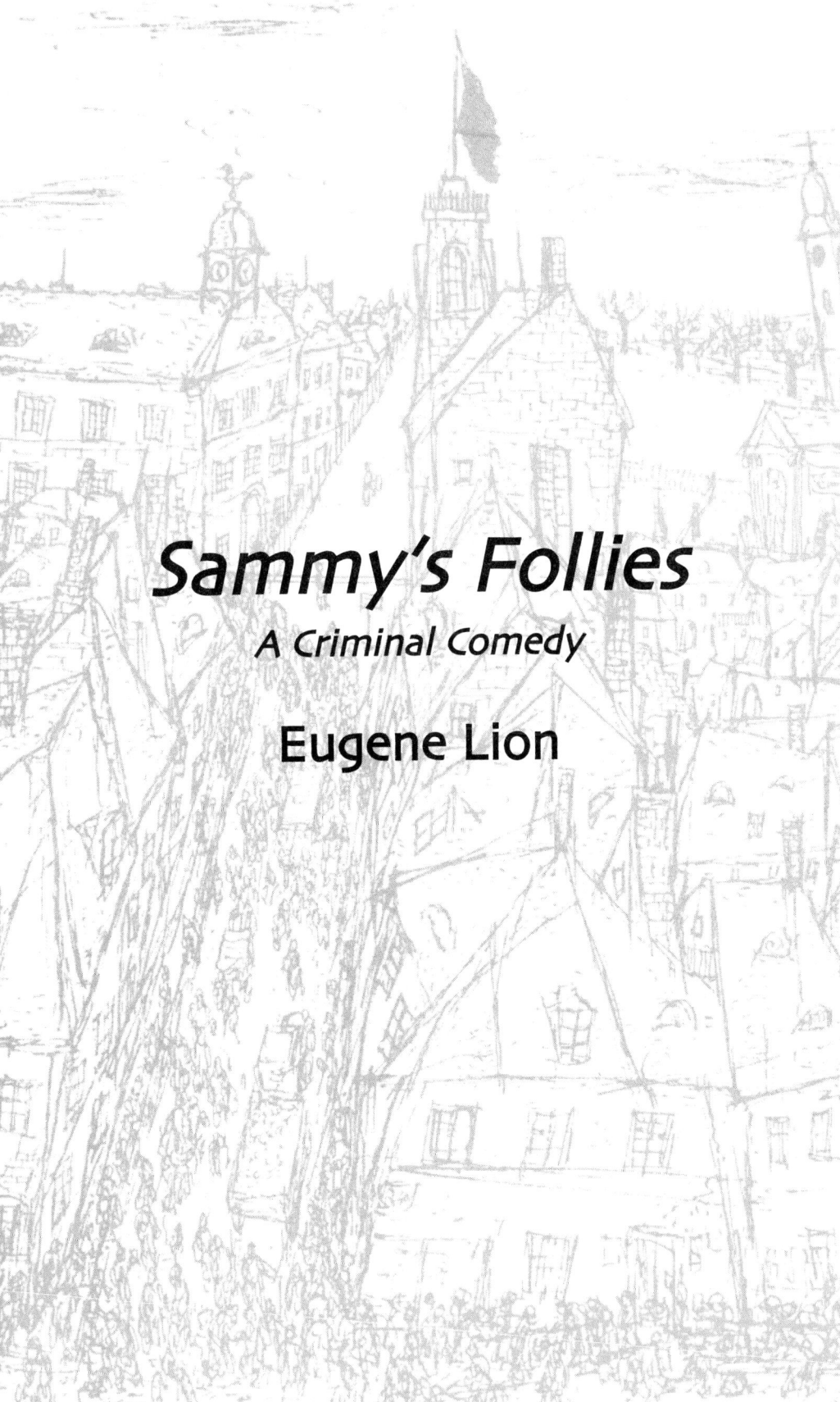

Sammy's Follies
A Criminal Comedy

Eugene Lion

Originally a New Yorker, now a playwright without borders, **Eugene Lion** has written, directed choreographed, acted and designed for theatre, film and television. He is the first North American to direct at The Abbey, Ireland's national theatre, and he has staged and written works at the Pushkin in Moscow, Dublin's Gate Theatre, The Advent in Nashville, Ottawa's National Arts Centre, the Edinburgh Festival, and on and off Broadway. He was artistic director of the Hawaii Public Theater and associate director of The Guthrie Theater in Minneapolis, as well as artistic director of Guthrie 2, its alternative stage. Among the authors he has directed are Jacques Audiberti, Samuel Beckett, Ugo Betti, Bertolt Brecht, Friedrich Dürrenmatt, Jean Genet, Michel de Ghelderode, Robert Hellman, Michael Ondaatje, George Bernard Shaw and Peter Weiss. He debuted as choreographer and designer in 1963 in New York, where during the Vietnam War he served as arts and political director of the Washington Square Methodist Church, which granted sanctuary to that war's first draft resisters; the church also reached national audiences via network television, while providing a home for insurgent theatre companies such as the Polish Lab and the Bread and Puppet Theatre. Paralleling Lion's independent efforts is a lifelong collaboration with his wife, dancer-actor-choreographer-painter Jo Lechay. Together they have pioneered experimental performing techniques and created more than 40 dance, theatre and multidisciplinary works, touring Canada, the United States and Europe. Among his produced translations are Betti's *The Burnt Flower-Bed* and *Queen and the Rebels*, Frisch's *The Physicists*, Genet's *The Maids*, Ghelderode's *Women at the Tomb* and Alexander Ostrovski's *Fools!*.Based in Montreal and British Columbia, he writes serious comedies and subversive musicals.

Sammy's Follies is scheduled to premiere in spring 2006 at the Persephone Theatre in Saskatoon, Saskatchewan and at Northern Stage Ensemble in Newcastle, England.

CHARACTERS

the director

SAMMY	barkeeper of the Follies	commandant

his troupe

SIMON	ex-civil servant	officer
ADDY	gay waiter	patient
JOCKO-ALI	black porter	escapee
FLIP	ex-GI	guard
MacIAN	former divinity student	surgeon
MAZO	retired quack	alter ego
AB	unpublished author	prosecutor
BERTIE	ex-high court judge	judge
KERR	lawyer, between clients	defender
ROSIE	ex-burlesque queen	newcomer

*and band**

JIMMY	the Follies cook, on drums
PARNELL	accordion
HEISEL	trumpet

* *choice of instruments is optional*

SETTING

Time: Now.
Place: A theatre.

NOTE

Indented dialogue indicates a song.

Sammy's Follies
A Criminal Comedy
by Eugene Lion

— — • — —

A bright light on a floor stand suddenly hits SAMMY, his hand on the switch, apron flung over one shoulder. Blinding white shirt. Histrionic eye makeup.

SAMMY
'Evening! Actually, up here it's morning. Either way may be too late, but we'll do our best. And as these are games best played after dark, you'll need more light —

Lights blaze up, disclosing their operators in varying stages of garish make-up and costuming: operatic TRAMP CLOWNS chronically incomplete. Other lights, on wheeled stands, are also operated by the performers.

Twelve low comics!

A tardy light reveals ROSIE, an aging ex-stripper, now a white-face clown navigating an eternal bacchanal.

One burlesque blonde! And me! Sworn this show to diversions more real than natural. Madcap athletes! Gutter *artistes*! Hired to rid an audience of its illusions. Trust in nothing. The spectacle is bait, the jokes a stratagem. Our performances? Sugar on the arsenic! *(presents his face)* This face? Samuel Kestor, owner-operator of a carefree corner bar called The Follies!

A platform explodes into view—a stage on stage—stools, misshapen bottles, sawdust, spittoon and bar, much of it in sulfurous yellows, fluorescent greens, radiant reds. Below and to the sides, in clear sight, items normally found offstage – wall phone, bulletin board, cable, rope, card table, folding chairs – where the ACTORS can be themselves when not playing derelicts. Small bandstand. Dead TV.

SAMMY
The time? Yours! The day? Election Day! Which means I'm closed. *(ties on his apron)* No walk-ins, this is a private party. In your world a day of deliverance. Here I guarantee you moments equally liberating.

Musical flourish: old accordion, OLDER MUSICIAN, orange hair parted by a white streak. Note: choice of all instruments is optional.

Parnell, our accordionist. Plays for drinks. Washed ashore from County Cork. Now, like any red pepper in ale, permanently afloat. *(to PARNELL)*

Stumble over to the bandstand, will you, and play something heroic while
I introduce the others.

> PARNELL *shuffles to the bandstand.* SAMMY *prods second musician,*
> JIMMY, *an ageless, greasy-haired capon.*

Smile for the crowd.

> JIMMY *grimaces.*

Jimmy, our cook, doubles on drums. His specialty? Yesterday's menu. *(pats* JIMMY*)* A treasure. Keeps the trade alive.

> *A third musician,* HEISEL, *in yellow fright wig plummets down a vertical light bar sounding a trumpet.*

Heisel! A tone-deaf mute on trumpet. My favourite: he has no lines.

> *Another* PERFORMER *steps forward, sporting the remains of a swagger and an elegant moustache.* SAMMY *hands him a pair of tattered gloves.*

Simon. Civil servant, statistician, at last count reduced to zeros.

SIMON
(icy smile) Civil but never servile.

SAMMY
(dryly) A supporting role dispatched with conspicuous modesty. *(music: crescendo)*

(picks up a pail and mop) Jocko–

JOCKO-ALI
Ali!

> JOCKO-ALI, *a veteran African-American, seated, works on an unfinished job of blackface. He flashes gleaming teeth inside huge white lips and wears a brimless Muslim cap.*

SAMMY
–of the wide nostril.

JOCKO-ALI
Desdemona's dessert!

SAMMY
(puts pail and mop down beside him) Make-believe Muslim!

JOCKO-ALI
On the trail of the white man's spoor—

SAMMY
Sent to heaven with a bullet.

JOCKO-ALI
Armed with a mop.

SAMMY
And a toilet brush!

ADDY, a carafe queen, lifts JOCKO-ALI's cap, buries his fingers in the BLACK MAN's hair.

ADDY
Love the feel of chocolate hair. One big candybox!

JOCKO-ALI
Careful, I'm the headache in your hell.

ADDY
Hush, li'l baby, don't you cry!
Papa's gonna buy you an oil well!

SAMMY
Presenting Addy. The family jewel.

ADDY
Up front 'n' down in back.

SAMMY
Addy, bow to the gentlemen in the house.

ADDY
(curtsies) Low enough? *(singles out AUDIENCE MALE)* Want that one.

SAMMY
Later, dear, we're about to start.

Music turns martial; ADDY ties on his apron.

SAMMY
(toes a prone figure in army cap and jacket) Dead.

Lifted by his fellows and tossed into the air, the dead soldier, FLIP, revives.

FLIP
Alive!

SAMMY
Flip! First in war!–

Shot by a percussion blast, FLIP dies again and is sent sprawling.

SIMON
Second everywhere else!

A tall derelict, MacIAN, is seated on the wreckage of FLIP.

SAMMY
Another crusader. *(turns MacIAN's collar around)* Only his side lost. In his youth a divinity student. More worldly now– *(smacks MacIAN out of his stupor)* –but still devoted to the spirits. Turn the other cheek.

MacIAN
(turns, is slapped almost alert) Ian MacIan!

SAMMY
Martyred in the wrong century.

MacIAN topples over.

SIMON
Now, as we move down the evolutionary scale, our intelligentsia.

Three standing DERELICTS abruptly lean on one another.

SAMMY
On bottom, Ambrose Bartley. Affectionately known as Bertie.

BERTIE
(opens one eye) British high court judge.

SAMMY
Lost his honour during the war. Paid with cash and his composure as well.

BERTIE
Chorus girl she was, with the bosom of Victoria and the bottom of m'mom!

ADDY
Moral: you always get it in the end.

Percussion as the three men wince.

SAMMY
On top, Yehudi Ab. Writer, refugee, professional victim.

> AB's pockets overflow with papers and notes. SAMMY plucks a scrap to read.

AB
> (snatches it back) Ver derhargt en a goyishe gass!

SAMMY
> Yiddish for "You should only drop dead–"

AB
> (heavy Jewish accent) "–on a gentile street!"

SAMMY
> (indicates the third of the trio) In the middle, Angus Kerr. Criminal lawyer, accessory after the fact. Between clients.

> > **ALL THREE**
> > (harmonize) Three gallants away from ho-o-ome
> > Blindfolded a babe in a bar-ro-om.
> > Spun 'round she chose "Justice" – poetic.
> > And they argued all night
> > Over who had the right
> > To do what and with which and to who-om!
> > (holding out their palms) Redeem us, pleeeeease!

SAMMY
> Where's Rosie?

ADDY
> (on bar-stage) In the can, saving her entrance for last.

SAMMY
> Get her.

> ADDY finishes hanging signs on either side of the bar-stage: "GENTS" and "LADEEZE."

SAMMY
> (wakes MAZO, asleep with his crutch) Salvatore Mazo. Anarchist, socialist, back-alley abortionist. Presently searching for the perfect anesthetic. (musical flourish) And introducing–

ADDY
> (under "LADEEZE" sign) From the tiled throne rooms of the world–!

SAMMY
> Stripper, *chanteusie*–!

MAZO
(*hauls himself up*) Mother of us all!

ADDY
The accessible–!

SAMMY
Miss Rosie Blossoms!

> *Led by her assets, an imperious profile and a grand manner, ROSIE sails in from under the "GENTS" sign, positions herself majestically, lifts her arms, throws back her head to sing – percussion–*

JOCKO-ALI
HEAR YE! HEAR YE! HEAR YE! DIS HONOURABLE COURT IS NOW–

> *FLIP, risen, crowns JOCKO-ALI—cymbal crash—with a bottle, which bends and bounces back. JOCKO-ALI looks around blankly.*

FLIP
I'm first.

ROSIE
(*suddenly fragile*) Shall I take it over again?

SAMMY
Absolutely. Here we go.

> *Musical reprise. SAMMY escorts ROSIE to the footlights. ROSIE lifts her arms, opens her mouth–*

FLIP
My shoes!!

> *Music halts again.*

ROSIE
(*flat*) I must be in the wrong play.

FLIP
Where the hell are my shoes?

ROSIE
Hey, it's my number!

FLIP
Up your number.

JOCKO-ALI
(reaches under a drum) Here. *(tosses FLIP a pair of shoes)*

FLIP
(stares at a loose sole) Ain't mine!

ROSIE
Oh can it!

FLIP
Somebody took my shoes.

JOCKO-ALI
(stands over FLIP with mop and pail) Let's go, Yankee-Doodle.

FLIP
There's a whole stage, you black bastard. Mop somewhere else.

JOCKO-ALI's mop turns club. FLIP aims a shoe.

SAMMY
Post time, gentlemen!

FLIP
Truce!

General run on the bar.

ROSIE
(dry) And so we begin.

Act One
— • —

MacIAN
(listing to port) A little courage, Sam.

SAMMY
No freebies this early. (BERTIE holds up a bill.)

MacIAN
Thanks, mate.

FLIP
C'mon, Rosie. Bertie's treatin'!

> HEISEL gets PARNELL and JIMMY their drinks.

MAZO
(claps BERTIE on the back) Pal!

BERTIE
Kiss off.

MAZO
Chum, bosom buddy, fellow constituent!

BERTIE
Last try.

MAZO
Comrade!!

BERTIE
(immediately in tears) Tovarich!!!

> BERTIE and MAZO fall into each other's arms.

KERR
(wry) They've just taken the Winter Palace.

BERTIE
Who do we kill first?

MacIAN
(turns toward AB) Yehudi.

> AB sits alone in ACTORS' area, collating scripts.

MAZO
   Hey, Ab!

BERTIE
   (*lifts his glass*) Cirrhosis for your liver!

AB
   (*without accent*) It's Election Day.

MAZO
   More reason to get crocked.

ADDY
   C'mon, Ab. Join the wake.

AB
   Announce the house rules.

SAMMY
   You're not ready.

AB
   (*gathers his papers, his accent returned*) God should be so ready.

   SAMMY nods.

ADDY
   (*rings up cash register*) Go, Simon!

SIMON
   I don't like following so immediately the sound of money.

ROSIE
   Why don't I do a quickie? (*starts to strip, sings*)

>   It's an art – with me.
>   Take heart – with me.
>   Y'know, y'know, y'know you can't live without me!

SIMON
   (*cuts ROSIE short*) We can, we do! Forgive her. You see, for drinks—one each scene—we degrade ourselves.

ADDY
   (*with trayful of drinks*) Whatever's necessary we do.

SIMON
And however depraved, however criminal our acts, no one onstage is subject to arrest, 'specially– (*ADDY hands him his drink.*) –on Election Day. For the simple reason–

ROSIE
(*bump and grind*) –there are no cops in the cast!

Percussion. Tossed sawdust.

SIMON
This charnel house? (*Behind him, lights and tables are rearranged, a stool placed on top of the bar.*) A gin-mill tribunal. Where Yehudi– (*Note: where comfortable, ACTORS' actual names may be used.*) (*AB raises a hand.*) –pursues his pound of flesh, Sammy– (*A spot hits SAMMY.*) –gambles for his humanity, and the author gets a run for your money! Me? Court stenographer to start. Our good shepherd– (*indicates SAMMY*) –likes a docile flock. But don't worry, I get my jollies in the end. Till then, have a ball, run amuck, go blind!

Cymbal crash. BERTIE steps forward, using JOCKO-ALI's mophead for a wig, which also serves him as handkerchief, worry beads and scourge.

BERTIE
I preside. (*ADDY supplies him with two drinks.*) In deference to my long experience before the bar. My good friend, Yehudi Ab, as playwright's proxy, will serve as counsel for the Prosecution. And taking on the singularly difficult role of defendant, our director and host, Mr. Samuel Kestor.

AB
(*with accent*) His crime–

KERR
As charged.

AB
–INdifference.

BERTIE
In time of need.

AB
Willful, personal, prolonged indifference.

KERR
(*quietly*) Motion is introduced here for mistrial. The charge is speculative, unparalleled and–

BERTIE
(*merrily*) Dee-nied! (*hands KERR his drink*) Mr. Kerr, genteel champion for the Defense. Which brings us to the delicate issue of the jury. (*to ACTORS*) Who's on tonight? (*hands are raised*) — two, three — four.

> *Note: Jury duty among the ACTORS is rotated, their number a minority on a full panel. ACTOR-JURORS seat and unseat themselves as needed, their verdicts unrehearsed.*

Less than half. Which– (*to AUDIENCE*) –dear hearts leaves us with but one recourse. *You.* Ladies and gentlemen, in the debauched cause of retribution, and on behalf of a band of players longing to be closer to their audience, I invoke your presence. Lights!!

> *House lights hit the AUDIENCE.*

BERTIE
(*recoils*) Lot of 'em, aren't there?!

SAMMY
Impanel them.

BERTIE
All of 'em?!

SAMMY
Just eight.

BERTIE
Done. (*to AUDIENCE*) Come thou and every clean beast! And be reminded, at play's end you must render a just verdict.

> *AB has given MacIAN a script open to his cue.*

MacIAN
Brethren! Cistern! (*holds out his palm*) Affirm the Epiderm!

SAMMY
No panhandling.

AB
Okay, okay. (*to MacIAN*) Change it to "Affirm the Infirm! Sit on our jury!"

> *MacIAN hurriedly pencils in the change.*

MacIAN
"–Infirm! Sit on–" (*fogged*) This the Sabbath?

ADDY
Every day's the Sabbath!

JOCKO-ALI
(*starts the Islamic call to prayer*) AAAllAAA AAAkkBAAA!! AAAnn–

MacIAN
(*cuts him off*) Wrong call! (*immediately malevolent*) Blow, wind!!

    HEISEL trumpets.

MacIAN
Let the earth bring forth living creatures after their kind! And every creeping thing that creepeth!

JOCKO-ALI
(*shakes bottle, sprays AUDIENCE with activated brew*) Excelsior Deo!

MacIAN
(*papal armspread*) Eight jurors! Eight! We need eight! Unbend thy knee! Cast off the shackles of passivity! Sit on our jury! (*waits, to JOCKO-ALI*) Try a little sex.

JOCKO-ALI
(*to AUDIENCE*) Last row! On the end! You, miss! I'm Black! I'm beautiful! I'm yours!

ADDY
(*presents a haunch*) Better yet, some white meat!

JOCKO-ALI
(*to AUDIENCE*) Fellow fundamentalists! Choose! (*raised index finger behind his own head*) Tonto here! Or– (*indicates ADDY*) –that Yankee studhoss Silver!

    ADDY whinnies.

JOCKO-ALI
(*to MAZO*) Give 'em some Carlos Marx. (*leaps into AUDIENCE*)

MAZO
(*to AUDIENCE*) Neighbours! Collaborators! Spectators of the world! Think! You have nothing to lose but your bad seats!

ADDY
Food and drinks on the house!

    Two approaches to an unpredictable section, the first if a game crowd, the second if not – combinations, additions & subtractions at the ACTORS' pleasure.

JOCKO-ALI
(*in aisle, victorious*)
Bingo! One juror!

JOCKO-ALI
(*beseeches*)
One juror!

Note: The first AUDIENCE-JUROR may have to be a plant.

MacIAN, with towel, is possessed by comatose moves of the High Mass. FLIP, as deacon, assists. SAMMY rings up cash register repeatedly.

Silence.

MacIAN
One, one, one, one!

Silence.

MacIAN
(*sonorous*) Introibo ad altare Dei!

ADDY is in the AUDIENCE, the better to hustle JURORS.

MacIAN
(*opens his eyes, yells*) Bertie!

BERTIE
(*hurries forward*) Chickadees, we need you! Help us lay the bloody egg. This is a court of last resort! There is no further appeal. Ah! Lovely! One volunteer! Is there a second? Someone to watch the watchers. A second, a second, a second juror! (*waits*) All right, fine. Now hear this! We guarantee each juror at least one onstage bowl of glorious third act chicken soup! Plus all the delicious bread you can eat! A second, a second, a second juror! Going once! – Going twice! – (*long pause, acrid horn, with wig over his heart*) Beloveds, it is my grievous duty to state that you have cast yourselves into the unbottom'd pit — and become one with the defendant!

JOCKO-ALI
(*working other side of the house*)
There's a staircase on the aisle, Miss* Gracias, gracias! Brave of you, but we're harmless. At this stage anyway. (*taking her hand*) We're in your debt–

KERR
Hold it!

BERTIE
One second, ma'am!

KERR
Excuse me. The lady will state her faith.

AB
Objection!

---

* *If a man:* **BERTIE**
Excuse me, sir. The court's partial to the fair sex. Would you mind if the honour of first juror falls to a female? But you're absolutely next. Terrific! Much obliged! (*doffs his wig*) Now, is there a lady in the house?

KERR
Defense maintains, as it has every night, that the juror's religion may prejudice her or his verdict.

AB
Bertie's ruled on that. The juror's religion is immaterial. Everybody died there.

BERTIE
You're getting repetitious. Mr. Kerr. *(takes JUROR's hand)* We're honoured. *(kisses her hand)* And in your debt! *(leads her to onstage seat)* This way, m'pet.

JOCKO-ALI
One down, seven to go. A second, a second! You, sir? Two it is! And a third!

MacIAN
Confiteor Deo! Do we have a fourth?

BERTIE
We do!

JOCKO-ALI
Then break open a new deck! *(They chortle, slap palms.)*

BERTIE!
A fifth! Is there a fifth? A fifth?

MacIAN
(elevates a flask) A fifth! *(sees a FIFTH JUROR)* Another fifth!

BERTIE
(sees a SIXTH JUROR) A sixth!

ADDY
Go for broke!

AB
His crime–

KERR
As charged.

AB
INdifference!

BERTIE
Willful, personal, prolonged indifference!

AB
In time of need.

BERTIE
Plead distaste, fear, disbelief. Your privilege – and ours to charge you with inertia, apathy, passivity. In a word, *indifference*. One reprieve. Those, who care to exempt themselves from said charge, will offer themselves at this time. The court will take all comers.

ADDY gyrates.

JOCKO-ALI
Here's one! This way!

ADDY
Anybody else?

BERTIE
Last call!

ADDY
Are there no *men* in the house?

SIMON
Sweet Judas!

MacIAN
Even Judas did his part. These are doubting Thomases!

JOCKO-ALI
  (*spits into his palms*) Seven, come seven! (*at sight of a SEVENTH JUROR*) Seven it is!

JIMMY
  Eight!

MacIAN
  Munda cor meum!

ADDY
  Nine!

MacIAN
  (*to NINTH VOLUNTEER*) Too late, miscreant! Back to your seat! Among the lily-livered passive-ists! (*swings an imaginary giant priapus*) DANG! BA-DONG-DONG!!

BERTIE
  (*scandalized*) My God! Convene the court!

  Trumpet.

BERTIE
  So be it! The remainder in this theatre may consider the defendant's cause their own. Convene the court!

  Trumpet.

ADDY
  Rise! Those of you who can!

JOCKO-ALI
  HEAR YE! HEAR YE! HEAR YE! ALL PERSONS DOING BUSINESS WITH THE FOLLIES, DRAW NEAR, PAY YOUR RESPECTS AND YOU SHALL BE HEARD! (*sour horn*)

BERTIE
  (*mounts the bar*) Hand out the parts. (*climbs stool atop the bar*)

  AB distributes remaining scripts, including one to an AUDIENCE-JUROR. ACTORS have moved into place, some relaxing offside. JOCKO-ALI, using his mop handle, pounds the floor for silence.

BERTIE
  Defendant will state his name.

SAMMY
Franz Ferdinand Höss.

SIMON
(*writing*) Spell the last name.

SAMMY
H – O – umlaut – S – S.

SIMON
Occupation?

SAMMY
Professional soldier.

SIMON
Place of business?

SAMMY
Oswiecim, Poland.

AB
Otherwise known as Auschwitz.

FLIP
(*scoops up handful of sawdust, showers the air*) HA-HAA!!

SIMON
Care to try something more recent?! (*SAMMY smiles evenly.*)

MAZO
(*grins at AUDIENCE*) Thought it was going to be all fun and pretzels, didn't you?!

BERTIE
(*orotund*) Franz Ferdinand Höss, you are charged with willful, personal, prolonged indifference for a period extending from– (*consults script*) –from June 1941 to November 1943. During which time you were commandant of the Auschwitz-Birkenau concentration camp complex. How do you plead?

SAMMY
(*simply*) Not guilty.

JOCKO-ALI
THE PEOPLE OPEN!

FLIP opens his fly – FANFARE – is immediately restrained.

AB

(*downs his drink*) May it please the Court, ladies and gentleman of the jury. We stand upon a mountain of skulls. We smile. We are alive, careful never to ask why. After the war, justice being conveniently blind, the defendant was found guilty of murder, mass murder, and executed. I say "blind" because another crime, a crime of greater significance, never came to trial. The crime of indifference. (*He motions for his glass to be refilled. SAMMY ignores him.*) Murder draws a tight circle: the killer, his victim, their families, a few friends. With indifference the circle of responsibility widens, its diameter, at first cry, being the length of a scream. (*hisses wildly*) IN-DIF-FER-ENCE!! (*pause, softly*) If I shouted, imagine how many more of you I would reach. Alongside indifference, hatred becomes benevolent. Hatred, by its vehemence, at least grants its victim some importance. He exists. (*lays script down*) And, existing, he can hate in return, he can fight back. (*motions again for a drink, without effect; puts down his glass*) Picture a butcher shop: sawdust to catch the blood, porcelain trays for the beef, the butcher cold as his knife, as impassive as his chopping block. What choice has a carcass, eh? (*grabs his chest through his clothes*) Here! Have some meat!! The defendant, as we will prove, treated his prisoners as mere beasts of burden fit mostly for slaughter. (*another plea for a refill is ignored*) Instead of names, numbers. Instead of human beings with individual identities, they became trainloads of flesh to be dispatched upon arrival and discarded upon use. Their suffering—as we shall demonstrate—their degradation, their dehumanization, their deaths meant nothing to the accused. No one mattered. *No one.* We resurrect the defendant, not as scapegoat for our remorse. We are beyond redress, as he is beyond penalty. Our wish, our only wish, is to see a crime *never fully examined* finally brought to justice. The crime of indifference. (*holds out his glass*) Please–

BERTIE

Fill his glass, dammit!

ADDY

One per scene.

BERTIE

Give him my next one. (*turns*) Mr. Kerr.

KERR

(*fumbles with his script, quietly*) Our defense is a simple one. Indifference does not exist. (*looks up*) To be alive is to be in pain. What we call indifference is really a – an armor each of us wears to shield us from the suffering around us. One's own misery is quite enough. Another's is unbearable. The defendant had no choice but to turn a deaf ear to the cries that assailed him from all sides. Anything more would have meant instant annihilation. (*addressing AUDIENCE*) Or does anyone here believe that one person alone could contain the nightmare that was Auschwitz? (*waits, gently*) To those who still turn away from the defendant, I ask – who among you, *who* is prepared at *this* moment to take on the torment, the agony of this – *our!* – world?

A silence.

(*carefully*) The silent voice, the face of stone, belong, as defense shall prove, to a man whose – whose feelings made him doubly sensitive to the horror around him. He had no choice but to hide his – his vulnerability under an impenetrable mask. The charge of indifference is itself proof of the defendant's innocence.

BERTIE
First witness.

AB
My lord, your indulgence. Our first witness, like the defendant, is no longer alive.

BERTIE
Oh! Sorry, old man!

AB
Which gives his testimony a somewhat unbelievable air. Unfortunately, most of my witnesses are dead. To lend their testimony more credibility, therefore, we ask the Court to allow a few graphic reenactments.

BERTIE
Objection?

KERR
Naturally. But since they've been rehearsed, I imagine I'm overruled.

BERTIE
Indeed. Lights!

MacIAN
(*sets lights*) Lights!

BERTIE
Stools!

MAZO
(*presents a pair of stools*) Stools!

BERTIE
Rope!

FLIP
(*produces a heavy rope*) Rope!

AB
The People call– *(checks his script)* A-one-thirty-four Zero-fifteen!

> *JOCKO-ALI adjusts his cap, starts into the scene. SAMMY halts the BLACK ACTOR.*

SAMMY
Winter, it's winter!

JOCKO-ALI
Right– *(pulls jacket tight about his throat, shivers violently, reenters, stops, turns, exits, grabs his script, returns, shivers, enters again)*

BERTIE
Swear in the witness.

MacIAN
(holds out a drink) Place your right hand upon the Word.

> *JOCKO-ALI covers the glass with his palm.*

MacIAN
YOUSOLEMNLYSWEARTOTELLTHETRUTHTHEWHOLETRUTHAND
NOTHIN'BUTTHETRUTHSOHELPYOUGOD?

JOCKO-ALI
I do.

MacIAN
Cheers! *(JOCKO-ALI downs the drink)* Hip-hip! *(–and surrenders the glass.)*

BERTIE
Take the stand.

> *JOCKO-ALI seizes one of the stools, starts to leave with it; halted by FLIP, he stands beside it.*

AB
I offer the witness's left forearm in evidence.

BERTIE
Mark it. *(MacIAN pens numbers on JOCKO-ALI's forearm.)*

AB
Number?

JOCKO-ALI
(reads from his arm) A-one-thirty-four Zero-fifteen.

AB
>Name?

JOCKO-ALI
>(*shivering*) Schneider. Chaim Schneider.

AB
>Place of birth?

JOCKO-ALI
>(*checks script*) Bu – Budejovice, Czechoslovakia.

AB
>Place of death?

JOCKO-ALI
>Oswiecim, Poland.

AB
>Kindly tell the court how you died.

JOCKO-ALI
>I was hanged.

AB
>Your crime, Zero-fifteen?

JOCKO-ALI
>Attempted escape.

AB
>Relate the facts of your death. Briefly.

JOCKO-ALI
>(*shivering*) We were discovered outside Buna, the factory camp, where my mother was. Snow had fallen during the night. Our tracks led them to us.

AB
>How many were you?

JOCKO-ALI
>Three. We were dragged back in time for morning roll call.

AB
>Your mother was at the hanging?

JOCKO-ALI
>She was forced to watch.

ROSIE
Here? *(SAMMY nods; ROSIE steps into place.)*

AB
(to JOCKO-ALI) Go on.

JOCKO-ALI
(reading) The camp stood at attention. SS Major Aumeier spoke of the importance of the camp's work and the danger posed by terrorists. Then the three of us were flogged and forced to climb the gallows. *(mounts the stool)* Aumeier signalled the camp orchestra.

> *SIMON signals MUSICIANS, who begin to play. FLIP tosses his rope over a bar in the flies, fits noose around JOCKO-ALI's neck, then mounts the second stool and stands at attention.*
>
> *ROSIE, in wringing one of her necklaces, snaps a strand: a length of loose pearls falls to the floor.*

ROSIE
Oh Jesus! *(drops to her knees; to MUSICIANS, who have stopped playing)* Cover me! *(begins retrieving pearls)*

> *The MUSICIANS resume playing.*
>
> *During the next exchange, MAZO turns, crosses, answers the wall phone, returns, whispers to SIMON, who rises and goes to the phone. MAZO takes over SIMON's stenographic duties.*

AB
(to ROSIE) Get up!

JOCKO-ALI
Rosie!

> **ROSIE**
> *(cockneys her way across the floor)*
> She was poor but she was honest,
> Victim of a rich man's whim.
> 'E seduced 'er and 'e left 'er–

ADDY
(barks) She walks, she talks, she crawls on her belly like a reptile!

MacIAN
(hisses) Rosie!

ROSIE
(stuffing pearls down her front) What?

MacIAN
You're his mother!

ROSIE
In a minute–

JOCKO-ALI
She's killing the scene!

FLIP
Rosie, it's a hanging!

ROSIE
Up your hanging.

JOCKO-ALI
I die here!!

ROSIE
In a hurry? Jump.

AB
(*to SAMMY*) Do something!

SAMMY
(*dryly*) Pearls before swine.

AB
Still a number, you two?

SAMMY & ROSIE
'E seduced 'er and 'e left 'er
And she 'ad a child by 'im!

AB
(*to FLIP*) Don't just stand there! Drown them out!

FLIP
–I've got a gal that lives on a hill–
Honey, honey!
I've got a gal that lives on a hill!
Babe, babe!

BERTIE
(*up and off the "bench," gavels the bar with a bottle*) Order! Order!

Countersinging, their voices rise.

ROSIE & SAMMY
    It's the syme the 'ole world over!

FLIP
    I've got a gal that lives on a hill!
    KILLLL! KILLLL!!

MAZO
    (*shouts*) –The President! The President!!

ROSIE & SAMMY
    It's the syme the 'ole world over!
    It's the poor what tykes the blyme!!

FLIP
    If she won't her sister will!
    Honey! Oh baby mine!!

BERTIE
    (*roars*) ORDER IN THE– (*staggers FLIP with a whack of his wig*)
    –GODDAMN COURT!!

    Silence.

BERTIE
    (*to MAZO*) What'd you just say?

MAZO
    Dunno, but it sounded great.

BERTIE
    Listen, m'rummies, I'm fully aware of the inspiriting proximity of the bar. Nevertheless, this court expects– (*replaces his wig crookedly*) –a certain sense of decorum. We will not continue until shown the proper contrition. (*ROSIE, FLIP and MAZO hang their heads.*) Very well. Places. (*positions are resumed*) Still with us, Zero-fifteen?

JOCKO-ALI
    Yeah, but I'm about at the end of my rope.

BERTIE
    Well, don't stretch it out.

AB
    Where were we?

SAMMY
    "Major Aumeier–"

AB
    Where?

SAMMY
    "–signalled the camp orchestra."

AB
    Page?

JOCKO-ALI
Thought you wrote this stuff. Three eighty-five.

AB finds the place. SAMMY nods: music.

(*reads*) They were professional musicians. Some had played with the best orchestras. The conductor was from the Warsaw Philharmonic. He tried to comfort us with an aria from a Czech opera–

BERTIE slips, topples off the bar.

BERTIE
(*from floor*) Go on, go on!

JOCKO-ALI
(*exasperated*) The aria was called, "Why Should We Not Be Merry When God Gives Us Strength."

AB
(*pause*) And?

JOCKO-ALI
(*checks his script*) That's it.

SAMMY
Doctor.

MAZO hobbles into scene. Drum roll. SAMMY nods. JOCKO-ALI hands MAZO his script. Gripping the rope, FLIP leaps off his stool – percussion – lifting the BLACK MUSLIM into the air. FLIP, with help, secures the rope. JOCKO-ALI jerks about: the latest dance craze.

KERR
Objection!

BERTIE
Hold it!!

JOCKO-ALI and MUSICIANS halt.

KERR
Defense strenuously objects to reenacting the moment of death. Such an exhibition is morbid and in questionable taste. It undermines all chance of a rational verdict.

AB
Has counsel ever witnessed a hanging?

KERR
No.

AB
I assure my learned adversary that hangings are, by definition, morbid. And always, I might add, in questionable taste. My lord, we've researched this scene with care and can attest to its accuracy.

BERTIE
(*augustly*) Objection overruled. Continue.

> *Music resumes. The BLACK ACTOR completes his dance – abrupt, convulsive, climactic end. Silence. MAZO reaches up, takes JOCKO-ALI's pulse; JOCKO-ALI jerks violently, then is immediately still.*

MAZO
Purely muscular. The witness is mortified.

AB
Thank you, Doctor. (*MAZO withdraws.*) Corporal!

FLIP
(*snaps to attention*) Yessir!

AB
Face the witness front.

FLIP
Yessir! (*turns JOCKO-ALI and stands at parade rest*)

AB
(*facing AUDIENCE*) Zero-fifteen?

JOCKO-ALI
(*now at the end of his rope*) Here!

AB
Tell us, Zero-fifteen. Was it a clear day the morning of your execution?

JOCKO-ALI
Yeah!

AB
Was the head – was your head covered?

JOCKO-ALI
No.

AB
A hood was not used?

JOCKO-ALI
No.

AB
Then you could see?

JOCKO-ALI
Yes.

AB
You had a clear view of the yard?

JOCKO-ALI
You bet.

AB
Beside your mother, Zero-fifteen, who was present at your hanging?

JOCKO-ALI
All of Block Eleven. The guards. Major Aumeier. The usual.

AB
Anybody in particular?

JOCKO-ALI
Yes.

AB
Is that person here?

JOCKO-ALI
Yes.

AB
Point him out to the Court, please.

JOCKO-ALI
Commander House.

SAMMY
Pardon, it's pronounced Höss.

JOCKO-ALI
Horse.

SAMMY
Höss.

JOCKO-ALI
Hearse.

SAMMY
Höss.

JOCKO-ALI
Suck ass, you were there.

SAMMY
Go on, Yehudi.

AB
To the grave. *(to JOCKO-ALI)* Tell them where our glorious benefactor was – during the ceremony. How far from the gallows?

JOCKO-ALI
About where he is now.

AB
No trouble seeing him?

JOCKO-ALI
None.

AB
He was there the whole time?

JOCKO-ALI
Oh, yeah.

AB
You could see him at – when Major Aumeier signalled the musicians?

JOCKO-ALI
I never took my eyes from his.

AB
To the last?

JOCKO-ALI
(nods) I wanted him to remember me.

AB
(voice rising) His reaction, what was his reaction?

KERR
   An absurd inquiry. The witness was dying.

AB
   Precisely. *(to JOCKO-ALI)* The last thing you saw?

JOCKO-ALI
   His face.

AB
   (indicates SAMMY) His face?

JOCKO-ALI
   His face.

AB
   And?

JOCKO-ALI
   (pause) He didn't seem interested.

KERR
   Conjecture.

BERTIE
   Sustained.

AB
   Did the defendant at any time attempt to stop the execution?

JOCKO-ALI
   No.

AB
   Did he in any way try to help you, comfort you?

JOCKO-ALI
   You kidding?

AB
   (driving) Did he make any sign, gesture, grimace of sympathy?

JOCKO-ALI
   Not that I saw.

AB
   And his face. What was its expression? Exactly. Enjoyment? Satisfaction? Exultation?

> JOCKO-ALI *laughs.*

Regret?

JOCKO-ALI
> You crazy?

AB
> Revulsion?

JOCKO-ALI
> No!

AB
> Or– (*jerks around*) –was it like it is *now*?

> SAMMY *looks on, politely impassive, his expression unchanging.*

JOCKO-ALI
> Same.

AB
> Your witness.

> SIMON *ends his phone conversation and, between lights, watches from the sidelines.* BERTIE, *via* MacIAN, *has passed his mophead to* JOCKO-ALI, *who puts it on.*

> KERR *rises, approaches the dangling, bemopped* BLACK MUSLIM *and studies him.*

KERR
> Funny. You don't look Jewish.

JOCKO-ALI
> Nobody's perfect.

KERR
> Comfortable?

JOCKO-ALI
> (*at his blackest*) It's an old family tradition.

KERR
> Then you can hang on a bit longer.

SAMMY
> Without the mophead. Zero-fifteen was not a Rasta.

> *JOCKO-ALI removes the mop head, tosses it to MacIAN who passes it back to BERTIE.*

KERR
You say, Mr. Schneider, it was a clear day, your eyes were uncovered, you could see easily, and your mother, SS Major Aumeier and most of the camp were there.

JOCKO-ALI
(adjusts his cap) Right.

KERR
Everybody was there?

JOCKO-ALI
You got it.

KERR
Including Höss.

JOCKO-ALI
Including.

KERR
(gently) And, as you say, he did nothing to help.

JOCKO-ALI
You know it, baby.

KERR
Did your mother?

> *ROSIE looks up, butts out her cigarette.*

JOCKO-ALI
'Scuse me?

KERR
Your mother. She was there. Did she help you?

ROSIE
I was outnumbered!

KERR
Supporting players will please be instructed.

SAMMY
No ad-libs, Rosie.

ROSIE
Whaddya talkin' about? He's my son!

KERR
You're a little late, Mrs. Schneider. Tell us, Chaim, were you very popular at camp?

JOCKO-ALI
(at a loss) Script!

KERR
(hands up his own script) Here, use mine. Popular. You know, did you have a lot of friends?

JOCKO-ALI
(looking for his line) Sure, a few.

KERR
Friends who cared, who would miss you afterwards?

JOCKO-ALI
What are you getting at?

KERR
Friends who, concerning your execution, you would not describe as "indifferent?"

JOCKO-ALI
(wary) Okay. So?

KERR
So on this day, on this clear, crisp morning, as you stood there with your life about to be snuffed out, did– *(looks toward AB)* –these "friends"—the ones who cared—did any of them attempt to help you?

AB
They couldn't.

KERR
(gently) The witness will kindly answer. Did any of them try to help you?

JOCKO-ALI
They were prisoners.

KERR
(patiently) You're not answering the question.

JOCKO-ALI
The question's ridiculous.

KERR
　You were about to die. Did anybody come to your aid?

JOCKO-ALI
　The guards would've opened fire–

KERR
　–at anyone who made the slightest effort to help you.

JOCKO-ALI
　You bet.

KERR
　(*calmly*) In other words, among all those thousands of people, most of whom had every reason to identify with you—friends, mothers, fellow prisoners, perhaps even some of those in uniform—no one, whatever their sympathies, *no single individual could do anything*.

　　Thwarted, JOCKO-ALI twists away.

KERR
　That's all, Your Honour. (*retrieves script from JOCKO-ALI*) Thank you.

BERTIE
　Cut the witness down!

　　Released, JOCKO-ALI hits the floor – percussion – and is unhitched by MAZO.

JOCKO-ALI
　(*taps FLIP on the shoulder*) Corporal.

FLIP
　(*coiling rope, turns*) Yessir?

JOCKO-ALI
　(*knocks FLIP down – cymbal crash*) ACHTUNG!

FLIP
　What's wrong with you!?!

JOCKO-ALI
　Nothin'. I just reached Mecca.

　　Music. JOCKO-ALI helps FLIP up. ACTORS assemble for curtain song.

ADDY
　Break time! Who's for stuffing ballot boxes?

MAZO
  How much they paying?

ADDY
  Enough to light up the night! (*pulls ROSIE along*) C'mon, luv–

> **SIMON**
>   (*sings*) A sociable race we barbarians!

> **JOCKO-ALI**
>   (*equally sardonic*) Have a little EYE-rack-ee-an!

> **BERTIE**
>   Especially jovial our diversions–

> **MacIAN**
>   Each one a deadly sin!

  Instant killing orgy.

> **ADDY**
>   (*dispatches MacIAN*) Have a permanent Mickey Finn!!

> **FLIP**
>   (*gets rid of KERR*) Good God! Another Ho Chi Minh!!!

> **SIMON**
>   We enliven the whole year
>   With camaraderie and beer–

AB
  (*cuts JOCKO-ALI down*) TERRORIST!

BERTIE
  (*dying grandiosely, slain by FLIP*) TRAGEDIAN!!

> **SIMON**
>   And save Election Day for perversions! (*decimates FLIP*)

  Bodies pile up.

> **MAZO**
>   Promises! Plots!! Assassination!!! (*kills SIMON*)

> **AB**
>   (*kills ADDY*) For every closet a skeleton!!

> **MAZO**
>   (*kills AB*) Each new war an old solution!

MacIAN
In Nomine Patris!

JOCKO-ALI
(killed again by FLIP) Father!

ROSIE
Son!!

KERR
Petrol-lee-UM!!!

SIMON
One small consideration.

BERTIE
We might not be alive to criticize–

FLIP
(pulls MAZO down) Traitor!

ADDY
(resurrecting himself) Comedienne!!

BERTIE
–the next administration!!

SIMON
Compete! Cheat! Defeat!

AB
(rising with the others) Remember the bottom line!!

FLIP
Forget the Alamo!!

JIMMY
We interrupt this program–

PARNELL
–to bring you a special bulletin!

ROSIE
Christ! What more?!

MAZO
PEACE!!

SIMON
FIRST, PREEMPTIVE WAR!!

JIMMY
Moonrock!!

PARNELL
Spaceballs!!!

BERTIE
Aspirin! Atropin!! Heroin!!!

AB
Follow me!!!!

KERR
No! no! no! No saviours!

FLIP
(*collars JOCKO-ALI*) No more illegal immigrants!!

JOCKO-ALI
HEY! I'M AMERICAN!!

OTHERS
Urban! Suburban!! Collateral!!!

ALL TOGETHER
VOTE!! VOTE!!! VOTE!!!!

FLIP
(*at SIMON*) Hey, you!

SIMON
Ex-officio!

MacIAN
(*to ROSIE*) And you?!

ROSIE
Mistress! Without portfolio!!

ALL & INDIVIDUALLY
A spirited tribe we Colonials!
Common-lawed, Magna-Charted liberals!
Said the King, "Use my wine!"
Said we, "Kiss our cordial behind!
We'll Bloody Mary our own aboriginals!!"

Lights aimed into the house. The ACTORS come at the AUDIENCE.

ROSIE
Mothers arise!

ADDY
Actors unite!

MAZO
(upends his crutch) Ream the Republic!!

BERTIE
CITIZENS! TO THE POLLS!!!

FLIP
(setting the pace as the ACTORS veer and march off) Left! Left! Left, right, left! One, two, three, four! One-two! *(ACTORS misstep)* Left!! Left!! Left, right, left!– *(off)*

SAMMY
(drys hands) So, the end of Act One. Our first atrocity is complete. And our little clutch of cupids is on its way to commit a few more, those at least who are able to vote. But they'll be back, this merely an aperitif. To those who care to return for the feast, one suggestion. While you're out – drink deep!

JOCKO-ALI
(back on, gavels the floor with his mopstick) HEAR YE! HEAR YE! HEAR YE! DIS HONOURABLE COURT IS RECESSED FOR FIFTEEN MINUTES!! *(and off)*

SAMMY mixes with AUDIENCE-JURORS and leads them off. The music swells. The curtain does not come down.

SIMON, at the bar, drinks, checks his pay. MAZO, unlit cigarette in his mouth, sits offside, reads a newspaper. AB and KERR sip coffee, quietly go over lines. Nearby, JOCKO-ALI, in nylon stocking-cap, clowns his mouth with ruby red. The drums are on the stage floor, and JIMMY and PARNELL put tables on the bandstand. SAMMY distributes pay envelopes. HEISEL, in ancient bowler, sits in the AUDIENCE muting his trumpet. ROSIE mummifies MacIAN with lengths of toilet paper.

JOCKO-ALI
Find your shoes?

FLIP
(accepts pay envelope from SAMMY) Not yet.

MacIAN
(swathed in toilet paper) How do I look?

FLIP
(signs SAMMY's clipboard) Ready for burial.

MacIAN
I'm alive! I'm alive!

ROSIE
(to MacIAN) Sure, Lazarus. Turn. *(steps back to view her handiwork)*

FLIP
(cups ROSIE's breasts from behind) Hi, Ma.

ROSIE
Hi, sugar. What's up?

FLIP
Me.

ROSIE
(hands him toilet roll) Not in the graveyard, doll.

MacIAN
(to ROSIE) Sign for me, will you?

ROSIE accepts two envelopes, signs for MacIAN and herself.

AB
Simon.

SIMON
Yeah?

AB
> Four thirty-nine. (*SIMON opens his script.*) Fourth speech from the top. "Sweating, wild-eyed–" Add "evasive." (*SIMON writes in his script.*)

ADDY
> (*enters, to SAMMY, leading AUDIENCE-JURORS*) We're back, Papa! The Heavenly Host! A round for the seraphim! (*to JURORS*) Don't worry, girls, it's only tea.

MAZO
> You vote?

ADDY
> Eight times.

JOCKO-ALI
> Long live social assistance!

ADDY
> (*accepting his pay envelope*) So long as they pay. (*waggles envelope*) Or are you up here outta love?

SAMMY
> Where's Heisel?

ADDY
> (*signing SAMMY's clipboard*) Fraternizing.

SAMMY
> Heisel!

> *HEISEL, in the AUDIENCE, raspberries SAMMY with his horn.*

> (*calls*) Wages!

SIMON
> (*getting up*) Our bargain with the devil.

SAMMY
> (*to ADDY, indicating SIMON*) Now he's playing Faust. Where's Bertie?

ADDY
> In the john going over lines.

SAMMY
> Run the Freight till he gets out.

ADDY
> Italian route?

SAMMY
　Sì.

　　HEISEL advances down the aisle.

MacIAN
　Paderewsi!

PARNELL
　Yeah?

MacIAN
　The wop track.

ADDY
　(taking mike out of its stand) Let's go, guys. *(to JOCKO-ALI)* Come on, Rufus, move it.

JOCKO-ALI
　Careful, whitey, I'm the explosive type.

　　Trumpet blast. SAMMY leans over footlights with HEISEL's pay envelope.

SAMMY
　Cut the overheads!

　　ADDY, with mike, mounts bar-stage. The lights change. Trumpet.

Act Two
— • —

Music.

> **ADDY**
> *(into mike, evenly)* ON YOUR FEET. TO THE STATION FOR RESETTLEMENT. NO EXCEPTIONS.

The ACTORS assemble. SAMMY moves to the side.

> BRING ONLY THOSE TOOLS NECESSARY TO THE EXERCISE OF YOUR PROFESSIONS.

ROSIE hikes up her skirt. JIMMY carts his drums.

> FAMILIES TOGETHER. CLOSE CORDON.

Music.

> FRIENDS. BY SUPERIOR ORDER YOU WILL BE RESETTLED IN HAMLETS WHERE YOU WILL BE MORE WELCOME. SUITABLE LODGINGS HAVE BEEN FOUND. THERE IS WORK FOR ALL. TRADESMEN WILL BE GIVEN SHOPS. UNSKILLED LABOUR WILL WORK IN FACTORIES.

MAZO
I'm a doctor! I don't belong here!

> **ADDY**
> DOCTORS WILL WORK IN CLINICS.

JIMMY
I'm a musician! I've got a gig!!

> **ADDY**
> ARTISTS WILL RECEIVE SPECIAL TREATMENT.

Trumpet. PARNELL sits, his script open on a music stand. MacIAN reads over his shoulder.

MacIAN
Col' soda! Oranges!–

> **ADDY**
> THE OLD AND THE SICK WILL BE MOVED TO SANATORIUMS. THERE WILL BE PLENTY TO EAT.

Music.

> WARNING. TO PROTECT YOU FROM ENEMY
> AIRCRAFT, GUNNERS ARE SITUATED ON THE
> ROOF OF EACH CAR. ANYONE ATTEMPTING
> TO LEAVE THEIR CAR WILL BE SHOT.

Percussion.

> DOORS – OPEN.

Music.

> INSIDE.

Trumpet.

ROSIE
Does he mean us!?!

KERR
Sigi! Stay here!–

JOCKO-ALI runs on.

FLIP
Quit pushing!

> **ADDY**
> HOLD ON TO YOUR LUGGAGE.

KERR
Come back! Sigi!

> **ADDY**
> TAKE ALL VALUABLES.

KERR
Sigi!

> **ADDY**
> LEAVE ALL PERISHABLES.

SIMON
There's no more room!

JOCKO-ALI
Here, hide this–!

ROSIE
   Oh, God!

         ADDY
            DOORS CLOSED.

MacIAN
   Sooooofff Drinks–! Sig Rettes–! Eye Scream–!

      Music builds. The "freight" lurches, shakes, changes shape rhythmically. SAMMY looks on, takes notes. ADDY serves AUDIENCE-JURORS.

ROSIE
   Where are we?

JIMMY
   Open a window!–

         PARNELL
            (*sings out*) Milano!!

KERR
   Where did he say?!

         PARNELL
            Bergamo!!

SIMON
   Rosie.

         PARNELL
            Brescia!!

ROSIE
   Water!

SIMON
   Rosie–

         PARNELL
            Rovereto!! Bolzano!! Merano!! Brennero!!

SIMON
   Rosie!

ROSIE
   What?!

SIMON
You're on my foot!

ROSIE
Oh. Sorry.

        PARNELL
        Innsbruck!!

JOCKO-ALI
We're stopping!

        PARNELL
        Innsbruck!!

FLIP
Ask him!

                KERR
                Officer, we've got no water!

                ADDY
                Drink your piss.

Trumpet.

        PARNELL
        Hopfgarten!!

JOCKO-ALI
Water!

JIMMY
I can't breathe!

MAZO
Smash the glass!

FLIP
Can't reach it!

        PARNELL
        Saalfelden!! Bruck!! Salzburg!!

ROSIE
He's not breathing!–

        PARNELL
        Linz!! Vienna!! Vienna!! Vienna!!!

ROSIE
   Ask through the window!

FLIP
   Stand on my shoulders–

KERR
   Sir! We need water!

MacIAN
   (reads) Forty watches.

ROSIE
   Ask him again!

MacIAN
   –And your wedding rings!

            PARNELL
               Bratislava!!

            KERR
               God's in heaven,
               We're in hell.
               Name the Devil,
               Who can tell!

            PARNELL
               Belusa!!

            MacIAN
               (sings) Dona–
                         nobis!–

            PARNELL
               Zilina!!

            MacIAN & ADDY
               PA–
                  –A

MAZO
   Help me up!
                  –A

FLIP
   Where you going?
                  –A

MAZO
Through the window!–

                    –CEM!

       PARNELL
        Cadca!!

MAZO leaps from the "freight" – rat-tat-tat of percussion – and crumples to the floor.

              JOCKO-ALI
               The deer are hungry.
               The grass is dry.
               Burn a leaf
               And the forest dies!

           MacIAN & ADDY
            Dona–
               nobis–
                  Pacem, pacem!
            Dona —
               nobis!
                  Pacem!

The "freight" and the music stop. A toilet is heard to flush. BERTIE appears under the "GENTS" sign, adjusting his pants, script under his arm, wig askew.

ROSIE
Are we here?

BERTIE
Where else, y'bleedin' twits! Well? Get on with it!

    Cymbals.

JOCKO-ALI
(*hoisted aloft*) HEAR YE! HEAR YE! HEAR YE! WELCOME TO THE FOLLIES, THE BAR THAT SERVES YOU RIGHT!!

    Musical flourish. ACTORS disperse. SAMMY pours, ADDY serves. SAMMY piles silverware on a cloth. BERTIE has climbed back on his stool.

BERTIE
Produce the witness.

AB
My Lord, our next witness is a noted surgeon. Given the nature of his testimony, he asks that we protect his present identity and reputation.

MAZO
(*aside*) Not to mention his bank account.

AB
As a professional courtesy.

KERR
Meaning what? That he appear in disguise?

AB
In uniform. Surgical mask and gown.

> *Lights. Vamp. ROSIE and MAZO enter the scene, escorting the papered MacIAN: his head, torso and the lower half of his face are covered with toilet paper.*

BERTIE
So that's where the bloody paper went!

ROSIE
(*wide-eyed, bucolic*) He was in the manger, sir. Under a cow.

BERTIE
How's he supposed to testify?

ROSIE
(*earnestly*) Oh, not with his mouth, m'lord. (*indicates MAZO*) With *his!*

AB
Dr. Salvatore Mazo. Noted authority. Colleague of the witness. Dr. Mazo has been given a script, so the witness need not speak at all.

KERR
Such an arrangement, your honour, is entirely without precedent.

BERTIE
Mr. Kerr, this whole trial is unprecedented.

KERR
But the law–

BERTIE
–is what the Court says it is! And if we can prosecute a dead defendant, I see no earthly reason why we cannot hear a silent witness. Flip!

FLIP
Yeah?

BERTIE
　　Swear in this turd! And his spokesman.

FLIP
　　(eyes one of three drinks SAMMY has poured) S'pleasure! *(stations himself)*

> The toileted MacIAN crosses to the witness stool, accompanied by MAZO, who favours a grossly bandaged foot.

ADDY
　　(with tray, serves the THREE DERELICTS) White Eye for the Doc! Snakehead for his go-between! And Cat's Piss for–

FLIP
　　(grabs his drink) –The Terminator! *(glass aloft)* 'SWEARTOLOVEHONOUR ANDOBEY–

AB
　　(cuts in) Wrong oath!

FLIP
　　–THEWHOLETRUTHNOTHIN'BUTTHETRUTHSOHELPYOUGOD?!

MAZO
　　He does.

FLIP
　　Skäl!

> MacIAN lowers his "surgical" mask – the drinks are downed in unison – then replaces it.

BERTIE
　　(to FLIP and ADDY) Scat!

> ADDY collects the glasses, leaves scene with FLIP. MacIAN, corseted in toilet paper, stands stiffly, always mute. MAZO, seated next to him, refers to his script as needed.

AB
　　(always to MacIAN, with transparent contempt) Profession?

MAZO
　　Physician.

AB
　　Specialty?

MAZO
Obstetrics.

AB
Length of practice?

MAZO
Twenty-eight years.

AB
And the defendant – you know him?

MAZO
(smiles at SAMMY) Yes.

AB
The nature of your relationship?

MAZO
Short-term fluids.

AB
(to MAZO) As *doctor!*

SAMMY
Yehudi–

AB
I know, I know! The ventriloquist.

SAMMY
Not the dummy.

AB
Fine. *(pointedly addresses the silent MacIAN, his disgust barely concealed)* Your relationship? To the defendant.

MAZO
I was his prisoner.

AB
Whose?

MAZO
Sammy's.

AB
Höss's.

MAZO
　　Right.

AB
　　You were? Specifically? (*always to MacIAN*) If you can't remember, read it.

MAZO
　　(*reads*) Surgeon-in-charge of Block 21's operating theatre.

AB
　　A large unit?

MAZO
　　Three hundred.

AB
　　In residence, so to speak.

MAZO
　　Most of us were prisoners, yes.

AB
　　Your purpose?

MAZO
　　To maintain the labour supply. A good part of the camp's population was on loan to neighbouring factories.

AB
　　Your duties, Doctor?

MAZZO
　　Normal day-to-day surgery.

AB
　　Anything else?

MAZO
　　It was a camp. We were under instruction–

AB
　　(*snarls, still to MacIAN*) Tell them!!

MAZO
　　(*pause*) We performed experiments.

> SAMMY *rings up the cash register – music – removes an icepick from the drawer, wraps it in an apron along with silverware.* JOCKO-ALI *and* ROSIE *have mounted the bandstand.* JOCKO-ALI *pulls on black rubber gloves.*

ROSIE
(slips on evening gloves) One female volunteer, please!

ADDY
(takes wrapped silverware from SAMMY) Coming, honey!

JOCKO-ALI
She said female.

ADDY
(hurries to bandstand) Right up my alley, luv! Lights! Action! Travesty! (hands ROSIE silverware) Your instruments, doll! (flings back his arms) Ruin me! (swoons into JOCKO-ALI's arms)

JOCKO-ALI
We need help!

BERTIE
Two jurors! To the bandstand!

Muffled drums. ADDY is lowered onto the tables on the bandstand. JOCKO-ALI and ROSIE put on aprons, lay out silverware. SIMON selects two AUDIENCE-JURORS, conducts them to the bandstand, amusing them with asides. Music halts. ADDY, now horizontal, shakes hands with the smiling JURORS.

BERTIE
(to JURORS) Please! Empty your faces. Sanitize your emotions. This is a sterile drama! (to AB) Proceed, counsellor.

SIMON positions the AUDIENCE-JURORS.

AB
(to MacIAN) You were saying you performed experiments.

MAZO
Yes.

AB
Their nature, Doctor?

MAZO
Sterilization. Mass sterilization of defectives.

ADDY
(sits up) What did he say?

MAZO
Gypsies. Jews. Perverts.

ADDY
　Watch your language!

AB
　(*sharply*) Secure the patient.

　　ADDY is slapped down and, upon instruction, the AUDIENCE-JURORS hold his limbs.

AB
　(*always to MacIAN*) "Defectives?" Was that the term?

MAZO
　Officially.

AB
　I call your attention to twenty of them. Twenty Greek women.

　　Music.

MAZO
　From Salonika.

AB
　You recall?

MAZO
　Some things one does not forget.

　　　　JOCKO-ALI
　　　　　Icepick.

　　　　ROSIE
　　　　　(*slaps icepick into JOCKO-ALI's palm*) 'Pick.

　　JOCKO-ALI and ROSIE's gestures are impeccable, hieratic.

AB
　(*to MacIAN*) What exactly do you recall?

MAZO
　(*closes script*) Young girls, Mediterranean types, fearful. There was no time for a general anæsthetic, just spinals.

　　　　ADDY
　　　　　("*stabbed*" with icepick) AIEE!!

MAZO
Conditions were rudimentary. No time to scrub down. Paper bandages. No sterilization of instruments between operations.

ROSIE wipes a large kitchen knife on her apron.

AB
(*always to MacIAN*) The girls were conscious?

MAZO
A shield was used. To keep them from seeing the operation.

ADDY's arms are freed and he is supplied a newspaper to read. The released AUDIENCE-JUROR is handed the kitchen knife.

The site of the incision was cleaned–

>   **JOCKO-ALI**
>   Alcohol.

Drinks are handed up.

MAZO
–preliminary opinions were exchanged–

>   **ROSIE**
>   (*toasts, drinks*) Bottoms up!

MAZO
–and the operation begun.

>   **JOCKO-ALI**
>   Knife.

>   **ROSIE**
>   (*moves AUDIENCE-JUROR-WITH-KNIFE between herself and JOCKO-ALI*) Slap it into his palm. And no smiling.

The "operation" on the bandstand competes for MAZO's attention.

MAZO
There'd been prior exposure of the organs to x-rays – an overdose. And the ovaries were needed for observation.

>   **JOCKO-ALI**
>   Lipstick.

ROSIE
'Stick. *(hands lipstick to JUROR, who passes it to JOCKO-ALI)* Faster.

MAZO
An incision was made.

JOCKO-ALI lipsticks ADDY's belly.

ADDY
(giggles) Lower! *(hides face under his newspaper)*

MAZO
(distracted by operation) A horizontal incision.

JOCKO-ALI "plunges" knife into ADDY – cymbal crash – ADDY guffaws.

(starts to laugh too, checks himself) Left to right.

A blossom of black blood has appeared in MacIAN's toilet paper mask.

AB
(into MacIAN's papered face) Go on!

MAZO
The peritoneum was cut. A forceps was inserted.

JOCKO-ALI
Fork.

ROSIE
Fork.

MAZO
(struggles against his amusement) Another forceps was inserted– *(ADDY: bursts of laughter throughout.)* –between the tup and the ovary – after which the ovary was excised.

JOCKO-ALI raises up a string of knockwurst.

SAMMY
Hold it!

Everything halts. SAMMY has entered the scene.

Where'd those come from?

JOCKO-ALI
(deep smell of the knockwurst) Hung-garee!

SAMMY
Hack-kneed.

ROSIE
(takes the knockwurst) Makes for great intestines.

SAMMY
You're removing ovaries.

JOCKO-ALI
Where's the mustard?

SAMMY
It's a low stock cliché.

ROSIE
So is the mad-doctor routine.

SAMMY
(suddenly intense) The doctor is more than mad. And the situation's hardly routine– *(takes the knockwurst)* –or gastronomic. *(leaves scene)* You know, taste isn't only in the mouth. Mazo, see if you can control yourself. *(hands knockwurst to JIMMY)* For the soup.

PARNELL
Sam.

SAMMY
Yeah?

PARNELL
The waltz?

SAMMY
Please.

A waltz is struck up.

MAZO
(suppresses his amusement) Ordinarily, one would use clamps, cut the pedicle, remove the ovary and tie the stump. To prevent arterial bleeding.

Black blood gushes through MacIAN's mask and down his papered chest.

JOCKO-ALI
Tray.

MAZO
(no longer able to suppress his mirth) But the object of these operations was not survival of the patient!–

Now a geyser of black blood bursts loose, spraying everyone within reach. Muffled cries from MacIAN.

    ROSIE
    (passes an ice bucket to JUROR) No tray.

MAZO
(tries to contain his laughter, works frantically over MacIAN: sotto voce) Jesus! Where's the tube!?!

SAMMY
Don't stop!

MAZO
(hit in the face with a black jet, struggles to return to the dialogue) In this – In this – In this–

SAMMY
Keep going!

MAZO
(suppresses his hilarity with growing difficulty) –In this situation–

    JOCKO-ALI
    Tongs.

MAZO
(struggles with MacIAN) –we simply removed!–

    ROSIE
    (passing ice-tongs) Tongs.

    JOCKO-ALI
    Tong you very much.

MAZO
(breaks into laughter, unable to stem MacIAN's hemorrhaging) –the – the – THE PATIENT'S – THE PATIENT'S OVARY!!

The music has stopped.

JOCKO-ALI
(plucks a gleaming, dripping apple from the ice bucket and holds it aloft) Ain't love grand!!

A momentary silence.

MAZO
(*suddenly sober*) –Then we stretched the incision up, secured the sutures–

JOCKO-ALI
Sutures.

ROSIE
Suit yourself.

MAZO
–and put the ovary into a specimen tray.

JOCKO-ALI drops apple and tongs into JUROR's ice bucket. At the sound of ice tongs and apple striking the bucket's bottom, MacIAN topples over like a block of ice. Percussion.

BERTIE
Smashing, Sammy! Brilliant! And to our– (*motions to the two AUDIENCE-JURORS*) –heroic helpmates the nectar of their choice!

SAMMY
Get rid of him.

MacIAN is hustled off. ROSIE and JOCKO-ALI blanket ADDY with newspaper, then retire along with the two AUDIENCE-JURORS, who have been given drinks. ROSIE, offside, returns to her crocheting.

BERTIE
(*to MAZO*) Go on, man! No one told you to stop!

Music resumes.

MAZO
(*reads quietly*) The first patient died within hours, another the following day, three days later a third.

AB
You operated with their consent?

MAZO
No one asked them, if that's what you mean.

AB
You operated against their will?

MAZO
We were not recruiting volunteers.

AB
    Bear with me, Doctor. Who was in charge of the camp? At the time of these experiments?

MAZO
    (*steady*) Commandant Höss.

AB
    Did he show any interest in the condition of the women? In your procedures? In the results of the program?

MAZO
    He seldom came to the hospital.

AB
    But when he did, did he demonstrate, if not supervisory concern, any personal curiosity?

MAZO
    No.

AB
    (*delighted*) Even about such experiments?

MAZO
    He didn't stay long. He had few questions.

AB
    His attitude then, generally speaking?

MAZO
    (*looks across at SAMMY*) Remote. Aloof. Distant.

AB
    Indifferent?

MAZO
    You could say.

AB
    Your witness!

KERR
    Return the *corpus delicti* to the stage, please.

> *Freshly laundered, totally toileted, with not an inch of flesh visible, MacIAN is hustled on and seated next to MAZO. MacIAN's paper snaps and loosens fitfully: a mummy reviving.*

KERR
To whom do I direct my examination? The doctor or the dummy?

AB
They come as a set.

KERR
What does either, alone or together, have to do with the charge against my client? Except an admission, on their part! of human vivisection.

BERTIE
Human vivisection?

KERR
How else would my good lord define the surgical mutilation of living human beings? Or does the Court also subscribe to the notion of "defectives?"

BERTIE
Angus–

KERR
How partial is this court? The jury has a right to know.

BERTIE
The Court, Mr. Kerr, is not on trial.

KERR
(erupts) Everybody's on trial here!!

BERTIE
Confine yourself to the witness, counsellor. Or you shall find yourself in contempt.

KERR
Meaning what?

ADDY
(pokes his head out from under a headline) No liquor!

KERR *looks at* SAMMY, *who quietly fills a glass and places it on the bar.*

KERR
(pause, dry-mouthed, to MacIAN) Tell us, Doctor, how many of these experiments were performed?

MAZO
Hard to say. There were other surgeons.

KERR
How many did you perform?

MAZO
(*motions toward MacIAN*) Let him answer that!

KERR
(*livid but controlled, always to MacIAN*) Play it out. How many did you perform?

MAZO
(*grim*) Several hundred.

KERR
No doubt you also object to the term "human vivisection?"

MAZO
(*willing the words*) Most of the hospital staff were prisoners. It was a concentration camp. Nobody considered anybody human. We were rats. One simply protected oneself against the other rats.

KERR
And if you refused to become a rat?

MAZO
You became a corpse.

KERR
Nobody opposed the experiments?

MAZO
They would've been dispatched.

KERR
No choice?

MAZO
(*frustrated*) None.

KERR
You're aware, Doctor, the SS operated under as merciless a standard.

MAZO
Presumably.

KERR
And that, possibly, the camp commander also had no choice?

AB
Calls for conjecture.

BERTIE
Quite.

KERR
(*to MacIAN*) Doctor, you recall the defendant's military rank?

MAZO
(*checks script*) Obersturmbannführer.

KERR
English? (*MAZO looks to SAMMY.*)

SAMMY
Lieutenant-Colonel.

KERR
Not a lowly private. Not top of the heap either. As for your experiments, Doctor, imagine what would've happened to this Lieutenant-Colonel had he shown any obvious scruples.

AB
Object–

KERR
Withdrawn. Is it not true, Doctor, that camp physicians, all of them, were accountable only to the–

SAMMY
(*prompts*) Standortarzt.

KERR
Chief of medical services.

MAZO
(*genuinely*) I'm not sure.

KERR
Well, look it up!

MAZO turns a page.

KERR
We'll take it again. (*back to MacIAN*) As a camp physician, were you independent of the camp commander's authority?

MAZO
It says, "Yes."

KERR
I suggest, then, that Sam – that Höss seldom visited the hospital block, not because he was uncaring or unconcerned, but because the hospital's work lay outside his command.

AB
Objection.

KERR
I further suggest, Doctor, that you've depicted the defendant as distant and remote–

AB
Objection!

KERR
–so that we– *(turns suddenly on MacIAN)* –but especially *you*–

AB
Objection!!

KERR
–will overlook your own extraordinary behaviour!

AB
Stop him!

KERR
Your own willful, personal, prolonged *in*difference!

MacIAN
(jerks to his feet) No-no! No!

KERR
Oh, no longer trying to hide your indifference?

MacIAN
(ripping paper away from his face) No, no – I was–! You can't–! That's not what I–!

KERR
(cuts him off) Yes, Doctor, we know. You're blameless, a reluctant bystander not a willing participant. Whose innocence and testimony cannot be questioned. *(steps away)*

AB
(to BERTIE) Where were you!

BERTIE
Trying to be impartial.

AB
At whose expense? *(MAZO starts off.)* Get back here, Mazo! *(to MacIAN)* Sit down, schmuck.

MacIAN sits. MAZO returns.

(to both) Tell them. You were, were you not, a member of the camp underground?

MAZO
(looks at MacIAN, who nods) I was, yes.

AB
And one of your jobs was to help escaping prisoners obtain medical supplies. Correct?

MAZO
(stares at his script) Is that here?!

AB
The answer is yes. And when you were able, when you were *able*, Doctor, did you not help sabotage the camp's extermination program?

MAZO
(at a loss) –Page?

MacIAN
Ask me that question!

AB
(turns to MacIAN at last) The truth! When you were able, Doctor, did you not help undermine the camp's extermination program?

MacIAN
Always!

AB
Thank you. *(stalks off)*

BERTIE
Recross?

KERR
(to MacIAN) Before there were only rats. Now, suddenly, there's an underground.

MacIAN
Organized to protect the larger rats.

KERR
(smiles, moves MAZO aside) Excuse me. Several resistance groups were active in the camp?

MacIAN
Yes.

KERR
(turns a page) You refused to join the largest, the single most effective group. Why?

MacIAN
That's my business.

KERR
And this court's. You refused to work with them. Why?

MacIAN
They were communists. *(indicates MAZO)* Like him.

KERR
They were prisoners.

MacIAN
They were extremists! I've never been political.

MAZO
But you were all fighting for your lives!

MacIAN
They were from the gutter. I was a professional.

KERR
(repulsed) No more questions.

MacIAN
Nor will I reply to any more. *(leaves, turns)* I was a gentleman. And a scholar.

MAZO
(in all his derelict splendor) A pity, isn't it, there are so few of us left.

MAZO limps offside, opposite MacIAN.

AB
The People have one other witness. We call A-Eighty-four One-eleven.

Music. ROSIE exchanges her crocheting for a script and, led by a regal bosom, makes a commanding entrance. Appreciative noises from the ACTORS.

BERTIE
Skip the preliminaries. The witness's virtue is well known.

ROSIE
My drink.

AB
After.

ROSIE
I'm better wet.

AB
(peremptory) Sit down.

ROSIE smiles patiently and sits.

AB
Number?

ROSIE
A-Eighty-four One-eleven.

AB
How long were you in Auschwitz?

ROSIE
Three years.

AB
You made it out alive?

ROSIE
'Fraid not.

AB
You know why you're here?

ROSIE
(lays aside her script) Totally.

AB
　Then begin.

ROSIE
　(*effortlessly*) We thanked God when they slid open the doors. We'd been travelling in locked boxcars for six days, the last three without water. No food. No light. Makeshift toilets. A number of us had died. Now, finally, the doors were open. The station outside was lit up– (*looks up into the lights*) –like here. It was strangely quiet– (*small smile*) –like here. (*SAMMY hands some drinks to ADDY.*) An officer across the platform—Sammy—spoke quietly to an officer next to him, who did the shouting.

ADDY
　(*hushed shout*) "Get out!"

ROSIE
　–he yelled.

ADDY
　(*hushed shout*) "Without your bags!"

ROSIE
　Those who refused were pulled out and clubbed to the ground. Several boys in the last car made a run for it. They were shot. "Leave everything in the cars!" we were told. "No holding hands!" they said. (*Her mouth has gone dry.*) We were lined up, women and children on one side of the tracks, men on the other. The women and children were told to step forward in threes. Some, those with families, began to weep. One officer, with a gold rosette in his lapel, divided us again. The young and strong were sent to the right. The old and the sick – and the children – went to the left. I could see my husband, with his white hair, among the men. They were also being divided. (*pause*) I was sent to the right. My husband, on his side of the tracks, was sent to the left.

AB
　Go on.

ROSIE
　Yehudi, I don't think – This – This isn't the place for it.

AB
　(*no longer looks at ROSIE*) It's perfect.

ROSIE
　But–

AB
　Finish!

ROSIE
(*subdued*) We were told the old people would take care of the children. Whoever resisted was beaten or shot. Those on the left were taken away in trucks. My husband – I waved– (*Her hand lifts almost imperceptibly.*) –till his truck turned a corner and was gone. (*pause*) Sammy – Sam, I – I'm not sure I want to do it now.

AB
(*savagely*) Yes, now! And stand up!

ROSIE hesitates, rises. SAMMY motions to the the MUSICIANS, who begin to play. MAZO, SIMON, MacIAN, FLIP and JOCKO-ALI close ranks behind ROSIE – as the CHORUS LINE for her production number.

ROSIE
Then – then the young men then were marched off. The women were taken to a large building. It was a sort of hall, a hangar, I think. Metal siding, no windows, with a curved tarpaper roof.

AB
The smell!–

ROSIE
(*hoarsely*) There was an odd smell. Something was burning. Before they led us inside, I saw a high brick chimney in the distance. The chimney must have caught fire. Flames were shooting out the top–

The line of men behind ROSIE has begun to sing and dance.

> **JOCKO-ALI**
> Ring around the gallows tree!
>
> **MAZO**
> Ready for another atrocity?
>
> **MacIAN**
> Ashes, ashes–
>
> **ALL**
> All fall down!

ROSIE
Please, Ab–

AB
Keep going!

ROSIE
(*tonelessly*) They closed the doors behind us. There were soldiers inside. They were drinking. One of them, younger than the rest, smiled shyly and said quietly, "Take off your clothes." We couldn't move. Suddenly he yelled, "All of you! Strip!"

The music continues. ADDY supplies the CHORUS LINE with drinks.

It was a huge space. A few of us tried to break out. The doors were bolted from the outside. We crowded into the corners, trying to hide behind one another. "Everything on the floor!" another soldier shouted. "Woolens on that side! Cottons over here!"

ROSIE begins to remove her clothes, her body moving to the music, her face like stone.

MacIAN
Ring around the rosary!

FLIP
Pocket full of prayers!

SIMON
Father, Son and Saint Marie!

JOCKO-ALI
But no one ever hears!

ROSIE
(*her face momentarily softens*) A few of the older women refused. The soldiers grabbed them by their hair, shouting. "Nothing is yours anymore! Not even your hair!" One of the soldiers said to take our time, that the more professional we were, the easier it would be–

MAZO
Ring around our Rosie–

ADDY
(*has joined the CHORUS LINE*) Fourth floor! Lingerie!

JOCKO-ALI
Oh, honey, let it all come down!

ROSIE
(*toneless*) We tried to hold on to little things – our rings, a locket – they tore them from us.

SIMON
(*toasts*) Ring around the rosé!

ADDY
   Here comes the negligee!

ROSIE *drops her slip.*

MacIAN
   Friends!

MAZO
   Romans!

FLIP
   Bosom buddies!

ALL
   Stick around!!

ROSIE
They stared and laughed. *(wan smile)* Some of us laughed too. I don't know why.

JOCKO-ALI
   Ring around the Rosie!

SIMON
   What are we bid–

ADDY
   –for this delicacy?

MAZO
   Come one!

JOCKO-ALI
   Come all!

FLIP
   (climaxing) C-C-C-C-COME!

MacIAN
   And see what made
   Adam climb the tree!

ROSIE
They walked among us, comparing us one to the other. The floor was cold. I couldn't find my shoes–

SIMON
   Ring around your Rosie–

MAZO
(at AUDIENCE MEMBER, who is exiting) Hey! Don't leave now!

ADDY
(with a glass) She goes further for a fee! (hands MacIAN his drink)

ALL
Drink up! In the end we all
Wind up *underground*!
O honey, let it all come down!!

MacIAN
(offers ROSIE a drink) Hey, gorgeous! (ROSIE reaches for the glass.) One Hebe! One christening! (splashes the drink in ROSIE's face)

A silence.

ROSIE
Sammy–

SAMMY
(implacable) Höss.

ROSIE's head drops. Then slowly—regally—she bares her breasts.

MacIAN and JOCKO-ALI fall to their knees before ROSIE. ADDY, shot glass in one eye, appraises first one breast, then the other.

ADDY
Demeter? Or is it Ishtar?

MacIAN and JOCKO-ALI sample ROSIE's breasts with their mouths. The music resumes.

(arms thrown wide) Tutti Frutti!!

MacIAN
God!

JOCKO-ALI
(blackfaced, kneeling, Jolsons the moment) She beats Mammy, pound for pound!

MacIAN
Aphrodite in the round!

MAZO
Lady, lady let's lie down!

JOCKO-ALI
Hit it, Charlie!

FLIP
Jesus! I'm on fire!

MacIAN
Help me drown!

FLIP
Lady, lady, let's lie down!

SIMON
(*roars*) How we doing, Yehudi!? Better than the script!?

AB stares out into the dark.

JOCKO-ALI
(*calypsodic*) All together!

ALL
Curtain call! Do it up brown!

FLIP
(*cries*) FIRE!! FIRE!!

MacIAN
Bring on the clowns!

SIMON & OTHERS
(*cry out*) TAKE IT OFF!!

The music continues, ROSIE completes her strip: an aging showgirl totally exposed.

JOCKO-ALI
There is but one God!!

FLIP
Come you, come me!

MacIAN
Come without grace!

SIMON
Like Adam, fall on your face!

ADDY
EVERYBODY!

> **ALL**
> Come one, come all! But come on time!
>
> **MacIAN**
> Less – Less! – LESS! is more of a crime!
>
> **SIMON**
> Ring 'er up! Ring 'er down!

BERTIE
(*bitterly*) On your knees for Queen and Crown!

> **ALL**
> Oh lady! Lady!
> Lady! Lady!
> Lady! Lady! Lady!!!
> Oh lady!! Let's lie down!!!

The song and music have ended.

ROSIE
Then we were taken into another room. Where we were examined–

SIMON
(*grabs ROSIE brutally by her hair*) –and shaved!!

ROSIE's hair comes away in SIMON's hand; her head is shaved to the skull. She stands frozen: a naked, old display mannequin.

AB
The People rest. Your witness.

MacIAN
(*raucous*) What's he mean, *his* witness? Rosie's everybody's witness!

FLIP
(*chants drunkenly*) Rosie is a duck, Rosie is a duck, Rosie is a duck–

SIMON
And she likes to–

FLIP
QUACK! QUACK!

ROSIE
(*stares out over the footlights*) Animals – We're all– (*words will not come*)

Pause.

MAZO
C'mon, let's find out who won the election.

FLIP
Turn on the TV!

ADDY
It's dead, dumbhead!!

SIMON
We're prehistoric!

KERR
(to AB, indicating ROSIE) Well–? Was it worth it?

AB
If it's clear – how easy it is.

KERR
Easy?

AB
(with precise, controlled fury) NOT – TO – GIVE – A – DAMN!!

AB leaves. KERR follows. The rest weave off, dragging MUSICIANS and AUDIENCE-JURORS with them. Cacophonic music. Raucous singing.

SEVERAL & ALL
Ring around sobriety!
Mammy!–
    God!–
        Debauchery!
O say can you see!
Cast a vote for democracy!
Lady, lady, lie down!
With me!
    Me!
        Me!
            Me!
It's free!–

FLIP
(juts his head back in) QUACK, QUACK! *(and off)*

The WOMAN weeps. SAMMY places a robe over her shoulders. ADDY puts a drink in her hand and follows SAMMY into the wings.

Alone, the ACTRESS examines her glass. Then, without drinking, she lifts her head and faces down her AUDIENCE – nakedly, soberly, dauntlessly.

The lights fail.

— • —

Late. ROSIE is gone. JIMMY doles out bowls of soup, ADDY distributes silverware, and JOCKO-ALI serves bread. SIMON talks with AB. Filling in as court stenographer, HEISEL, in grimy Stetson, dozes fitfully. Offside, MacIAN and PARNELL, joined later by JOCKO-ALI, play cards. Following SAMMY's occasional cues, the ACTORS drink, eat, listen.

Sounds of eating throughout. Note: The sight and sound of AUDIENCE-JURORS and PERFORMERS eating is meant as unsavoury counterpoint. Genuinely delicious soup and bread, therefore, would be a mischief.

SIMON
(*nudged by AB, sees AUDIENCE*) Hah! I see taste has lost out to curiosity: you've come back. (*grins*) Remember me? Court stenographer? Well, I'm on to bigger things.

AB
(*to SIMON, handing him additional pages*) No deviations.

SIMON
(*lays pages on the floor; to AUDIENCE*) Be warned. Words are secondary. It's performance that counts.

SIMON turns away – drum roll – covert gestures. He turns back – cymbal crash. A pair of glasses has been pencilled around his eyes; FLIP's army cap sits at a jaunty angle on his head. A stool has been placed nearby.

(*with martial gaiety*) Major Aumeier! *Sturmbannführer* Aumeier! Presently being examined by the Defense–

Act Three
— • —

KERR
    You were saying?

SIMON
    (sits; cheerfully) –That, technically, we failed. Oh, elimination was easy enough. *(refers occasionally to AB's pages on the floor)* Three to 15 minutes, depending on the humidity, another 15 minutes to clear the air. Figure half an hour, all told. No, the problem was one of disposal. That's where the process broke down.

    JIMMY pulls up other stool, puts a soup bowl on it.

SIMON
    What's today?

JIMMY
    Chicken noodle.

KERR
    The particulars. Please.

SIMON
    (uses a page of script as a bib, toes the remaining pages on the floor) Capacity was 140,000. Truth of the matter is when we housed more than a hundred-thou', the place went to pieces. Typhus, scarlet fever, dysentery. *(stirs soup)* The greater part of the transports had to be dispatched immediately upon arrival.

    AUDIENCE-JURORS are served.

MAZO
    (ravenous) Hey, *paisano!*

JIMMY
    Coming!

KERR
    Go on, Major.

SIMON
    According to calculations– *(blows on soup)* –the two smaller units, Crema III and IV, could handle fifteen-hundred daily. With I and II running full blast, we were assured of between eight and 10,000 a day. *(eats meticulously)* Rot. The multiple-retort ovens never met specifications. Crema IV kept burning out its chimney and had to be repeatedly shut down. Surprising, eh? Bidding

on the contracts, after all, had been competitive. Höss had been— *(rubs thumb and fingers together)* —swindled.

KERR
Facilities aside, Major, as second-in-command, what troubled you most?

SIMON
(breaks bread) My own execution.

KERR
I mean the camp, its administration.

SIMON
(straightens the script on the floor with his foot, dips bread in his soup) We had no clear-cut purpose. One day we were— *(eats)* —depopulating Europe, the next we were manufacturing munitions. Or trying to. Everybody had a finger in the pie. Paper, carbon paper, orders, counter-orders. We even built a synthetic rubber factory. *(laughs)* Didn't produce enough elastic to stretch a garter strap. We should've decided on a single course of action and let the fanatics at Supreme Headquarters fight it out. The Commandant didn't have the backbone for that.

KERR
Höss?

SIMON
(smiles) I can still see him on the reviewing stand, as he ordered the gassing. *(picks at his back teeth)* Before us passed weeping millions. And he— *(with relish)* —absolutely impassive. As if his face had been lifted off a coin. You couldn't see past the profile. A performance unfortunately. At heart, Höss was a sentimentalist.

BERTIE
(bleary-eyed) A what?

SIMON
(spoons his soup) A sentimentalist.

BERTIE
(suddenly wide-eyed) A sentimentalist?!

HEISEL
(spells as he writes) S – E – N–

BERTIE
Shut up, Heisel!

HEISEL retorts with trumpeted raspberry.

KERR
  Please, Major.

SIMON
  Of course– (*swallows, savours the taste*) –one's always on the alert for weaknesses in superior officers. Höss had one dramatic peculiarity. He would disappear at odd moments. For hours. One morning, after a particularly trying incident– (*SAMMY, at the bar, rinses his hands.*) –outside the women's barracks, he was gone again. I set out to find him.

KERR
  And?

SIMON
  (*spoons soup*) He was in the woods, alone, riding madly, his mount in a lather. And Höss? Sweating, wild-eyed, evasive. (*SAMMY dries his hands.*) I felt it my duty to watch our commander more closely.

KERR
  Your observations.

SIMON
  He was a washer.

BERTIE
  A what?

SIMON
  His hands – he was constantly washing his hands. He wore gloves, of course, we all did. But his hands were always dirty – or so it seemed to him. Also, he was inordinately fond of children. When he wasn't escaping to the stables, he was off with his children, swimming, motoring, touring the countryside. Then I discovered he was obtaining extra rations for the youngsters in the gypsy compound. (*spoons soup*) Someone of lesser rank would've been shot.

KERR
  Shot?

SIMON
  For conduct unbecoming an SS Elite. Children are useless, tire quickly, are fit only for the most rudimentary labour.

BERTIE
  No mercy?

SIMON
  (*benignly*) I'm a military man. I wasn't trained to raise flowers.

BERTIE
It's you, sir, who should've been shot.

SIMON
So quick to pity, so quick to kill. I've had a taste of your justice, m'lord, and I find your notion of mercy– *(mimes being hung)* –rather constricting. Another bowl, please.

JOCKO-ALI
(calls) Soup!

KERR
(nettled) On the double! *(ADDY hurries off.)* Major–

SIMON
Call me, Hansel.

AB
Stick to the script, Simon.

KERR
Major, you and Höss disagreed on a number of issues–

SIMON
The Commandant was not one for idle chit-chat.

KERR
(thrown, picks up a script) Chit-chat? *(aside to AB)* Where is he?

AB
He's your witness. Control him.

KERR
You never argued camp politics, the war?

SIMON
Me?

KERR
(raps the script) Come on, Simon. You never lack for an opinion.

SIMON
Only one opinion was allowed in the SS–

ADDY
(sails in) YANKEE BEAN!

BERTIE
Yankee bean?

ADDY
We ran out of chicken noodle. But dere ist ka-knock of da worsht mitt da bean!

KERR
It was agreed in rehearsals you had differences with Höss.

SIMON
C'mon, the guy was highly secretive. (*ADDY changes soup bowls.*) Thanks. Look, don't you understand? This was no ordinary lunatic. In actual fact, if you want the truth, I should be playing Höss.

KERR
In actual fact – to get back to the script – you disagreed with Höss–

SIMON
Openly?

KERR
–about the camp.

SIMON
(*spoons more soup, eats*) With a superior officer? Never. Though I admit it was hard to stomach all those absurd arabesques. Injections of benzene, whippings, scourgings

AB
Where is he?

SIMON
(*merrily*) Just entering the gas chambers, darling. Oh, you should've seen us afterwards, crawling about among the corpses like grave robbers, snatching watches, rings, gold fillings. Anything for the greater glory of the Reich National Bank. They even had us looking up assholes for the Holy Grail.

KERR
Can we return to Höss?

SIMON
Höss? Iron Cross, First War. Liked to charge about on horseback, slicing up Iraqi natives.

AB
(*incensed, to SAMMY*) He's using his own material!

SIMON
(*pulls foolscap from an inside pocket*) You left out a few delicacies.

AB
  (*to SAMMY*) Stop him.

SAMMY
  (*amused*) Simon.

SIMON
  (*blows SAMMY a kiss*) His kind never comes home from the wars. Even as old men in bed, they hunger after the great blood-feast.

  AB advances on SIMON.

  (*rises, retreats*) Toy soldiers under the quilts, dreaming of arms grappling in the dark, their bayonets buried to the hilt in some young man's breast. Battlefield Casanovas lusting after inamoratas. And God! How suggestive a wounded body is. Stab it, shoot it, slash it, blow it up, and it opens like hungry pussy. Red, wet, warm and quivering! (*sings out, in SAMMY's direction*) CARNAGE!! Well, shall we toast our apron-stringed Pyrrhus over there? – who dreamed of the greatest orgy of all. Hail the huntsman-hero, he brings us flesh! (*moves behind lights as AB stalks him*) Pity we don't eat our meat raw anymore. The world's progressed since Torquemada and Siegfried. Personal combat's been laid to rest. Poor Höss. Faced by death in the abstract, with one hand on his dress sword, the other on his fly, our romantic little knight fell down in a fit, overcome by his own baroque obsolescence! Indifferent? Hardly.

AB
  (*flings himself upon SIMON*) A choleria zol dir chappen!

JOCKO-ALI
  Ab!

AB
  (*raves*) Schveig! None of that was mine!

  JOCKO-ALI and MAZO grab AB.

SIMON
  (*laughing*) Get him off me!

AB
  You're not the writer! I am!!

MAZO
  Hold him!

AB
  Putz!

JOCKO-ALI
Okay, Ju-Jubes–

AB
(*dragged away*) Does it every time! Sonuvabitch! *A klug iz mir!* Bastard!

> AB is seated and consoled with a drink. ROSIE has entered, fully dressed, her makeup garishly complete.

ADDY
Ah, madame. Just in time.

ROSIE
(*smashed*) What's with those two?

ADDY
The usual.

> FLIP passes ROSIE his cigarette.

ADDY
Election returns in yet?

ROSIE
Yeah.

MacIAN
(*looks up from his cards*) Who won? Syphilis or gonorrhea?

ROSIE
(*picks up a glass*) Who cares. They're all a bunch of empty bottles.

PARNELL
(*wry*) Perfect spot for a song!

> Music.

    ROSIE
        (*sings*) The winners won, the losers lost.
        Nothing's changed except the cost.
        The ins are out, the outs are in.
        Light a match!

(FLIP puts a match to ROSIE's drink: EXPLOSION) It's nitroglycerin!!

    ADDY
        (*sings*) Lift your glass, toast the elite.
        Asskiss another victorious defeat.
        Sweeter smells the seat of power–

>   *(extends her glass to ADDY)*
>   Rescued by a whiskey sour!

Pause. Music halts.

ROSIE
> Well?

ADDY
> *(raises bottle)* Muscatel.

ROSIE
> Go to hell. *(ADDY fills ROSIE's glass anyway. ROSIE stares at it.)* Know why the old days were rosier? They had bigger glasses.

Music.

JOCKO-ALI
> But for those with cash and conscience–

>   **BERTIE**
>   *(sings)* Who want privilege without its price,
>   Who season their neutrality
>   With luncheon revolutions
>   And after-dinner anarchy
>   Warmed with a little ice–
>   Cheers! Politics grows more comic
>   With each succeeding gin and tonic!

>   **MAZO**
>   *(sings)* As for the rest, the bourgeoisie,
>   White collars, intellectuals, you know, the brotherly–
>   Nothing sugars social esprit
>   Like a bottle of Burgundy!
>   Should these solutions leave you dry
>   And History continue to intensify–

JOCKO-ALI
> HEAR YE! HEAR YE! HEAR YE!

>   **SIMON**
>   One crème de menthe!

>   **BERTIE**
>   One absinthe!

>   **MacIAN**
>   Three cherry brandies!

FLIP
Four Sneaky Petes!

MAZO
Three Bacardis!

ROSIE
Two ryes!

SIMON
A Benedictine!

BERTIE
Plus a tall Madeira!

ADDY
Taken within the hour—

MAZO
And we guarantee you, friends, the answer!

MacIAN
You Sons of Babylon!

JOCKO-ALI & OTHERS
INSTANT OMNIPOTENT O-O-O-O-BLIV-I-ON!!!

KERR
May we resume?

SIMON
(*small smile*) I want protection. And a shot.

AB
Between the eyes!

KERR
Make it two. Corporal.

FLIP
Yessir!

KERR
Stand by the witness.

> *FLIP plants himself unsteadily next to SIMON, notices his cap on SIMON's head, reclaims it.*

FLIP
    Prick!

ADDY
    (*supplied by SAMMY, hurries over with two drinks*) Tea for two! Comedy versus depravity!

SIMON
    L'chaim!

KERR
    Prosit!

    They down their drinks. SIMON smashes his glass, KERR follows suit.

    (*pugnacious*) Aumeier, where were you the morning of the execution?

SIMON
    Which one? There were so many.

KERR
    (*nods toward JOCKO-ALI*) His.

SIMON
    I was on the phone.

KERR
    No, at the end. You were on the side, watching. (*SIMON smiles broadly.*) Was it that amusing?

SIMON
    (*laughs*) No. Boring.

KERR
    (*indicates SAMMY*) And the Commandant? What was his reaction?

SIMON
    Ask him!

KERR
    I'm asking you! You two usually go to executions together?

SIMON
    When required.

KERR
    His reaction this time?

SIMON
(*looks at SAMMY*) The Commandant? Or Sammy?

KERR
You know who. Was he bored? Blasé? Unconcerned? Indifferent?

SIMON
As I recall, he cast his eyes toward Heaven, undid his libido and assaulted the victim's mother.

KERR
Simon!

SIMON
What do you expect? For him to burst into tears? He's an officer. It's a point of honour not to show emotion. The firing squad fires, the hangman hangs, a few papers are signed, and everybody goes home and has lunch.

MacIAN
(*playing cards offside, spreads a winning hand*) Including the worms!

KERR
(*pale*) Major.

SIMON
Yes?

KERR
(*drained*) Would you say, given your knowledge of the defendant, that he put his heart into his work? (*thrusts the script into SIMON's face*) Your answer!

SIMON
(*laughs, pushes script aside, looks directly at SAMMY*) The truth? I would have been more enterprising.

AB
Cocksucker, play Aumeier!

SIMON
I *am*! We were at war! And, as Aumeier, I say we should have done everything but lose!

KERR
(*lays down script*) That's not Aumeier. You're improvising. I'm finished, your honour.

SIMON
A shame. I was about to come over to Ab's side of the graveyard.

> KERR, AB and BERTIE *are immediately alert.*

BERTIE
> Heisel! *(HEISEL, asleep, starts up.)* Write!

SIMON
> I share your disgust. Not on moral grounds. Purely as a technician. Logistically, Höss was an asshole, and his camps were a disaster. I repudiate the whole exercise.

HEISEL
> *(writing laboriously)* –lo – gis – tic – al – ly–

SIMON
> The executions, the experiments, the crematoria. One unmitigated calamity! From morning till night. Ever consider the–

HEISEL
> *(louder)* –ca – lam – i – ty–

SIMON
> *(grimaces)* –the personnel and the effort it takes to torture the living? It was a waste of their tears and our time. There's a lesson to be learned–

HEISEL
> *(voice rising)* –o – u – R T – I – M – E–

SIMON
> *(voice rising)* –to be learned from your democracies. You don't kill your minorities. You work them!

HEISEL
> *(writes, emphatically)* –DEMOCRA–

SIMON
> *(explodes)* Shut up, Heisel! You're a mute!

HEISEL
> *(grins triumphantly)* True.

SIMON
> *(turns back, hoarsely)* Think of the labour force we would've had! Add the occupied populations, and we'd have been unbeatable. Put to work on the outside, however, our prisoners lasted a month, maybe two. In peacetime we would've gone bankrupt.

KERR
> *(emptied)* No more. Your witness.

BERTIE
　　Get him, Yehudi. He's dangerous.

　　SAMMY rings up his cash register. JOCKO-ALI dashes water over AB and releases him like a boxer into the ring.

AB
　　(squares off) Ready, bubela?

FLIP
　　(referees) You know the rules, boys. Keep it clean–!

　　Rabbit-punched by AB, kneed by KERR, grabbed and thrown by both, FLIP is catapulted from the scene.

AB
　　(to SIMON) Suddenly against killing, are you?

SIMON
　　In general, yes. With aberrations like you–

AB
　　No more crematoria?

SIMON
　　Cumbersome.

AB
　　(moving in) You renounce it all?

SIMON
　　Yes. *(motions for his drink)*

AB
　　Unconditionally?

SIMON
　　Yes.

AB
　　But during the killing, during the torture, while you were doing it, Simon, where was your opposition then?

BERTIE
　　(momentarily without accent) Remember, chum, you said you didn't openly oppose Höss.

SIMON
　　Cruelty has its satisfactions.

AB
You enjoyed it?

SIMON
I was young.

ADDY hands SIMON his drink.

AB
(*drops his accent*) And the years have changed you. (*SIMON looks at his glass, smiles ruefully.*) Sobered you. Altered your perspective.

SIMON drains his glass, does not reply.

AB
So that today, looking back, you claim it was all a mistake.

Pause.

SIMON
(*staring inward, desolate*) Yes.

AB
Impractical?

SIMON
(*distant*) Yes.

AB
Uneconomical?!

SIMON
(*looks down at his shabby clothes, laughs wryly*) Very.

AB
(*still without accent*) But we know, Simon, don't we, if you had to, you'd do it again, wouldn't you?

SIMON
Yes, but–

AB
(*cuts in, his accent returned in full*) Differently from the defendant!

SIMON
Given today's methods.

AB
    (*purrs*) "Given *today's* methods." (*to JURY*) *I've had a chance to think*, he says. *He's older*, he says. *Today* he believes this. *Now* he knows this. *Looking back* he realizes – You hear what I'm hearing? Hindsight! He's operating out of hindsight. This witness is asking us, based on what he knows now, to conclude, along with him, that Höss was some sort of saber-toothed romantic sunk up to his eyeballs in a tarpit of incompetent emotionalism. But he's dead! He cannot know that. Aumeier's stand-in here has violated the rules. He's judging history *after the fact*.

SIMON
    Know a better way?

AB
    (*trembling*) I move that the testimony of this Judas—all of it!—be stricken from the record.

KERR
    Wait a minute!

AB
    Current events, current considerations do not apply. And we—counsel, witnesses, the jury—are duty bound to judge the crime of indifference for what it *was!* – unburdened, unbiased! by what it may have become. The present has nothing whatsoever to do with this case. I move, therefore, that this witness, in his entirety, be cancelled, deleted, obliterated, erased!

KERR
    In his entirety?!

AB
    Totally! On grounds that he's injecting into these proceedings a totally inadmissible point of view!

KERR
    That's mad.

BERTIE
    The whole world is mad, Mr. Kerr. Join the party. (*to SIMON*) And you! Get off the bloody stool!

AB
    Bertie, rule! The present!–

BERTIE
    (*fighting for clarity but losing the battle*) Yes! Oh, yes! Yes!! The present!! The present?!? Right, right!! *The present!!!* Yes!! Absolutely!! The present!!! Nothing in this case has anything to do with the present!! The present is

irrelevant! immaterial!!– *(cries out)* –UNBEARABLE!!! Strike it out!! All of it!!!

> *HEISEL rips up SIMON's testimony, stuffs the pieces into his trumpet.*

AB
Bertie! The witness!

BERTIE
The witness? Ha-ha! the witness! The witness!!! The jury is instructed to disregard the witness. The witness never testified. In fact, he no longer exists. Remove yourself from the Court, sir. You're a flaming menace!

SIMON
No more, it seems, than his lordship.

BERTIE
And thank God you're dead!

SIMON
(steps away) A rum world, isn't it?

> *HEISEL, with a blast, showers the Court with SIMON's testimony.*

BERTIE
(to card-players, losing his accent) You too! Cut out the fucking card game! Distracts me, distracts the audience! *(mutters)* Talk about indifference! *(casts about, regains his accent)* Where's the bloody script?

ADDY
(supplies it) Here, m'good lord.

BERTIE
(grabs script, swats ADDY with it) We'll have none o' your lip either! *(to KERR, seething)* Next scoundrel.

AB
Which one?

BERTIE
The one!

> *Sour horn.*

KERR
We call the defendant, Lieutenant-Colonel Franz Ferdinand Höss to the stand.

Ragged fanfare. SAMMY calmly walks into place. PARNELL positions a music stand with a script near SAMMY.

MacIAN
(*staggers into the scene with a drink*) 'SWEARTOTELLTHETRUTHTHE WHOLETRUTHAN'NUTHIN'BUTTHE TRUTH – S'HELPYOUGOD?

SAMMY
(*mildly*) I do not. (*MacIAN is dumbfounded.*) I do not believe in God.

BERTIE
Then go to the devil!

AB
(*tumbles BERTIE from his perch*) Move over! (*installs himself*) What manner of oath would the defendant find binding?

SAMMY
My honour as an officer.

AB
So sworn.

SAMMY
(*accepts the glass, does not drink*) Thank you. (*sits by the music stand; occasionally, casually turns a page of his script*)

SIMON
(*returned as court clerk and stenographer*) Date of birth?

SAMMY
November 4, 1900.

SIMON
Date of death?

SAMMY
April 17th, 1947.

SIMON
Cause of death?

SAMMY
Public hanging.

KERR
You accept your sentence?

SAMMY
I'd rather have died as a soldier.

AB
(*intervenes*) No other regrets?

KERR
Don't answer. (*to AB*) You'll have your turn.

AB
Normal cross-examination is at an end. The People will question as Defense rolls along.

KERR
No you won't.

AB
In order to more closely pursue the truth.

BERTIE
(*gavels the floor*) Oh, pursue, pursue!

AB
(*to KERR*) So ruled. Bravo! A parallel examination! (*trumpet blast, to SAMMY*) Colonel, we trust you won't lower yourself with a plea of higher orders.

SAMMY
(*evenly*) I'm responsible for my acts. But I remind Prosecution that without its own obedient soldiers our positions here might be reversed.

>**MAZO**
>(*sings*) Cups and saucers plates and wishes!

>**JOCKO-ALI**
>All the boys are wearing–

>**BOTH**
>Knickerbocker bitches!

BERTIE
(*from the floor*) Confess!!

SAMMY
(*dispassionately*) I grew up on the outskirts of Baden. An isolated place. Forests, a few scattered farmhouses. I was left mostly to myself.

AB
Siblings?

SAMMY
Two sisters.

AB
Were you close?

SAMMY
We played together, but we had nothing in common.

KERR
Education?

SAMMY
I was expected to enter the priesthood. My schooling was arranged accordingly.

KERR
Your parents?

SAMMY
My mother did what mothers do. My father was a strict, devout man, who took me with him on his annual pilgrimage. After his death I joined the regiment he had served in, as his father had before him. The 21st Baden Dragoons. I was sixteen.

AB
Never to take the cloth.

SAMMY
The baptism of war made the notion of God a rather precious sentiment.

AB
And for the loss of Paradise, let's see, you were awarded – the Iron Crescent, the Iron Cross, 1st and 2nd Class, the Baden Service Medal–

SAMMY
Trophies. Of an acquired realism.

AB
On the contrary, a witness testified that you were a romantic–

KERR
Stricken from the record.

AB
–who gloried in personal combat.

SAMMY
I will not dispute non-existent testimony.

AB
You deny your part in the atrocities committed under your command?

SAMMY
A great deal was done without my sanction. However–

FLIP, half-conscious, moans, grimaces, bangs his soup bowl on the floor.

(flinches perceptibly) –as they occurred under my authority, I am responsible.

KERR
In name. In rank. Were you responsible *in fact*?

SAMMY
I was surrounded by small men. Camp service for many was a way to satisfy perverse appetites. My instructions were often disregarded.

FLIP trembles violently.

AB
Are you saying you could not control your own staff?

SAMMY
(patiently) My first duty was to construct and maintain a prison camp. We often lacked the most basic materials. Field fortifications had to be plundered. Even our barbed wire was stolen. Time was short. I had to delegate the prisoners' welfare to subordinates.

AB
Who did not share your humanitarian impulses?

SAMMY
Their behaviour speaks for itself.

AB
Why didn't you replace them?

SAMMY
Half the staff would've had to go. The Camp Inspectorate would never have agreed.

KERR
Colonel, I call your attention to an incident toward the end of the war. On the road near– *(consults script)* –Liebesnest.

SAMMY
  Yes.

KERR
  Tell them.

SAMMY
  I was away from the camp at the time. *(turns a page)* In Lower Silesia. Our major cities had been bombed. Berlin was in ruins. The Russians were advancing in the East. My orders were to return immediately. Everything had to be destroyed.

  FLIP, convulsed, gags.

FLIP
  ARGHHH!

SAMMY
  (tight-lipped) Shut him up.

  A bottle is slammed down beside FLIP, who promptly appropriates it.

  (regains his composure) Our armor was in full retreat. Thousands of prisoners had been evacuated from the camps. Driven by a few exhausted soldiers, they trudged through the snow, clogging the roads. I had to turn back. Where possible, I gave strict orders that prisoners were not to be killed. Those unable to march were to be handed over to local militias. On my way back however, I found a never-ending trail of dead prisoners. Most had been shot.

  SAMMY drinks for the first time.

  Near Liebesnest I came across a non-commissioned officer. His motorcycle was at the side of the road. He was holding his pistol to the head of a prisoner, who'd stopped to lean against a tree. I leaped from my car and shouted at him to stop. He fired, blew the smoke from the barrel of his pistol, then inquired into the state of my health.

KERR
  What did you do?

SAMMY
  I drew my own pistol and shot him.

AB
  On the spot?

SAMMY
  Yes.

AB
    (*consults his script*) A sergeant-major in the air force.

SAMMY
    Correct.

AB
    And you a lieutenant-colonel.

SAMMY
    Right.

KERR
    The question, of course, is did you pull the trigger for the dead prisoner's sake–

AB
    –or because the Sergeant-Major had been impertinent? Remember, Colonel, you're on your honour.

KERR
    (*after no reply*) Sam?

SAMMY
    I shot him for both of us.

AB
    And behind the wire, in camp? What happened to your gallantry there?

SAMMY
    (*evenly*) I was never indifferent to the condition of the prisoners.

AB
    Are you claiming you were unsuited for camp work?

SAMMY
    Possibly.

AB
    Why didn't you request a transfer?

SAMMY
    I did. It was refused.

KERR
    Ever consider deserting?

SAMMY
    No.

KERR
(*impulsively*) Never?

SAMMY
I joined the SS voluntarily. I believed—I still believe—the State has the right to safeguard itself against its enemies. I swore loyalty to my country, the SS, to the Führer. To desert was unthinkable.

KERR
Did anyone know of your sympathies? Someone who could testify on your behalf?

SAMMY
No.

KERR
You must have confided in somebody.

SAMMY
(*quietly*) No. No one.

KERR
Not even your wife?

ROSIE
(*saturated*) Tha's none of your business!

SAMMY
The camp claimed most of my energies. As the smell from the crematoria grew more noticeable, my wife and I drifted apart. To all appearances, we were a normal family. The children went to school, my wife worked in the garden, I went about my duties. Over time we turned into strangers.

ROSIE cackles.

KERR
As commandant, Sammy, how many–

AB
–deaths!–

KERR
Yes – how many deaths were you directly responsible for?

SAMMY
(*contained*) It is a matter of record that I personally arranged the gassing of two million people.

KERR
(*awed*) Two million?!

SAMMY
Give or take a hundred thousand.

FLIP
(*half-comatose, laughs*) Kill 'em all! The Infidels!

KERR
(*to SAMMY*) You're sweating.

SAMMY
The lights are hot.

KERR
"Give or take a hundred thousand?"

SAMMY
Thought you missed the line. Was I too casual?

KERR
Ever occur to you to kill yourself?

SAMMY
An indulgence. (*suddenly, quietly ardent*) The camps were an unalterable fact of life. Dead, I would've been replaced. Alive, I assisted those who chose to live. Prisoners who couldn't work had to be dispatched. I created work, even if it meant digging graves. Those who dug lived a little longer.

> *Unseen, JOCKO-ALI holds up a brass spittoon—a halo—behind SAMMY's head.*

The sick? Their diseases spread to the able-bodied. They wasted rations. They undermined the camp. They had to be eliminated–

> *JOCKO-ALI has placed the spittoon upside down on SAMMY's head. SAMMY rises abruptly, spilling his drink, and smashes JOCKO-ALI to the floor with a back-handed blow.*

SAMMY
(*turns back, furiously tearing off the spittoon*) You moralists!! Full of self-righteous accusations, denouncing the world but doing nothing to change it! (*savagely*) I did something!

KERR
(*softly*) We noticed.

SAMMY
No longer defending me, Angus?

KERR
You're beyond defense.

SAMMY
(elated) As Höss? Or Sammy?

KERR
You wanted to play both. Curious ambition.

SAMMY
To edge us – over the edge.

AB
What edge?!

The stain from SAMMY's drink has spread across his apron.

SAMMY
The nightmare of charity.

AB
(appalled) Charity?!

SAMMY
Abiding, overriding charity.

AB
(outraged) Whose? Yours?!

SAMMY
Mine! And others like me! All of us caring more than you would like to know. Imagine that nightmare! Eh, Yehudi? To be deprived of your grievances? Suddenly no more villains.

AB
Suddenly I'm tired.

SAMMY
What would you do without all your villains?

BERTIE
No more villains? Oh, I like it, I like it!

AB
(disgusted) Spare us, will you.

BERTIE
No! Pursue, pursue!

SAMMY
All the way! (*looks down at the floored JOCKO-ALI*) Even Li'l Black Sambo – give us a smile, luv–

> *JOCKO-ALI lifts his head. Grimaces, only to be ground down under SAMMY's heel.*

SAMMY
–even Jocko's agreed we're here to be extreme. (*AB starts to leave.*) Heading home, Yehudi? Afraid of what I might say? Leave and you lose by default. (*AB grinds to a halt.*)

KERR
(*quietly*) Take your foot off him.

SAMMY
For whose sake? His or the jury's?

KERR
Win on testimony. Not last-minute posturing.

> *Pause. SAMMY releases JOCKO-ALI.*

JOCKO-ALI
(*rises, stares SAMMY in the eye*) To be continued.

SAMMY
You bet.

AB
What's left?

KERR
The truth.

BERTIE
Which one?!

KERR
The one he knows by heart.

AB
Oh no, that speech is a fabrication. Rule, Bertie!

BERTIE
Hn–?

AB
  Sammy's speech!

BERTIE
  (*lost*) Which speech–?

AB
  (*hauls BERTIE to his feet*) Sam's confession!

BERTIE
  I adore confessions!

AB
  Disallow it! It's a fiction!

BERTIE
  (*holds onto his wig, as he retreats*) Better be. It is my firm opinion– (*staggers*) –that Western juris – juris – jurisprudence has always been too prudent! Truth is – fiction is a helluva lot more fun than the f-f-f-facts! Objection denied!! (*weaves away*)

FLIP
  (*still shoeless, stares at BERTIE*) Stop!

BERTIE
  Oh dear.

FLIP
  You rotten cockroach.

BERTIE
  Me?

FLIP
  Take 'em off.

BERTIE
  Here?

FLIP
  Now.

BERTIE
  (*slips off a shoe, surrenders it*) One.

FLIP
  (*takes it*) One.

BERTIE
(*second shoe*) Two.

FLIP
(*takes it*) Two.

BERTIE
(*produces a third matching shoe*) Three! (*He clubs FLIP over the head with it, and reclaims the first two shoes. FLIP collapses.*) Inherit the Earth! (*steps over FLIP's body*) Yessiree! (*reels away*) Prudent! Too prudent! (*sings*)

> When Britain at Satan's command
> Arose from out the azure main–!
> Arose! Arose!! (*collapses*)

ADDY
Rapunzel's out.

SAMMY
Bury him. With his wig.

KERR
(*to AUDIENCE*) This is one speech– (*directs a light*) –that will brook no interruptions.

ADDY
A last-minute confession– (*directs another light*) –designed to prove a tactical, radical–

KERR
CHARITY!

A quiet stage. Most of the Bar has succumbed. Soft music.

SAMMY
It was a normal evening. An east wind was blowing. Fruit trees blossomed in the camp orchard. For once the night air was fresh. I stood on the loading platform half-listening to the cries, as families were broken up. I don't know why it came to me then. Nothing unusual had happened. But, as I looked up into that clear spring night and watched the stars shiver, I knew I belonged there. I had found my place. Not that I expect anyone to understand my exhilaration. How many of us extract from the fates exactly what we want? We eat, squirm about, move our bowels and, in the end, like maggots, leave nothing behind but a hole in the dark rot of existence. I stood there– (*gazes directly at the AUDIENCE*) –their faces were as close as yours – I stood there looking out from my place on the platform, and I thought, in a few moments — *you* and *you* and *you* will not be here. And it was so. With the smallest gesture– (*flicks his fingertips*) –I disposed of a hundred, a thousand, a million human beings. For one brief moment I articulated a few muscles– (*flicks his*

fingers again) –and startled all of history. Not an unprecedented gesture. Each one of the august conquerors was an exterminator. But I went beyond their parochial efforts. My aim was global. I would rid the world of its refuse. *(strolls among the silent and the still)* The office of commandant was privileged It gave me the chance to observe our species stripped of its disguises. And I tell you the human being is a ravenous beast that will commit any crime, given the proper incentive. With some it's money. With others, hunger. Promise a small bonus and a sentry's aim always improves. *(looks down at a body)* In winter, when rations ran low, we sometimes found, stuffed under the huts, bodies half-buried in the frozen mud, pieces chewed out of their thighs. Oh yes. Prisoners would push each other into the electrified fence over mere scraps. And the hope of a few more days of life led the most moral to inform on their neighbours. *(unequivocal)* I think you will believe me when I say I never grew indifferent to the day-by-day annihilation of my fellow man. I welcomed it.

> ADDY *steps forward, hands* SAMMY *a towel, waits, a jar of face cream at the ready.*

I was not without allies. *(sits)* An unspoken conspiracy sprang up between us, between our so-called victims and we, their executioners, to end this obscenity called Life. *(removes an eyelash)* A gentlemen's agreement unburdened by the usual hypocrisies. Naturally, a few allowed ideals to deny what instincts craved. A few fought. *(removes other eyelash)* They were the exception. The great majority cooperated. For example, when the crematoria were working beyond capacity– *(creams his face, then wipes off an eyebrow)* –shovels were handed to the surplus prisoners and they were ordered to dig a long pit. That done, they were called forward in twos and, upon instruction, they climbed down, lay with their faces to the earth and were shot. *(other eyebrow)* The next two shovelled a bit of earth over the first two, lay down and in turn were shot. So on. No resistance. Often there was just one soldier sitting there, smoking a cigarette, cradling his weapon, his feet dangling over the edge of the pit. He could easily have been overpowered by the hundreds waiting in line. *(wipes away the rest of his make-up)* But – you see – they wanted it.

ROSIE
    (derisive) His story.

SAMMY
    (avid, directly to the AUDIENCE*)* Surely some of you recognize the urge, the impulse, the craving that hungers for an end to the uselessness, the emptiness, the indifference of our civilized lives. My prisoners were sunk up to their nostrils in existence, and the only undeniable truth they could discern was the stench of their own bodies. It's at that point—when futility stands at the edge of the abyss—that finalities become irresistible. (ROSIE *comes up behind him, waits quietly. He finishes his face.)* Reminds me of an evening at the National. The show was over, the audience gone. The female lead stopped by my dressing room. We were both young – she, a vain little

ingenue in her first big role. (ROSIE: *small smile.*) We chatted till the building went quiet. I watched her in the mirror watching me. I got up, walked over to her and forced her down onto the floor. (*hands ROSIE the towel*) She struggled exquisitely. Without uttering a sound, she thrashed about and tore at my face. Then, gasping, lay on her back trembling, her neck arched. (*pause*) She wanted it. She had wanted it all along.

ROSIE
(*dryly*) He says.

SAMMY
I was nauseated. I reached for her throat. She screamed. She had finally found her voice. (*rises*) I left her sobbing theatrically under the dressing table. There are few victims who are not party to their own violation. The sheep bleats, you cut its throat, its very helplessness invites its slaughter. (*suddenly with a terrible anguish*) Oh God, is there no other role to play in this stockyard of a world but butcher?! (*looks out into the AUDIENCE*) And you?! You! What are you?! Lamb or executioner?!!

Waits.

SAMMY
(*impassioned*) That is the question, isn't it!?!!

Searches the AUDIENCE for a response.

(*appalled*) No one – with an answer?!

Waits. Note: Should anyone in the AUDIENCE be moved to reply, they might be welcomed onstage to more openly declare themselves—and others urged to join them—before resuming: "Wonderful! Great! Stupendous! Any more? Surely. No? (*Waits. Silence.*)

SAMMY
So it goes. Until the final butchery.

ADDY steps out of the shadows, puts a hand on SAMMY's shoulder.

ADDY
(*gently*) Sam.

SAMMY
Yes?

ADDY
The summations.

SAMMY
Be brief.

Lights.

ADDY
(*with mischievous congeniality*) The accused is yours. To be judged according to the evidence. Our performances are incidental. If there's anyone you've become fond of– (*winsome smile*) –like me – great! (*drops the smile*) But it's not relevant. In fact, every sympathy now is inadmissible. You're obliged instead to render an objective verdict. Based, I repeat, entirely upon the evidence presented here. Follow that instruction and you will find the defendant innocent of indifference. By his own admission he wanted the worst, hungered for it, gloried in it. Pitiless, perhaps. Relentless, yes. Indifferent? Never. If that admission fails to persuade you, then heed his other confession, that he did his worst to prevent the worst, his mission to help the living. Either way, as apocalyptic executioner or kind administrator, the defendant was eager, ardent, zealous. Call him "monster," but he was never an indifferent monster. To those who still insist on a guilty verdict, one question. Does indifference even exist? Is anyone ever indifferent? Remember, too, you are judging an historical figure. The epoch surrounding him cannot be ignored. If the defendant was indifferent, so, too, is the world that produced him. Condemn him and you condemn an entire civilization.

SAMMY
(*with dry vehemence*) Forget civilization. Your obligation is not to be humane but just. The defendant lived among us and we were forever diminished by his actions. Clemency now would be gross. The facts alone merit your attention; the rest is supposition. The accused superintended a campaign of torture, pillage and extermination. All of it, according to the witnesses—remember them?!—all of it performed without pity or remorse. No mercy. No regret. And none except the defendant and a non existent witness have testified to the contrary. You have one duty, to render an objective verdict. Given the evidence, there can be but one judgement. Of the crime of indifference – guilty!

AB
The charge? Willful, personal, prolonged indifference.

ADDY
No time to deliberate. An audience waits.

KERR
Majority rules!

SAMMY moves among AUDIENCE- and ACTOR-JURORS, rousing the sleepy, extracting verdicts, goading the soft-spoken into shouting their decisions, sometimes repeating verdicts for ADDY, who keeps score on the bar, lining up bottles – "GUILTY" to one side, "INNOCENT" to the other, a smashed bottle representing an indecisive or reluctant JUROR. Sour and jubilant music accompanies the announcements.

SAMMY
(after the LAST JUROR's verdict) The count?

ADDY
Seven for, five against! *(Or whatever. In the event of a tie, ADDY calls out, "Tie score!" or "a dead heat!")*

SAMMY
Wake Bertie.

> ADDY crosses to BERTIE with a waterpail, upends it over the unconscious judge.

BERTIE
(sits upright, streaming water) Pardon?!

ADDY
(helps BERTIE up) Pronounce the verdict.

BERTIE
Verdict? *(behind his hand)* What is it?

ADDY
(a stage whisper)
Guilty!   (or)   Innocent!   (or)   A well-hung jury!

BERTIE
What?

SAMMY
(a frustrated cry)
Guilty!!   (or)   Innocent!!   (or)   No decision!!

ADDY
Fanfare!

> Music. A pay envelope falls to the floor, retrieved by BERTIE. Wig askew. BERTIE assumes a vestigial dignity and issues one of three pronouncements.

BERTIE
It is the judgment of this court, freely arrived at and without duress, that the accused – is – guilty as charged!

(or)

It is the judgement of this court, freely arrived at and without duress that the accused – is – innocent! He stands acquitted!

(or)

It is the judgement of this court, freely arrived at and without duress, that its judgement – is – without conviction!

Fanfare.

ADDY
As for the question of charity, we're still debating it. Now it's your turn. Have fun. And since this performance is punishment enough–

BERTIE
The Verdict is all!!

MacIAN
The Lord be with you!

ROSIE
(*toasts*) And with thy Spirits!

ALL & INDIVIDUALLY
(*sing*) The winners won, the losers lost.
Nothing's changed except the cost.
The ins are out, the outs are in!
Do it! Kill the competition!
(*an enormous explosion rocks the building*)

SAMMY
(*his voice rising over the music*) And so our end! Again! Indeed, we're here every show – my sentence to secure your judgement!

The curtain begins to fall.

SIMON
Wait! Stop!

The curtain halts.

We didn't finish the song!

SAMMY
(*regaining some of his humour*) What a loss! Well? Do it!

SIMON
(*indicates AUDIENCE*) With them?!

SAMMY
Always!

SIMON
(*to AUDIENCE*) Hey! You're invited to sing along! We'll feed you the lines!

SIMON sings, leads the AUDIENCE and is joined by the ACTORS.

Lift your glass! Toast the elite!
(with AUDIENCE) Lift your glass! Toast the elite!
Asskiss another glorious defeat!
(laughs) C'mon, c'mon! We can't hear you!
(with AUDIENCE) Asskiss another glorious defeat!
Sweeter smells the seat of power
Scented with a whiskey sour!
(prompts) Scented!–
(with AUDIENCE) Scented with a whiskey sour!
That's it!

Cheers! Politics grows more comic
With each succeeding gin and tonic!
As for the rest, the bourgeoisie,
White collars, intellectuals,
Y'know the brotherly.
Nothing sugars social esprit
Like a bottle of Burgundy!

AB

(soliciting spare change) Give us a hand, friends. No one'll notice.

SIMON & OTHERS

Should these solutions leave you dry
And history continue to intensify–
HEAR YE! HEAR YE! HEAR YE!
One crème de menthe!
One absinthe!
Three cherry brandies!
Four Sneaky Petes!
Three Bacardies!
Two ryes!
A Benedictine!
Plus a tall Madeira! Taken within the hour–
And we guarantee you, friends, the answer!
Are you listening, ye children of Babylon?!
INSTANT OMNIPOTENT O-O-O-O-BLIV-I-ON!!!

SAMMY

(to AUDIENCE) And for those who like a bit of pepper on their apple pie, let's end the night with a little bite by demonstrating—with your help!—that indifference belongs to history and not to the theatre! (signals PARNELL) Forte, Mæstro! (music builds, to AUDIENCE) Applause! Cheers! Catcalls! Anything'll do! But we'll prove, won't we, that no one here is indifferent! First our valiant guests! (to AUDIENCE-JURORS) Step forward, ladies and gentlemen! Don't be modest! This is your curtain call!

SAMMY leads applause as AUDIENCE-JURORS and BRAVE NEWCOMERS (if any) bow. Then SAMMY presents MUSICIANS, ACTORS and himself.

(ending applause) Wonderful! Marvelous! Terrific! Magnificent! You've been a good audience! A glorious *(or just "grand" – depending)* audience! Thank you for coming! Thank you also for your laughter! Come again! Bring friends! Next month we do Rwanda! To those who have lived in this world and are alive– *(hand to heart)* –we the dead salute you! *(raises his arm)* You have survived!

SAMMY surveys the AUDIENCE. A patriotic strain has fouled the music.

(Author's note. "The end" normally appears at the close of a printed play. Not here. The final curtain has been halted, the AUDIENCE invited back, the ACTORS ready with another atrocity-filled performance. At the Follies, as in life, there is no end to the killing.)

Also Available:

A Terrible Truth   Anthology of Holocaust Drama   Volume II
compiled by Irene N. Watts

Includes:

Good	None is	Playing	Still	The Trials
C.P.	Too Many	for Time	the Night	of John
Taylor	Jason	Arthur	Theresa	Demjanjuk
	Sherman	Miller	Tova	Jonathan
				Garfinkel

0-88754-714-1
$45.00

Playwrights Canada Press
215 Spadina Avenue, Suite 230, Toronto, Ontario CANADA M5T 2C7
416-703-0013
orders@playwrightscanada.com • www.playwrightscanada.com